COBIT for Small and Medium Enterprises

Using COBIT 2019

COBIT®
An ISACA® Framework

ISACA®

About ISACA

For more than 50 years, ISACA® (*www.isaca.org*) has advanced the best talent, expertise and learning in technology. ISACA equips individuals with knowledge, credentials, education and community to progress their careers and transform their organizations, and enables enterprises to train and build quality teams that effectively drive IT audit, risk management and security priorities forward. ISACA is a global professional association and learning organization that leverages the expertise of more than 150,000 members who work in information security, governance, assurance, risk and privacy to drive innovation through technology. It has a presence in 188 countries, including more than 220 chapters worldwide. In 2020, ISACA launched One In Tech, a philanthropic foundation that supports IT education and career pathways for under-resourced, under-represented populations.

Disclaimer

ISACA has designed and created *COBIT for Small and Medium Enterprises* (the "Work") primarily as an educational resource for enterprise governance of information and technology (EGIT), assurance, risk and security professionals. ISACA makes no claim that use of any of the Work will assure a successful outcome. The Work should not be considered inclusive of all proper information, procedures and tests or exclusive of other information, procedures and tests that are reasonably directed to obtaining the same results. In determining the propriety of any specific information, procedure or test, enterprise governance of information and technology (EGIT), assurance, risk and security professionals should apply their own professional judgment to the specific circumstances presented by the particular systems or information technology environment.

ISACA
1700 E. Golf Road, Suite 400
Schaumburg, IL 60173, USA
Phone: +1.847.660.5505
Fax: +1.847.253.1755
Contact us: https://support.isaca.org
Website: www.isaca.org

Participate in the ISACA Online Forums: https://engage.isaca.org/onlineforums

Twitter: http://twitter.com/ISACANews
LinkedIn: www.linkedin.com/company/isaca
Facebook: www.facebook.com/ISACAGlobal
Instagram: www.instagram.com/isacanews/

COBIT for Small and Medium Enterprises
ISBN 978-1-60420-900-6

Acknowledgments

ISACA would like to recognize:

Lead Developer
Greet Volders, CGEIT, Voquals NV, Belgium

Expert Reviewers
Leela Dhulipalla, CGEIT, CDPSE, COBIT Assessor, AWS Certified Cloud Practitioner, CDMP, CITAM, CSAM, IAITAM–CHAMP, NCSP Practitioner, PMP, TOGAF, Accredited Trainer–CGEIT, COBIT, CHAMP, CITAM and CSAM, Process Governance Manager, First Abu Dhabi Bank, UAE
Adham Etoom, CISM, CRISC, PMP, GCIH, FAIR, Government of Jordan, Jordan
J. Winston Hayden, CISA, CRISC, CISM, CGEIT, CDPSE, South Africa
Jimmy Heschl, CISA, CISM, CGEIT, Head of Digital Security, Red Bull, Austria
Alberto Piamonte, COBIT Trainer, Implementor and Assessor, Senior GRC Consultant, Key Map Team, Italy
Andre Pitkowski, CGEIT, CRISC, Data Protection Officer, Santos Port Authority, Brazil
Abdul Rafeq, CISA, FCA, DISA (ICAI), Managing Director, WINCER Infotech, Ltd, India
Dirk Steuperaert, CISA, CRISC, CGEIT, Managing Consultant, IT In Balance, Belgium
Manuel Yrigoyen, CISM, CGEIT, CRISC, ISO 3100O LRM, IT Governance Consultant, Independent, Peru
Tichaona Zororo, CISA, CRISC, CISM, CGEIT, CDPSE, CIA, CRMA, COBIT Certified Assessor, Director Digital Transformation & Innovation Advisory, EGIT | Enterprise Governance of IT, South Africa
Guodong Zou, CISA, CISM, CGEIT, CRISC, CDPSE, CISSP, CBRM, CBAP, CBPP, TOGAF, ITIL, LSS Black Belt, Strategic Advisor, IT Practices, Cisco Systems, Inc., China

Board of Directors
Gregory Touhill, Chair, CISM, CISSP, Director, CERT Center, Carnegie Mellon University, USA
Pamela Nigro, Vice-Chair, CISA, CGEIT, CRISC, CDPSE, CRMA, Vice President–Information Technology, Security Officer, Home Access Health, USA
John De Santis, Former Chairman and Chief Executive Officer, HyTrust, Inc., USA
Niel Harper, CISA, CRISC, CDPSE, Chief Information Security Officer, UNOPS, Denmark
Gabriela Hernandez-Cardoso, Independent Board Member, Mexico
Maureen O'Connell, Board Chair, Acacia Research (NASDAQ), Former Chief Financial Officer and Chief Administration Officer, Scholastic, Inc., USA
David Samuelson, Chief Executive Officer, ISACA, USA
Gerrard Schmid, President and Chief Executive Officer, Diebold Nixdorf, USA
Veronica Rose, CISA, CDPSE, Founder, Encrypt Africa, Kenya
Asaf Weisberg, CISA, CRISC, CISM, CGEIT, Chief Executive Officer, introSight Ltd., Israel
Tracey Dedrick, ISACA Board Chair, 2020-2021, Former Chief Risk Officer, Hudson City Bancorp, USA
Brennan P. Baybeck, CISA, CRISC, CISM, CISSP, ISACA Board Chair, 2019-2020, Vice President and Chief Information Security Officer for Customer Services, Oracle Corporation, USA
Rob Clyde, CISM, ISACA Board Chair, 2018-2019, Independent Director, Titus, and Executive Chair, White Cloud Security, USA

Page intentionally left blank

TABLE OF CONTENTS

LIST OF FIGURES

Chapter 1. Introduction to Enterprise Governance of Information and Technology

Chapter 2. Introduction to COBIT as an I&T Governance Framework

Chapter 3. Scope and Intended Audience

Chapter 4. How to Start an I&T Governance Program

Chapter 5. Structure of COBIT Governance and Management Objectives

Chapter 6. Practical Example Using This Publication

Appendix A. Suitability Test

Appendix B. Design Factors

Appendix C. Applying Design Factors

Appendix D. Goals Cascade—Overview

Appendix E. Goals Cascade—Mapping Tables

Appendix F. Example Metrics

Appendix G. Organizational Structures

Chapter 1
Introduction to Enterprise Governance of Information and Technology

1.1 What Is Governance?

This publication uses the term governance to refer to enterprise governance of information and technology (EGIT).

Given the centrality of information and technology (I&T) for enterprise risk management and value generation, a specific focus on EGIT has arisen over the last three decades.

EGIT is an integral part of corporate governance. It is exercised by the board, which oversees the definition and implementation of organizational processes, structures and relational mechanisms that enable both business and IT professionals to execute their responsibilities in support of business/information technology (IT) alignment and the creation of business value from I&T-enabled business investments (**figure 1.1**).

Figure 1.1—The Context of Enterprise Governance of Information and Technology

Source: De Haas, S.; W. Van Grembergen; *Enterprise Governance of Information Technology: Achieving Alignment and Value, Featuring COBIT® 5*, 2nd ed., Springer International Publishing, Switzerland, 2015, *https://www.springer.com/us/book/9783319145464*

EGIT is complex and multifaceted. There is no ideal way to design, implement and maintain effective EGIT within an enterprise. Members of governing boards and senior management typically need to tailor EGIT measures and implementation to their own specific strategies, contexts and needs. They must also be willing to accept more accountability for I&T and drive a different mindset and culture for delivering value from I&T.

Enterprise governance of information and technology is a term that is carefully chosen, and the meaning has changed over time. It encompasses nuances that ISACA sees as important for effective EGIT, for example:

- Commonly speaking, the term IT governance is often used, but this focuses too much on the IT department and gives the impression that responsibility for governance lies within the IT department.
- Referring to I&T emphasizes that governance is about information management and the use of technology to support information management. While the management of information is not the sole responsibility of IT, the management of the technology is.
- IT is the term used for the IT department. I&T (by contrast) often extends beyond the IT department (and/or areas under its control).

Enterprise governance indicates that the governance of I&T is a responsibility of the business, not just of IT.

1.2 Importance of I&T and I&T Governance

During the last few decades, I&T has become crucial in the support, sustainability and growth of enterprises. Previously, governing boards (boards of directors) and senior management could delegate, ignore or avoid I&T-related decisions. In most sectors and industries, such attitudes are now ill-advised, to put it mildly.

Enterprises are increasingly dependent on technology and digitization. I&T are essential for survival and growth.

Therefore, top management needs to understand whether managers of I&T assets are:

- Likely to achieve enterprise objectives
- Resilient enough to learn and adapt
- Thoughtfully managing the I&T risk the enterprise faces
- Appropriately recognizing opportunities and acting upon them

Boards and executive management need to extend their business governance to I&T and provide the leadership, organizational structures and processes that ensure that the enterprise's I&T sustains and extends enterprise strategies and objectives.

EGIT is not an isolated discipline. It is an integral part of overall enterprise governance. The need to integrate IT governance with overall I&T governance is similar to the need to integrate IT across the enterprise rather than relegate it to remote corners or ivory towers.

Chapter 2
Introduction to COBIT as an I&T Governance Framework

2.1 Introduction

Over the years, best practice frameworks have been developed and promoted to assist in the process of understanding, designing and implementing EGIT principles and objectives. COBIT® 2019 builds on and integrates more than 25 years of development in this field, incorporating new scientific insights and operationalizing them as practices. From its foundation in the IT audit community, COBIT has broadened to become more comprehensive and has established itself as a generally accepted I&T governance and management framework.

Some view COBIT as an excellent resource for larger enterprises but see it as difficult to implement in small and medium enterprise (SME) settings. This publication adapts COBIT to small and medium enterprise contexts, allowing SMEs to adopt pertinent COBIT concepts tailored to their size, scope and industry, thus enabling them to enjoy the benefits afforded by implementing COBIT.

2.2 What Is COBIT and What Is It Not?

COBIT is a framework for the governance and management of enterprise information and technology[1] aimed at the whole enterprise. Enterprise I&T means all the technology and information processing the enterprise puts in place to achieve its goals, regardless of where it occurs in the enterprise. In other words, enterprise I&T includes the IT department of an enterprise but certainly are not limited to it.

The COBIT framework makes a clear distinction between governance and management. These two disciplines encompass different types of activities, require different organizational structures and serve different purposes.

COBIT establishes a key distinction between governance and management:

- **Governance** ensures that stakeholder needs, conditions and options are evaluated to determine balanced, agreed-on enterprise objectives to be achieved; that direction is set through prioritization and decision making; and that performance and compliance are monitored against agreed-on direction and objectives. In most SMEs, governance is the responsibility of the directors of the enterprise, who are—in some cases—also the owners of the enterprise.
- **Management** plans, builds, runs and monitors activities, in alignment with the direction set by the governance body, to achieve the enterprise objectives. In most enterprises, management is the responsibility of the executive management under the leadership of the chief executive officer (CEO).

  In some instances, the directors of the enterprise are also involved in its management. They are, therefore, responsible for both governance and management. However, there is still a distinction between governance and management.

2.3 COBIT Components

To satisfy governance and management objectives, each enterprise needs to establish, tailor and sustain a governance system from a combination of components (**figure 2.1**). Basic concepts pertaining to components of governance systems follow:

[1] Throughout this document, references to the framework for the governance of I&T imply the entirety of the description here.

- Components are factors that, individually and collectively, contribute to the good operations of the enterprise's I&T governance system.
- Components interact with each other, resulting in a holistic I&T governance system.
- Components can be of different types. The most familiar components are processes, but other components of a governance system (**figure 2.1**) also must be considered:
  - **Processes** describe an organized set of practices and activities to achieve certain objectives and produce a set of outputs in support of overall IT-related goals.
  - **Organizational structures** are the key decision-making entities in an enterprise.
  - **Information flows and items** are pervasive and include all information produced and used by the enterprise. COBIT focuses on the information required for the effective functioning of the enterprise governance system.
  - **People, skills and competencies** are required for successful completion of all activities and for making correct decisions and taking corrective actions.
  - **Principles, policies and procedures** are the vehicles that translate desired behavior into practical guidance for day-to-day management.
  - **Culture, ethics and behavior** of individuals and of the enterprise are very often underestimated as success factors in governance and management activities.
  - **Services, infrastructure and applications** include the technology services, hardware and software applications that provide the enterprise with the governance system for I&T processing.

Figure 2.1—COBIT Components of a Governance System

Source: ISACA, *COBIT® 2019 Framework: Introduction and Methodology*, USA, 2018, *https://store.isaca.org/s/store#/store/browse/detail/a2S4w000004Ko5dEAC*

2.4 Design Factors

COBIT defines the design factors that should be considered by each enterprise to build a best-fit governance system focusing on the context, objectives and needs of the enterprise. Design factors include any combination of the factors shown in **figure 2.2**.

Descriptions and selection criteria for design factors are described in Appendix B. Applying Design Factors can focus an enterprise on where it can focus a governance program when building a governance program to achieve the greatest value from that program.

Figure 2.2—COBIT Design Factors

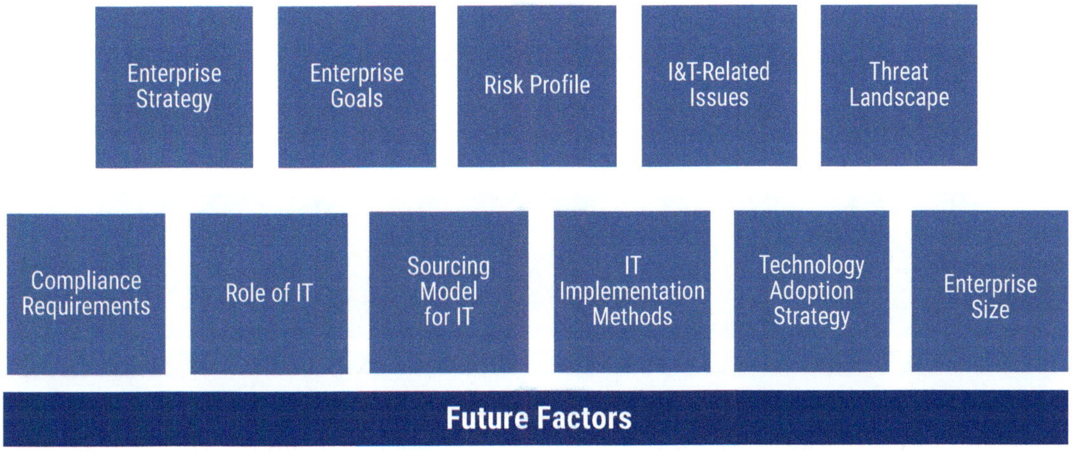

Source: ISACA, *COBIT® 2019 Framework: Introduction and Methodology*, USA, 2018, *https://store.isaca.org/s/store#/store/browse/detail/a2S4w000004Ko5dEAC*

2.5 Governance and Management Objectives

For I&T to contribute to enterprise goals, several governance and management objectives should be achieved.

A governance or management objective always relates to one process (with an identical or similar name) and a series of related component types to help achieve the objective. A governance objective relates to governance processes (depicted on the dark blue background in **figure 2.3**), while a management objective relates to management processes (depicted on the lighter blue background in **figure 2.3**). Governance processes typically are the purview of boards and executive management, whereas management processes are the domain of senior and middle management. Within SMEs, the governance processes are the responsibility of the enterprise directors and owners (the governing body). However, within some SMEs, the directors and owners are also responsible for the management processes.

The governance and management objectives in COBIT are grouped into five domains. Domain names identify the objectives' key purposes and areas of activity (when looking at I&T at the enterprise level).

- Governance objectives are grouped in one domain: **Evaluate, Direct and Monitor** (EDM). In this domain, the governing body evaluates strategic options, directs senior management on chosen strategic options and monitors achievement of the strategy.
- Management objectives are grouped in four domains:
  - **Align, Plan and Organize** (APO)—This domain addresses the overall organization, strategy and supporting activities for I&T.
  - **Build, Acquire and Implement** (BAI)—This domain deals with the definition, acquisition and implementation of I&T solutions and their integration into business processes.
  - **Deliver, Service and Support** (DSS)—This domain addresses the operational delivery and support of I&T services, including security.
  - **Monitor, Evaluate and Assess** (MEA)—This domain deals with monitoring the performance and conformance of I&T with internal performance targets, internal control objectives and external requirements.

There are 40 governance and management objectives in COBIT (the core model; see **figure 2.3**).

Figure 2.3—COBIT Core Model

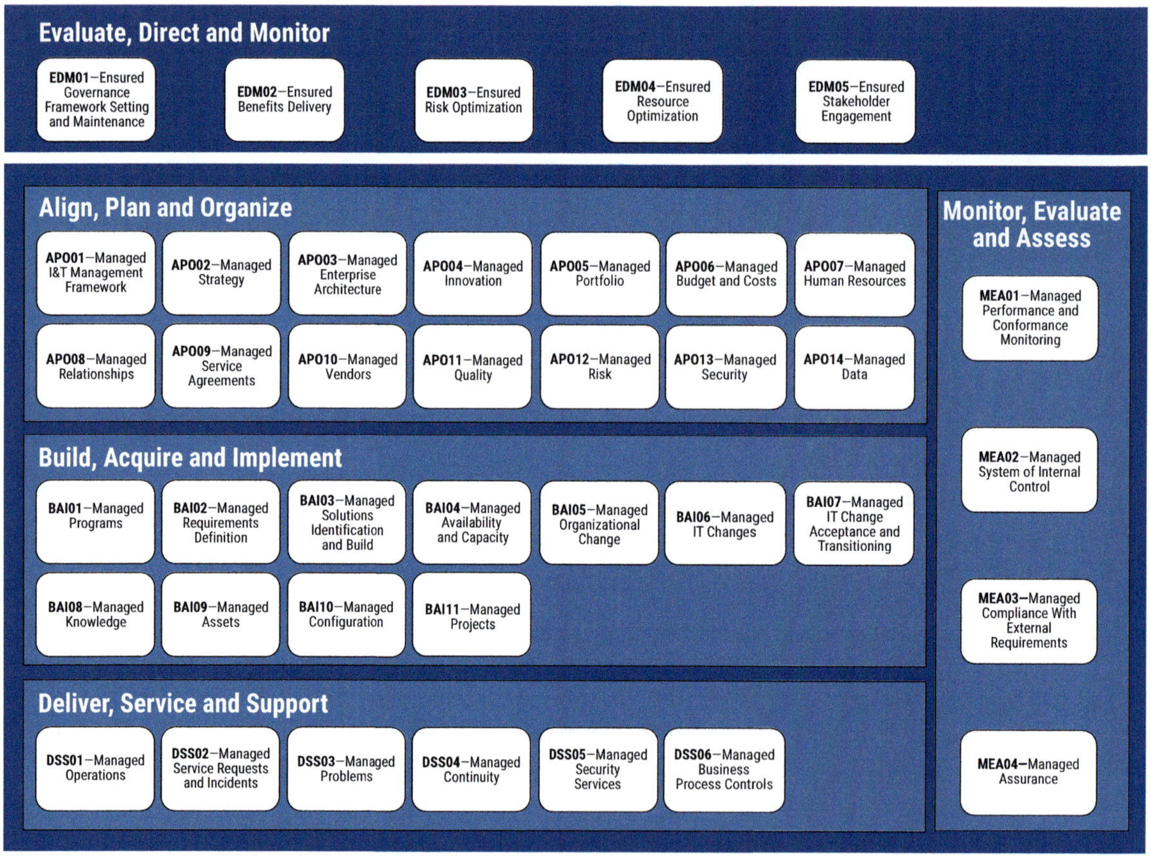

Source: ISACA, *COBIT® 2019 Framework: Introduction and Methodology*, USA, 2018, *https://store.isaca.org/s/store#/store/browse/detail/a2S4w000004Ko5dEAC*

Each governance and management objective consists of a number of related components (see **figure 2.1**). They are intrinsically interdependent; there is no natural order of priority among them. However, design factors can influence their significance and make some governance and management objectives more important than others. As a consequence, some governance and management objectives may become negligible, particularly for SMEs.

More information and detailed guidance on how to use the design factors for designing a governance system can be found in *COBIT® 2019 Design Guide: Designing an Information and Technology Governance Solution.*[2]

[2] ISACA, *COBIT® 2019 Design Guide: Designing an Information and Technology Governance Solution*, USA, 2019, *https://store.isaca.org/s/store#/store/browse/detail/a2S4w000004Ko9bEAC*

Page intentionally left blank

Chapter 3
Scope and Intended Audience

3.1 Introduction

This publication provides specific guidance that is related to small and medium enterprises (SME). In prior COBIT 2019 publications, this title was referred to as the COBIT Focus Area: Small and Medium Enterprises.[3]

The target audience for this guide includes different functions in an SME, including business managers, IT managers, quality and security professionals, internal audit, and others who require detailed guidance on developing and implementing governance practices in their enterprises.

In this publication, the official definition[4] of SME specifies enterprises with 50 to 250 full-time employees (FTEs) and an annual turnover of up to US$59 million (€ 50 million) or an annual balance sheet total up to US$51 million (€ 43 million).

In addition to enterprises captured by this official definition of an SME, this guide also applies to those with a significant number of employees who use IT systems and services, relative to the total number of FTEs.

For enterprises that have up to 250 FTEs and that are highly dependent on IT systems and services, *COBIT® 2019 Framework: Governance and Management Objectives*[5] may be more relevant and appropriate than this SME guidance.

For other enterprises that have up to 250 FTEs, including approximately 30 to 70 employees who work daily with IT systems and services, this guide is applicable.

For enterprises that have fewer than 100 FTEs and are not strongly dependent on IT systems and services, COBIT might not be entirely appropriate. Some aspects of COBIT may be adopted, but the application of this complete SME guidance may not be needed. Each SME will need to determine the extent to which COBIT governance and management objectives are developed and deployed for the enterprise. Enterprises that may benefit from this guide typically:

- Have limited in-house IT skills and/or capacity
- Do not have a complex IT infrastructure
- Outsource complex tasks
- Aim more to buy (and potentially tailor) tools rather than build them
- Have a relatively high risk tolerance, because of their low risk capacity
- Are very cost-conscious
- Have a simple command structure and limited organizational structures in place
- Have a short span of control

The specific guidance included in this publication is driven by the assumption that these characteristics will match most users. In addition, the suitability test, explained in Appendix A, can help an enterprise determine whether this guidance is appropriate for its use.

[3] Unlike other COBIT Focus Areas which are intended to be used in conjunction with the COBIT core model, this publication is designed to be used as standalone guidance to aid small and medium enterprise users who are looking for a quick reference for I&T governance and quick wins to implement good governance I&T practices.

[4] European Commission, "SME definition," Internal Market, Industry, Entrepreneurship and SMEs, *http://ec.europa.eu/growth/smes/business-friendly-environment/sme-definition_en*

[5] ISACA, *COBIT® 2019 Framework: Governance and Management Objectives,* USA, 2019, *https://store.isaca.org/s/store#/store/browse/detail/a2S4w000004Ko5aEAC*

3.2 How to Apply This SME Guidance

SMEs are not all the same, so the specific governance and management decisions and I&T setup may vary from one SME to another. Some may have one or two employees who focus exclusively on basic IT services, while others may have substantial in-house IT departments that provide specialized expertise for both operations and new projects.

Some may decide to allocate IT costs back to the business, while others may keep an overall I&T budget overview at the enterprise level. Some may consistently choose off-the-shelf solutions and limit tailoring and changes, while others may work with external partners to tailor specific solutions to their requirements. The role of the I&T function depends on the enterprise's core business, priorities, available resources, industry and other factors. The following ranking of governance and management objectives (**figure 3.1**)—based on a survey of COBIT governance advisors—can serve as a predefined list of SME-specific objectives from which to begin the prioritization process. As the specific I&T setup may vary from one SME to another, it is up to the enterprise to apply this guidance to its specific context and to select the governance and management objectives that are most relevant to its situation.

Figure 3.1—COBIT Governance and Management Objectives: Relevance and Priority for SMEs

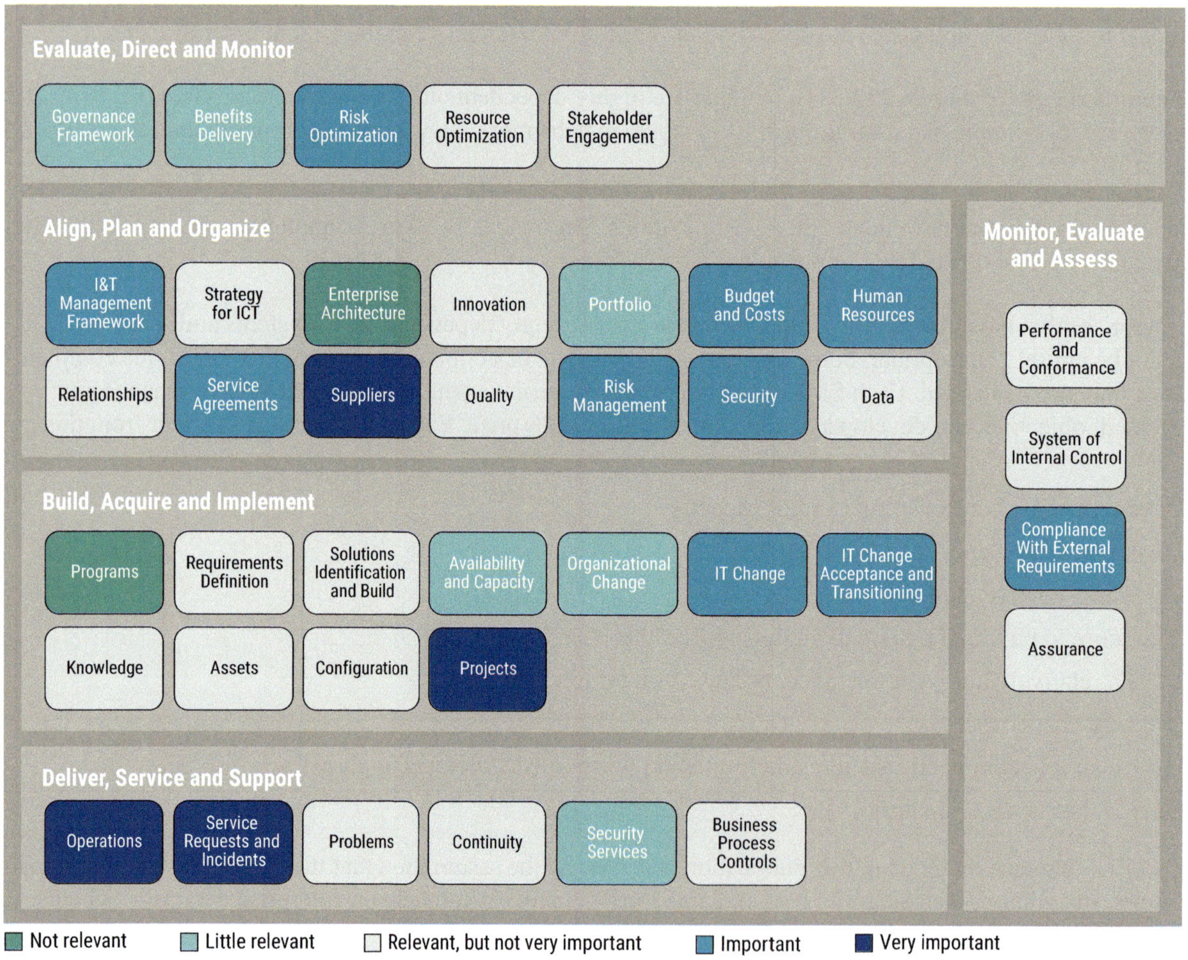

An enterprise can assign its own relevance and priority to the objectives by applying the design factors described in Appendix B or by executing the goals cascade described in Appendix D.

This publication can serve as a starting point and a working guide to develop a tailored enterprise governance system for I&T. Some experience in setting up governance practices might be required to take full advantage of this SME guidance.

Page intentionally left blank

Chapter 4

How to Start an I&T Governance Program

4.1 Getting Started

There is no one-size-fits-all governance system for enterprise I&T. This applies to SMEs just as it does to large enterprises. Every enterprise has a distinct character and profile and will differ from other organizations in several critical respects: size, industry sector, regulatory landscape, threat landscape, role of IT in the enterprise and tactical technology-related decision making, among others. All these aspects—which COBIT references collectively as design factors—require enterprises to tailor their governance systems to realize the most value from their use of I&T.

To develop a feasible road map, it is important to scope the program well from the start, following the governance system design workflow illustrated in **figure 4.1**.

Figure 4.1—Governance System Design Workflow

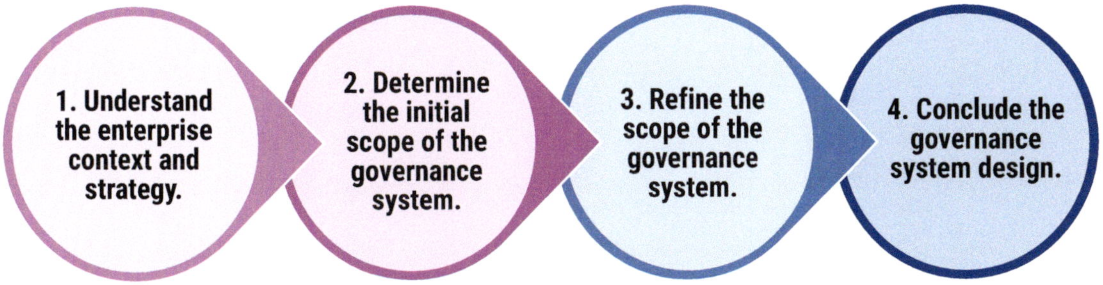

- 1.1 Understand enterprise strategy.
- 1.2 Understand enterprise goals.
- 1.3 Understand the risk profile.
- 1.4 Understand current I&T-related issues.

- 2.1 Consider enterprise strategy.
- 2.2 Consider enterprise goals and apply the COBIT goals cascade.
- 2.3 Consider the risk profile of the enterprise.
- 2.4 Consider current I&T-related issues.

- 3.1 Consider the threat landscape.
- 3.2 Consider compliance requirements.
- 3.3 Consider the role of IT.
- 3.4 Consider the sourcing model.
- 3.5 Consider IT implementation methods.
- 3.6 Consider the IT adoption strategy.
- 3.7 Consider enterprise size.

- 4.1 Resolve inherent priority conflicts.
- 4.2 Conclude the governance system design.

Source: ISACA, *COBIT® 2019 Framework: Introduction and Methodology*, USA, 2018, *https://store.isaca.org/s/store#/store/browse/detail/a2S4w000004Ko5dEAC*

Following the stages and steps in the design process, as illustrated in **figure 4.1**, will generate recommendations, e.g., for prioritizing governance and management objectives or related governance system components to address target capability levels, or for adopting specific variants of a governance system component. Some steps or substeps may lead to conflicting guidance, which is inevitable due to the large number of design factors and the overall generic nature of the design factor guidance and mapping tables.

One useful approach is to put all guidance obtained during this process on a design canvas and then, as the last stage of the design process, resolve conflicts among the elements to the degree possible and conclude. There is no magic formula. The final design will be the result of case-by-case decision making, based on all the elements on the design canvas. Following these steps while using the COBIT® 2019 governance system design tool kit[6] will enable an enterprise to establish a governance system tailored to its needs.

To develop an executable road map, it is important to evaluate the outcome of the design tool kit with knowledge of the specific situation and context of the enterprise. It is also useful to refer to the general relevance overview for SMEs of the 40 COBIT objectives shown in **figure 3.1**).

The prioritization must result in one design for the governance system for enterprise I&T. The design will include prioritized governance and management objectives, with the number of high-priority objectives limited at a reasonable level. Once the enterprise determines the relative importance of the 40 COBIT objectives, it can start developing the related components or begin integrating different components into one project.

An example of the prioritization process for a medium-sized innovative company can be found in Appendix C.

The practical implementation of a governance program for SMEs is discussed in Chapter 6.

[6] The COBIT® 2019 governance system design tool kit can be downloaded at *https://www.isaca.org/-/media/files/isacadp/project/isaca/knowledge-and-insights/zips/cobit-2019-design-toolkit_tkt_eng_1218.zip?la=en&hash=0E8BC92071EF5FDF474A979F75A0F78CBC775E54.*

Chapter 5
Structure of COBIT Governance and Management Objectives

5.1 Introduction

This chapter describes the paradigmatic structure of COBIT governance and management objectives, and explains—at a high descriptive level—how the following key components of each objective will be further subdivided and elaborated throughout this publication.

- Processes
- Organizational structures
- Information flows and items
- People, skills and competencies
- Principles, policies and procedures
- Culture, ethics and behavior
- Services, infrastructure and applications

A subsequent chapter—Chapter 7—outlines detailed guidance relevant to SMEs for all domains and objectives, following the order of components whose general exposition begins at Section 5.3 below.

5.2 Governance and Management Objectives

The COBIT SME model consists of 40 governance and management objectives, split into five domains (see **figure 2.3**).

5.2.1 Naming of the Objectives

For each objective, the following information is included in the top section of the detailed guidance (**figure 5.1**):

- **Domain name** (aligning to responsibility for objectives within the domain)
  - **Governance domain**—Evaluate, Direct and Monitor (EDM)
  - **Management domains**—For most SMEs, governance will include I&T management domains:
    - Align, Plan and Organize (APO)
    - Build, Acquire and Implement (BAI)
    - Deliver, Service and Support (DSS)
    - Monitor, Evaluate and Assess (MEA)
- **Governance or management objective name**
- **Focus Area**
- **Description**
- **Purpose statement**—The purpose statement elaborates on the governance or management objective.
- **Focus Area relevance statement**—This statement provides more information about the relevance of each objective, specifically for SMEs. This general guidance should be evaluated in the context of each enterprise.

Figure 5.1—Display of Governance and Management Objectives	
Domain: <NAME> Governance/Management Objective: <NAME>	Focus Area: Small and Medium Enterprises
Description	
<TEXT>	
Purpose	
<TEXT>	
Small and Medium Enterprise Focus Area Relevance	
<TEXT>	
Source: ISACA, *COBIT® 2019 Framework: Governance Management and Objectives*, USA, 2018, *https://store.isaca.org/s/store#/store/browse/detail/a2S4w000004Ko5aEAC*	

5.3 Component A: Process

Each governance and management objective includes several process practices. Each process has one or more activities. A limited number of example metrics accompanies each process practice, to measure the achievement of the practice and its contribution to the achievement of the overall objective. Following is a detailed explanation of the process component within each objective (**figure 5.2**).

Figure 5.2—Display of Process Component		
A. Component: Process		
Governance/Management Practice	**Small and Medium Enterprise-specific Metrics**	
<REF> <NAME> <DESCRIPTION>	<METRIC>	
Small and Medium Enterprise-specific Activities		**Capability Level**
1. <TEXT>		<NR>
2. <TEXT>		<NR>
n. <TEXT>		<NR>
Related Guidance (Standards, Frameworks, Compliance Requirements)	**Detailed Reference**	
<STANDARD NAME>	<TEXT>	
<STANDARD NAME>	<TEXT>	
Source: ISACA, *COBIT® 2019 Framework: Governance Management and Objectives*, USA, 2018, *https://store.isaca.org/s/store#/store/browse/detail/a2S4w000004Ko5aEAC*		

Assignment of capability levels to all process activities enables clear definitions. A process reaches a certain capability level as soon as all activities at that level are performed successfully.

COBIT® 2019 supports a CMMI-based process capability scheme. Processes within each governance and management objective can operate at various capability levels, ranging from 0 to 5. The capability level is a measure of how well a process is implemented and performing. **Figure 5.3** depicts the model, the increasing capability levels and the general characteristics of each capability level.

Figure 5.3—Capability Levels for Processes

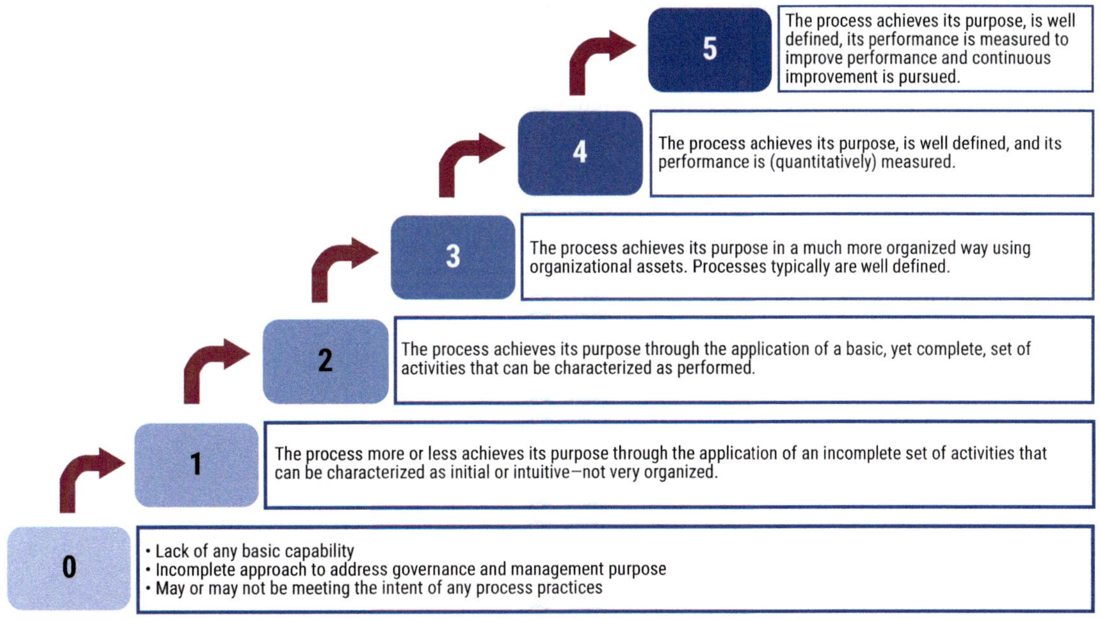

Source: ISACA, *COBIT® 2019 Framework: Introduction and Methodology*, USA, 2018, *https://store.isaca.org/s/store#/store/browse/detail/a2S4w000004Ko5dEAC*

5.3.1 References to Other Standards and Guidance

References relevant to other standards and guidance are included in Component A (see **figure 5.2**). The related guidance refers to standards, frameworks, compliance requirements and other guidance relevant to the process at hand. The detailed reference area cites specific chapters or sections within related guidance. A complete list of sources for the related guidance is included in Appendix H. If no related guidance is listed for a particular component, no applicable references are known from the sources mapped.

5.3.2 Rating Process Activities

A capability level can be achieved to varying degrees, which can be expressed by ratings. The range of available ratings depends on the context in which the performance assessment is made:

- Some formal methods leading to independent certification use a binary pass/fail set of ratings.
- Less formal methods (often used in performance improvement contexts) work better with a larger range of ratings, such as the following set, in which each descriptor defines the degree of achievement of capability levels:
  - **Fully**—The capability level is more than 85 percent achieved. (This remains a judgment call, but it can be substantiated by the examination or assessment of the components of the enabler, such as process activities, process goals and organizational structure good practices.)
  - **Largely**—The capability level is achieved between 50 percent and 85 percent.
  - **Partially**—The capability level is achieved between 15 percent and 50 percent.
  - **Not**—The capability level is achieved less than 15 percent.

5.4 Component B: Organizational Structures

Organizational structures are the committees, functions and roles that make decisions or manage parts of the enterprise. For each practice, levels of responsibility and accountability are suggested (**figure 5.4**).

Small- and medium-sized enterprises are assumed to have a simple command structure and limited organizational structures in place. Responsibilities are concentrated in a limited number of roles and structures as opposed to those defined in *COBIT® 2019 Framework: Governance and Management Objectives*[7] (i.e., the core publication). The following roles and organizational structures have been defined in the context of this SME guidance:

- Board
- Executive Committee
- General Manager
- Financial Manager
- Operations Manager
- Security Manager
- Security Expert
- Business Process Owners
- Steering Committee
- Project Manager
- Head Human Resources
- Head of IT
- IT Development Coordinator
- IT Operations Coordinator
- Privacy Officer
- Legal Department
- Compliance or Quality
- Audit

A detailed description of each of these roles and organizational structures is included in Appendix G.

Specific responsibilities per management objective are included in responsible (R)/ accountable (A) charts in the detailed component guidance. These two levels of involvement are:

- **Responsible** (R)—These roles take the main operational obligation of fulfilling the practice and creating the intended outcome. Who is getting the task done? Who drives the task?
- **Accountable** (A)—These roles carry overall and final accountability. As a principle, accountability cannot be shared. Who accounts for the success and achievement of the task?

The SME can customize this chart by adding two levels of involvement for roles and organizational structures that should be:

- **Consulted** (C)—These roles provide input for the task. Who provides input?
- **Informed** (I)—These roles are informed of the achievements and/or deliverables of the task. Who receives information?

[7] *Op cit* ISACA, *COBIT® 2019 Framework: Governance and Management Objectives*

Since attribution of C and I depends on the organizational context and priorities, they are not included in this detailed guidance.

It is recommended that each enterprise review the suggested levels of responsibility and accountability and consider additional levels of involvement, such as C and I.

Before starting to work on these organizational structures, each enterprise should update the naming of the proposed roles and organizational structures according to its own organizational context, priorities and preferred terminology.

Figure 5.4—Display of Organizational Structures Component

B. Component: Organizational Structures								
Key Governance/Management Practice	Organizational Structure 1	Organizational Structure 2	Organizational Structure 3	Organizational Structure 4	Organizational Structure 5	Organizational Structure 6	Organizational Structure 7	Organizational Structure 8, etc.
<REF> <NAME>								

Source: ISACA, *COBIT® 2019 Framework: Governance Management and Objectives*, USA, 2018, *https://store.isaca.org/s/store#/store/browse/detail/a2S4w000004Ko5aEAC*

5.5 Component C: Information Flows and Items

The third governance component provides guidance on the information flows and items linked to process practices. For each practice, inputs and outputs—with indications of origin and destination—are provided.

In general, each output is sent to one or a limited number of destinations, typically another COBIT process practice. That output then becomes an input to its destination (**figure 5.5**).

Figure 5.5—Display of Information Flows and Items Component

C. Component: Information Flows and Items				
Governance/Management Practice	Small and Medium Enterprise-specific Inputs		Small and Medium Enterprise-specific Outputs	
<REF> <NAME>	**From**	**Description**	**Description**	**To**
	<REF>	<TEXT>	<REF>	<TEXT>

Source: ISACA, *COBIT® 2019 Framework: Governance Management and Objectives*, USA, 2018, *https://store.isaca.org/s/store#/store/browse/detail/a2S4w000004Ko5aEAC*

For some inputs/outputs, "internal" is mentioned as a destination. This means that the input/output is between activities within the same process.

There are a number of outputs that have many destinations, such as all COBIT processes or all processes within a domain. For readability reasons, these outputs are not listed as inputs in these processes. A complete list of such outputs is included in **figure 5.6.**

Figure 5.6—Outputs to Multiple Processes		
Outputs to All Processes		
From Key Practice	**Output Description**	**Destination**
APO13.02	Information security risk treatment plan	All EDM, All APO, All BAI, All DSS, All MEA
From Governance Practice	**Output Description**	**Destination**
EDM01.01	Decision-making model	All EDM
EDM01.01	Authority levels	All EDM
Outputs to All Management Processes		
From Management Practice	**Output Description**	**Destination**
APO01.01	Management system design	All APO; All BAI; All DSS; All MEA
APO01.01	Priority governance and management objectives	All APO; All BAI; All DSS; All MEA
APO01.02	Communication on I&T objectives	All APO; All BAI; All DSS; All MEA
APO01.03	Targets for gap analysis	All APO; All BAI; All DSS; All MEA
APO01.11	Process improvement opportunities	All APO; All BAI; All DSS; All MEA
APO11.03	Quality management standards	All APO; All BAI; All DSS; All MEA
APO11.05	Examples of good practice to be shared	All APO; All BAI; All DSS; All MEA
MEA01.02	Monitoring targets	All APO; All BAI; All DSS; All MEA
MEA01.04	Performance reports	All APO; All BAI; All DSS; All MEA
MEA01.05	Remedial actions and assignments	All APO; All BAI; All DSS; All MEA
MEA02.01	Results of internal control monitoring and reviews	All APO; All BAI; All DSS; All MEA
MEA02.03	Self-assessment plans and criteria	All APO; All BAI; All DSS; All MEA
MEA02.04	Control deficiencies	All APO; All BAI; All DSS; All MEA
MEA02.04	Remedial actions	All APO; All BAI; All DSS; All MEA
MEA03.02	Communications of changed compliance requirements	All APO; All BAI; All DSS; All MEA
MEA04.02	Assurance plans	All APO; All BAI; All DSS; All MEA
MEA04.08	Assurance review report	All APO; All BAI; All DSS; All MEA
MEA04.08	Assurance review results	All APO; All BAI; All DSS; All MEA
MEA04.09	Remedial actions	All APO; All BAI; All DSS; All MEA

5.6 Component D: People, Skills and Competencies

The people, skills and competencies governance component identifies the human resources and skills required to achieve a governance or management objective. COBIT® 2019 based this guidance on the Skills Framework for the Information Age (SFIA®) V6 (version 6).[8] All listed skills are described in detail in the SFIA framework. The detailed reference provides a unique code that correlates to SFIA guidance on the skill (**figure 5.7**). In addition, references are included for several governance and management objectives to *e-Competence Framework (e-CF) – A common European Framework for ICT Professionals in all industry sectors – Part 1: Framework*[9] and the Institute of Internal Auditors' "Core Principles for the Professional Practice of Internal Auditing."[10]

[8] SFIA Foundation, "SFIA V6, the sixth major version of the Skills Framework for the Information Age," *https://sfia-online.org/en/legacy-sfia/sfia-6*

[9] European Committee for Standardization (CEN), *e-Competence Framework (e-CF) – A common European Framework for ICT Professionals in all industry sectors – Part 1: Framework*, EN 16234-1:2016, *https://ec.europa.eu/esco/portal/escopedia/European_e-Competence_Framework__40_e-CF_41_*

[10] The Institute of Internal Auditors® (IIA®), "Core Principles for the Professional Practice of Internal Auditing," *https://na.theiia.org/standards-guidance/mandatory-guidance/Pages/Core-Principles-for-the-Professional-Practice-of-Internal-Auditing.aspx*

Figure 5.7—Display of People, Skills and Competencies Component

D. Component: People, Skills and Competencies		
Skill	**Related Guidance (Standards, Frameworks, Compliance Requirements)**	**Detailed Reference**
<NAME>	Skills Framework for the Information Age, V6 (SFIA 6), 2015	<SFIA CODE>
<NAME>	Skills Framework for the Information Age, V6 (SFIA 6), 2015	<SFIA CODE>

Source: ISACA, *COBIT® 2019 Framework: Governance Management and Objectives*, USA, 2018, *https://store.isaca.org/s/store#/store/browse/detail/a2S4w000004Ko5aEAC*

5.7 Component E: Principles, Policies and Procedures

This component includes suggested principles, policies, standards and procedures relevant to the governance or management objective. The names of relevant principles, policies, standards and procedures are provided, with a description of their purpose and content (**figure 5.8**).

Figure 5.8—Display of Principles, Policies and Procedures Component

E. Component: Principles, Policies and Procedures	
Relevant Policy	**Policy Description**
<NAME>	<DESCRIPTION>

Source: ISACA, *COBIT® 2019 Framework: Governance Management and Objectives*, USA, 2018, *https://store.isaca.org/s/store#/store/browse/detail/a2S4w000004Ko5aEAC*

5.8 Component F: Culture, Ethics and Behavior

The governance component on culture, ethics and behavior provides detailed guidance on cultural elements within the enterprise that support the achievement of a governance or management objective (**figure 5.9**). Where relevant, references to other standards and additional guidance are included. The related guidance cites specific chapters or sections wherein more information may be consulted. A complete list of sources is included in Appendix H.

Figure 5.9—Display of Culture, Ethics and Behavior Component

F. Component: Culture, Ethics and Behavior
Key Culture Elements
<NAME>

Source: ISACA, *COBIT® 2019 Framework: Governance Management and Objectives*, USA, 2018, *https://store.isaca.org/s/store#/store/browse/detail/a2S4w000004Ko5aEAC*

5.9 Component G: Services, Infrastructure and Applications

The services, infrastructure and applications component provides detailed guidance on third-party services, types of infrastructure and categories of applications that support the achievement of a governance or management objective. Guidance operates at a generic level. The intention is to provide direction for enterprises to build their governance system for I&T (**figure 5.10**) without naming specific vendors or products.

Figure 5.10—Display of Services, Infrastructure and Applications Component

G. Component: Services, Infrastructure and Applications

- <CATEGORY OF SERVICES, INFRASTRUCTURE OR APPLICATIONS>
- <CATEGORY OF SERVICES, INFRASTRUCTURE OR APPLICATIONS>

Source: ISACA, *COBIT® 2019 Framework: Governance Management and Objectives*, USA, 2018, *https://store.isaca.org/s/store#/store/browse/detail/a2S4w000004Ko5aEAC*

Page intentionally left blank

Chapter 6
Practical Example Using This Publication

6.1 Introduction

EGIT does not occur in a vacuum. Implementation takes place under different conditions and in circumstances determined by numerous factors in the external and internal environment, such as:

- Governing laws, regulations and policies
- International standards
- Industry practices
- The economic and competitive environment
- Technology advancements and evolution
- The threat landscape
- The community's culture and ethics
- The enterprise's:
  - Reason for existence, mission, vision, goals and values
  - Governance policies and practices
  - Culture and management style
  - Models for roles and responsibilities
  - Business plans and strategic intentions
  - Operating model and level of maturity

The implementation of EGIT for each enterprise is different, therefore, and the context needs to be understood and considered to design the optimal new or improved EGIT environment.

6.2 Creating the Appropriate Environment

It is important to implement EGIT improvements in the appropriate context. This helps ensure that the initiative is adequately governed and guided, and supported by management. Major I&T initiatives often fail due to inadequate management direction, support and oversight. EGIT implementations have a greater chance of success if they are well governed and well managed.

Inadequate support and direction from key stakeholders can result in EGIT initiatives that produce new policies and procedures lacking proper ownership or lasting effect, for example. Improvements are unlikely to become normal business practices without a management structure that assigns roles and responsibilities, commits to the continued operation of the practices, and monitors conformance.

An appropriate environment should be created and maintained to ensure that EGIT is implemented as an integral part of an overall governance approach within the enterprise. It should include adequate direction and oversight of the implementation initiative, based on guiding principles. The objective is to provide sufficient commitment, direction and control of activities to ensure alignment with enterprise objectives and to garner appropriate implementation support from the board and executive management.

6.3 Starting With the Design Canvas

Implementation of a comprehensive governance system can be overwhelming. It is important to identify quick wins and scale the governance system—both in terms of how robust it needs to be to meet current business needs and how much activity should be implemented at any given point.

As outlined in Chapter 4, the enterprise needs to scope the governance program using the design factors, which allow the enterprise to tailor its governance system to realize the most value from its I&T assets:

1. Prioritized governance and management objectives, together with their target capability levels. (Once the governance system design workflow schema has been applied, specifically the different stages and steps in the design process, as illustrated in **figure 6.1,** the enterprise will have a list of its highest-priority governance and management objectives, based on the enterprise's unique circumstances.)
2. Related or specific variant governance system components
3. Other focus areas such as information security, risk or DevOps

As noted in Chapter 4, following the design process will result in a design canvas based on the prioritization, keeping the number of high-priority objectives to a reasonable level. See Appendix C for the details of the design process used for this example medium-sized company.

The design process is just the first step in establishing a good governance system in an enterprise. Once the list of priorities is understood, an enterprise can begin implementing or enhancing its governance system.

6.4 Establishing an Implementation Team

In order to work the prioritized objectives, the enterprise must establish an implementation team. In an SME, this team may be very small. It is important to include people from the business and IT functions and identify the knowledge, expertise, experience, credibility and authority of team members.

The team should commit to:

- A clear vision of success and desired goals
- Clarity and transparency of team processes, accountabilities and communications
- Integrity, mutual support and commitment to each other's success
- Mutual accountability and collective responsibility
- Venturing out of comfort zones, always looking for ways to improve, uncovering new possibilities and embracing change

Some enterprises may engage consultants to aid in prioritization and implementation. The use of consultants is not required but it may be helpful, given an SME's resource constraints.

6.5 Working the Prioritized Objectives

Once the list of prioritized objectives has been determined, the enterprise can simply use the detailed guidance described in Chapter 7 for each of the identified objectives. Specifically, the enterprise should:

1. Assess each objective as it relates to the enterprise and determine the baseline.
2. Determine the target capability level for each identified objective.
3. Identify the gaps using the practices and activities for each objective.

4. Create a plan to close the identified gaps (a business case may be needed, and involving a project manager is key).
5. Implement the plan.
6. Monitor the governance system to ensure that it operates at the desired capability level.

6.6 Conclusions of the Design Exercise

The design exercise example (see Appendix C) allows a conclusion to be drawn on the relative importance of COBIT objectives for the enterprise. For example:

- The most important objectives in the APO domain are APO03 *Managed Enterprise Architecture* (100) and APO04 *Managed Innovation* (95). APO07 *Managed Human Resources* is next (75).
- Among the BAI objectives, BAI03 *Managed Solutions Identification and Build* (75), BAI07 *Managed IT Change Acceptance and Transitioning* (75) and BAI06 *Managed IT Changes* (60) are the most important objectives.
- From the DSS domain, DSS01 *Managed Operations* is the most important (80), followed by DSS03 *Managed Problems* (45) and DSS02 *Managed Service Requests and Incidents* (30).
- MEA01 *Managed Performance and Conformance Monitoring* (40) also should receive some attention.

6.7 How to Use Conclusions to Develop a Road Map

Although the design exercise (see Appendix C) resulted in relative importance scores of 100 for APO03 *Managed Enterprise Architecture* and 95 for APO04 *Managed Innovation*, it is not practical to start with these objectives, since the example organization needs a solid base to guarantee good, efficient and effective management. Therefore, the example organization is advised to start with two tracks:

- Ensuring the most essential operational processes are developed and the related objectives reached
- Initiating building and implementation processes, since this is the example organization's core business

6.7.1 Operational Processes

A solid set of operational processes can be developed in the sequence shown in **figure 6.1**.

Figure 6.1—Developing Operational Processes

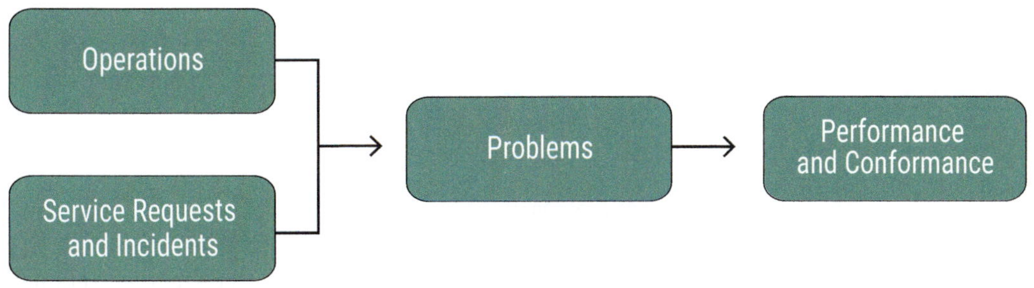

6.7.2 Building and Implementation Processes

Pragmatic building and implementation-related processes can be developed in the sequence illustrated by **figure 6.2**.

Figure 6.2—Building and Implementation Processes

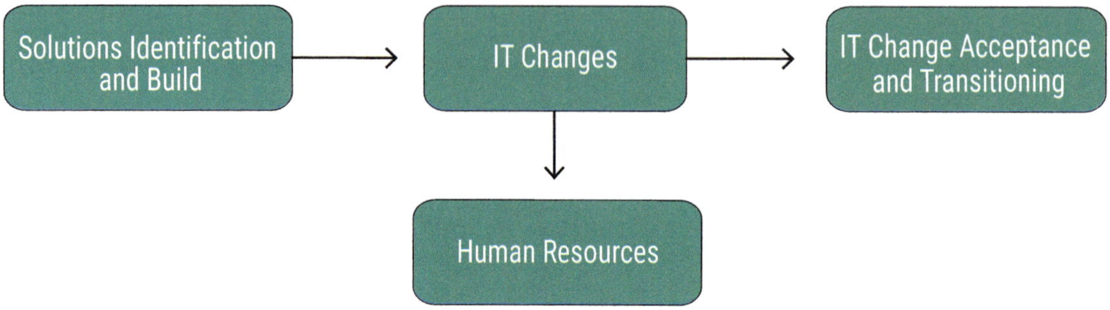

6.7.3 Detailed Steps, Using the COBIT Guidance

If this is the enterprise's first project in the implementation and use of COBIT, it should begin by looking at the organizational structures, which are listed for each objective in component B (**figure 6.3**).

Figure 6.3—Example Component B: Organizational Structures (Objective DSS01)

B. Component: Organizational Structures

Key Management Practice	Chief Operating Officer	Chief Information Officer	Chief Technology Officer	Head IT Operations	Information Security Manager	Privacy Officer
DSS01.01 Perform operational procedures.	R	A	R	R		
DSS01.02 Manage outsourced I&T services.		A	R	R	R	R
DSS01.03 Monitor I&T infrastructure.		R	A	R	R	
DSS01.04 Manage the environment.		R	A	R	R	
DSS01.05 Manage facilities.		R	A	R	R	

Source: ISACA, *COBIT® 2019 Framework: Governance and Management Objectives*, USA, 2018, *https://store.isaca.org/s/store#/store/browse/detail/a2S4w000004Ko5aEAC*

The enterprise should determine which governance and management objectives in its own organizational structure correspond with the functions mentioned in component B (organizational structures) and replace them with its own functions. The next steps are to check the practices and their related activities. **Figure 6.4** shows an example of the first practice in DSS01.

Figure 6.4—Example Component A: Process Activities (DSS01.01)

Small and Medium Enterprise-specific Activities	Capability Level
1. Develop and maintain operational procedures and related activities to support all delivered services.	2
2. Maintain a schedule of operational activities and perform the activities.	
3. Verify that all data expected for processing are received and processed completely, accurately and in a timely manner. Deliver output in accordance with enterprise requirements. Support restart and reprocessing needs. Ensure that users are receiving the right outputs in a secure and timely manner.	3
4. Manage the performance and throughput of the scheduled activities.	4
5. Monitor incidents and problems dealing with operational procedures and take appropriate action to improve reliability of operational tasks performed.	5

Source: ISACA, *COBIT® 2019 Framework: Governance and Management Objectives*, USA, 2018, *https://store.isaca.org/s/store#/store/browse/detail/a2S4w000004Ko5aEAC*

The enterprise should:

1. Evaluate whether the practice is relevant and needs to be developed and implemented.
2. Check all activities for relevance, and adapt the wording to make the practice understandable in the enterprise context.

General guidance is that:

- Activities at capability level 2 are basic and should be implemented.
- Activities at capability level 3 move the enterprise to a higher maturity level and thus help it move forward.
- Activities at capability levels 4 and 5 can be considered optional and may be implemented in a later phase.

It is important in this step (defining the activities for the enterprise) to consider the inputs and outputs defined in the guide, listed in component C for each practice (**figure 6.5**).

Figure 6.5—Example Component C: Information Flows and Items (DSS01 Inputs and Outputs)

C. Component: Information Flows and Items				
Management Practice	Small and Medium Enterprise-specific Inputs		Small and Medium Enterprise-specific Outputs	
	From	Description	Description	To
DSS01.01 Perform operational procedures.	BAI05.05	Operation and use plan	Backup log	Internal
			Operational schedule	Internal
DSS01.02 Manage outsourced I&T services.	APO09.03	• SLAs • OLAs	Independent assurance plans	MEA04.02
	BAI05.05	Operation and use plan		
DSS01.03 Monitor I&T infrastructure.	BAI03.11	Service definitions	Asset monitoring rules and event conditions	DSS02.01; DSS02.02
			Incident tickets	DSS02.02
			Event logs	Internal
DSS01.04 Manage the environment.			Environmental policies	APO01.09
			Insurance policy reports	MEA03.03
DSS01.05 Manage facilities.			Health and safety awareness	Internal
			Facilities assessment reports	MEA01.03

Source: ISACA, *COBIT® 2019 Framework: Governance and Management Objectives*, USA, 2018, *https://store.isaca.org/s/store#/store/browse/detail/a2S4w000004Ko5aEAC*

The enterprise may not use all inputs specified nor produce all outputs listed. Therefore, the enterprise must indicate in its own processes which inputs are used and which outputs are generated.

The other components (**figure 6.6**) provided for each governance or management objective can be used to:

- Select the persons with the adequate skills to collaborate in the project/process (component D)
- Check whether there is a policy in place in the enterprise that reflects the content of the suggested policy (component E)
- Provide guidance or attention points to implement the changes needed for the enterprise, as an outcome of this road map (component F)
- Consider the services, infrastructure and applications for relevancy in the enterprise (component G)

The steps described in this section should be repeated for each objective selected in the road map.

NOTE

The enterprise can plan to work on different objectives or projects in parallel but must make sure there is one person (the project manager) who coordinates the initiatives and helps the teams work with each other's outputs and results.

Figure 6.6—Example Components D Through G (Objective DSS01)

D. Component: People, Skills and Competencies		
Skill	**Related Guidance (Standards, Frameworks, Compliance Requirements)**	**Detailed Reference**
Database administration	Skills Framework for the Information Age V6, 2015	DBAD
Facilities management	Skills Framework for the Information Age V6, 2015	DCMA
IT infrastructure	Skills Framework for the Information Age V6, 2015	ITOP
Methods and tools	Skills Framework for the Information Age V6, 2015	METL
Service delivery	e-Competence Framework (e-CF)—A common European Framework for ICT Professionals in all industry sectors—Part 1: Framework, 2016	C. Run—C.3. Service Delivery
Storage management	Skills Framework for the Information Age V6, 2015	STMG

E. Component: Principles, Policies and Procedures	
Relevant Policy	**Policy Description**
Service management policy	Provides direction and guidance to ensure effective management and implementation of all I&T services to meet business and customer requirements, within a framework of performance measurement. Covers management of risk related to I&T services. (The ITIL V3 framework offers detailed guidance on service management and optimization of risk related to services.)

F. Component: Culture, Ethics and Behavior
Key Culture Elements
Create a culture of habitual excellence throughout the organization. Encourage employees to excel. Create an environment in which operational procedures deliver (more than) the necessary services while also allowing employees to question the status quo and try new ideas. Manage operational excellence through employee engagement and continuous improvement. Apply a customer-centric approach (for both internal and external customers).

G. Component: Services, Infrastructure and Applications
• Cloud hosting services • Infrastructure monitoring tools • Service level monitoring tools

Source: ISACA, *COBIT® 2019 Framework: Governance and Management Objectives*, USA, 2018, *https://store.isaca.org/s/store#/store/browse/detail/a2S4w000004Ko5aEAC*

6.8 Continuing the Governance Journey

Once the first set of prioritized governance and management objectives has been implemented, the team can turn its attention to the next set of prioritized governance and management objectives and work on those. The objectives that have been implemented should be monitored to ensure they are operating as targeted and expected. Once a governance system is in place to the satisfaction of stakeholders in the enterprise, the team can begin to focus on its continuous improvement. As an enterprise grows, the team should periodically review the design factor canvas to ensure the enterprise is shifting its priorities as necessitated by the changing business landscape and organizational goals.

More detailed guidance on governance system implementation can be found in ISACA's publication *COBIT® 2019 Implementation Guide: Implementing and Optimizing an Information and Technology Governance Solution.*[11]

[11] ISACA, *COBIT® 2019 Implementation Guide: Implementing and Optimizing an Information and Technology Governance Solution*, USA, 2018, *https://store.isaca.org/s/store#/store/browse/detail/a2S4w000004Ko5gEAC*

Page intentionally left blank

Chapter 7
COBIT Governance and Management Objectives—Detailed Small and Medium Enterprise-Specific Guidance

7.1 Evaluate, Direct and Monitor (EDM)

01 Ensured Governance Framework Setting and Maintenance

02 Ensured Benefits Delivery

03 Ensured Risk Optimization

04 Ensured Resource Optimization

05 Ensured Stakeholder Engagement

Page intentionally left blank

Domain: Evaluate, Direct and Monitor Governance Objective: EDM01 — Ensured Governance Framework Setting and Maintenance	Focus Area: Small and Medium Enterprises
Description	
Analyze and articulate the requirements for the governance of enterprise I&T. Put in place and maintain governance components with clarity of authority and responsibilities to achieve the enterprise's mission, goals and objectives.	
Purpose	
Provide a consistent approach integrated and aligned with the enterprise governance approach. I&T-related decisions are made in line with the enterprise's strategies and objectives and desired value is realized. To that end, ensure that I&T-related processes are overseen effectively and transparently; compliance with legal, contractual and regulatory requirements is confirmed; and the governance requirements for board members are met.	
Small and Medium Enterprise Focus Area Relevance	
Analyze and articulate the requirements for enterprise governance. Put in place and maintain governance components with clarity of authority and responsibilities to achieve the enterprise's mission, goals and objectives. Ensure that all business and IT processes are overseen effectively and transparently; that compliance with legal, contractual and regulatory requirements is confirmed; and that governance requirements for board members are met.	

A. Component: Process		
Governance Practice	**Small and Medium Enterprise-specific Metrics**	
EDM01.01 Evaluate the governance system. Continually identify and engage with the enterprise's stakeholders, document an understanding of the requirements, and evaluate the current and future design of governance of enterprise I&T.	a. Number of guiding principles defined for governance and decision making	
Small and Medium Enterprise-specific Activities		**Capability Level**
1. Analyze and identify the internal and external environmental factors (legal, regulatory and contractual obligations) and trends in the business environment that may influence governance design.		2
2. Determine the significance of I&T and its role with respect to the business.		
3. Consider external regulations, laws and contractual obligations and determine how they should be applied within the governance of enterprise I&T.		
4. Articulate principles that will guide the design of governance and decision making.		3
5. Determine the appropriate levels of authority delegation, including threshold rules, for I&T decisions.		
Related Guidance (Standards, Frameworks, Compliance Requirements)	**Detailed Reference**	
CMMI Cybermaturity Platform, 2018	GE.AG Apply Governance System; GE.MG Monitor Governance System	
ISO/IEC 38500:2015(E)	5.2 Principle 1: Responsibility (Evaluate)	
ITIL V3, 2011	Service Strategy, 2.3 Governance and management systems	
National Institute of Standards and Technology Special Publication 800-37, Revision 2 (Draft), May 2018	3.1 Preparation (Tasks 2, 3, 4, 5)	
Governance Practice	**Small and Medium Enterprise-specific Metrics**	
EDM01.02 Direct the governance system. Inform leaders on I&T governance principles and obtain their support, buy-in and commitment. Guide the structures, processes and practices for the governance of I&T in line with the agreed governance principles, decision-making models and authority levels. Define the information required for informed decision making.	a. Frequency of governance reporting to the board b. Number of roles, responsibilities and authorities for governance that are defined, assigned and accepted by appropriate business and IT management	
Small and Medium Enterprise-specific Activities		**Capability Level**
1. Ensure that governance of I&T is on the agenda of the board and that it is adequately addressed. Ensure that strategic direction and prioritization of I&T-enabled investments are in line with the enterprise's business strategy and priorities.		2
2. Allocate responsibility, authority and accountability for I&T decisions.		3
3. Define relevant guidelines for ethical and professional behavior and ensure that consequences of noncompliance are known and enforced.		
4. Direct the establishment of a reward system to promote desirable cultural change, if relevant.		

A. Component: Process *(cont.)*	
Related Guidance (Standards, Frameworks, Compliance Requirements)	**Detailed Reference**
CMMI Cybermaturity Platform, 2018	GE.DG Direct Governance System
ISF, The Standard of Good Practice for Information Security 2016	SG1.1 Security Governance Framework
ISO/IEC 38500:2015(E)	5.2 Principle 1: Responsibility (Direct)
ISO/IEC 38502:2017(E)	Governance of IT - Framework and model (all chapters)
King IV Report on Corporate Governance for South Africa, 2016	Part 5.4: Governance functional areas - Principle 12
National Institute of Standards and Technology Special Publication 800-53, Revision 5 (Draft), August 2017	3.14 Planning (PL-2, PL-10)
Governance Practice	**Small and Medium Enterprise-specific Metrics**
EDM01.03 Monitor the governance system. Monitor the effectiveness and performance of the enterprise's governance of I&T. Assess whether the governance system and implemented mechanisms (including structures, principles and processes) are operating effectively and provide appropriate oversight of I&T to enable value creation.	a. Actual vs. target cycle time for key decisions b. Frequency of independent reviews of governance of I&T c. Number of governance system components that are monitored

Small and Medium Enterprise-specific Activities	Capability Level
1. Assess the effectiveness and performance of those stakeholders given delegated responsibility and authority for governance of enterprise I&T.	3
2. Periodically assess whether agreed-on governance mechanisms (structures, principles, processes, etc.) are established and operating effectively.	4
3. Oversee the extent to which the organization satisfies obligations (regulatory, legislative, common law, contractual), internal policies, standards and professional guidelines.	

Related Guidance (Standards, Frameworks, Compliance Requirements)	Detailed Reference
ISO/IEC 38500:2015(E)	5.2 Principle 1: Responsibility (Monitor)
National Institute of Standards and Technology Special Publication 800-53, Revision 5 (Draft), August 2017	3.14 Planning (PL-11)

B. Component: Organizational Structures

Key Governance Practice	Board	Executive Committee	General Manager	Head of IT
EDM01.01 Evaluate the governance system.	A	R	R	R
EDM01.02 Direct the governance system.	A	R	R	
EDM01.03 Monitor the governance system.	A	R	R	R

C. Component: Information Flows and Items				
Governance Practice	Small and Medium Enterprise-specific Inputs		Small and Medium Enterprise-specific Outputs	
	From	Description	Description	To
EDM01.01 Evaluate the governance system.	MEA03.02	Communications of changed compliance requirements	Decision-making model	All EDM APO01.01 APO01.04
	Outside COBIT	• Constitution/bylaws/ statutes of organization • Laws/regulations • Business environment trends	Authority levels	All EDM APO01.05
EDM01.02 Direct the governance system.	There are no small and medium enterprise-specific inputs for this practice.		Guidelines for ethical and professional behavior	Internal
			Reward system approach	APO07.03 APO07.04
EDM01.03 Monitor the governance system.	MEA01.04	Performance reports	Feedback on governance effectiveness and performance	All EDM APO01.11
	MEA01.05	Status and results of actions		
	MEA02.01	Results of internal control monitoring and reviews		
	MEA02.03	Results of self-assessments		
	MEA03.03	Compliance confirmations		
	MEA03.04	• Compliance assurance reports • Reports of noncompliance issues and root causes		
	MEA04.02	Assurance plans		

D. Component: People, Skills and Competencies		
Skill	**Related Guidance (Standards, Frameworks, Compliance Requirements)**	**Detailed Reference**
IS governance	e-Competence Framework (e-CF)—A common European Framework for ICT Professionals in all industry sectors—Part 1: Framework, 2016	E. Manage—E.9. IS Governance
IT governance	Skills Framework for the Information Age V6, 2015	GOVN

E. Component: Principles, Policies and Procedures	
Relevant Policy	**Policy Description**
There are no small and medium enterprise-specific principles, policies and procedures for this objective.	

F. Component: Culture, Ethics and Behavior
Key Culture Elements
Identify and communicate the decision-making culture, and the organizational ethics and individual behaviors that embody enterprise values. Demonstrate ethical leadership and set the tone at the top.

G. Component: Services, Infrastructure and Applications
• COBIT and related products/tools • Equivalent frameworks and standards

Domain: Evaluate, Direct and Monitor Governance Objective: EDM02 — Ensured Benefits Delivery	Focus Area: Small and Medium Enterprises
Description	
Optimize the value to the business from investments in business processes, I&T services and I&T assets.	
Purpose	
Secure optimal value from I&T-enabled initiatives, services and assets; cost-efficient delivery of solutions and services; and a reliable and accurate picture of costs and likely benefits so that business needs are supported effectively and efficiently.	
Small and Medium Enterprise Focus Area Relevance	
Secure optimal value from I&T-enabled initiatives, services and assets. Ensure cost-efficient delivery of solutions and services so that business needs are supported effectively and efficiently.	

A. Component: Process	
Governance Practice	**Small and Medium Enterprise-specific Metrics**
EDM02.01 Establish the target investment mix. Review and ensure clarity of the enterprise and I&T strategies and current services. Define an appropriate investment mix based on cost, alignment with strategy, type of benefit for the programs in the portfolio, degree of risk, and financial measures such as cost and expected return on investment (ROI) over the full economic life cycle. Adjust the enterprise and I&T strategies where necessary.	a. Percent of I&T investments that are evaluated based on cost, alignment with strategy and financial measures (e.g., based on costs and benefits) b. Number of updates to enterprise and I&T strategies

Small and Medium Enterprise-specific Activities	Capability Level
1. Validate that I&T-enabled investments and current I&T services and assets are aligned with enterprise vision, strategic goals and objectives, and enterprise architecture vision and priorities.	2
2. Create and maintain portfolios of I&T-enabled investment programs, IT services and IT assets, which form the basis for the current IT budget.	
3. Identify the broad categories of information systems, applications, data, IT services, infrastructure, IT assets, resources, skills, etc., needed to support the enterprise strategy.	
4. Agree on I&T goals, taking into account the interrelationships between the enterprise strategy and IT services, assets and other resources.	
5. Define an investment mix that achieves the right balance among a number of dimensions, including short- and long-term returns, financial and nonfinancial benefits, and high- and low-risk investments.	3

Related Guidance (Standards, Frameworks, Compliance Requirements)	Detailed Reference
King IV Report on Corporate Governance for South Africa, 2016	Part 5.5: Stakeholder relationships—Principle 17
The Open Group IT4IT Reference Architecture, Version 2.0	3.2 IT Value Chain and IT4IT Reference Architecture

Governance Practice	Small and Medium Enterprise-specific Metrics
EDM02.02 Evaluate value optimization. Continually evaluate the portfolio of I&T-enabled investments, services and assets to determine the likelihood of achieving enterprise objectives and delivering value. Identify and evaluate any changes in direction to management that will optimize value creation.	a. Deviation between target and actual investment mix b. Number of business goals that are supported by alignment goals and/or IT strategies.

Small and Medium Enterprise-specific Activities	Capability Level
1. Understand strategic I&T issues, such as dependence on I&T, and technology insights and capabilities regarding the actual and potential significance of I&T for the enterprise's strategy.	2
2. Understand the key elements of governance required for the reliable, secure and cost-effective delivery of optimal value from the use of existing and new I&T services, assets and resources.	3
3. Evaluate how effectively the enterprise and I&T strategies have been integrated and are aligned with enterprise goals for delivering value.	4
4. Understand and consider the effectiveness of current roles, responsibilities, accountabilities and decision-making bodies in ensuring value creation from I&T-enabled investments, services and assets.	
5. Evaluate the portfolio of investments, services and assets for alignment with the enterprise's strategic objectives; risk appetite; effectiveness in terms of usability, availability and responsiveness; and efficiency in terms of cost, redundancy and technical health.	

A. Component: Process *(cont.)*		
Related Guidance (Standards, Frameworks, Compliance Requirements)	**Detailed Reference**	
COSO Enterprise Risk Management, June 2017	7. Strategy and Objective-Setting—Principle 8	
ISF, The Standard of Good Practice for Information Security 2016	SG2.2 Stakeholder Value Delivery	
ISO/IEC 38500:2015(E)	5.3 Principle 2: Strategy (Evaluate)	
King IV Report on Corporate Governance for South Africa, 2016	Part 5.2: Strategy, performance and reporting—Principle 4	
The Open Group IT4IT Reference Architecture, Version 2.0	5. Strategy to Portfolio (S2P) Value Stream	
Governance Practice	**Small and Medium Enterprise-specific Metrics**	
EDM02.03 Direct value optimization. Direct value management principles and practices to enable optimal value realization from I&T-enabled investments throughout their full economic life cycle.	a. Percent of I&T initiatives in the overall portfolio where value is being managed through the full life cycle	
Small and Medium Enterprise-specific Activities		**Capability Level**
1. Define and communicate portfolio and investment types, categories, criteria and relative weightings to the criteria to allow for overall relative value scores.		2
2. Define requirements for stage-gates and other reviews to assess the significance of the investment to the enterprise and associated risk; project schedules; funding plans; and the delivery of key capabilities, benefits and ongoing contributions to value.		3
3. Direct any required changes in assignment of accountabilities and responsibilities for executing the investment portfolio and delivering value from business processes and services.		
4. Direct any required changes to the portfolio of investments and services to realign with current and expected enterprise objectives and/or constraints.		
5. Define and communicate value delivery goals and outcome measures to enable effective monitoring.		4
Related Guidance (Standards, Frameworks, Compliance Requirements)	**Detailed Reference**	
ISO/IEC 38500:2015(E)	5.3 Principle 2: Strategy (Direct)	
Governance Practice	**Small and Medium Enterprise-specific Metrics**	
EDM02.04 Monitor value optimization. Monitor key goals and metrics to determine whether the enterprise receives expected value and benefit from I&T-enabled investments and services. Identify significant issues and consider corrective actions.	a. Percent of strategic enterprise objectives obtained as a result of strategic I&T initiatives b. Percent of expected value realized	
Small and Medium Enterprise-specific Activities		**Capability Level**
1. Define a balanced set of performance objectives, metrics, targets and benchmarks. Metrics should cover activity and outcome measures, with an appropriate balance of financial and nonfinancial measures.		4
2. Review and agree on a balanced set of performance objectives, metrics, targets and benchmarks with relevant IT and business stakeholders.		
3. Collect relevant, timely, complete, credible and accurate data to report on progress in delivering value against targets. Obtain a concise, high-level view of portfolio performance that supports decision making. Ensure that expected results are being achieved and risk is mitigated.		
4. Upon review of reports, ensure that appropriate management corrective action is initiated and controlled.		5
Related Guidance (Standards, Frameworks, Compliance Requirements)	**Detailed Reference**	
ISO/IEC 38500:2015(E)	5.3 Principle 2: Strategy (Monitor)	

B. Component: Organizational Structures						
Key Governance Practice	Board	Executive Committee	General Manager	Financial Manager	Operations Manager	Head of IT
EDM02.01 Establish the target investment mix.	A	R	R	R	R	R
EDM02.02 Evaluate value optimization.	A	R	R	R	R	R
EDM02.03 Direct value optimization.	A	R	R	R	R	R
EDM02.04 Monitor value optimization.	A	R	R	R	R	R

C. Component: Information Flows and Items				
Governance Practice	Small and Medium Enterprise-specific Inputs		Small and Medium Enterprise-specific Outputs	
	From	Description	Description	To
EDM02.01 Establish the target investment mix.	APO02.05	• Risk assessment initiatives • Strategic road map, with definition of the defined initiatives	Feedback on strategy and goals	APO02.05
	APO09.01	Definitions of standard services	Identified resources and capabilities required to support strategy	Internal
	BAI03.11	Service definitions	Defined investment mix	Internal EDM02.03
	EDM02.03	Investment types and criteria		
EDM02.02 Evaluate value optimization.	APO02.05	Strategic road map, with definition of the defined initiatives	Evaluation of strategic alignment	APO02.04 APO05.02
	APO05.01	Investment return expectations	Evaluation of investment and services portfolios	APO05.02 APO05.03 APO06.02
	APO05.02	Selected programs with ROI milestones		
	APO05.05	Benefit results and related communications		
EDM02.03 Direct value optimization.	APO05.03	Investment portfolio performance reports	Requirements for stage-gate reviews	BAI11.01
	EDM02.01	Defined investment mix	Investment types and criteria	APO05.02 EDM02.01
EDM02.04 Monitor value optimization.	APO05.03	Investment portfolio performance reports	Actions to improve value delivery	APO05.03 APO06.02 BAI11.01 EDM05.01
			Feedback on portfolio performance	APO05.03 APO06.05

D. Component: People, Skills and Competencies		
Skill	**Related Guidance (Standards, Frameworks, Compliance Requirements)**	**Detailed Reference**
Benefits management	Skills Framework for the Information Age V6, 2015	BENM

E. Component: Principles, Policies and Procedures	
Relevant Policy	**Policy Description**
There are no small and medium enterprise-specific principles, policies and procedures for this objective.	

F. Component: Culture, Ethics and Behavior
Key Culture Elements
The value that I&T adds depends on the degree to which I&T is aligned with the business and meets its expectations. Optimize I&T value by establishing a culture in which I&T services are delivered on time and within budget, with appropriate quality.

G. Component: Services, Infrastructure and Applications
• Cost accounting system • Program management tool

Domain: Evaluate, Direct and Monitor Governance Objective: EDM03 — Ensured Risk Optimization	Focus Area: Small and Medium Enterprises
Description	
Ensure that the enterprise's risk appetite and tolerance are understood, articulated and communicated, and that risk to enterprise value related to the use of I&T is identified and managed.	
Purpose	
Ensure that I&T-related enterprise risk does not exceed the enterprise's risk appetite and risk tolerance, the impact of I&T risk to enterprise value is identified and managed, and the potential for compliance failures is minimized.	
Small and Medium Enterprise Focus Area Relevance	
Define and communicate the enterprise's risk appetite and tolerance. Ensure that I&T-related risk does not exceed the enterprise's risk appetite and risk tolerance and that the impact of I&T risk to enterprise value is identified and managed. Ensure the potential for compliance failures is minimized.	

A. Component: Process		
Governance Practice	**Small and Medium Enterprise-specific Metrics**	
EDM03.01 Evaluate risk management. Continually examine and evaluate the effect of risk on the current and future use of I&T in the enterprise. Consider whether the enterprise's risk appetite is appropriate and ensure that risk to enterprise value related to the use of I&T is identified and managed.	a. Percent of I&T risk that exceeds enterprise risk tolerance b. Refreshment rate of risk factor evaluation	
Small and Medium Enterprise-specific Activities		**Capability Level**
1. Understand the organization and its context related to business and I&T Risk.		2
2. Determine the Risk Appetite of the organization, i.e., the level of risks that the enterprise is willing to take in its pursuit of enterprise objectives.		
3. Determine risk tolerance levels against the risk appetite, i.e., temporarily acceptable deviations from the risk appetite.		
4. Proactively evaluate business and I&T risk factors before taking strategic enterprise decisions and ensure that risk considerations are part of the strategic enterprise decision process.		3
5. Attract and maintain necessary skills for business and I&T Risk Management.		
Related Guidance (Standards, Frameworks, Compliance Requirements)	**Detailed Reference**	
COSO Enterprise Risk Management, June 2017	Strategy and Objective-Setting—Principles 6 and 7; 9. Review and Revision—Principle 16	
Governance Practice	**Small and Medium Enterprise-specific Metrics**	
EDM03.02 Direct risk management. Direct the establishment of risk management practices to provide reasonable assurance that I&T risk management practices are appropriate and that actual I&T risk does not exceed the board's risk appetite.	a. Percent of enterprise projects that consider business and I&T risk	
Small and Medium Enterprise-specific Activities		**Capability Level**
1. Direct the translation and integration of the risk strategy into risk management practices and operational activities.		2
2. Direct the development of risk communication plans (covering all levels of the enterprise).		
3. Direct implementation of the appropriate mechanisms to respond quickly to changing risk, supported by agreed-on principles of escalation (what to report, when, where and how).		
4. Direct that risk, opportunities, issues and concerns may be identified and reported by anyone at any time and escalated to the relevant decision makers.		
5. Identify key goals and metrics related to risk management, and approve the approaches, methods, techniques and processes for capturing and reporting the measurement information.		3
Related Guidance (Standards, Frameworks, Compliance Requirements)	**Detailed Reference**	
CMMI Cybermaturity Platform, 2018	RS.AS Apply Risk Management Strategy; BC.RO Determine Strategic Risk Objectives	
ISF, The Standard of Good Practice for Information Security 2016	IR1.1 Information Risk Assessment—Management Approach	
King IV Report on Corporate Governance for South Africa, 2016	Part 5.4: Governance functional areas—Principle 11	
National Institute of Standards and Technology Special Publication 800-37, Revision 2 (Draft), May 2018	3.5 Assessment (Task 2)	

A. Component: Process *(cont.)*	
Governance Practice	Small and Medium Enterprise-specific Metrics
EDM03.03 Monitor risk management. Monitor the key goals and metrics of the risk management processes. Determine how deviations or problems will be identified, tracked and reported for remediation.	a. Number of potential business and I&T risk issues identified and managed b. Percent of critical risk effectively mitigated c. Percent of risk action plans executed on time

Small and Medium Enterprise-specific Activities	Capability Level
1. Report any risk management issues to the board or executive committee.	2
2. Monitor the extent to which the risk profile is managed within the risk appetite and tolerance thresholds.	3
3. Monitor key goals and metrics of risk against targets, analyze the cause of any deviations, and initiate remedial actions to address the underlying causes.	4
4. Enable key stakeholders' review of the enterprise's progress towards identified goals.	

Related Guidance (Standards, Frameworks, Compliance Requirements)	Detailed Reference
COSO Enterprise Risk Management, June 2017	9. Review and Revision—Principle 17
National Institute of Standards and Technology Special Publication 800-37, Revision 2 (Draft), May 2018	3.1 Preparation (Task 7); 3.5 Assessment (Task 1); 3.6 Authorization (Task 1)
The Open Group IT4IT Reference Architecture, Version 2.0	6. Requirement to Deploy (R2D) Value Stream; 7. Request to Fulfill (R2F) Value Stream

B. Component: Organizational Structures

Key Governance Practice	Board	Executive Committee	General Manager	Financial Manager Operations Manager	Operations Manager	Head of IT	Security Manager
EDM03.01 Evaluate risk management.	A	R	R	R	R	R	
EDM03.02 Direct risk management.	A	R	R	R	R	R	
EDM03.03 Monitor risk management.	A	R	R	R	R	R	R

C. Component: Information Flows and Items				
Governance Practice	Small and Medium Enterprise-specific Inputs		Small and Medium Enterprise-specific Outputs	
	From	Description	Description	To
EDM03.01 Evaluate risk management.	APO12.01	Identified risk issues and factors	Risk appetite guidance	APO12.03
	Outside COBIT	Enterprise risk management (ERM) principles	Evaluation of risk management activities	APO12.01
			Approved risk tolerance levels	APO12.03
EDM03.02 Direct risk management.	APO12.03	Documented risk profile, including status of risk management actions	Approved process for measuring risk management	APO12.01
	Outside COBIT	Enterprise risk management (ERM) profiles and mitigation plans	Key objectives to be monitored for risk management	APO12.01
			Risk management policies	APO12.01
EDM03.03 Monitor risk management.	APO12.02	Risk analysis results	Remedial actions to address risk management deviations	APO12.06
	APO12.04	• Risk analysis and risk profile reports for stakeholders • Results of third-party risk assessments	Risk management issues for the board	EDM05.01

D. Component: People, Skills and Competencies		
Skill	Related Guidance (Standards, Frameworks, Compliance Requirements)	Detailed Reference
Business risk management	Skills Framework for the Information Age V6, 2015	BURM
Risk management	e-Competence Framework (e-CF)—A common European Framework for ICT Professionals in all industry sectors—Part 1: Framework, 2016	E. Manage—E.3. Risk Management

E. Component: Principles, Policies and Procedures	
Relevant Policy	Policy Description
Enterprise risk policy	Defines at strategic, tactical and operational levels how the risk of an enterprise needs to be governed and managed pursuant to enterprise business objectives. This policy should support enterprise risk governance principles and elaborate on risk management activities.

F. Component: Culture, Ethics and Behavior
Key Culture Elements
Promote an I&T risk-aware culture at all levels of the organization and empower the enterprise proactively to identify, report and escalate I&T risk, opportunity and potential business impacts. Senior management sets direction and demonstrates visible and genuine support for risk practices. Additionally, management must clearly define risk appetite and ensure an appropriate level of debate as part of business-as-usual activities. Desirable behaviors include encouraging employees to raise issues or negative outcomes and show transparency with regard to I&T risk. Business owners should accept ownership of I&T risk when applicable and demonstrate genuine commitment to I&T risk management by providing adequate resource levels.

G. Component: Services, Infrastructure and Applications
Risk management system

Page intentionally left blank

Domain: Evaluate, Direct and Monitor Governance Objective: EDM04 — Ensured Resource Optimization	Focus Area: Small and Medium Enterprises
Description	
Ensure that adequate and sufficient business and I&T-related resources (people, process and technology) are available to support enterprise objectives effectively and, at optimal cost.	
Purpose	
Ensure that the resource needs of the enterprise are met in the optimal manner, I&T costs are optimized, and there is an increased likelihood of benefit realization and readiness for future change.	
Small and Medium Enterprise Focus Area Relevance	
Ensure that adequate and sufficient business and I&T-related resources (e.g., people, information, processes and technology) are available to support enterprise objectives effectively and organize the required monitoring to ensure that enterprise objectives are realized at optimal cost.	

A. Component: Process		
Governance Practice	**Small and Medium Enterprise-specific Metrics**	
EDM04.01 Evaluate resource management. Continually examine and evaluate the current and future need for business and I&T resources (financial and human), options for resourcing (including sourcing strategies), and allocation and management principles to meet the needs of the enterprise in the optimal manner.	a. Number of deviations from the resource plan	
Small and Medium Enterprise-specific Activities		**Capability Level**
1. Starting from the current strategy and considering future needs, examine the potential options for providing I&T-related resources (technology, financial and human resources).		2
2. Define preferred sourcing options for certain services and set financial boundaries per sourcing option.		
3. Review and approve the resource and procurement plans and enterprise architecture strategies for delivering value and mitigating risk with the allocated resources.		
4. Align I&T resource management with enterprise financial and human resources (HR) planning.		
Related Guidance (Standards, Frameworks, Compliance Requirements)	**Detailed Reference**	
CMMI Cybermaturity Platform, 2018	GR.DR Direct Resource Management Needs	
ISO/IEC 38500:2015(E)	5.4 Principle 3: Acquisition (Evaluate)	
Governance Practice	**Small and Medium Enterprise-specific Metrics**	
EDM04.02 Direct resource management. Ensure the adoption of resource management principles to enable optimal use of business and I&T resources throughout their full economic life cycle.	a. Number of deviations from, and exceptions to, resource management principles	
Small and Medium Enterprise-specific Activities		**Capability Level**
1. Assign responsibilities for executing resource management.		2
2. Establish principles related to safeguarding resources.		
3. Communicate and drive the adoption of the resource management strategies, principles, and agreed resource plan and enterprise architecture strategies.		3
4. Align resource management with enterprise financial and HR planning.		
5. Define key goals, measures and metrics for resource management.		4
Related Guidance (Standards, Frameworks, Compliance Requirements)	**Detailed Reference**	
CMMI Cybermaturity Platform, 2018	GR.ER Evaluate Resource Management Needs	
COSO Enterprise Risk Management, June 2017	6. Governance and Culture—Principle 5	
ISO/IEC 38500:2015(E)	5.4 Principle 3: Acquisition (Direct)	
National Institute of Standards and Technology Special Publication 800-53, Revision 5 (Draft), August 2017	3.14 Planning (PL-4)	

A. Component: Process *(cont.)*		
Governance Practice	**Small and Medium Enterprise-specific Metrics**	
EDM04.03 Monitor resource management. Monitor the key goals and metrics of the resource management processes. Determine how deviations or problems will be identified, tracked and reported for remediation.	a. Percent of projects with a medium- or high-risk status due to resource management issues b. Percent of projects with appropriate resource allocations	
Small and Medium Enterprise-specific Activities		**Capability Level**
1. Use agreed-on goals and metrics to monitor the allocation and optimization of resources in accordance with enterprise objectives and priorities.		4
2. Monitor I&T-related sourcing strategies and business and IT-related capabilities to ensure that current and future needs and objectives of the enterprise can be met.		
3. Monitor resource performance against targets, analyze the cause of deviations, and initiate remedial action to address the underlying causes.		
Related Guidance (Standards, Frameworks, Compliance Requirements)	**Detailed Reference**	
CMMI Cybermaturity Platform, 2018	GR.MR Monitor Resource Management Needs	
ISO/IEC 38500:2015(E)	5.4 Principle 3: Acquisition (Evaluate)	

B. Component: Organizational Structures						
Key Governance Practice	**Board**	**Executive Committee**	**General Manager**	**Financial Manager**	**Operations Manager**	**Head of IT**
EDM04.01 Evaluate resource management.	A	R	R	R	R	R
EDM04.02 Direct resource management.	A	R	R	R	R	R
EDM04.03 Monitor resource management.	A	R	R	R	R	R

C. Component: Information Flows and Items				
Governance Practice	**Small and Medium Enterprise-specific Inputs**		**Small and Medium Enterprise-specific Outputs**	
EDM04.01 Evaluate resource management.	**From**	**Description**	**Description**	**To**
	AP002.04	Gaps and changes required to realize target capability	Guiding principles for allocation of resources and capabilities	AP002.01 AP007.01
	AP007.03	Skill development plans	Approved resources plan	AP002.05 AP007.01 AP009.02
	AP010.02	Decision results of vendor evaluations		

C. Component: Information Flows and Items *(cont.)*			
Governance Practice	Small and Medium Enterprise-specific Inputs	Small and Medium Enterprise-specific Outputs	
EDM04.02 Direct resource management.	There are no small and medium enterprise-specific inputs for this practice.	Principles for safeguarding resources	APO01.02
		Assigned responsibilities for resource management	APO01.05
		Communication of resourcing strategies	APO02.06 APO07.05 APO09.02
EDM04.03 Monitor resource management.	There are no small and medium enterprise-specific inputs for this practice.	Remedial actions to address resource management deviations	APO07.01 APO07.03 APO09.04
		Feedback on allocation and effectiveness of resources and capabilities	EDM05.01 APO02.02 APO07.05 APO09.05

D. Component: People, Skills and Competencies		
Skill	**Related Guidance (Standards, Frameworks, Compliance Requirements)**	**Detailed Reference**
Portfolio management	Skills Framework for the Information Age V6, 2015	POMG
Resourcing	Skills Framework for the Information Age V6, 2015	RESC

E. Component: Principles, Policies and Procedures	
Relevant Policy	**Policy Description**
Performance measurement policy	Identifies the need for a performance measurement system beyond conventional accounting. This system encompasses measurement of relationships and knowledge-based assets necessary to compete in the information age, including customer focus, process efficiency and the ability to learn and grow (balanced scorecard). The balanced scorecard translates strategy into action to achieve enterprise goals, taking into account intangibles like customer satisfaction, streamlining of internal functions, creation of operational efficiencies and development of staff skills. This holistic view of operations helps link long-term strategic objectives and short-term actions.

F. Component: Culture, Ethics and Behavior
Key Culture Elements
Establish a culture in which resources are valued and the investment, use and allocation of resources (whether people, information, applications, technology or facilities) align with organizational needs. Illustrate these values by ensuring that appropriate methods and adequate skills exist in the organization; for example, ensure that benefits from service procurement are real and achievable, and implement sound performance measurement systems (e.g., the balanced scorecard).

G. Component: Services, Infrastructure and Applications
Performance measurement system (e.g., balanced scorecard, skills management tools)

Page intentionally left blank

Domain: Evaluate, Direct and Monitor Governance Objective: EDM05 — Ensured Stakeholder Engagement	Focus Area: Small and Medium Enterprises
Description	
Ensure that stakeholders are identified and engaged in the I&T governance system and that enterprise I&T performance and conformance measurement and reporting are transparent, with stakeholders approving the goals and metrics and necessary remedial actions.	
Purpose	
Ensure that stakeholders are supportive of the I&T strategy and road map, communication to stakeholders is effective and timely, and the basis for reporting is established to increase performance. Identify areas for improvement, and confirm that I&T-related objectives and strategies are in line with the enterprise's strategy.	
Small and Medium Enterprise Focus Area Relevance	
Ensure that stakeholders are identified and engaged in the governance system, that enterprise performance and conformance measurement and reporting are transparent, and that stakeholders approve and support relevant goals and metrics which support the strategy and road map.	

A. Component: Process		
Governance Practice	**Small and Medium Enterprise-specific Metrics**	
EDM05.01 Evaluate stakeholder engagement and reporting requirements. Continually examine and evaluate current and future requirements for stakeholder engagement and reporting (including reporting mandated by regulatory requirements), and communication to other stakeholders. Establish principles for engaging and communicating with stakeholders.	a. Frequency of revisions to reporting requirements b. Percent of stakeholders covered in reporting requirements	
Small and Medium Enterprise-specific Activities		**Capability Level**
1. Identify all relevant stakeholders within and outside the enterprise. Group stakeholders in stakeholder categories with similar requirements.		2
2. Examine the current and future mandatory reporting requirements related to the use of I&T within the enterprise (regulatory, legislative, common law, contractual), and define the extent and frequency of reporting.		
3. Determine the current and future communication and reporting requirements for stakeholders regarding the use of I&T within the enterprise, including required level of involvement/consultation, extent of communication, and level of detail and conditions.		
4. Maintain principles for communication with external and internal stakeholders, including communication formats and communication channels. Include stakeholder acceptance and sign-off of reporting.		3
Related Guidance (Standards, Frameworks, Compliance Requirements)	**Detailed Reference**	
CMMI Cybermaturity Platform, 2018	SR.DR Direct Stakeholder Communication and Reporting	
Governance Practice	**Small and Medium Enterprise-specific Metrics**	
EDM05.02 Direct stakeholder engagement, communication and reporting. Ensure the establishment of effective stakeholder involvement, communication and reporting, including mechanisms for ensuring the quality and completeness of information, overseeing mandatory reporting, and creating a communication strategy for stakeholders.	a. Percent of stakeholder satisfaction with communication and reporting	
Small and Medium Enterprise-specific Activities		**Capability Level**
1. Direct the establishment and implementation of mechanisms for engagement and communication with external and internal stakeholders.		2
2. Establish mechanisms for validation and approval of mandatory reporting.		
3. Establish reporting escalation mechanisms.		3
Related Guidance (Standards, Frameworks, Compliance Requirements)	**Detailed Reference**	
CMMI Cybermaturity Platform, 2018	SR.AR Apply Stakeholder Reporting Requirements	
King IV Report on Corporate Governance for South Africa, 2016	Part 5.5: Stakeholder relationships—Principle 16	
King IV Report on Corporate Governance for South Africa, 2016	Part 5.2: Strategy, performance and reporting—Principle 5	
National Institute of Standards and Technology Framework for Improving Critical Infrastructure Cybersecurity V1.1, April 2018	3.3 Communicating Cybersecurity Requirements with Stakeholders	

A. Component: Process *(cont.)*		
Governance Practice	**Small and Medium Enterprise-specific Metrics**	
EDM05.03 Monitor stakeholder engagement. Monitor stakeholder engagement levels and the effectiveness of stakeholder communication. Assess mechanisms for ensuring accuracy, reliability and effectiveness, and ascertain whether the requirements of different stakeholders in terms of reporting and communication are met.	a. Percent of reports containing inaccuracies b. Percent of reports not delivered on time	
Small and Medium Enterprise-specific Activities		**Capability Level**
1. Periodically assess the effectiveness of the mechanisms for ensuring the accuracy and reliability of mandatory reporting.		4
2. Periodically assess the outcomes from, involvement of and communication with external and internal stakeholders.		
3. Determine whether the requirements of different stakeholders are met and assess stakeholder engagement levels.		
Related Guidance (Standards, Frameworks, Compliance Requirements)	**Detailed Reference**	
CMMI Cybermaturity Platform, 2018	SR.MC Monitor Stakeholder Communication	

B. Component: Organizational Structures

Key Governance Practice	Board	Executive Committee	General Manager	Financial Manager	Operations Manager	Head of IT
EDM05.01 Evaluate stakeholder engagement and reporting requirements.	A	R	R	R	R	R
EDM05.02 Direct stakeholder engagement communication and reporting.	A	R	R	R	R	R
EDM05.03 Monitor stakeholder engagement.	A	R	R	R	R	R

C. Component: Information Flows and Items

Governance Practice	Small and Medium Enterprise-specific Inputs		Small and Medium Enterprise-specific Outputs	
	From	**Description**	**Description**	**To**
EDM05.01 Evaluate stakeholder engagement and reporting requirements.	EDM02.04	Actions to improve value delivery	Reporting and communications principles	MEA01.01
	EDM03.03	Risk management issues for the board	Evaluation of enterprise reporting requirements	MEA01.01
	EDM04.03	Feedback on allocation and effectiveness of resources and capabilities		
EDM05.02 Direct stakeholder engagement, communication and reporting.	APO12.04	Risk analysis and risk profile reports for stakeholders	Rules for validating and approving mandatory reports	MEA01.01 MEA03.04
			Escalation guidelines	MEA01.05
EDM05.03 Monitor stakeholder engagement.	MEA04.08	• Assurance review results • Assurance review report	Assessment of reporting effectiveness	MEA01.01

D. Component: People, Skills and Competencies		
Skill	**Related Guidance (Standards, Frameworks, Compliance Requirements)**	**Detailed Reference**
Relationship management	e-Competence Framework (e-CF)—A common European Framework for ICT Professionals in all industry sectors—Part 1: Framework, 2016	E. Manage—E.4. Relationship Management

E. Component: Principles, Policies and Procedures	
Relevant Policy	**Policy Description**
There are no small and medium enterprise-specific principles, policies and procedures for this objective.	

F. Component: Culture, Ethics and Behavior
Key Culture Elements
Create a culture in which open and structured communication is provided to key stakeholders, in line with their requirements.

G. Component: Services, Infrastructure and Applications
• Communication tools and channels • IT dashboarding • Stakeholder survey tools

Page intentionally left blank

7.2 Align, Plan and Organize (APO)

01 Managed I&T Management Framework

02 Managed Strategy

03 Managed Enterprise Architecture

04 Managed Innovation

05 Managed Portfolio

06 Managed Budget and Costs

07 Managed Human Resources

08 Managed Relationships

09 Managed Service Agreements

10 Managed Vendors

11 Managed Quality

12 Managed Risk

13 Managed Security

14 Managed Data

Page intentionally left blank

Domain: Align, Plan and Organize Management Objective: APO01 — Managed I&T Management Framework	Focus Area: Small and Medium Enterprises
Description	
Design the management system for enterprise I&T based on enterprise goals and other design factors. Based on this design, implement all required components of the management system.	
Purpose	
Implement a consistent management approach for enterprise governance requirements to be met, covering governance components such as management processes; organizational structures; roles and responsibilities; reliable and repeatable activities; information items; principles, policies and procedures; skills and competencies; culture and behavior; and services, infrastructure and applications.	
Small and Medium Enterprise Focus Area Relevance	
The description and purpose of this COBIT objective is fully applicable to SMEs. No SME-specific focus area relevance statement is required.	

A. Component: Process	
Management Practice	**Small and Medium Enterprise-specific Metrics**
APO01.01 Design the management system for enterprise I&T. Design a management system tailored to the needs of the enterprise. Management needs of the enterprise are defined through the use of the goals cascade and by application of design factors. Ensure the governance components are integrated and aligned with the enterprise's governance and management philosophy and operating style.	a. Percent of senior executives involved in the goals cascade to define priorities b. Number of business stakeholders and IT staff involved in determining priorities using design factors c. Number of strategic goals that can be translated as new projects to achieve these goals d. Percent of governance components integrated and aligned with the enterprise's governance and management philosophy and operating style

Small and Medium Enterprise-specific Activities	Capability Level
1. Obtain an understanding of the enterprise vision, mission and strategic priorities as well as the current enterprise context and challenges.	2
2. Consider the enterprise's internal environment, including management culture and philosophy, risk tolerance, security and privacy policy, ethical values, code of conduct, accountability, and requirements for management integrity.	
3. Apply the COBIT goals cascade and design factors to the enterprise strategy and context to decide on priorities for the management system and thus for the implementation of management objective priorities.	
4. Validate the selected priorities for implementation of management objectives with industry-specific good practices or requirements (e.g., industry-specific regulations) and with the executive committee.	3
5. Revise at least annually the priorities defined based on changes in external and internal environment.	5

Related Guidance (Standards, Frameworks, Compliance Requirements)	Detailed Reference
COSO Enterprise Risk Management, June 2017	7. Strategy and Objective-Setting—Principle 9
ISO/IEC 27001:2013/Cor.2:2015(E)	International standard for establishing, implementing and maintaining a management system (all chapters)
ITIL V3, 2011	Service Strategy, 2.3 Governance and management systems

Management Practice	Small and Medium Enterprise-specific Metrics
APO01.02 Communicate management objectives, direction and decisions made. Communicate awareness and promote understanding of alignment and I&T objectives to stakeholders throughout the enterprise. Communicate at regular intervals on important I&T-related decisions and their impact for the organization.	a. Frequency (at least yearly) of communication on management objectives and decisions made for I&T

Small and Medium Enterprise-specific Activities	Capability Level
1. Provide skilled resources to support the communication process.	2
2. Establish a consistent communication plan.	
3. Communicate at regular intervals IT objectives and direction and their impact on the enterprise.	3
4. Ensure that the information communicated encompasses a clearly articulated mission, service objectives, roles and responsibilities, and relevant policies, if any. Communicate the information at the appropriate level of detail for the respective audiences within the enterprise.	

Related Guidance (Standards, Frameworks, Compliance Requirements)	Detailed Reference
No related guidance for this management practice	

A. Component: Process *(cont.)*		
Management Practice	**Small and Medium Enterprise-specific Metrics**	
APO01.03 Implement management processes (to support the achievement of governance and management objectives). Define target process capability levels and implementation priority based on the management system design.	a. Number of priority processes to be implemented or improved to meet the target capability level vs. total number of processes b. Percent of processes successfully implemented or improved	
Small and Medium Enterprise-specific Activities		**Capability Level**
1. Develop the I&T selected processes based on the priority defined (output of goals cascade and design factors exercise).		2
2. Analyze the gap between the target process model for the organization and current practices and activities that are in place.		3
3. Draft a road map for implementation of missing process practices and activities. Use practice metrics to follow up and determine successful implementation.		4
Related Guidance (Standards, Frameworks, Compliance Requirements)	**Detailed Reference**	
No related guidance for this management practice		
Management Practice	**Small and Medium Enterprise-specific Metrics**	
APO01.04 Define and implement the organizational structures. Put in place the required internal and extended organizational structures (e.g., committees) per the management system design, enabling effective and efficient decision making. Ensure that required technology and information knowledge is included in the composition of management structures.	a. Percent of senior management involved in the approval of the organizational structures b. Number of organizational issues identified and resolved to reduce escalations	
Small and Medium Enterprise-specific Activities		**Capability Level**
1. Define the scope of all organizational structures, including those performed by third parties.		2
2. Change the organizational structures, as defined by COBIT, to the organizational reality of the organization.		
3. Direct the executive committee to steer I&T direction, track status of projects and resolve resource conflicts.		3
4. Regularly verify the adequacy and effectiveness of the organizational structures.		4
Related Guidance (Standards, Frameworks, Compliance Requirements)	**Detailed Reference**	
No related guidance for this management practice		
Management Practice	**Small and Medium Enterprise-specific Metrics**	
APO01.05 Establish roles and responsibilities. Define and communicate roles and responsibilities for enterprise I&T, including authority levels, responsibilities and accountability.	a. Percent of completed role descriptions	
Small and Medium Enterprise-specific Activities		**Capability Level**
1. Establish, agree on and communicate I&T-related roles and responsibilities, in alignment with business needs and objectives. Pay attention to responsibilities in the areas of security and quality.		2
2. Ensure that responsibilities and accountabilities, especially for decision making and approvals, are clearly delineated.		
3. Consider requirements for business continuity, while defining sufficient backup for key roles and critical functions.		
4. Include in role and responsibility descriptions adherence to management policies and procedures, the code of ethics, and professional practices.		
5. Implement adequate supervisory practices to ensure that roles and responsibilities are properly exercised. The level of supervision should be in line with the sensitivity of the position and extent of responsibilities assigned.		3
6. Ensure that accountability is defined through roles and responsibilities. Structure roles and responsibilities to reduce the possibility for a single role to compromise a critical process.		4
Related Guidance (Standards, Frameworks, Compliance Requirements)	**Detailed Reference**	
No related guidance for this management practice		

A. Component: Process *(cont.)*		
Management Practice	**Small and Medium Enterprise-specific Metrics**	
APO01.06 Optimize the placement of the IT function. Position the IT capabilities in the overall organizational structure to reflect the strategic importance and operational dependency of IT within the enterprise. The reporting line of the CIO and representation of IT within senior management should be commensurate with the importance of I&T within the enterprise.	a. Percent of stakeholders with a favorable opinion of the position of IT in the organizational structure b. Number of refresher courses in IT and business risk management carried out annually	
Small and Medium Enterprise-specific Activities		**Capability Level**
1. Clarify the placement of the IT function, including assessment of enterprise strategy and operating model (centralized, federated, decentralized, hybrid), importance of I&T, and sourcing situation and options.		3
2. Define and prioritize options for organizational placement, sourcing and operating models.		
3. Define placement of the IT function and obtain agreement.		
4. Evaluate the placement of the IT function and update, if required.		4
Related Guidance (Standards, Frameworks, Compliance Requirements)	**Detailed Reference**	
ISO/IEC 27002:2013/Cor.2:2015(E)	8.2 Information classification	
Management Practice	**Small and Medium Enterprise-specific Metrics**	
APO01.07 Define information (data) and system ownership. Define and maintain responsibilities for ownership of information (data) and information systems. Ensure that owners classify information and systems and protect them in line with their classification.	a. Percent of data assets that have a clearly defined owner b. Percent of information systems that have a clearly defined owner c. Percent of classified information items according to the agreed classification levels d. Number of systems that have an owner outside the enterprise	
Small and Medium Enterprise-specific Activities		**Capability Level**
1. Create an inventory of information (data) and systems.		2
2. Indicate owners, custodians and classifications within the inventory of information (data) and systems.		
3. Define appropriate and consistent classification rules for information items.		3
4. Maintain the inventory of information (systems and data). Include systems that are outsourced and those for which ownership should stay within the enterprise.		
5. Assess and distinguish between critical (high value) and noncritical data, information and systems, and ensure appropriate protection for each category.		
Related Guidance (Standards, Frameworks, Compliance Requirements)	**Detailed Reference**	
No related guidance for this management practice		
Management Practice	**Small and Medium Enterprise-specific Metrics**	
APO01.08 Define target skills and competencies. Define the required skills and competencies to achieve relevant management objectives.	a. Percent of staff who attend training or awareness sessions for selected skills, competencies, desired behaviors b. Percent of staff with required skills and competencies aligned to selected management objectives c. Number of business and IT-resource needs that are addressed annually; number of review meetings held annually d. Number of roles defined for IT resource management	
Small and Medium Enterprise-specific Activities		**Capability Level**
1. Identify the required skills and competencies to achieve selected management objectives.		2
2. Analyze the gap between the enterprise's target skills and capabilities and the current skills of the workforce. Refer to APO07 *Managed Human Resources* for skills development and management practices.		
Related Guidance (Standards, Frameworks, Compliance Requirements)	**Detailed Reference**	
No related guidance for this management practice		

A. Component: Process *(cont.)*	
Management Practice	**Small and Medium Enterprise-specific Metrics**
APO01.09 Define and communicate policies and procedures. Put in place procedures to maintain compliance with and performance measurement of policies and other components of the control framework. Enforce the consequences of noncompliance or inadequate performance. Track trends and performance and consider these in the future design and improvement of the control framework.	a. Frequency for updating I&T policies b. Percent of active policies and procedures that are documented and up to date

Small and Medium Enterprise-specific Activities	Capability Level
1. Identify the required policies for the organization.	2
2. Create a set of policies to drive IT control expectations on relevant key topics such as quality, security, privacy, internal controls, usage of I&T assets, ethics and intellectual property (IP) rights.	3
3. Roll out and enforce the I&T policy to all relevant staff.	
4. Evaluate and update I&T policies at least yearly to accommodate changing operating or business environments.	4

Related Guidance (Standards, Frameworks, Compliance Requirements)	Detailed Reference
No related guidance for this management practice	

Management Practice	Small and Medium Enterprise-specific Metrics
APO01.10 Define and implement infrastructure, services and applications to support the governance and management system. Define and implement infrastructure, services and applications to support the governance and management system (e.g., architecture repositories, risk management system, project management tools, cost-tracking tools and incident monitoring tools).	a. Number of tools to support priority processes b. Adequacy/coverage of key I&T processes by selected tools c. Satisfaction of recipients with the accuracy, completeness and timeliness of information d. Percent of stakeholder satisfaction with tools selected to support their needs

Small and Medium Enterprise-specific Activities	Capability Level
1. Identify the processes in which automated services, applications or infrastructure could help to support key processes.	2
2. Select and implement the most appropriate tools and communicate tool selection to stakeholders.	
3. Provide training on selected tools, as required.	3
4. Regularly assess the performance of the supporting tools.	4

Related Guidance (Standards, Frameworks, Compliance Requirements)	Detailed Reference
No related guidance for this management practice	

Management Practice	Small and Medium Enterprise-specific Metrics
APO01.11 Manage continual improvement of the I&T management system. Continually improve processes and other management system components to ensure that they can deliver against governance and management objectives. Consider COBIT implementation guidance, emerging standards, compliance requirements, automation opportunities and the feedback of stakeholders.	a. Frequency of updating and validating updates to the framework and components b. Percentage of IT programs and projects sponsored by senior business executives

Small and Medium Enterprise-specific Activities	Capability Level
1. Identify business-critical processes based on performance and conformance drivers and related risk.	2
2. Organize periodic reviews of I&T structure and components.	4
3. Assess capability of business-critical processes and identify improvement targets. Prioritize initiatives for improvement based on potential benefits and costs.	
4. Implement and operationalize agreed-on improvements to the current I&T management system; set performance goals and metrics to enable monitoring of improvements.	5
5. Consider ways to improve efficiency and effectiveness (e.g., through training, documentation, standardization and/or process automation).	
6. Retire outdated governance components (processes, information items, policies, etc.).	

Related Guidance (Standards, Frameworks, Compliance Requirements)	Detailed Reference
ITIL V3, 2011	Continual Service Improvement, 4.1 The 7-Step Improvement Process

B. Component: Organizational Structures									
Key Management Practice	Executive Committee	General Manager	Head Human Resources	Business Process Owners	Head of IT	Security Expert	IT Development Coordinator	IT Operations Coordinator	Privacy Officer
APO01.01 Design the management system for enterprise I&T.	A				R				
APO01.02 Communicate management objectives, direction and decisions made.		A			R	R			
APO01.03 Implement management processes (to support the achievement of governance and management objectives).		A			R	R			
APO01.04 Define and implement the organizational structures.		A	R		R				
APO01.05 Establish roles and responsibilities.			A		R				
APO01.06 Optimize the placement of the IT function.		A			R				
APO01.07 Define information (data) and system ownership.		A		R	R				
APO01.08 Define target skills and competencies.			A		R		R	R	
APO01.09 Define and communicate policies and procedures.		A	R	R	R		R	R	R
APO01.10 Define and implement infrastructure, services and applications to support the governance and management system.	A				R		R	R	R
APO01.11 Manage continual improvement of the I&T management system.		A		R	R		R	R	R

C. Component: Information Flows and Items				
Management Practice	Small and Medium Enterprise-specific Inputs		Small and Medium Enterprise-specific Outputs	
	From	Description	Description	To
APO01.01 Design the management system for enterprise I&T.	APO02.05	Strategic road map	Priority governance and management objectives	All APO All BAI All DSS All MEA
	APO12.01	Emerging risk issues and factors	Management system design	All APO All BAI All DSS All MEA
	APO12.02	Risk analysis results		
	EDM01.01	Decision-making model		
APO01.02 Communicate management objectives, direction and decisions made.	APO12.06	Risk impact communication	Communication on I&T objectives	All APO All BAI All DSS All MEA
	DSS04.01	Policy and objectives for business continuity		
	DSS05.03	Security policies for endpoint devices		
	EDM04.02	Principles for safeguarding resources		

Align, Plan and Organize

C. Component: Information Flows and Items *(cont.)*				
Management Practice	Small and Medium Enterprise-specific Inputs		Small and Medium Enterprise-specific Outputs	
	From	Description	Description	To
APO01.03 Implement management processes (to support the achievement of governance and management objectives).	APO02.04	Gaps and changes required to realize target capability	Targets for gap analysis	All APO All BAI All DSS All MEA
			Current process capability levels	APO01.11
APO01.04 Define and implement the organizational structures.	APO03.02	Process architecture model	Definition of organizational structure and functions	APO03.02
APO01.05 Establish roles and responsibilities.	APO07.03	• Skills and competencies matrix • Skill development plans	Guidance on supervisory practices	APO07.01
	DSS06.03	• Allocated levels of authority • Allocated roles and responsibilities	Definition of I&T-related roles and responsibilities	DSS05.04
	EDM01.01	Authority levels		
APO01.06 Optimize the placement of the IT function.	Outside COBIT	Enterprise strategy	Defined operational placement of IT function	APO03.02
APO01.07 Define information (data) and system ownership.	There are no small and medium enterprise-specific inputs for this practice.		Data classification guidelines	APO03.02 APO14.01 BAI02.01 DSS05.02 DSS06.01
			Data security and control guidelines	APO14.04 APO14.10 BAI02.01
			Data inventory	APO14.04 BAI02.01 DSS06.01
APO01.08 Define target skills and competencies.	There are no small and medium enterprise-specific inputs for this practice.		Target skills and competencies matrix	APO07.03
APO01.09 Define and communicate policies and procedures.	MEA03.02	Updated policies, principles, procedures and standards	Suggestions for updating policies and procedures	MEA01.05

C. Component: Information Flows and Items *(cont.)*				
Management Practice	Small and Medium Enterprise-specific Inputs		Small and Medium Enterprise-specific Outputs	
	From	Description	Description	To
APO01.10 Define and implement infrastructure, services and applications to support the governance and management system.	Outside COBIT	Assessment of IT services, applications and infrastructure, used for managing the I&T management system	Identified supporting tools	APO02.02 APO02.03
APO01.11 Manage continual improvement of the I&T management system.	APO01.03	Process capability levels	Process improvement opportunities	All APO All BAI All DSS All MEA
	MEA03.02	Updated I&T policies, procedures and standards	Performance goals and metrics for process improvement tracking	MEA01.02
			Process capability assessments	MEA01.03

D. Component: People, Skills and Competencies		
Skill	**Related Guidance (Standards, Frameworks, Compliance Requirements)**	**Detailed Reference**
IT governance	Skills Framework for the Information Age V6, 2015	GOVN
IT management	Skills Framework for the Information Age V6, 2015	ITMG

E. Component: Principles, Policies and Procedures	
Relevant Policy	**Policy Description**
I&T policy	Summarizes all relevant information for staff concerning the use of information and technology (i.e., the use of IT assets, security and privacy policies, the integrity of IT systems, IP rights related to proprietary software and enterprise data)

F. Component: Culture, Ethics and Behavior
Key Culture Elements
Set an internal culture of alignment between business and IT, establishing the necessary management objectives, structures, processes, and roles and responsibilities that enable decision making and value creation in the most effective and efficient manner.

G. Component: Services, Infrastructure and Applications
• COBIT and related products/tools • Equivalent frameworks and standards

Page intentionally left blank

Domain: Align, Plan and Organize Management Objective: APO02 — Managed Strategy	Focus Area: Small and Medium Enterprises
Description	
Provide a holistic view of the current business and I&T environment, the future direction, and the initiatives required to migrate to the desired future environment. Ensure that the desired level of digitization is integral to the future direction and the I&T strategy. Assess the organization's current digital maturity and develop a road map to close the gaps. With the business, rethink internal operations as well as customer-facing activities. Ensure focus on the transformation journey across the organization. Leverage enterprise architecture building blocks, governance components and the organization's ecosystem, including externally provided services and related capabilities, to enable reliable but agile and efficient response to strategic objectives.	
Purpose	
Support the digital transformation strategy of the organization and deliver the desired value through a road map of incremental changes. Use a holistic I&T approach, ensuring that each initiative is clearly connected to an overarching strategy. Enable change in all different aspects of the organization, from channels and processes to data, culture, skills, operating model and incentives.	
Small and Medium Enterprise Focus Area Relevance	
The I&T strategy should be aligned with the business strategy and should provide a road map to realize the enterprise digital transformation strategy. It is important to use a holistic approach to enable changes in all aspects of the I&T-related organization. Assessing the enterprise's current capabilities, performance and digital maturity is typically carried out by the top level of management.	

A. Component: Process	
Management Practice	**Small and Medium Enterprise-specific Metrics**
APO02.01 Understand enterprise context and direction. Understand the enterprise context (industry drivers, relevant regulations, basis for competition), its current way of working and its ambition level in terms of digitization.	a. IT management's level of understanding of current enterprise organization and context b. IT management's level of knowledge of enterprise goals and direction

Small and Medium Enterprise-specific Activities	Capability Level
1. Develop and maintain an understanding of the external environment of the enterprise.	2
2. Develop and maintain an understanding of the current way of working: the operational environment, the enterprise architecture (processes, data, applications and technology domains), organizational culture, and current challenges.	
3. Develop an understanding of future direction, i.e., the enterprise strategy, goals and objectives.	
4. Identify key stakeholders.	
5. Obtain insight on the requirements of key stakeholders.	3
6. Periodically evaluate and maintain an understanding of future direction, i.e., the enterprise strategy, goals and objectives.	4
7. Strategically evaluate the risk profile of the enterprise.	

Related Guidance (Standards, Frameworks, Compliance Requirements)	Detailed Reference
COSO Enterprise Risk Management, June 2017	7. Strategy and Objective-Setting—Principle 6

Management Practice	Small and Medium Enterprise-specific Metrics
APO02.02 Assess current capabilities, performance and digital maturity of the enterprise. Assess the performance of current I&T services and develop an understanding of current business and I&T capabilities (both internal and external). Assess current digital maturity of the enterprise and its appetite for change.	a. Percent of staff satisfied with current I&T capabilities b. Percent of business owner satisfaction with investment in and utilization of the internal and external asset base to meet critical success factors c. Number of observations on the management system by regulatory authorities

Small and Medium Enterprise-specific Activities	Capability Level
1. Assess current business and I&T capabilities and services, including external service provision and enterprisewide I&T-related skills and competencies.	2
2. Assess the organization's digital maturity across different dimensions (e.g., leadership's ability to leverage technology, level of accepted technology risk, culture, knowledge level of users, approach to innovation) and its appetite for change.	3

Related Guidance (Standards, Frameworks, Compliance Requirements)	Detailed Reference
COSO Enterprise Risk Management, June 2017	7. Strategy and Objective-Setting—Principle 6; 9. Review and Revision—Principle 15

A. Component: Process *(cont.)*

Management Practice	Small and Medium Enterprise-specific Metrics
APO02.03 Define target digital capabilities. Based on the understanding of enterprise context and direction, define the target I&T products and services and required capabilities. Consider reference standards, best practices and validated emerging technologies.	a. Percent of enterprise objectives addressed by the I&T goals/objectives

Small and Medium Enterprise-specific Activities	Capability Level
1. Identify specific I&T aspects of the enterprise strategy (digitizing processes, implementing new technology, supporting legacy architecture, applying new digital business models, developing digital product portfolio, etc.).	2
2. Define high-level I&T objectives/goals and how they will contribute to the enterprise's business objectives.	
3. Detail required I&T services and products to realize high-level I&T objectives. Consider validated emerging technology or innovations, reference standards, competitor business and I&T capabilities, and comparative benchmarks of good practice and emerging IT service provision.	3
4. Consider different I&T organization methodologies (Agile, scrum, waterfall, bimodal IT) depending on business requirements.	

Related Guidance (Standards, Frameworks, Compliance Requirements)	Detailed Reference
No related guidance for this management practice	

Management Practice	Small and Medium Enterprise-specific Metrics
APO02.04 Conduct a gap analysis. Identify gaps between current and target environments and describe the high-level changes in the enterprise architecture.	a. Number of gaps assessed between current and desired state

Small and Medium Enterprise-specific Activities	Capability Level
1. Identify all gaps and changes required to realize the target environment.	3
2. Describe the high-level changes in the enterprise architecture (processes, data, applications and technology domains).	
3. Assess the impact of potential changes on I&T investment programs.	
4. Consider the value of potential changes to I&T services, products and capabilities and the implications if no changes are realized.	4
5. Refine the target environment definition and prepare a value statement with the benefits of the target environment.	5

Related Guidance (Standards, Frameworks, Compliance Requirements)	Detailed Reference
No related guidance for this management practice	

Management Practice	Small and Medium Enterprise-specific Metrics
APO02.05 Define the strategic plan and road map. Develop a holistic digital strategy, in cooperation with relevant stakeholders, and detail a road map that defines the incremental steps required to achieve the goals and objectives. Ensure focus on the transformation journey through the appointment of a person who helps spearhead the digital transformation and drives alignment between business and I&T.	a. Percent of initiatives in the I&T strategy that are self-funding (i.e., financial benefits exceed costs) b. Degree of correspondence between enterprise strategy and I&T strategy and objectives

A. Component: Process *(cont.)*

Small and Medium Enterprise-specific Activities	Capability Level
1. Identify the initiatives required to close gaps between the current and target environment and translate them into a coherent I&T strategy that will integrate information & technology into all aspects of the business.	2
2. Detail a road map that defines the incremental steps required to achieve the goals and objectives of the I&T strategy. Ensure actions are included to train people with new skills, support adoption of new technology, sustain change throughout the organization, etc.	3
3. Consider the external ecosystem of the enterprise (partners, suppliers, start-ups, etc.) to help support execution of the road map.	
4. Group actions into projects with clear goals or deliverables. For each project, identify high-level resource requirements, create a schedule, determine investment/operational budget, calculate risk, assess change impact, etc.	
5. Determine and prioritize project dependencies, overlaps, synergies and impacts.	
6. Finalize the road map and indicate the relative scheduling and interdependencies of projects.	
7. Appoint a person from the executive committee to help spearhead the digital transformation and drive alignment.	
8. Formally obtain support and approval for the plan from the executive committee.	
9. Translate the objectives into outcome measures represented by metrics (what) and targets (how much) that can be related to enterprise benefits.	4

Related Guidance (Standards, Frameworks, Compliance Requirements)	Detailed Reference
ISF, The Standard of Good Practice for Information Security 2016	SG2.1 Information Security Strategy
ITIL V3, 2011	Service Strategy, 4.1 Strategy management for IT services

Management Practice	Small and Medium Enterprise-specific Metrics
AP002.06 Communicate the I&T strategy and direction. Create awareness and understanding of the business and I&T objectives and direction, as captured in the I&T strategy, through communication to appropriate stakeholders and users throughout the enterprise.	a. Frequency of updates to the I&T strategy communication plan

Small and Medium Enterprise-specific Activities	Capability Level
1. Communicate the IT direction and objectives to the organization and explain alignment to the overall business strategy.	2
2. Encourage responsiveness in staff with regard to the I&T direction and objectives, I&T risk, protection of IT resources, integrity of IT systems, etc.	

Related Guidance (Standards, Frameworks, Compliance Requirements)	Detailed Reference
No related guidance for this management practice	

B. Component: Organizational Structures

Key Management Practice	General Manager	Business Process Owners	Head of IT	IT Operations Coordinator	Privacy Officer	Legal Department
AP002.01 Understand enterprise context and direction.			A	R	R	R
AP002.02 Assess current capabilities, performance and digital maturity of the enterprise.			A	R	R	R
AP002.03 Define target digital capabilities.		R	A	R	R	R
AP002.04 Conduct a gap analysis.	A	R	R	R	R	R
AP002.05 Define the strategic plan and road map.		R	A	R	R	R
AP002.06 Communicate the I&T strategy and direction.	A		R			

C. Component: Information Flows and Items				
Management Practice	Small and Medium Enterprise-specific Inputs		Small and Medium Enterprise-specific Outputs	
	From	Description	Description	To
APO02.01 Understand enterprise context and direction.	APO04.02	Innovation opportunities linked to business drivers	Inventory of stakeholders and their expectations	Internal
	Outside COBIT	Enterprise strategy and strengths, weaknesses, opportunities, threats (SWOT) analysis		
APO02.02 Assess current capabilities, performance and digital maturity of the enterprise.	APO06.05	Cost optimization opportunities	Gaps and risk related to current capabilities	APO12.01
	APO09.01	Identified gaps in IT services to the business	Capability SWOT analysis	Internal
	APO12.02	Risk analysis results		
	BAI04.03	Prioritized improvements		
	BAI09.04	Results of cost optimization reviews		
	EDM04.03	Feedback on allocation and effectiveness of resources and capabilities		
APO02.03 Define target digital capabilities.	APO04.05	Results and recommendations from proof-of-concept initiatives	Proposed enterprise architecture changes	APO03.03
			Required business and IT capabilities	Internal
			High-level I&T-related goals	Internal
APO02.04 Conduct a gap analysis.	APO05.01	Investment return expectations	Gaps and changes required to realize target capability	APO01.03 APO13.02 BAI03.11 EDM04.01
	BAI11.09	Post-implementation review results	Estimated values related to target environment	BAI03.11
			Gaps and changes required to realize target capability	APO01.03 APO13.02 BAI03.11 EDM04.01
APO02.05 Define the strategic plan and road map.	APO03.01	Defined scope of architecture	I&T strategy and objectives	All APO All BAI All DSS All MEA
	APO03.03	Transition architectures	Strategic road map, with definition of the identified initiatives	APO01.01 APO03.01 APO08.01 EDM02.01 EDM02.02
	APO06.03	I&T budget		
	DSS04.02	Approved strategic options		
	EDM02.01	Feedback on strategy and goals	Risk assessment initiatives	EDM02.01 APO12.01
	EDM04.01	Approved resources plan		
APO02.06 Communicate the I&T strategy and direction.	EDM04.02	Communication of resourcing strategies	Communication plan	Internal

D. Component: People, Skills and Competencies		
Skill	**Related Guidance (Standards, Frameworks, Compliance Requirements)**	**Detailed Reference**
Business plan development	e-Competence Framework (e-CF)—A common European Framework for ICT Professionals in all industry sectors—Part 1: Framework, 2016	A. Plan—A.3. Business Plan Development
Emerging technology monitoring	Skills Framework for the Information Age V6, 2015	EMRG
I&T strategy and planning	Skills Framework for the Information Age V6, 2015	ITSP
Strategy alignment	e-Competence Framework (e-CF)—A common European Framework for ICT Professionals in all industry sectors—Part 1: Framework, 2016	A. Plan—A.1. IS and Business Strategy Alignment

E. Component: Principles, Policies and Procedures	
Relevant Policy	**Policy Description**
I&T strategy policy and principles	Provide strategic direction and initiatives required to transition to the desired future environment. Ensure that business and I&T strategy reflect the target level of digitization.

F. Component: Culture, Ethics and Behavior
Key Culture Elements
Establish a culture and underlying values that fit the overall business strategy (i.e., customer-oriented, innovation-driven, product-based). Find ways to inject speed into processes, and introduce the supporting culture and behavior that allow moving at a faster pace. This could start with changing basic habits, such as having more frequent strategy leadership meetings or automating certain activities.

G. Component: Services, Infrastructure and Applications
• Customer analytics • Industry benchmarks • Performance measurement system (e.g., balanced scorecard, skills management tools) • Technology watch services and tools

Page intentionally left blank

Domain: Align, Plan and Organize Management Objective: APO03 — Managed Enterprise Architecture	Focus Area: Small and Medium Enterprises
Description	
Establish a common architecture consisting of business process, information, data, application and technology architecture layers. Create key models and practices that describe the baseline and target architectures, in line with the enterprise and I&T strategy. Define requirements for taxonomy, standards, guidelines, procedures, templates and tools, and provide a linkage for these components. Improve alignment, increase agility, improve quality of information and generate potential cost savings through initiatives such as re-use of building block components.	
Purpose	
Represent the different building blocks that make up the enterprise and its interrelationships as well as the principles guiding their design and evolution over time, to enable a standard, responsive and efficient delivery of operational and strategic objectives.	
Small and Medium Enterprise Focus Area Relevance	
Establish a common architecture consisting of business capabilities, business processes, information, data, applications and technology architecture layers to effectively and efficiently realize the enterprise business strategies, as relevant and applicable.	

A. Component: Process	
Management Practice	**Small and Medium Enterprise-specific Metrics**
APO03.01 Develop the enterprise architecture vision. The architecture vision provides a first-cut, high-level description of the baseline and target architectures, covering the business, information, data, application and technology domains. The architecture vision provides the sponsor with a key tool to sell the benefits of the proposed capabilities to stakeholders within the enterprise. The architecture vision describes how the new capabilities (in line with I&T strategy and objectives) will meet enterprise goals and strategic objectives and address stakeholder concerns when implemented.	a. Degree to which the baseline and target architectures cover the business, information, data, application and technology domains, and frequency of updates

Small and Medium Enterprise-specific Activities	Capability Level
1. Identify the key stakeholders and their concerns/objectives, and define the key enterprise requirements to be addressed to satisfy their objectives.	2
2. Identify the enterprise goals and strategic drivers. Define the constraints that must be dealt with, including enterprisewide constraints and project-specific constraints (time, schedule, resources, etc.).	
3. Understand the capabilities and desires of the business, then identify options to realize those capabilities (based on the I&T strategy and road map).	
4. Based on stakeholder concerns, business capability requirements, scope, constraints and principles, create the architecture vision: a high-level view of the baseline and target architectures.	
5. Confirm and elaborate architecture principles, including enterprise principles. Ensure that any existing definitions are current and clarify any areas of ambiguity.	3

Related Guidance (Standards, Frameworks, Compliance Requirements)	Detailed Reference
National Institute of Standards and Technology Special Publication 800-53, Revision 5 (Draft), August 2017	3.15 Program management (PM-7)
The Open Group Standard TOGAF version 9.2, 2018	6. Phase A: Architecture Vision

A. Component: Process *(cont.)*

Management Practice	Small and Medium Enterprise-specific Metrics
APO03.02 Define reference architecture. The reference architecture describes the current and target architectures for the business, information, data, application and technology domains.	a. Number of exceptions and/or changes to architecture standards applied for and granted

Small and Medium Enterprise-specific Activities	Capability Level
1. Develop baseline architectural domain descriptions using the scope and level of detail necessary to support the target architecture.	2
2. Maintain a process architecture model as part of the baseline and target domain descriptions. Standardize the descriptions and documentation of processes.	3
3. Maintain an information architecture model as part of the baseline and target domain descriptions, consistent with the enterprise's strategy, to enable optimal acquisition, storage and use of data for decision making.	
4. Finalize business, information, data, applications and technology domain architectures, and create an architecture definition document.	
5. Verify the architecture models for internal consistency and accuracy and perform a gap analysis between the baseline and target. Prioritize gaps and define new or modified components that must be developed for the target architecture. Resolve potential impacts such as incompatibilities, inconsistencies or conflicts within the envisioned architecture.	4
6. Periodically conduct a formal stakeholder review by checking the proposed architecture against the original motivation for the architecture project and the statement of architecture work.	5

Related Guidance (Standards, Frameworks, Compliance Requirements)	Detailed Reference
CMMI Data Management Maturity Model, 2014	Platform and Architecture—Architectural Approach; Platform and Architecture—Data Integration
ITIL V3, 2011	Service Strategy, 5.4 IT service strategy and enterprise architecture
National Institute of Standards and Technology Special Publication 800-37, Revision 2 (Draft), May 2018	3.1 Preparation (Task 9)
National Institute of Standards and Technology Special Publication 800-53, Revision 5 (Draft), August 2017	3.5 Configuration management (CM-8)
The Open Group Standard TOGAF version 9.2, 2018	7. Phase B: Business Architecture; 8. Phase C: Information Systems Architectures; 9. Phase C: Information Systems Architectures Data Architecture; 10. Phase C: Information Systems Architectures Application Architecture; 11. Phase D: Technology Architecture

Management Practice	Small and Medium Enterprise-specific Metrics
APO03.03 Select opportunities and solutions. Rationalize the gaps between baseline and target architectures, accounting for both business and technical perspectives, and logically group them into project work packages. Integrate the project with any related I&T-enabled investment programs to ensure that the architectural initiatives are aligned with and enable these initiatives as part of overall enterprise change. Make this a collaborative effort with key enterprise stakeholders from business and IT to assess the enterprise's transformation readiness, and identify opportunities, solutions and all implementation constraints.	a. Number of identified gaps in models across enterprise, information, data, application and technology architecture domains

Small and Medium Enterprise-specific Activities	Capability Level
1. Review and consolidate the gap analysis results between the baseline and target architectures and assess their implications with respect to potential solutions/opportunities, interdependencies and alignment with current I&T-enabled projects.	2
2. Confirm the enterprise's readiness for transformation and the associated risk.	
3. Formulate a high-level implementation and migration strategy that will guide the target architecture implementation and structure the transition architectures in alignment with enterprise strategic objectives and time scales.	3
4. Identify and group major work packages into a coherent set of projects that align with the enterprise's direction and approach to strategic implementation.	
5. Develop a series of transition architectures for use when the scope of change required to realize the target architecture requires an incremental approach.	4

A. Component: Process *(cont.)*		
Related Guidance (Standards, Frameworks, Compliance Requirements)	**Detailed Reference**	
CMMI Data Management Maturity Model, 2014	Platform and Architecture—Architectural Approach; Platform and Architecture—Data Integration	
The Open Group Standard TOGAF version 9.2, 2018	12. Phase E: Opportunities and Solutions	
Management Practice	**Small and Medium Enterprise-specific Metrics**	
APO03.04 Define architecture implementation. Create a viable implementation and migration plan in alignment with the program and project portfolios. Ensure the plan is closely coordinated to deliver value and that the required resources are available to complete the necessary work.	a. Number of stakeholder comments on the implementation and migration plan	
Small and Medium Enterprise-specific Activities		**Capability Level**
1. Establish, as part of project planning, what the implementation and migration plan should include, and ensure that it aligns with the requirements of the executive committee.		3
2. Confirm transition architecture increments and phases. Update the architecture definition document.		
3. Communicate the defined architectural road map to relevant stakeholders.		
Related Guidance (Standards, Frameworks, Compliance Requirements)	**Detailed Reference**	
CMMI Data Management Maturity Model, 2014	Platform and Architecture—Architectural Approach; Platform and Architecture—Data Integration	
The Open Group Standard TOGAF version 9.2, 2018	13. Phase F: Migration Planning	
Management Practice	**Small and Medium Enterprise-specific Metrics**	
APO03.05 Provide enterprise architecture services. Provide enterprise architecture services within the enterprise that include guidance to and monitoring of implementation projects, formalizing ways of working through architecture contracts, and measuring and communicating architecture's value and compliance monitoring.	a. Percent of projects that utilize the framework and methodology to reuse defined components b. Project benefits realized that can be traced back to architecture involvement (e.g., cost reduction through reuse)	
Small and Medium Enterprise-specific Activities		**Capability Level**
1. Maintain a portfolio of enterprise architecture services and ensure alignment with strategic objectives and solution development as required.		3
2. Identify enterprise architecture priorities.		4
3. Align priorities to value drivers. Define and collect value metrics and measure and update architecture services as required.		
Related Guidance (Standards, Frameworks, Compliance Requirements)	**Detailed Reference**	
CMMI Data Management Maturity Model, 2014	Platform and Architecture—Architectural Standards	
ITIL V3, 2011	Service Design, 3.9 Service Oriented Architecture	
The Open Group Standard TOGAF version 9.2, 2018	14. Phase G: Implementation Governance; 15. Phase H: Architecture Change Management	

B. Component: Organizational Structures				
Key Management Practice	**Executive Committee**	**General Manager**	**Operations Manager**	**Head of IT**
APO03.01 Develop the enterprise architecture vision.	A	R		R
APO03.02 Define reference architecture.		R		A
APO03.03 Select opportunities and solutions.	A	R		R
APO03.04 Define architecture implementation.			R	A
APO03.05 Provide enterprise architecture services.			R	A

C. Component: Information Flows and Items				
Management Practice	**Small and Medium Enterprise-specific Inputs**		**Small and Medium Enterprise-specific Outputs**	
	From	**Description**	**Description**	**To**
APO03.01 Develop the enterprise architecture vision.	APO02.05	Strategic road map	Architecture principles and scope	BAI02.01 BAI03.01 BAI03.02
	Outside COBIT	Enterprise strategy		
APO03.02 Define reference architecture.	APO01.04	Definition of organizational structure and functions	Process architecture model	APO01.04
	APO01.07	Data classification guidelines	Information architecture model	APO13.02 BAI02.01 BAI03.01 BAI03.02 BAI03.12
	APO14.01	Data management strategy		
APO03.03 Select opportunities and solutions.	APO02.03	Proposed enterprise architecture changes	Transition architectures	APO02.05
	Outside COBIT	Enterprise strategies		
APO03.04 Define architecture implementation.	There are no small and medium enterprise-specific inputs for this practice.		Implementation phase descriptions	BAI01.01
APO03.05 Provide enterprise architecture services.	There are no small and medium enterprise-specific inputs for this practice.		There are no small and medium enterprise-specific outputs for this practice.	

D. Component: People, Skills and Competencies		
Skill	**Related Guidance (Standards, Frameworks, Compliance Requirements)**	**Detailed Reference**
Architecture design	e-Competence Framework (e-CF)—A common European Framework for ICT Professionals in all industry sectors—Part 1: Framework, 2016	A. Plan—A.5. Architecture Design
Data analysis	Skills Framework for the Information Age V6, 2015	DTAN
Enterprise and business architecture	Skills Framework for the Information Age V6, 2015	STPL
Product / service planning	e-Competence Framework (e-CF)—A common European Framework for ICT Professionals in all industry sectors—Part 1: Framework, 2016	A. Plan—A.4. Product/Service Planning
Solution architecture	Skills Framework for the Information Age V6, 2015	ARCH

E. Component: Principles, Policies and Procedures	
Relevant Policy	**Policy Description**
There are no small and medium enterprise-specific principles, policies and procedures for this objective.	

F. Component: Culture, Ethics and Behavior
Key Culture Elements
Create an environment in which management understands architectural needs relative to business goals and objectives. Drive effective practice of enterprise architecture throughout the organization (not only by enterprise architects). Ensure a holistic approach that links components more seamlessly (e.g., by moving away from dedicated teams of application specialists).

G. Component: Services, Infrastructure and Applications
Architecture repository

Page intentionally left blank

Domain: Align, Plan and Organize Management Objective: APO04 — Managed Innovation	Focus Area: Small and Medium Enterprises
Description	
Maintain an awareness of I&T and related service trends and monitor emerging technology trends. Proactively identify innovation opportunities and plan how to benefit from innovation in relation to business needs and the defined I&T strategy. Analyze what opportunities for business innovation or improvement can be created by emerging technologies, services or I&T-enabled business innovation; through existing established technologies; and by business and IT process innovation. Influence strategic planning and enterprise architecture decisions.	
Purpose	
Achieve competitive advantage, business innovation, improved customer experience, and improved operational effectiveness and efficiency by exploiting I&T developments and emerging technologies.	
Small and Medium Enterprise Focus Area Relevance	
Consider innovation as a facilitator to achieve competitive advantage and thereby generate more business. Make sure there are efficient mechanisms in place to react to market opportunities, competition and customer requests.	

A. Component: Process		
Management Practice	**Small and Medium Enterprise-specific Metrics**	
APO04.01 Create an environment conducive to innovation. Create an environment that is conducive to innovation, considering methods such as culture, reward, collaboration, technology forums, and mechanisms to promote and capture employee ideas.	a. Executive committee interest in I&T innovation	
Small and Medium Enterprise-specific Activities		**Capability Level**
1. Create an innovation plan that includes risk appetite, the envisioned budget to spend on innovation initiatives, and innovation objectives.		2
2. Set up a program enabling staff to submit innovation ideas. Create an appropriate decision-making structure to assess and move innovative ideas forward.		
3. Maintain the program that enables staff to submit innovation ideas.		3
4. Encourage innovation ideas from customers, suppliers and business partners.		
Related Guidance (Standards, Frameworks, Compliance Requirements)	**Detailed Reference**	
No related guidance for this management practice		
Management Practice	**Small and Medium Enterprise-specific Metrics**	
APO04.02 Maintain an understanding of the enterprise environment. Work with relevant stakeholders to understand their challenges. Maintain an adequate understanding of enterprise strategy, competitive environment and other constraints, so that opportunities enabled by new technologies can be identified.	a. Percent of I&T investments that are evaluated based on cost, alignment with strategy and financial measures (e.g., based on costs and benefits) b. Percent of opportunities enabled by new technologies identified	
Small and Medium Enterprise-specific Activities		**Capability Level**
1. Maintain an understanding of the business drivers, enterprise and I&T strategy, industry drivers, and enterprise operations and current challenges so that the potential value-add of technologies or I&T innovation can be identified.		2
2. Understand current business problems, process bottlenecks or other constraints that may create opportunities for emerging technologies or I&T innovations.		
3. Understand enterprise investment parameters for innovation and new technologies in order to develop appropriate strategies.		3
Related Guidance (Standards, Frameworks, Compliance Requirements)	**Detailed Reference**	
No related guidance for this management practice		
Management Practice	**Small and Medium Enterprise-specific Metrics**	
APO04.03 Monitor and scan the technology environment. Set up a technology watch process to perform systematic monitoring and scanning of the enterprise's external environment to identify emerging technologies that have the potential to create value (e.g., by realizing the enterprise strategy, optimizing costs, avoiding obsolescence, and better enabling enterprise and I&T processes). Monitor the marketplace, competitive landscape, industry sectors, and legal and regulatory trends to be able to analyze emerging technologies or innovation ideas in the enterprise context.	a. Frequency of environmental research activities and scans performed to identify innovative ideas and trends	

A. Component: Process *(cont.)*	
Small and Medium Enterprise-specific Activities	**Capability Level**
1. Understand the enterprise's interest and potential for adopting new technology innovations and focus awareness efforts on the most opportunistic technology innovations.	2
2. Set up technology watch initiatives for performing research and scanning the external environment, including appropriate web sites, journals and conferences, to identify emerging technologies and their potential value to the enterprise. Alternatively, buy this service from an external provider.	
3. Consult with third-party experts as needed to confirm research findings or as a source of information on emerging technologies.	
4. Capture I&T-innovation ideas from staff and review for potential implementation.	
Related Guidance (Standards, Frameworks, Compliance Requirements)	**Detailed Reference**
No related guidance for this management practice	
Management Practice	**Small and Medium Enterprise-specific Metrics**
APO04.04 Assess the potential of emerging technologies and innovative ideas. Analyze identified emerging technologies and/or other I&T innovative suggestions to understand their business potential. Work with stakeholders to validate assumptions on the potential of new technologies and innovation.	a. Percent of implemented initiatives that realize the envisioned benefits b. Percent of successful proof-of-concept initiatives to test emerging technologies or other innovation ideas
Small and Medium Enterprise-specific Activities	**Capability Level**
1. Evaluate identified technologies, considering aspects such as time to reach maturity, inherent risk of new technologies (including potential legal implications), fit with the enterprise architecture, and potential to provide additional value in line with enterprise and I&T strategy.	2
2. Identify any issues that may need to be resolved or proven through a proof-of-concept initiative.	3
3. Scope the proof-of-concept initiative, including desired outcomes, required budget, time frames and responsibilities.	
4. Obtain approval for the proof-of-concept initiative.	
5. Conduct proof-of-concept initiatives to test emerging technologies or other innovation ideas, identify any issues, and determine whether further implementation or rollout should be considered based on feasibility and potential ROI.	
Related Guidance (Standards, Frameworks, Compliance Requirements)	**Detailed Reference**
No related guidance for this management practice	
Management Practice	**Small and Medium Enterprise-specific Metrics**
APO04.05 Recommend appropriate further initiatives. Evaluate and monitor the results of proof-of-concept initiatives and, if favorable, generate recommendations for further initiatives. Gain stakeholder support.	a. Number of proof-of-concept initiatives evaluated and approved for further rollout b. Number of proof-of-concept initiatives that have been leveraged in actual investment
Small and Medium Enterprise-specific Activities	**Capability Level**
1. Document proof-of-concept results, including guidance and recommendations for trends and innovation programs.	3
2. Include viable innovation opportunities in the I&T strategy and enterprise architecture processes.	
3. Analyze and communicate reasons for rejected proof-of-concept initiatives.	
4. Follow up on proof-of-concept initiatives to measure the degree to which they have been leveraged in actual investment.	4
Related Guidance (Standards, Frameworks, Compliance Requirements)	**Detailed Reference**
No related guidance for this management practice	
Management Practice	**Small and Medium Enterprise-specific Metrics**
APO04.06 Monitor the implementation and use of innovation. Monitor the implementation and use of emerging technologies and innovations during adoption, integration and for the full economic life cycle to ensure that the promised benefits are realized and to identify lessons learned.	a. Number of lessons learned and opportunities for improvement captured for future use

A. Component: Process *(cont.)*		
Small and Medium Enterprise-specific Activities		**Capability Level**
1. Capture lessons learned and opportunities for improvement.		3
2. Ensure innovation initiatives are in line with the enterprise and I&T strategy. Adjust the innovation plan, if required.		
3. Assess the implementation of the new innovations.		4
4. Identify and evaluate the potential value to be realized from the use of innovation.		
Related Guidance (Standards, Frameworks, Compliance Requirements)	**Detailed Reference**	
No related guidance for this management practice		

B. Component: Organizational Structures							
Key Management Practice	**Executive Committee**	**Financial Manager**	**Head Human Resources**	**Business Process Owners**	**Head of IT**	**IT Development Coordinator**	**IT Operations Coordinator**
APO04.01 Create an environment conducive to innovation.	A	R	R	R	R	R	R
APO04.02 Maintain an understanding of the enterprise environment.	A			R	R	R	R
APO04.03 Monitor and scan the technology environment.	A			R	R	R	R
APO04.04 Assess the potential of emerging technologies and innovative ideas.	A			R	R	R	R
APO04.05 Recommend appropriate further initiatives.	A			R	R	R	R
APO04.06 Monitor the implementation and use of innovation.	A	R		R	R	R	R

C. Component: Information Flows and Items				
Management Practice	Small and Medium Enterprise-specific Inputs		Small and Medium Enterprise-specific Outputs	
	From	**Description**	**Description**	**To**
APO04.01 Create an environment conducive to innovation.	EDM03.01	Enterprise risk appetite	Recognition and reward program	APO07.04
			Innovation plan	Internal
APO04.02 Maintain an understanding of the enterprise environment.	Outside COBIT	Enterprise strategy and SWOT analysis	Innovation opportunities	APO02.01
APO04.03 Monitor and scan the technology environment.	Outside COBIT	Emerging technologies	Research analyses of innovation possibilities	BAI03.01
APO04.04 Assess the potential of emerging technologies and innovative ideas.	There are no small and medium enterprise-specific inputs for this practice.		Proof-of-concept scope and high-level business case	APO05.02 APO06.02
			Evaluations of innovation ideas	BAI03.01
			Test results from proof-of-concept initiatives	Internal

C. Component: Information Flows and Items *(cont.)*				
Management Practice	Small and Medium Enterprise-specific Inputs		Small and Medium Enterprise-specific Outputs	
AP004.05 Recommend appropriate further initiatives.	From	Description	Description	To
	There are no small and medium enterprise-specific inputs for this practice.		Results and recommendations from proof-of-concept initiatives	AP002.03 BAI03.09
AP004.06 Monitor the implementation and use of innovation.	There are no small and medium enterprise-specific inputs for this practice.		Evaluation of innovation benefits	AP005.03
			Adjusted innovation plans	Internal

D. Component: People, Skills and Competencies		
Skill	**Related Guidance (Standards, Frameworks, Compliance Requirements)**	**Detailed Reference**
Business plan development	e-Competence Framework (e-CF)—A common European Framework for ICT Professionals in all industry sectors—Part 1: Framework, 2016	A. Plan—A.3. Business Plan Development
Emerging technology monitoring	Skills Framework for the Information Age V6, 2015	EMRG
Innovating	e-Competence Framework (e-CF)—A common European Framework for ICT Professionals in all industry sectors—Part 1: Framework, 2016	A. Plan—A.9. Innovating
Innovation	Skills Framework for the Information Age V6, 2015	INOV
Research	Skills Framework for the Information Age V6, 2015	RSCH
Technology trend monitoring	e-Competence Framework (e-CF)—A common European Framework for ICT Professionals in all industry sectors—Part 1: Framework, 2016	A. Plan—A.7. Technology Trend Monitoring

E. Component: Principles, Policies and Procedures	
Relevant Policy	**Policy Description**
Innovation principle	Ensures that new and innovative ideas and their impacts are considered and assessed in strategic goal setting and decision making

F. Component: Culture, Ethics and Behavior
Key Culture Elements
Create an environment that is conducive to innovation by maintaining relevant HR initiatives, such as innovation recognition and reward programs, appropriate job rotation, and discretionary time for experimentation. Ensure close collaboration and coordination of initiatives across the organization.

G. Component: Services, Infrastructure and Applications
• Collaboration platforms • Industry benchmarks • Technology watch services and tools

Domain: Align, Plan and Organize Management Objective: APO05 — Managed Portfolio	Focus Area: Small and Medium Enterprises
Description	
Execute the strategic direction set for investments in line with the enterprise architecture vision and I&T road map. Consider the different categories of investments and the resource and funding constraints. Evaluate, prioritize and balance programs and services, managing demand within resource and funding constraints, based on their alignment with strategic objectives, enterprise worth and risk. Move selected programs into the active products or services portfolio for execution. Monitor the performance of the overall portfolio of products and services and programs, proposing adjustments as necessary in response to program, product or service performance or changing enterprise priorities.	
Purpose	
Optimize the performance of the overall portfolio of programs in response to individual program, product and service performance and changing enterprise priorities and demand.	
Small and Medium Enterprise Focus Area Relevance	
The investments in programs and projects should be effectively managed in accordance with enterprise objectives, priorities and demands.	

A. Component: Process		
Management Practice	**Small and Medium Enterprise-specific Metrics**	
APO05.01 Determine the availability and sources of funds. Determine potential sources of funds, different funding options and the implications of the funding source on the investment return expectations.	a. Ratio between funds allocated and funds used b. Ratio between retained earnings and funds allocated	
Small and Medium Enterprise-specific Activities		**Capability Level**
1. Identify options for obtaining funds for I&T-enabled investments, internally and from external sources.		2
Related Guidance (Standards, Frameworks, Compliance Requirements)	**Detailed Reference**	
No related guidance for this management practice		
Management Practice	**Small and Medium Enterprise-specific Metrics**	
APO05.02 Evaluate and select programs to fund. Based on requirements for the overall investment portfolio mix and the I&T strategic plan and road map, evaluate and prioritize program business cases and decide on investment proposals. Allocate funds and initiate programs.	a. Percent of projects evaluated as positive and approved for initiation b. Percent of business units involved in the evaluation and prioritization process	
Small and Medium Enterprise-specific Activities		**Capability Level**
1. Recognize investment opportunities and classify them in alignment with the enterprise's investment categories.		2
2. Develop project business cases, referring to strategic alignment, enterprise benefits, risk and availability of resources.		
3. Assess the impact of project initiations, identifying any changes that might be required to other projects.		3
4. Decide which candidate projects can be launched. Decide whether rejected projects should be held for future consideration or provided with some seed funding to determine whether the business case can be improved or should be discarded.		
Related Guidance (Standards, Frameworks, Compliance Requirements)	**Detailed Reference**	
PMBOK Guide Sixth Edition, 2017	Part 1: 1.2.3 Relationship of project, program, portfolio and operations management	
Management Practice	**Small and Medium Enterprise-specific Metrics**	
APO05.03 Monitor, optimize and report on investment portfolio performance. On a regular basis, monitor and optimize the performance of the investment portfolio and individual programs throughout the entire investment life cycle. Ensure continuous follow-up on the alignment of the portfolio with I&T strategy.	a. Trends in ROI of initiatives included in the I&T strategy	

A. Component: Process *(cont.)*		
Small and Medium Enterprise-specific Activities		**Capability Level**
1. Review the portfolio on a regular basis to identify and exploit synergies, eliminate duplication between projects, and identify and mitigate risk.		3
2. Develop metrics for measuring I&T contribution to the enterprise, and establish appropriate performance targets reflecting the required IT and enterprise capability targets. Use guidance from external experts and benchmark data to develop metrics.		4
3. Provide the executive committee with an accurate view of the performance of the investment portfolio.		
4. Identify and report deviations between budget and actual spend, and any adjustments to expected ROI.		
Related Guidance (Standards, Frameworks, Compliance Requirements)	**Detailed Reference**	
No related guidance for this management practice		
Management Practice	**Small and Medium Enterprise-specific Metrics**	
APO05.04 Maintain portfolios. Maintain portfolios of investment programs and projects, I&T products and services, and I&T assets.	a. Frequency of service portfolio updates	
Small and Medium Enterprise-specific Activities		**Capability Level**
1. Create and maintain portfolios of I&T-enabled investment projects, IT services and IT assets, which form the basis for the current IT budget and support the I&T tactical and strategic plans.		3
2. Maintain the service and asset portfolios in alignment with the investment projects that were executed successfully.		
3. Remove a project from the active investment portfolio when the desired enterprise benefits have been achieved or when it is clear that benefits will not be achieved within the value criteria set for the project.		
Related Guidance (Standards, Frameworks, Compliance Requirements)	**Detailed Reference**	
ITIL V3, 2011	Service Strategy, 4.2 Service portfolio management	
Management Practice	**Small and Medium Enterprise-specific Metrics**	
APO05.05 Manage benefits achievement. Monitor the benefits of providing and maintaining appropriate I&T products, services and capabilities, based on the agreed and current business case.	a. Percent of stakeholders satisfied with efforts to monitor the benefits of providing and maintaining appropriate IT services and capabilities, based on the agreed-on and current business case b. Number of escalations to higher management for resolution c. Percent of investments with measurable realized benefits compared to the business case	
Small and Medium Enterprise-specific Activities		**Capability Level**
1. Using the agreed-on metrics, track how benefits are achieved, how they evolve throughout the project life cycle, how they are delivered by IT products and services, and how they compare to internal and industry benchmarks. Communicate results to stakeholders.		4
2. Implement corrective action when achieved benefits significantly deviate from expected benefits. Update the business case for new initiatives and implement business process and service improvements as required.		5
3. Consider obtaining guidance from external experts, industry leaders and comparative benchmarking data to test and improve the metrics and targets.		
Related Guidance (Standards, Frameworks, Compliance Requirements)	**Detailed Reference**	
No related guidance for this management practice		

B. Component: Organizational Structures					
Key Management Practice	General Manager	Financial Manager	Business Process Owners	Project Manager	Head of IT
APO05.01 Determine the availability and sources of funds.	A	R			R
APO05.02 Evaluate and select programs to fund.		R			A
APO05.03 Monitor, optimize and report on investment portfolio performance.					A
APO05.04 Maintain portfolios.					A
APO05.05 Manage benefits achievement.	A	R	R		R

C. Component: Information Flows and Items				
Management Practice	Small and Medium Enterprise-specific Inputs		Small and Medium Enterprise-specific Outputs	
	From	Description	Description	To
APO05.01 Determine the availability and sources of funds.	There are no small and medium enterprise-specific inputs for this practice.		Investment return expectations	APO02.04 APO06.02 BAI01.06 EDM02.02
APO05.02 Evaluate and select programs to fund.	APO06.02	• Budget allocations • Prioritization and ranking of I&T initiatives	Business case assessments	APO06.02
	APO06.03	IT budget	Selected programs with ROI milestones	EDM02.02
	APO09.01	Identified gaps in IT services to the business		
	APO09.03	Service level agreements (SLAs)		
	APO13.02	Information security business cases		
	EDM02.02	Evaluation of investment and services portfolios		
	EDM02.03	Investment types and criteria		

C. Component: Information Flows and Items *(cont.)*				
Management Practice	Small and Medium Enterprise-specific Inputs		Small and Medium Enterprise-specific Outputs	
	From	Description	Description	To
APO05.03 Monitor, optimize and report on investment portfolio performance.	APO04.06	Evaluation of innovation benefits	Investment portfolio performance reports	EDM02.03 EDM02.04 MEA01.03
	EDM02.02	Evaluation of investment and services portfolios		
	EDM02.04	• Feedback on portfolio and program performance • Actions to improve delivery of value		
APO05.04 Maintain portfolios.	BAI03.11	Updated service portfolio	Updated service and project portfolio	APO09.02 BAI01.01
	BAI01.09 BAI11.07	Communication on status of programs and projects		
APO05.05 Manage benefits achievement.	There are no small and medium enterprise-specific inputs for this practice.		Benefit results and related communications	EDM02.02

D. Component: People, Skills and Competencies		
Skill	Related Guidance (Standards, Frameworks, Compliance Requirements)	Detailed Reference
Benefits management	Skills Framework for the Information Age V6, 2015	BENM
Portfolio management	Skills Framework for the Information Age V6, 2015	POMG
Product/service planning	e-Competence Framework (e-CF)—A common European Framework for ICT Professionals in all industry sectors—Part 1: Framework, 2016	A. Plan—A.4. Product/Service Planning

E. Component: Principles, Policies and Procedures	
Relevant Policy	Policy Description
Portfolio principles	Define general principles that ensure selection of diverse programs and projects well suited to achieve I&T strategy; consider alignment with business strategy, appropriate investment mix, etc.

F. Component: Culture, Ethics and Behavior
Key Culture Elements
Promote systematic management of I&T investments; measure and evaluate investment scenarios objectively.
To support speed and agility, ensure that leaders manage the active investment portfolio decisively. If a prototype does not work, leadership must end the project decisively, incorporate lessons learned and move on. Quickly devote additional resources to successful projects so they can be appropriately scaled.

G. Component: Services, Infrastructure and Applications
Portfolio/investment management tools

Domain: Align, Plan and Organize Management Objective: APO06 – Managed Budget and Costs	Focus Area: Small and Medium Enterprises
Description	
Manage the I&T-related financial activities in both the business and IT functions, covering budget, cost and benefit management and prioritization of spending through the use of formal budgeting practices and a fair and equitable system of allocating costs to the enterprise. Consult stakeholders to identify and control the total costs and benefits within the context of the I&T strategic and tactical plans. Initiate corrective action where needed.	
Purpose	
Foster a partnership between IT and enterprise stakeholders to enable the effective and efficient use of I&T-related resources and provide transparency and accountability of the cost and business value of solutions and services. Enable the enterprise to make informed decisions regarding the use of I&T solutions and services.	
Small and Medium Enterprise Focus Area Relevance	
Management of budget and cost can be integrated in the enterprise processes for financial management. Effective and efficient use of I&T-related resources is achieved by setting priorities based on business and IT priorities. Cost allocation is highly dependent on the complexity of the organization. Vary the complexity of cost allocation based on organizational strategy and the desired level of formality.	

A. Component: Process		
Management Practice	**Small and Medium Enterprise-specific Metrics**	
APO06.01 Manage finance and accounting. Establish and maintain a method to manage and account for all I&T-related costs, investments and depreciation as an integral part of enterprise financial systems and accounts. Report using the enterprise's financial measurement systems.	a. Number of deviations between expected and actual budget categories b. Usefulness of financial information as input to business cases for new investment in I&T assets and services	
Small and Medium Enterprise-specific Activities		**Capability Level**
1. Define processes, inputs, outputs and responsibilities for the financial management and accounting of I&T in alignment with the enterprise budgeting and cost accounting policies and approach. Define how to analyze and report (to whom and how) on the IT budget control process.		2
2. Define a classification scheme to identify all I&T-related cost elements (capital expenditures [capex] vs. operating expenses [opex], hardware, software, people, etc.) and identify how they are captured.		
3. Use financial information to support business cases for new investments in I&T assets and services.		3
4. Ensure that costs are maintained in the I&T asset and service portfolios.		
5. Establish and maintain practices for financial planning and the optimization of recurring operational costs to deliver maximum value to the enterprise for the least expenditure.		4
Related Guidance (Standards, Frameworks, Compliance Requirements)	**Detailed Reference**	
ITIL V3, 2011	Service Strategy, 4.3 Financial management for IT services	
Management Practice	**Small and Medium Enterprise-specific Metrics**	
APO06.02 Prioritize resource allocation. Implement a decision-making process to prioritize the allocation of resources and establish rules for discretionary investments by individual business units. Include the potential use of external service providers and consider the buy, develop and rent options.	a. Number of resource allocation issues escalated b. Percent of IT resources aligned with high-priority initiatives	
Small and Medium Enterprise-specific Activities		**Capability Level**
1. Rank all I&T initiatives and budget requests based on business cases and strategic and tactical priorities, and establish procedures to determine budget allocations and cut-off.		2
2. Agree with business the required IT resources (including external service providers) for I&T-enabled projects, IT services and IT assets. Consider the options for buying or developing capitalized assets and services vs. externally utilized assets and services on a pay-for-use basis.		
3. Communicate budget decisions and review them with the budget holders.		
4. Obtain ratification from the business management for the I&T budget implications that negatively impact the entity's strategic or tactical plans and offer suggested actions to resolve these impacts.		3
Related Guidance (Standards, Frameworks, Compliance Requirements)	**Detailed Reference**	
No related guidance for this management practice		

A. Component: Process *(cont.)*		
Management Practice	**Small and Medium Enterprise-specific Metrics**	
APO06.03 Create and maintain budgets. Prepare a budget reflecting investment priorities based on the portfolio of I&T-enabled programs and I&T services.	a. Number of budget changes due to omissions and errors	
Small and Medium Enterprise-specific Activities		**Capability Level**
1. Implement a formal IT budget, including all expected I&T costs of I&T-enabled projects, services and assets.		2
2. When creating the budget, consider the following components: alignment with the business; internal resource costs, including personnel, accommodations and information assets; third-party costs, including outsourcing contracts, consultants and service providers; capex and opex; and cost elements that depend on the workload.		
3. Compile and adjust the budget based on changing enterprise needs and financial considerations.		3
4. Record, maintain and communicate the current IT budget, including committed expenditures and current expenditures for approved and planned I&T projects, operations and maintenance.		
5. Evaluate the effectiveness of the method for managing the I&T budgeting.		4
6. Use the monitoring results to implement improvements and ensure that future budgets are more accurate, reliable and cost-effective.		5
Related Guidance (Standards, Frameworks, Compliance Requirements)	**Detailed Reference**	
ISO/IEC 20000-1:2011(E)	6.4 Budgeting and accounting for services	
PMBOK Guide Sixth Edition, 2017	Part 1: 7. Project cost management	
Management Practice	**Small and Medium Enterprise-specific Metrics**	
APO06.04 Model and allocate costs. Establish and use an I&T costing model based, for example, on the service definition. This approach ensures that allocation of costs for services is identifiable, measurable and predictable, and encourages the responsible use of resources, including those provided by service providers. Regularly review and benchmark the cost/chargeback model to maintain its relevance and appropriateness for evolving business and IT activities.	a. Percent of overall IT costs that are allocated according to the agreed-upon cost models	
Small and Medium Enterprise-specific Activities		**Capability Level**
1. Decide on a cost allocation model that enables fair, transparent, repeatable and comparable allocation of I&T-related costs to users. For example, a basic allocation model is the even spread of shared I&T-related costs. This is a very simple allocation model that is easy to apply. However, depending on the context of the enterprise, it is often considered to be unfair and it does not encourage responsible use of resources. An activity-based costing scheme in which costs are allocated to IT services and charged to users of those services enables a more transparent and comparable allocation of cost.		2
2. Inspect service definition catalogs to identify services subject to user chargeback and those that are shared services.		3
3. Design the cost model to be transparent enough to allow users to identify their actual usage and charges by identifying categories and cost drivers that make sense to the user (e.g., cost per help desk call, cost per software license). An effective cost model will enable predictability of I&T costs and efficient and effective utilization of IT resources. Analyze cost drivers (time spent per activity, expenses, portion of fixed vs. variable costs, etc.), decide on appropriate differentiation (e.g., different categories of users with different weights), and use cost approximations or averages in case actual costs are highly variable in nature.		
4. Explain the cost model principles and expected outcomes to key stakeholders and obtain their feedback for further fine-tuning to achieve a transparent and comprehensive model.		
5. Obtain approval of key stakeholders and communicate the I&T costing model to management.		
6. Communicate important changes in the cost/chargeback model principles to key stakeholders and management.		
Related Guidance (Standards, Frameworks, Compliance Requirements)	**Detailed Reference**	
No related guidance for this management practice		

A. Component: Process *(cont.)*	
Management Practice	**Small and Medium Enterprise-specific Metrics**
APO06.05 Manage costs. Implement a cost management process that compares actual costs against budget. Costs should be monitored and reported. Deviations from budget should be identified in a timely manner and their impact on enterprise processes and services assessed.	a. Percent of variance among budgets, forecasts and actual costs b. Timeliness of monitoring and reporting deviations and their impact on assessed enterprise processes and services

Small and Medium Enterprise-specific Activities	Capability Level
1. Ensure proper authority and independence between IT budget holders and the individuals who capture, analyze and report financial information.	2
2. Define a method for collecting relevant data to identify deviations between budget and actuals, ROI, service cost trends, etc.	
3. Instruct those responsible for cost management to capture, collect and consolidate the data, and present and report the data to the appropriate budget owners. Ensure that budget analysts and owners jointly analyze deviations and compare performance to internal and industry benchmarks. The analysis should explain significant deviations and suggest corrective actions.	3
4. Ensure that the appropriate levels of management review the results of the analysis and approve suggested corrective actions.	
5. Ensure that changes in cost structures and enterprise needs are identified and budgets and forecasts are revised as required.	4
6. At regular intervals, and especially when budgets are cut due to financial constraints, identify ways to optimize costs and introduce efficiencies without jeopardizing services.	5

Related Guidance (Standards, Frameworks, Compliance Requirements)	Detailed Reference
No related guidance for this management practice	

B. Component: Organizational Structures

Key Management Practice	Financial Manager	Head of IT	IT Development Coordinator	IT Operations Coordinator
APO06.01 Manage finance and accounting.	A			
APO06.02 Prioritize resource allocation.	R	A		
APO06.03 Create and maintain budgets.	R	A	R	R
APO06.04 Model and allocate costs.	R	A	R	R
APO06.05 Manage costs.	R	A	R	R

C. Component: Management Flows and Items				
Management Practice	Small and Medium Enterprise-specific Inputs		Small and Medium Enterprise-specific Outputs	
	From	Description	Description	To
APO06.01 Manage finance and accounting.	BAI09.01	Asset register	I&T costs classification scheme	Internal
APO06.02 Prioritize resource allocation.	APO04.04	Proof-of-concept scope and outline business case	Budget allocations	APO02.05 APO05.02 APO07.05 BAI03.11
	APO05.01	Investment return expectations	Prioritization and ranking of I&T initiatives	APO05.02
	APO05.02	• Program business case • Business case assessments		
	EDM02.02	Evaluation of investment and services portfolios		
	EDM02.04	Actions to improve value delivery		
APO06.03 Create and maintain budgets.	There are no small and medium enterprise-specific inputs for this practice.		I&T budget	APO02.05 APO05.02 APO07.01 BAI03.11
			Budget communications	APO05.02 APO07.01 BAI03.11
APO06.04 Model and allocate costs.	There are no small and medium enterprise-specific inputs for this practice.		Categorized IT costs	Internal
APO06.05 Manage costs.	EDM02.04	Feedback on portfolio and program performance	Cost optimization opportunities	APO02.02

D. Component: People, Skills and Competencies		
Skill	Related Guidance (Standards, Frameworks, Compliance Requirements)	Detailed Reference
Financial management	Skills Framework for the Information Age V6, 2015	FMIT

E. Component: Principles, Policies and Procedures	
Relevant Policy	Policy Description
Budgeting policy (can be a responsibility of finance department)	Develop a budgeting policy that addresses the preparation and timeline of the annual budget, informs the forecasting of the annual financial position, and provides an overview of the required management reporting process. The budgeting policy should establish accountability and responsibility for the budget plan and other financial documents.

F. Component: Culture, Ethics and Behavior
Key Culture Elements
Effective and efficient management of I&T is supported by a culture of transparency on budget, costs and benefits throughout the organization. Management enables a culture of fact-based decision making through, for example, comparable estimations of business and IT costs and benefits for input to portfolio management, fair cost allocation of IT assets and resources, and repeatable budgeting of IT budgets.

G. Component: Services, Infrastructure and Applications
Cost accounting system

Domain: Align, Plan and Organize Management Objective: APO07 — Managed Human Resources	Focus Area: Small and Medium Enterprises
Description	
Provide a structured approach to ensure optimal recruitment/acquisition, planning, evaluation and development of human resources (both internal and external).	
Purpose	
Optimize human resources capabilities to meet enterprise objectives.	
Small and Medium Enterprise Focus Area Relevance	
Management of human resources can be integrated into the enterprise processes for personnel management. Focus attention on key IT personnel and their critical role in the organization.	

A. Component: Process		
Management Practice	**Small and Medium Enterprise-specific Metrics**	
APO07.01 Acquire and maintain adequate and appropriate staffing. Evaluate internal and external staffing requirements on a regular basis or upon major changes to the enterprise or operational or IT environments to ensure that the enterprise has sufficient human resources to support enterprise goals and objectives.	a. Average duration of vacancies b. Percent of IT posts vacant c. Percent of staff turnover	
Small and Medium Enterprise-specific Activities		**Capability Level**
1. Evaluate staffing requirements on a regular basis or upon major changes to ensure that both the business and IT have sufficient resources to adequately and appropriately support enterprise goals and objectives, business processes and controls, and I&T-enabled initiatives.		2
2. Maintain business and IT personnel recruitment and retention processes in line with the overall enterprise's personnel policies and procedures.		
3. Include background checks in the IT recruitment process for employees, contractors and vendors. Base the extent and frequency of checks on the sensitivity or criticality of the function.		3
Related Guidance (Standards, Frameworks, Compliance Requirements)	**Detailed Reference**	
COSO Enterprise Risk Management, June 2017	6. Governance and Culture—Principle 5	
Skills Framework for the Information Age V6, 2015	SFIA and skills management—Acquire	
Management Practice	**Small and Medium Enterprise-specific Metrics**	
APO07.02 Identify key IT personnel. Identify key IT personnel. Use knowledge capture (documentation), knowledge sharing, succession planning and staff backup to minimize reliance on a single individual performing a critical job function.	a. Percent of critical jobs held by a single individual b. Number of staff backup plans in place	
Small and Medium Enterprise-specific Activities		**Capability Level**
1. Minimize reliance on a single individual performing a critical job function through knowledge capture (documentation), knowledge sharing, succession planning, staff backup, cross-training and job rotation initiatives.		2
2. Regularly review staff backup plans.		3
3. Conduct regular reviews to assess the evolution of the skills and competencies of the internal and external resources. Review succession planning.		4
Related Guidance (Standards, Frameworks, Compliance Requirements)	**Detailed Reference**	
CMMI Cybermaturity Platform, 2018	RI.RR Identification of Roles and Responsibilities	
Skills Framework for the Information Age V6, 2015	SFIA and skills management—Acquire	
Management Practice	**Small and Medium Enterprise-specific Metrics**	
APO07.03 Maintain the skills and competencies of personnel. Define and manage the skills and competencies required of personnel. Regularly verify that personnel have the competencies to fulfill their roles on the basis of their education, training and/or experience. Verify that these competencies are being maintained, using qualification and certification programs where appropriate. Provide employees with ongoing learning and opportunities to maintain their knowledge, skills and competencies at a level required to achieve enterprise goals.	a. Percentage of key skills and competencies missing in the resource matrix b. Number of identified gaps between required and available skills c. Number of training programs provided	

A. Component: Process *(cont.)*	
Small and Medium Enterprise-specific Activities	**Capability Level**
1. Identify currently available skills and competencies of internal and external resources.	2
2. Identify gaps between required and available skills. Develop action plans to address gaps on an individual and collective basis, including recruitment of skilled personnel and training of existing staff in technical and behavioral skills.	
3. Review training materials and programs on a regular basis to ensure alignment with changing enterprise requirements and to ensure that they convey necessary knowledge, skills and abilities. Promote and support learning and development with enterprise staff.	3
4. Provide access to knowledge repositories to support the development of skills and competencies.	
5. Conduct regular reviews to assess the evolution of the skills and competencies of the internal and external resources. Review succession planning.	4

Related Guidance (Standards, Frameworks, Compliance Requirements)	Detailed Reference
ISF, The Standard of Good Practice for Information Security 2016	PM2.3 Security Education/Training
ISO/IEC 27001:2013/Cor.2:2015(E)	7.2 Competence
National Institute of Standards and Technology Framework for Improving Critical Infrastructure Cybersecurity V1.1, April 2018	PR.AT Awareness and Training
National Institute of Standards and Technology Special Publication 800-53, Revision 5 (Draft), August 2017	3.2 Awareness and training (AT-3, AT-4)
Skills Framework for the Information Age V6, 2015	SFIA and skills management—Deploy
The CIS Critical Security Controls for Effective Cyber Defense Version 6.1, August 2016	CSC 17: Security Skills Assessment and Appropriate Training to Fill Gaps

Management Practice	Small and Medium Enterprise-specific Metrics
AP007.04 Assess and recognize/reward employee job performance. Conduct timely, regular performance evaluations against individual objectives derived from enterprise goals, established standards, specific job responsibilities, and the skills and competency framework. Implement a remuneration/recognition process that rewards successful attainment of performance goals.	a. Percentage of official feedback moments and 360-degree evaluations performed b. Number and value of rewards given to staff

Small and Medium Enterprise-specific Activities	Capability Level
1. Consider functional/enterprise goals as the context for setting individual goals.	2
2. Set individual goals to align with relevant I&T and enterprise goals. Base goals on specific, measurable, achievable, relevant and time-bound (SMART) objectives that reflect core competencies, enterprise values and skills required for the role(s).	
3. Provide specific instructions for the use and storage of personal information in the evaluation process, in compliance with applicable personal data and employment legislation.	
4. Provide timely feedback regarding performance against the individual's goals.	3
5. Provide professional development plans based on the results of the evaluation process to encourage competency development and opportunities for personal advancement and to reduce dependence on key individuals.	
6.Provide employee coaching on performance and conduct whenever appropriate.	
7. Implement a remuneration/recognition process that rewards appropriate commitment, competency development and successful attainment of performance goals. Ensure that the process is applied consistently and in line with organizational policies.	4

Related Guidance (Standards, Frameworks, Compliance Requirements)	Detailed Reference
Skills Framework for the Information Age V6, 2015	SFIA and skills management—Develop

A. Component: Process *(cont.)*		
Management Practice	**Small and Medium Enterprise-specific Metrics**	
APO07.05 Plan and track the usage of IT and business human resources. Understand and track the current and future demand for business and IT human resources with responsibilities for enterprise I&T. Identify shortfalls and provide input into sourcing plans, enterprise and IT recruitment processes, and business and IT recruitment processes.	a. Time spent per full-time equivalent (FTE) employee on assignments and projects	
Small and Medium Enterprise-specific Activities		**Capability Level**
1. Create and maintain an inventory of business and IT human resources.		2
2. Understand the current and future demand for human resources to support the achievement of I&T objectives and to deliver services and solutions based on the portfolio of current I&T-related initiatives, the future investment portfolio and day-to-day operational needs.		3
3. Identify shortfalls and provide input into sourcing plans as well as enterprise and IT recruitment processes. Create and review the staffing plan, keeping track of actual usage.		
4. Maintain adequate information on the time spent on different tasks, assignments, services or projects.		4
Related Guidance (Standards, Frameworks, Compliance Requirements)	**Detailed Reference**	
Skills Framework for the Information Age V6, 2015	SFIA and skills management—Assess; Reward	
Management Practice	**Small and Medium Enterprise-specific Metrics**	
APO07.06 Manage contract staff. Ensure that consultants and contract personnel who support the enterprise with I&T skills know and comply with the organization's policies and meet agreed contractual requirements.	a. Percent of contractors signing off on the enterprise code of conduct b. Frequency of periodic reviews conducted to ensure accuracy of the enterprise's contractor staff records and compliance of contractor staff	
Small and Medium Enterprise-specific Activities		**Capability Level**
1. Implement contract staff policies and procedures.		2
2. Obtain formal agreement from contractors at the commencement of the contract that they are required to comply with the enterprise's IT control framework, such as policies for security clearance, physical and logical access control, use of facilities, information confidentiality requirements, and nondisclosure agreements.		
3. Advise contractors that management reserves the right to monitor and inspect all usage of IT resources, including email, voice communications, and all programs and data files.		
4. Provide contractors with a clear definition of their roles and responsibilities as part of their contracts, including explicit requirements to document their work to agreed-on standards and formats.		
5. Review contractors' work and base the approval of payments on the results.		3
6. Define all work performed by external parties in formal and unambiguous contracts.		
7. Conduct periodic reviews to ensure that contract staff have signed all necessary agreements.		4
8. Conduct periodic reviews to ensure that contractors' roles and access rights are appropriate and in line with agreements.		
Related Guidance (Standards, Frameworks, Compliance Requirements)	**Detailed Reference**	
Skills Framework for the Information Age V6, 2015	SFIA and skills management—Deploy	

B. Component: Organizational Structures									
Key Management Practice	**Financial Manager**	**Operations Manager**	**Head Human Resources**	**Head of IT**	**Security Expert**	**IT Development Coordinator**	**IT Operations Coordinator**	**Privacy Officer**	**Legal Department**
APO07.01 Acquire and maintain adequate and appropriate staffing.			R	A		R	R		
APO07.02 Identify key IT personnel.			R	A	R	R	R	R	R
APO07.03 Maintain the skills and competencies of personnel.			R	A		R	R		
APO07.04 Assess and recognize/reward employee job performance.			R	A		R	R		
APO07.05 Plan and track the usage of IT and business human resources.	R	R	A	R		R	R		
APO07.06 Manage contract staff.			R	A		R	R		R

C. Component: Information Flows and Items				
Management Practice	**Small and Medium Enterprise-specific Inputs**		**Small and Medium Enterprise-specific Outputs**	
	From	**Description**	**Description**	**To**
APO07.01 Acquire and maintain adequate and appropriate staffing.	APO01.05	Guidance on supervisory practices	Job descriptions and personnel sourcing plans	Internal
	APO06.03	• IT budget • Budget communications	Staffing requirement evaluations	Internal
	EDM04.01	• Guiding principles for allocating resources and capabilities • Approved resources plan	Competency and career development plans	Internal APO07.02
	Outside COBIT	• Enterprise HR policies and procedures • Enterprise goals and objectives		
APO07.02 Identify key IT personnel.	APO07.01	Competency and career development plans	Inventory of critical functions and backup scenarios	

C. Component: Information Flows and Items *(cont.)*				
Management Practice	Small and Medium Enterprise-specific Inputs		Small and Medium Enterprise-specific Outputs	
	From	Description	Description	To
AP007.03 Maintain the skills and competencies of personnel.	AP001.08	Target skills and competencies matrix	Skills and competencies matrix	AP001.05 AP014.01 BAI01.02 BAI03.12
	BAI08.02	Published knowledge repositories	Skill development plans	AP001.05 EDM04.01
	BAI08.03	Knowledge awareness and training schemes	Review reports	Internal
	EDM01.02	Reward system approach		
	Outside COBIT	Enterprise goals and objectives		
AP007.04 Assess and recognize/reward employee job performance.	AP004.01	Recognition and reward program	Improvement plans	Internal
			Performance evaluations	Internal
	BAI05.06	HR performance review results		
	Outside COBIT	Enterprise goals and objectives		
AP007.05 Plan and track the usage of IT and business human resources.	AP006.02	Budget allocations	Resource utilization records	BAI01.06 BAI11.08
	BAI11.08	Project resource requirements		
AP007.06 Manage contract staff.	BAI11.08	Project resource requirements	Contract agreement reviews	Internal
			Contract agreements	Internal

D. Component: People, Skills and Competencies		
Skill	Related Guidance (Standards, Frameworks, Compliance Requirements)	Detailed Reference
Education and training provision	e-Competence Framework (e-CF)—A common European Framework for ICT Professionals in all industry sectors—Part 1: Framework, 2016	D. Enable—D.3. Education and Training Provision
Learning and development management	Skills Framework for the Information Age V6, 2015	ETMG
Performance management	Skills Framework for the Information Age V6, 2015	PEMT
Personnel development	e-Competence Framework (e-CF)—A common European Framework for ICT Professionals in all industry sectors - Part 1: Framework, 2016	D. Enable—D.9. Personnel Development
Professional development	Skills Framework for the Information Age V6, 2015	PDSV
Resourcing	Skills Framework for the Information Age V6, 2015	RESC

E. Component: Principles, Policies and Procedures	
Relevant Policy	**Policy Description**
Contract staff policy	Enumerates criteria for augmenting staff with third-party consultants and/or contractors in accordance with the enterprise IT procurement policy and the I&T control framework. Specifies what type of work can be performed or augmented by third parties, under what conditions, and when.

F. Component: Culture, Ethics and Behavior
Key Culture Elements
Describe the roles and responsibilities of users toward information, media and network usage, security, and privacy. Encourage and communicate a common culture that prescribes expected behaviors for all individuals in the enterprise and establishes zero tolerance for unethical behaviors.

G. Component: Services, Infrastructure and Applications
• HR management system • Performance measurement system (e.g., balanced scorecard, skills management tools) • Resource planning tools

Domain: Align, Plan and Organize Management Objective: APO08 — Managed Relationships	Focus Area: Small and Medium Enterprises
Description	
Manage relationships with business stakeholders in a formalized and transparent way that ensures mutual trust and a combined focus on achieving the strategic goals within the constraints of budgets and risk tolerance. Base relationships on open and transparent communication, a common language, and the willingness to take ownership and accountability for key decisions on both sides. Business and IT must work together to create successful enterprise outcomes in support of the enterprise objectives.	
Purpose	
Enable the right knowledge, skills and behaviors to create improved outcomes, increased confidence, mutual trust and effective use of resources that stimulate a productive relationship with business stakeholders.	
Small and Medium Enterprise Focus Area Relevance	
Management of relationships is mainly through direct contacts between IT and the business departments. Ensure that the business understands and respects the role and responsibilities of IT and that IT sufficiently understands the needs of the business.	

A. Component: Process		
Management Practice	**Small and Medium Enterprise-specific Metrics**	
APO08.01 Understand business expectations. Understand current business issues, objectives and expectations for I&T. Ensure that requirements are understood, managed and communicated, and their status agreed and approved.	a. Number of identified current business issues related to I&T	
Small and Medium Enterprise-specific Activities		**Capability Level**
1. Identify interests and areas of responsibilities for each business department.		2
2. Identify process constraints or issues for each business department.		
3. Agree on demand patterns that relate to service volumes and use.		
4. Manage expectations by ensuring that business units understand priorities, dependencies, financial constraints and the need to schedule requests.		3
5. Clarify business expectations for I&T-enabled services and solutions.		4
6. Ensure that requirements are defined with associated business acceptance criteria and metrics.		
Related Guidance (Standards, Frameworks, Compliance Requirements)	**Detailed Reference**	
No related guidance for this management practice		
Management Practice	**Small and Medium Enterprise-specific Metrics**	
APO08.02 Align I&T strategy with business expectations and identify opportunities for IT to enhance the business. Align I&T strategies with current business objectives and expectations to enable IT to be a value-add partner for the business and a governance component for enhanced enterprise performance.	a. Percentage of IT involvement in business investment proposals	
Small and Medium Enterprise-specific Activities		**Capability Level**
1. Position IT as a partner to the business. Play a proactive role in identifying and communicating with key stakeholders on opportunities, risk and constraints. This includes current and emerging technologies, services and business process models.		3
2. Ensure the involvement of the IT organization from the start of a new business initiative by providing advice and recommendations (e.g., for business case development, requirements definition, solution design) and taking ownership of I&T-related tasks or work streams.		
Related Guidance (Standards, Frameworks, Compliance Requirements)	**Detailed Reference**	
ITIL V3, 2011	Service Strategy, 4.4 Demand management	
Management Practice	**Small and Medium Enterprise-specific Metrics**	
APO08.03 Manage the business relationship. Manage the relationship between the IT service organization and its business partners. Ensure that relationship roles and responsibilities are defined and assigned, and communication is facilitated.	a. Ratings of business user and IT personnel satisfaction surveys	
Small and Medium Enterprise-specific Activities		**Capability Level**
1. Define and communicate a complaints and escalation procedure to resolve any relationship issues.		2
2. Ensure that key decisions are agreed on and approved by relevant accountable stakeholders.		3

A. Component: Process *(cont.)*	
Related Guidance (Standards, Frameworks, Compliance Requirements)	**Detailed Reference**
ISO/IEC 20000-1:2011(E)	7.1 Business relationship management
ITIL V3, 2011	Service Strategy, 4.5 Business relationship management
Management Practice	**Small and Medium Enterprise-specific Metrics**
APO08.04 Coordinate and communicate. Work with all relevant stakeholders and coordinate the end-to-end delivery of I&T services and solutions provided to the business.	a. Percent of business managers' satisfaction with delivery of IT services and solutions

Small and Medium Enterprise-specific Activities	Capability Level
1. Coordinate and communicate planned changes and project activities.	2
2. Coordinate and communicate operational activities, roles and responsibilities, including definition of request types, criteria for escalation and protocols for response to major outages (planned and unplanned).	
3. Organize awareness training.	3
4. Maintain periodic communication with business departments on service delivery, project status, changes and identified risk.	

Related Guidance (Standards, Frameworks, Compliance Requirements)	Detailed Reference
No related guidance for this management practice	
Management Practice	**Small and Medium Enterprise-specific Metrics**
APO08.05 Provide input to the continual improvement of services. Continually improve and evolve I&T-enabled services and service delivery to the enterprise to align with changing enterprise objectives and technology	a. Percent of root causes identified and resolved for any issues

Small and Medium Enterprise-specific Activities	Capability Level
1. Perform satisfaction analysis at both the business and IT levels. Ensure that issues are addressed and results and status are reported.	4
2. Work with business departments to identify, communicate and implement improvement initiatives.	5
3. Work with service management and business process owners to ensure that I&T-enabled services and service management processes are continually improved and the root causes of any issues are identified and resolved.	

Related Guidance (Standards, Frameworks, Compliance Requirements)	Detailed Reference
No related guidance for this management practice	

B. Component: Organizational Structures

Key Management Practice	General Manager	Financial Manager	Operations Manager	Business Process Owners	Head of IT	IT Development Coordinator	IT Operations Coordinator	Privacy Officer
APO08.01 Understand business expectations.				R	A	R	R	R
APO08.02 Align I&T strategy with business expectations and identify opportunities for IT to enhance the business.				R	A	R	R	
APO08.03 Manage the business relationship.	R	R	R	R	A	R	R	
APO08.04 Coordinate and communicate.	R	R	R	R	A	R	R	
APO08.05 Provide input to the continual improvement of services.				R	A	R	R	

C. Component: Information Flows and Items				
Management Practice	Small and Medium Enterprise-specific Inputs		Small and Medium Enterprise-specific Outputs	
	From	Description	Description	To
APO08.01 Understand business expectations.	APO02.05	Strategic road map	Clarified and agreed business expectations	Internal
APO08.02 Align I&T strategy with business expectations and identify opportunities for IT to enhance the business.	APO09.04	• Service level performance reports • Improvement action plans and remediations	List of agreed business requirements	Internal
	APO11.03	Root causes of failure to deliver quality		
APO08.03 Manage the business relationship.	DSS02.02	Classified and prioritized incidents and service requests	Complaint and escalation status	Internal
	DSS02.06	Closed service requests and incidents		
	DSS02.07	Incident status and trends report		
APO08.04 Coordinate and communicate.	APO09.03	SLAs	Periodic communications on changes and status of incidents	Internal
	APO12.06	Risk impact communication		
	BAI05.05	Operation and use plan		
	BAI09.02	Communications of planned maintenance downtime		
APO08.05 Provide input to the continual improvement of services.	APO09.02	Service catalogs	Definition of potential improvement projects	APO02.02 BAI03.11
	APO11.02	Customer requirements for quality management	Satisfaction analyses	APO09.04
	APO11.04	Results of quality reviews and audits		
	BAI03.10	Maintenance plan		

D. Component: People, Skills and Competencies		
Skill	Related Guidance (Standards, Frameworks, Compliance Requirements)	Detailed Reference
Relationship management	e-Competence Framework (e-CF)—A common European Framework for ICT Professionals in all industry sectors—Part 1: Framework, 2016	E. Manage—E.4. Relationship Management
Relationship management	Skills Framework for the Information Age V6, 2015	RLMT

E. Component: Principles, Policies and Procedures	
Relevant Policy	**Policy Description**
There are no small and medium enterprise-specific principles, policies and procedures for this objective.	

F. Component: Culture, Ethics and Behavior
Key Culture Elements
Establish a culture based on mutual trust, transparent communication, open and understandable terms, a common language, ownership, and accountability. Good relationships must exist between the business and IT within the enterprise to achieve a shared goal.

G. Component: Services, Infrastructure and Applications
• Collaboration platforms • Internal training and awareness building services

Domain: Align, Plan and Organize Management Objective: APO09 – Managed Service Agreements	Focus Area: Small and Medium Enterprises
Description	
Align I&T-enabled products and services and service levels with enterprise needs and expectations, including identification, specification, design, publishing, agreement, and monitoring of I&T products and services, service levels and performance indicators.	
Purpose	
Ensure that I&T products, services and service levels meet current and future enterprise needs.	
Small and Medium Enterprise Focus Area Relevance	
Manage service agreements at the enterprise level to meet current and future enterprise needs. Address the management of I&T products, services and service levels.	

A. Component: Process		
Management Practice	**Small and Medium Enterprise-specific Metrics**	
APO09.01 Identify I&T services. Analyze business requirements and the degree to which I&T-enabled services and service levels support business processes. Discuss and agree with the business on potential services and service levels. Compare potential service levels against the current service portfolio; identify new or changed services or service level options.	a. Percent of business activities that are not supported by any IT service b. Percent of obsolete services identified	
Small and Medium Enterprise-specific Activities		**Capability Level**
1. Assess current IT services and service levels to identify gaps between existing services and the business activities they support.		2
2. Estimate future demand and confirm capacity of existing IT-enabled services.		
3. Analyze business process activities to identify the need for new or redesigned IT services.		3
4. Regularly review the portfolio of IT services with business management to identify obsolete services. Agree on retirement and propose change.		
Related Guidance (Standards, Frameworks, Compliance Requirements)	**Detailed Reference**	
ITIL V3, 2011	Service Strategy, 4.4 Demand management	
Management Practice	**Small and Medium Enterprise-specific Metrics**	
APO09.02 Catalog I&T-enabled services. Define and maintain one or more service catalogs for relevant target groups. Publish and maintain live I&T-enabled services in the service catalogs.	a. Percent of updates in service catalogs b. Time since last service portfolio update	
Small and Medium Enterprise-specific Activities		**Capability Level**
1. Publish catalogs of relevant IT-enabled services, service packages and service level options.		2
2. Ensure that service catalogs are complete and continuously updated.		3
3. Inform business management of any updates to the service catalogs.		
Related Guidance (Standards, Frameworks, Compliance Requirements)	**Detailed Reference**	
ITIL V3, 2011	Service Design, 4.2 Service Catalogue Management	
Management Practice	**Small and Medium Enterprise-specific Metrics**	
APO09.03 Define and prepare service agreements. Define and prepare service agreements based on options in the service catalogues. Include internal operational agreements.	a. Percent of business processes without service agreements b. Percent of IT services covered by service agreements	
Small and Medium Enterprise-specific Activities		**Capability Level**
1. Analyze requirements for new or changed service agreements received from business management to ensure that the requirements can be matched. Consider aspects such as service times, availability, performance, capacity, security, privacy, continuity, compliance and regulatory issues, usability, demand constraints, and data quality.		2
2. Draft customer service agreements based on the required services, with related service levels.		
3. Finalize customer service agreements with business management.		
4. Ensure that supplier contracts with external service providers underpin the customer service agreements, if applicable.		3

A. Component: Process *(cont.)*	
Related Guidance (Standards, Frameworks, Compliance Requirements)	**Detailed Reference**
ISF, The Standard of Good Practice for Information Security 2016	SY2.1 Service Level Agreements
ISO/IEC 20000-1:2011(E)	4.5 Establish and improve the SMS; 6.1 Service level management
ITIL V3, 2011	Service Design, 4.3 Service Level Management
National Institute of Standards and Technology Special Publication 800-53, Revision 5 (Draft), August 2017	3.18 System and services acquisition (SA-9)
Management Practice	**Small and Medium Enterprise-specific Metrics**
APO09.04 Monitor and report service levels. Monitor service levels, report on achievements and identify trends. Provide the appropriate management information to aid performance management.	a. Percent of service targets being met b. Percent of services being monitored to service levels

Small and Medium Enterprise-specific Activities	**Capability Level**
1. Define how to monitor and collect service level data.	4
2. Evaluate performance and provide regular and formal reporting of service agreements, including deviations from the agreed-on values. Distribute this report to business management.	
3. Perform regular reviews to forecast and identify trends in service level performance.	
4. Agree on action plans and remediations for any performance issues or negative trends.	5

Related Guidance (Standards, Frameworks, Compliance Requirements)	**Detailed Reference**
HITRUST CSF version 9, September 2017	09.02 Control Third Party Service Delivery
ISO/IEC 20000-1:2011(E)	6.2 Service reporting
Management Practice	**Small and Medium Enterprise-specific Metrics**
APO09.05 Review service agreements and contracts. Conduct periodic reviews of the service agreements and revise when needed.	a. Percent of reviews of the service agreements performed b. Percent of service agreements revised, as needed

Small and Medium Enterprise-specific Activities	**Capability Level**
1. Regularly review service agreement terms to ensure that they are effective and up to date. When appropriate, take into account changes in business requirements, IT services provided or related service levels.	3
2. Revise agreements with service providers when needed.	4

Related Guidance (Standards, Frameworks, Compliance Requirements)	**Detailed Reference**
No related guidance for this management practice	

B. Component: Organizational Structures

Key Management Practice	Operations Manager	Business Process Owners	Head of IT	IT Operations Coordinator	Privacy Officer	Legal Department
APO09.01 Identify I&T services.	R	R	A			
APO09.02 Catalog I&T-enabled services.			A	R		
APO09.03 Define and prepare service agreements.			A	R	R	R
APO09.04 Monitor and report service levels.		R	A	R		R
APO09.05 Review service agreements and contracts.	R		A	R		

C. Component: Information Flows and Items				
Management Practice	Small and Medium Enterprise-specific Inputs		Small and Medium Enterprise-specific Outputs	
	From	Description	Description	To
APO09.01 Identify I&T services.	There are no small and medium enterprise-specific inputs for this practice.		Identified gaps in I&T services to the business	APO01.10 APO02.02 APO05.02 APO08.02
			Definitions of standard services	EDM02.01
APO09.02 Catalog I&T-enabled services.	APO05.04	Updated portfolios of programs, services and assets	Service catalogs	APO08.05
APO09.03 Define and prepare service agreements.	APO11.02	Customer requirements for quality management	There are no small and medium enterprise-specific outputs for this practice.	
APO09.04 Monitor and report service levels.	APO08.05	Satisfaction analyses	Improvement action plans and remediations	APO02.02 APO08.02
	APO11.04	Results of quality reviews and audits	Service level performance reports	APO08.02; MEA01.03
	DSS02.02	Classified and prioritized incidents and service requests		
	DSS02.06	Closed service requests and incidents		
	DSS02.07	• Incident status and trends report • Status of request fulfilment and trends report		

C. Component: Information Flows and Items *(cont.)*				
Management Practice	Small and Medium Enterprise-specific Inputs		Small and Medium Enterprise-specific Outputs	
APO09.05 Review service agreements and contracts.	**From**	**Description**	**Description**	**To**
	APO11.02	Results of quality of service, including customer feedback	Updated SLAs	Internal
	APO11.04	Results of quality reviews and audits		
	BAI04.01	Evaluations against SLAs		

D. Component: People, Skills and Competencies		
Skill	**Related Guidance (Standards, Frameworks, Compliance Requirements)**	**Detailed Reference**
Service level management	e-Competence Framework (e-CF)—A common European Framework for ICT Professionals in all industry sectors—Part 1: Framework, 2016	A. Plan—A.2. Service Level Management
Service level management	Skills Framework for the Information Age V6, 2015	SLMO

E. Component: Principles, Policies and Procedures	
Relevant Policy	**Policy Description**
SLA policy	Describes general standards and criteria to inform specific requirements and terms for delivery of services, whether between entities within the enterprise or between the enterprise and a third party

F. Component: Culture, Ethics and Behavior
Key Culture Elements
Establish a contract between a service provider (internal or external) and the end user that defines the expected level of service. Make sure this service level is based on output, specifically defining what the customer will receive in SMART objectives. Establish a culture in which service levels are respected. Discourage noncompliance through a penalty system.

G. Component: Services, Infrastructure and Applications
• Contract management system • Service level monitoring tools

Domain: Align, Plan and Organize Management Objective: APO10 — Managed Vendors	Focus Area: Small and Medium Enterprises
Description	
Manage I&T-related products and services provided by all types of vendors to meet enterprise requirements. This includes the search for and selection of vendors, management of relationships, management of contracts, and reviewing and monitoring of vendor performance and vendor ecosystem (including upstream supply chain) for effectiveness and compliance.	
Purpose	
Optimize available I&T capabilities to support the I&T strategy and road map, minimize the risk associated with nonperforming or noncompliant vendors, and ensure competitive pricing.	
Small and Medium Enterprise Focus Area Relevance	
Vendor or supplier management needs to be formalized, especially when the organization is outsourcing critical services to external providers. Evaluation of pricing and performance is essential to ensure the required service level and quality of services. Potential vendors can be identified when there is a need for a new supplier and periodically for ongoing evaluation.	

A. Component: Process	
Management Practice	**Small and Medium Enterprise-specific Metrics**
APO10.01 Identify and evaluate vendor relationships and contracts. Continuously search for and identify vendors and categorize them into type, significance and criticality. Establish criteria to evaluate vendors and contracts. Review the overall portfolio of existing and alternative vendors and contracts.	a. Percent of positive evaluations for existing vendors and contracts b. Percent of vendors or contracts changed due to negative evaluation

Small and Medium Enterprise-specific Activities	Capability Level
1. Establish and maintain criteria relating to type, significance and criticality of vendors and vendor contracts, enabling a focus on preferred and important vendors.	3
2. Identify, record and categorize existing vendors and contracts according to defined criteria to maintain a detailed register of preferred vendors that need to be managed carefully.	
3. Establish and maintain vendor and contract evaluation criteria to enable overall review and comparison of vendor performance in a consistent way.	4
4. Periodically evaluate and compare the performance of existing vendors and evaluate alternative vendors to identify opportunities or a compelling need to reconsider current vendor contracts.	5

Related Guidance (Standards, Frameworks, Compliance Requirements)	Detailed Reference
No related guidance for this management practice	

A. Component: Process *(cont.)*		
Management Practice	**Small and Medium Enterprise-specific Metrics**	
APO10.02 Select vendors. Select suppliers according to a fair and formal practice to ensure a viable best fit based on specified requirements. Requirements should be optimized with input from potential suppliers.	a. Percent of vendor selections that respect the procedure for vendor selection b. Percent of stakeholders satisfied with vendor products and/or services	
Small and Medium Enterprise-specific Activities		**Capability Level**
1. Review all requests for information (RFIs) and requests for proposal (RFPs) to ensure that they clearly define requirements (e.g., enterprise requirements for security and privacy of information, operational business and I&T processing requirements, priorities for service delivery), include a procedure to clarify requirements, allow vendors sufficient time to prepare their proposals, and clearly define award criteria and the decision process.		2
2. Use a standard vendor selection procedure. Evaluate RFIs and RFPs in accordance with the approved evaluation process/criteria and maintain documentary evidence of the evaluations. Verify the references of candidate vendors.		
3. Select the vendor that best fits the RFP. Document and communicate the decision, and sign the contract.		
4. In the specific case of software acquisition, include and enforce the rights and obligations of all parties in the contractual terms. These rights and obligations may include ownership and licensing of IP; maintenance; warranties; arbitration procedures; upgrade terms; and fit for purpose, including security, escrow and access rights.		3
5. In the specific case of acquisition of development resources, include and enforce the rights and obligations of all parties in the contractual terms. These rights and obligations may include ownership and licensing of IP; fit for purpose, including development methodologies; testing; quality management processes, including required performance criteria; performance reviews; basis for payment; warranties; arbitration procedures; human resource management; and compliance with the enterprise's policies.		
6. Obtain legal advice on resource development acquisition agreements regarding ownership and licensing of IP.		
7. In the specific case of acquisition of infrastructure, facilities and related services, include and enforce the rights and obligations of all parties in the contractual terms. These rights and obligations may include service levels, maintenance procedures, access controls, security, performance review, basis for payment and arbitration procedures.		
Related Guidance (Standards, Frameworks, Compliance Requirements)	**Detailed Reference**	
No related guidance for this management practice		
Management Practice	**Small and Medium Enterprise-specific Metrics**	
APO10.03 Manage vendor relationships and contracts. Formalize and manage the supplier relationship for each supplier. Manage, maintain and monitor contracts and service delivery. Ensure that new or changed contracts conform to enterprise standards and legal and regulatory requirements. Deal with contractual disputes.	a. Percent of third-party vendors who have contracts including control requirements b. Percent of formal disputes with vendors c. Percent of disputes resolved amicably in a reasonable time frame	
Small and Medium Enterprise-specific Activities		**Capability Level**
1. Assign ownership for vendor management, with accountability for the quality of service(s) provided.		3
2. Manage, maintain and renew formal contracts with vendors. Ensure that contracts conform to enterprise standards and legal and regulatory requirements.		
3. Where relevant, include provisions in contracts for the review of the vendor's site by management or independent third parties. Agree on independent audit and assurance controls applicable to the operational environments of vendors providing outsourced services to confirm that agreed-on requirements are being adequately addressed.		
4. Manage contract disputes with the aim of resolving service problems without legal or financial consequences.		
5. Evaluate the effectiveness of the contracts and services provided and identify necessary improvements.		4
6. Define, communicate and agree on ways to implement required improvements to the contract and relationship.		5
Related Guidance (Standards, Frameworks, Compliance Requirements)	**Detailed Reference**	
ISO/IEC 20000-1:2011(E)	7.2 Supplier management	
ITIL V3, 2011	Service Design, 4.8 Supplier Management	
Management Practice	**Small and Medium Enterprise-specific Metrics**	
APO10.04 Manage vendor risk. Identify and manage risk relating to vendors' ability to continually provide secure, efficient and effective service delivery. This also includes the subcontractors or upstream vendors that are relevant in the service delivery of the direct vendor.	a. Percent of formal disputes with vendors	

A. Component: Process *(cont.)*

Small and Medium Enterprise-specific Activities	Capability Level
1. When defining the contract, avoid potential service risk by clearly defining service requirements, including software escrow agreements, alternative vendors or standby agreements to mitigate possible vendor failure; security and protection of IP; and any legal or regulatory requirements.	3
2. Identify, monitor and, where appropriate, manage risk relating to the vendor's ability to deliver service efficiently, effectively, securely, reliably and continually. Integrate critical internal IT management processes with those of outsourced service providers—for example, internal processes covering performance and capacity planning, change management and configuration management.	4
3. Identify, monitor and, where appropriate, manage risk related to the sub-contractors and upstream vendors influencing the vendor's ability to deliver service efficiently, effectively, securely, reliably and continually.	

Related Guidance (Standards, Frameworks, Compliance Requirements)	Detailed Reference
CMMI Cybermaturity Platform, 2018	RM.MP Manage External Participation
ISF, The Standard of Good Practice for Information Security 2016	SC1.1 External Supplier Management Process
ISO/IEC 27002:2013/Cor.2:2015(E)	15. Supplier relationships
National Institute of Standards and Technology Framework for Improving Critical Infrastructure Cybersecurity v1.1, April 2018	D.SC Supply Chain Risk Management

Management Practice	Small and Medium Enterprise-specific Metrics
AP010.05 Monitor vendor performance and compliance. Periodically review overall vendor performance, compliance to contract requirements and value for money. Address identified issues.	a. Percent of vendor reviews executed b. Percent of vendors meeting agreed requirements

Small and Medium Enterprise-specific Activities	Capability Level
1. Define and document criteria to monitor vendor performance aligned with service level agreements.	2
2. Organize independent reviews of vendor internal practices and controls, if necessary.	3
3. Ensure that the vendor regularly and transparently reports on agreed criteria.	4
4. Monitor and review service delivery to ensure that the vendor is providing an acceptable quality of service, meeting requirements and adhering to contract conditions.	
5. Record and assess review results periodically and discuss them with the vendor to identify needs and opportunities for improvement.	5

Related Guidance (Standards, Frameworks, Compliance Requirements)	Detailed Reference
No related guidance for this management practice	

B. Component: Organizational Structures

Key Management Practice	Head of IT	IT Development Coordinator	IT Operations Coordinator	Privacy Officer	Legal Department	Compliance or Quality
AP010.01 Identify and evaluate vendor relationships and contracts.	A				R	
AP010.02 Select vendors.	A	R	R	R		R
AP010.03 Manage vendor relationships and contracts.	A	R	R		R	
AP010.04 Manage vendor risk.	A	R	R	R		R
AP010.05 Monitor vendor performance and compliance.	A	R	R		R	

C. Component: Information Flows and Items				
Management Practice	Small and Medium Enterprise-specific Inputs		Small and Medium Enterprise-specific Outputs	
	From	Description	Description	To
APO10.01 Identify and evaluate vendor relationships and contracts.	Outside COBIT	Vendor contracts	Vendor catalog	BAI02.02
			Potential revisions to vendor contracts	Internal
			Vendor significance and evaluation criteria	Internal
APO10.02 Select vendors.	BAI02.02	High-level acquisition/ development plan	Vendor RFIs and RFPs	BAI02.01 BAI02.02
			RFI and RFP evaluations	BAI02.02
			Decision results of vendor evaluations	BAI02.02 EDM04.01
APO10.03 Manage vendor relationships and contracts.	There are no small and medium enterprise-specific inputs for this practice.		Results and suggested improvements	Internal
			Vendor roles and responsibilities	Internal
APO10.04 Manage vendor risk.	APO12.04	• Risk analysis and risk profile reports for stakeholders • Results of third-party risk assessments	Identified vendor delivery risk	APO12.01 APO12.03 BAI01.01
			Identified contract requirements to minimize risk	Internal
APO10.05 Monitor vendor performance and compliance.	There are no small and medium enterprise-specific inputs for this practice.		Vendor compliance monitoring criteria	Internal
			Vendor compliance monitoring review results	MEA01.03

D. Component: People, Skills and Competencies		
Skill	**Related Guidance (Standards, Frameworks, Compliance Requirements)**	**Detailed Reference**
Contract management	e-Competence Framework (e-CF)—A common European Framework for ICT Professionals in all industry sectors - Part 1: Framework, 2016	D. Enable—D.8. Contract Management
Contract management	Skills Framework for the Information Age V6, 2015	ITCM
Purchasing	e-Competence Framework (e-CF)—A common European Framework for ICT Professionals in all industry sectors—Part 1: Framework, 2016	D. Enable—D.4. Purchasing
Sourcing	Skills Framework for the Information Age V6, 2015	SORC

E. Component: Principles, Policies and Procedures	
Relevant Policy	**Policy Description**
Third-party IT service delivery management policy	Sets guidelines for managing risk related to third-party services. Establishes framework of expectations for behavior and enumerates security precautions required of third-party service providers in managing related risk.

F. Component: Culture, Ethics and Behavior
Key Culture Elements
Build and manage an ecosystem of vendors that can assist the organization in its digital transformation and innovation. Continuously scan the landscape in search of new and effective partners.

G. Component: Services, Infrastructure and Applications
• Contract management system • Third-party assurance services

Page intentionally left blank

Domain: Align, Plan and Organize Management Objective: APO11 — Managed Quality	Focus Area: Small and Medium Enterprises
Description	
Define and communicate quality requirements in all processes, procedures and related enterprise outcomes. Enable controls, ongoing monitoring, and the use of proven practices and standards in continuous improvement and efficiency efforts.	
Purpose	
Ensure consistent delivery of technology solutions and services to meet the quality requirements of the enterprise and satisfy stakeholder needs.	
Small and Medium Enterprise Focus Area Relevance	
Quality management must be integrated in all processes by defining controls, performing ongoing monitoring and executing specific quality assurance actions, where relevant. The quality management system can be integrated into the I&T management framework or can be incorporated as an integral part of the enterprisewide quality management system. Use the guidance of this objective to optimize the enterprisewide quality management system.	

A. Component: Process		
Management Practice	**Small and Medium Enterprise-specific Metrics**	
APO11.01 Establish a quality management system (QMS). Establish and maintain a quality management system (QMS) that provides a standard, formal and continuous approach to quality management of information. The QMS should enable technology and business processes to align with business requirements and enterprise quality management.	a. Percent of effectiveness of quality management reviews b. Percent of key stakeholder satisfaction with quality management review program	
Small and Medium Enterprise-specific Activities		**Capability Level**
1. Include a standard, formal and continuous approach to quality management in the I&T management framework.		3
2. Within the I&T control framework, the business and IT processes, identify quality requirements and criteria (e.g., based on legal requirements and requirements from customers).		
3. Define roles, tasks, decision rights and responsibilities for quality management in the organizational structure.		
4. Obtain input from management and external and internal stakeholders on the definition of quality requirements and quality management criteria.		
5. Regularly monitor and review the QMS against agreed-on acceptance criteria. Include feedback from customers, users and management.		4
6. Respond to discrepancies in review results to continuously improve the QMS.		5
Related Guidance (Standards, Frameworks, Compliance Requirements)	**Detailed Reference**	
PMBOK Guide Sixth Edition, 2017	Part 1: 8.1 Plan quality management	
Management Practice	**Small and Medium Enterprise-specific Metrics**	
APO11.02 Focus quality management on customers. Focus quality management on customers by determining their requirements and ensuring integration in quality management practices.	a. Percent of customer satisfaction b. Percent of customer requirements and expectations communicated throughout the business and IT organization	
Small and Medium Enterprise-specific Activities		**Capability Level**
1. Focus quality management on customers by determining internal and external customer requirements and ensuring alignment of the I&T standards and practices.		3
2. Manage the business needs and expectations for each business process, IT operational service and new solution, and define their quality acceptance criteria.		
3. Communicate customer requirements and expectations throughout the business and IT organization.		
4. Periodically obtain customer views on business process and service provisioning and IT solution delivery, to determine the impact on I&T standards and practices and to ensure that customer expectations are met and are acted upon.		4
5. Capture quality acceptance criteria for inclusion in SLAs.		
Related Guidance (Standards, Frameworks, Compliance Requirements)	**Detailed Reference**	
No related guidance for this management practice		

A. Component: Process *(cont.)*	
Management Practice	**Small and Medium Enterprise-specific Metrics**
APO11.03 Manage quality standards, practices and procedures and integrate quality management into key processes and solutions. Identify and maintain standards, procedures and practices for key processes to guide the enterprise in meeting the intent of the agreed quality management standards. This activity should align with I&T control framework requirements. Consider certification for key processes, organizational units, products or services.	a. Percent of processes with defined quality requirements b. Percent of defects uncovered prior to production c. Number of SLAs that include quality acceptance criteria
Small and Medium Enterprise-specific Activities	**Capability Level**
1. Define the quality management standards, practices and procedures in line with the I&T control framework's requirements and with enterprise quality management criteria and policies.	2
2. Integrate the required quality management practices in key processes and solutions across the organization.	3
3. Consider the benefits and costs of quality certifications.	
4. Effectively communicate the quality management approach (e.g., through regular, formal quality training programs).	
5. Record and monitor quality data. Use industry good practices for reference when improving and tailoring the enterprise's quality practices.	4
6. Regularly review the continued relevance, efficiency and effectiveness of specific quality management processes. Monitor the achievement of quality objectives.	
Related Guidance (Standards, Frameworks, Compliance Requirements)	**Detailed Reference**
PMBOK Guide Sixth Edition, 2017	Part 1: 8.2 Manage quality
Management Practice	**Small and Medium Enterprise-specific Metrics**
APO11.04 Perform quality monitoring, control and reviews. Monitor the quality of processes and services on an ongoing basis, in line with quality management standards. Define, plan and implement measurements to monitor customer satisfaction with quality as well as the value provided by the quality management system (QMS). The information gathered should be used by the process owner to improve quality.	a. Percent of solutions and services delivered with formal quality certification b. Percent of processes with a formal quality assessment report c. Percent of projects reviewed that meet target quality goals and objectives
Small and Medium Enterprise-specific Activities	**Capability Level**
1. Prepare and conduct quality reviews for key organizational processes and solutions.	3
2. For these key organizational processes and solutions, monitor goal-driven quality metrics aligned to overall quality objectives.	4
3. Ensure that management and process owners regularly review quality management performance against defined quality metrics.	
4. Analyze overall quality management performance results.	
5. Report the quality management performance review results and initiate improvements where appropriate.	5
Related Guidance (Standards, Frameworks, Compliance Requirements)	**Detailed Reference**
PMBOK Guide Sixth Edition, 2017	Part 1: 8.3 Control quality
Management Practice	**Small and Medium Enterprise-specific Metrics**
APO11.05 Maintain continuous improvement. Maintain and regularly communicate an overall quality plan that promotes continuous improvement. The plan should define the need for, and benefits of, continuous improvement. Collect and analyze data about the quality management system (QMS) and improve its effectiveness. Correct nonconformities to prevent recurrence.	a. Percent of root cause analyses performed

A. Component: Process *(cont.)*	
Small and Medium Enterprise-specific Activities	**Capability Level**
1. Establish a platform to share good practices and to capture information on defects and mistakes, to enable learning from them.	2
2. Identify examples of excellent quality delivery processes that can benefit other services or projects, and share these with the service and project delivery teams to encourage improvement.	3
3. Identify recurring quality defects, determine their root cause, evaluate their impact and result, and agree on improvement actions with the service and/or project delivery teams.	
4. Benchmark the results of the quality reviews against internal historical data, industry guidelines, standards and data from similar types of enterprises.	4

Related Guidance (Standards, Frameworks, Compliance Requirements)	Detailed Reference
National Institute of Standards and Technology Framework for Improving Critical Infrastructure Cybersecurity v1.1, April 2018	DE.DP Detection Processes

B. Component: Organizational Structures

Key Management Practice	Operations Manager	Business Process Owners	Project Manager	Head of IT	IT Development Coordinator	IT Operations Coordinator
APO11.01 Establish a quality management system (QMS).	A			R		
APO11.02 Focus quality management on customers.	A	R		R		
APO11.03 Manage quality standards, practices and procedures and integrate quality management into key processes and solutions.	A	R	R	R	R	R
APO11.04 Perform quality monitoring, control and reviews.	A	R		R		
APO11.05 Maintain continuous improvement.	A	R	R	R	R	R

C. Component: Information Flows and Items

Management Practice	Small and Medium Enterprise-specific Inputs		Small and Medium Enterprise-specific Outputs	
APO11.01 Establish a quality management system (QMS).	**From**	**Description**	**Description**	**To**
	Outside COBIT	Enterprisewide quality system	QMS roles, responsibilities and decision rights	DSS06.03
			Quality management plans	APO14.04 APO14.06 BAI11.05

C. Component: Information Flows and Items *(cont.)*				
Management Practice	Small and Medium Enterprise-specific Inputs		Small and Medium Enterprise-specific Outputs	
APO11.02 Focus quality management on customers.	From	Description	Description	To
	Outside COBIT	Business and customer quality requirements	Customer requirements for quality management	APO08.05 APO09.03 BAI11.06
			Results of quality of service, including customer feedback	APO08.05 APO09.05 BAI05.01 BAI07.07
			Acceptance criteria	BAI02.01 BAI02.02
APO11.03 Manage quality standards, practices and procedures and integrate quality management into key processes and solutions.	BAI02.04	Approved quality reviews	Quality management standards	All APO All BAI All DSS All MEA
	Outside COBIT	• Available quality certifications • Industry good practices	Root causes of quality delivery failures	APO08.02 APO09.04 BAI07.08 MEA02.04 MEA04.04
			Results of quality monitoring	APO08.05 APO09.04 BAI07.08
APO11.04 Perform quality monitoring, control and reviews.	BAI03.06	Quality review results, exceptions and corrections	Results of quality reviews and audits	APO08.05 APO09.04 APO09.05 BAI07.08
	DSS02.07	Incident status and trends report		
APO11.05 Maintain continuous improvement.	There are no small and medium enterprise-specific inputs for this practice.		Examples of good practice to be shared	All APO All BAI; All DSS All MEA

D. Component: People, Skills and Competencies		
Skill	Related Guidance (Standards, Frameworks, Compliance Requirements)	Detailed Reference
ICT quality strategy development	e-Competence Framework (e-CF)—A common European Framework for ICT Professionals in all industry sectors—Part 1: Framework, 2016	D. Enable—D.2. ICT Quality Strategy Development
Quality assurance	Skills Framework for the Information Age V6, 2015	QUAS
Quality management	Skills Framework for the Information Age V6, 2015	QUMG
Quality standards	Skills Framework for the Information Age V6, 2015	QUST

E. Component: Principles, Policies and Procedures	
Relevant Policy	Policy Description
Quality management policy	Captures management's vision of enterprise quality objectives, acceptable level of quality, and duties of specific teams and entities to ensure quality.

F. Component: Culture, Ethics and Behavior
Key Culture Elements
Promote a culture of quality and continual improvement. Maintain and regularly communicate the need for, and benefits of, quality and continuous improvement.

G. Component: Services, Infrastructure and Applications
• QMS • Third-party quality assurance services

Page intentionally left blank

Domain: Align, Plan and Organize Management Objective: APO12 — Managed Risk	Focus Area: Small and Medium Enterprises
Description	
Continually identify, assess and reduce I&T-related risk within tolerance levels set by enterprise executive management.	
Purpose	
Integrate the management of I&T-related enterprise risk with overall enterprise risk management (ERM) and balance the costs and benefits of managing I&T-related enterprise risk.	
Small and Medium Enterprise Focus Area Relevance	
A risk management approach for I&T can be integrated into overall enterprise risk management, including management of actions required to mitigate identified risk. The risk profile can be limited to managing and maintaining a detailed risk inventory. As such, not all activities for maintaining a risk profile will be relevant for SMEs.	

A. Component: Process		
Management Practice	**Small and Medium Enterprise-specific Metrics**	
APO12.01 Collect data. Identify and collect relevant data to enable effective I&T-related risk identification, analysis and reporting.	a. Percent of identified risk with complete data, as defined in the risk method b. Percent of critical systems with known issues	
Small and Medium Enterprise-specific Activities		**Capability Level**
1. Establish and maintain a method for the collection, classification and analysis of I&T risk-related data, aligned with the enterprise's approach to risk identification.		2
2. Record relevant and significant I&T risk-related data regarding the enterprise's internal and external operating environment. At appropriate times, discuss with key staff what can go wrong with I&T that would impact business objectives significantly. Give special consideration to data, assets and services that are critical for the success of the business.		
3. Align the I&T-risk taxonomy with the organization's risk taxonomy to establish consistent definitions of risk scenarios and impact and likelihood categories.		3
4. Record data on risk events that have caused or may cause business impacts as per the impact categories defined in the risk taxonomy. Capture relevant data from related issues, incidents, problems and investigations.		
5. Determine the specific conditions that existed or were absent when risk events occurred and the way the conditions affected event frequency and loss magnitude.		4
6. Perform periodic event and risk factor analysis to identify new or emerging risk issues and to gain an understanding of the associated internal and external risk factors.		
Related Guidance (Standards, Frameworks, Compliance Requirements)	**Detailed Reference**	
CMMI Data Management Maturity Model, 2014	Supporting Processes - Risk Management	
COSO Enterprise Risk Management, June 2017	8. Performance—Principle 10	
ISO/IEC 27005:2011(E)	8.2 Risk identification; 12. Information security risk monitoring and review	
National Institute of Standards and Technology Special Publication 800-37, Revision 2 (Draft), May 2018	3.1 Preparation (Task 7)	

A. Component: Process *(cont.)*		
Management Practice	**Small and Medium Enterprise-specific Metrics**	
APO12.02 Analyze risk. Develop a substantiated view on actual I&T risk, in support of risk decisions.	a. Percent of identified I&T risk scenarios b. Time since last update of I&T risk scenarios	
Small and Medium Enterprise-specific Activities		**Capability Level**
1. Define the appropriate scope for performing risk analysis.		3
2. Build and regularly update I&T risk scenarios, including compound scenarios of cascading and/or coincidental threat types and events.		
3. Estimate the frequency (or likelihood) and magnitude of loss or gain associated with I&T risk scenarios. Take into account all applicable risk factors, evaluate known operational controls.		
4. Compare current risk (I&T-related loss exposure) to risk appetite and acceptable risk tolerance, and identify unacceptable or elevated risk.		
5. Propose risk responses for risk exceeding risk appetite and tolerance levels. Consider cost-effective means to manage risk identified through insurance coverage and protection practices (e.g., effective backup, basic access control, virus protection, firewalls).		
6. Manage the risk mitigation actions as projects.		4
7. Analyze the cost-benefit of potential risk response options, including avoid, reduce/mitigate, transfer/share, and accept and exploit/seize. Confirm the optimal risk response.		5
Related Guidance (Standards, Frameworks, Compliance Requirements)	**Detailed Reference**	
CMMI Data Management Maturity Model, 2014	Supporting Processes—Risk Management	
COSO Enterprise Risk Management, June 2017	8. Performance—Principle 11	
ISF, The Standard of Good Practice for Information Security 2016	IR2.1 Risk Assessment Scope; IR2.2 Business Impact Assessment	
ISO/IEC 27001:2013/Cor.2:2015(E)	8.2 Information security risk assessment	
ISO/IEC 27005:2011(E)	8.3 Risk analysis	
National Institute of Standards and Technology Framework for Improving Critical Infrastructure Cybersecurity v1.1, April 2018	ID.RA Risk Assessment	
National Institute of Standards and Technology Special Publication 800-37, Revision 2 (Draft), May 2018	3.6 Authorization (Task 3)	
National Institute of Standards and Technology Special Publication 800-53, Revision 5 (Draft), August 2017	3.17 Risk assessment (RA-3)	
Management Practice	**Small and Medium Enterprise-specific Metrics**	
APO12.03 Maintain a risk profile. Maintain an inventory of known risk and risk attributes, including expected frequency, potential impact and responses. Document related resources, capabilities and current control activities related to risk items.	a. Completeness of attributes and values in the risk inventory b. Percent of key business processes included in the risk inventory	
Small and Medium Enterprise-specific Activities		**Capability Level**
1. Inventory business processes and document their dependency on IT service management processes and IT infrastructure resources. Identify supporting personnel, applications, infrastructure, facilities, critical manual records, vendors, suppliers and outsourcers.		2
2. Determine and agree on which IT services and IT infrastructure resources are essential to sustain the operation of business processes. Analyze dependencies and identify weak links.		
3. Aggregate current risk scenarios by category, business line and functional area.		
4. Capture all risk profile information and consolidate it into an aggregated risk profile on a regular basis.		3
5. Capture information on the status of the risk action plan, for inclusion in the I&T risk profile of the enterprise.		
6. Based on all risk profile data, define a set of risk indicators that allow the quick identification and monitoring of current risk and risk trends.		4
7. Capture information on I&T risk events that have materialized, for inclusion in the IT risk profile of the enterprise.		

A. Component: Process *(cont.)*		
Related Guidance (Standards, Frameworks, Compliance Requirements)	**Detailed Reference**	
CMMI Cybermaturity Platform, 2018	RS.DT Define Organizational Risk Tolerance	
COSO Enterprise Risk Management, June 2017	8. Performance—Principle 12	
National Institute of Standards and Technology Special Publication 800-53, Revision 5 (Draft), August 2017	3.17 Risk assessment (RA-7)	
Management Practice	**Small and Medium Enterprise-specific Metrics**	
APO12.04 Articulate risk. Communicate information on the current state of I&T-related exposures and opportunities in a timely manner to all required stakeholders for appropriate response.	a. Completeness of risk profile reporting (including information in alignment with stakeholder requirements) b. Frequency of risk reporting to decision-making management	
Small and Medium Enterprise-specific Activities		**Capability Level**
1. Report the results of risk analysis to all affected stakeholders in terms and formats useful to support enterprise decisions. Wherever possible, include probabilities and ranges of loss or gain along with confidence levels that enable management to balance risk-return.		3
2. Provide decision makers with an understanding of worst-case and most probable scenarios; I&T-related loss exposures; significant reputational, legal and regulatory considerations; or any other impact category based on the risk taxonomy.		
3. Report the current risk profile to all stakeholders, including information on control effectiveness, gaps, inconsistencies, redundancies, remediation status, and their impacts on the risk profile.		
4. Review the results of objective third-party assessments, internal audit and quality assurance reviews, and include them in the risk inventory. Review identified gaps and I&T-related loss exposures to determine the need for additional risk analysis.		4
Related Guidance (Standards, Frameworks, Compliance Requirements)	**Detailed Reference**	
CMMI Cybermaturity Platform, 2018	RS.CR Determine Critical Infrastructure Requirements	
COSO Enterprise Risk Management, June 2017	10. Information, Communication, and Reporting—Principle 19	
ISO/IEC 27005:2011(E)	11. Information security risk communication and consultation	
National Institute of Standards and Technology Framework for Improving Critical Infrastructure Cybersecurity v1.1, April 2018	ID.RM Risk Management Strategy	
National Institute of Standards and Technology Special Publication 800-53, Revision 5 (Draft), August 2017	3.15 Program management (PM-32)	
Management Practice	**Small and Medium Enterprise-specific Metrics**	
APO12.05 Define a risk management action portfolio. Manage opportunities to reduce risk to an acceptable level as a portfolio.	a. Percent of risk management project proposals rejected due to lack of consideration of other related risk	
Small and Medium Enterprise-specific Activities		**Capability Level**
1. Maintain an inventory of activities that are in place to mitigate risk and that enable risk to be taken in line with risk appetite and tolerance.		2
2. Define a balanced set of project proposals designed to reduce risk and/or projects that enable strategic enterprise opportunities, considering cost/benefits, effect on current risk profile and regulations.		3
Related Guidance (Standards, Frameworks, Compliance Requirements)	**Detailed Reference**	
CMMI Data Management Maturity Model, 2014	Supporting Processes—Risk Management	
COSO Enterprise Risk Management, June 2017	8. Performance—Principle 14	
HITRUST CSF version 9, September 2017	03.01 Risk Management Program	

A. Component: Process *(cont.)*	
Management Practice	**Small and Medium Enterprise-specific Metrics**
APO12.06 Respond to risk. Respond in a timely manner to materialized risk events with effective measures to limit the magnitude of loss.	a. Percent of I&T risk action plans executed as designed

Small and Medium Enterprise-specific Activities	Capability Level
1. Prepare, maintain and test plans that document the specific steps to take when a risk event may cause serious business impact. Ensure that plans include pathways of escalation across the enterprise.	3
2. Apply the appropriate response plan to minimize the impact when risk incidents occur.	
3. Examine past adverse events/losses and missed opportunities and determine root causes.	4
4. Communicate root cause, additional risk response requirements and process improvements to appropriate decision makers.	5
5. Ensure that the cause, response requirements and process improvement are included in risk governance processes.	

Related Guidance (Standards, Frameworks, Compliance Requirements)	Detailed Reference
COSO Enterprise Risk Management, June 2017	8. Performance—Principle 13
ISF, The Standard of Good Practice for Information Security 2016	IR2.9 Risk Treatment
ISO/IEC 27001:2013/Cor.2:2015(E)	6.1 Action to address risk and opportunities
ISO/IEC 27005:2011(E)	9. Information security risk treatment
National Institute of Standards and Technology Special Publication 800-37, Revision 2 (Draft), May 2018	3.6 Authorization (Task 4)
National Institute of Standards and Technology Special Publication 800-53, Revision 5 (Draft), August 2017	3.15 Program management (PM-9, PM-31)

B. Component: Organizational Structures

Key Management Practice	Business Process Owners	Head of IT	Security Expert	IT Development Coordinator	IT Operations Coordinator	Privacy Officer
APO12.01 Collect data.	R	A	R	R	R	R
APO12.02 Analyze risk.	R	A				
APO12.03 Maintain a risk profile.	R	A				
APO12.04 Articulate risk.	R	A				
APO12.05 Define a risk management action portfolio.	R	A				
APO12.06 Respond to risk.	R	A	R	R	R	R

C. Component: Information Flows and Items				
Management Practice	Small and Medium Enterprise-specific Inputs		Small and Medium Enterprise-specific Outputs	
	From	Description	Description	To
APO12.01 Collect data.	APO02.02	Gaps and risk related to current capabilities	Identified risk issues and factors	APO01.01 APO02.02 EDM03.01
	APO02.05	Risk assessment initiatives	Data on risk events and contributing factors	Internal
	APO10.04	Identified vendor delivery risk		
	DSS02.07	Incident status and trends report		
	EDM03.01	Evaluation of risk management activities		
	EDM03.02	Approved process for measuring risk management		
APO12.02 Analyze risk.	DSS04.02	Business impact analyses (BIAs)	Risk analysis results	APO01.01 APO02.02 BAI11.06 EDM03.03
	DSS05.01	Evaluations of potential threats		
	Outside COBIT	Threat advisories		
APO12.03 Maintain a risk profile.	APO10.04	Identified vendor delivery risk	Documented risk profile, including status of risk management actions	APO02.02 EDM03.02
	DSS05.01	Evaluations of potential threats		
	EDM03.01	• Risk appetite guidance • Approved risk tolerance levels		
APO12.04 Articulate risk.	There are no small and medium enterprise-specific inputs for this practice.		Risk analysis and risk profile reports for stakeholders	APO10.04 EDM03.03 EDM05.02 MEA04.05
			Results of third-party risk assessments	APO10.04 EDM03.03 MEA02.01
APO12.05 Define a risk management action portfolio.	There are no small and medium enterprise-specific inputs for this practice.		Project proposals for reducing risk	APO13.02
APO12.06 Respond to risk.	EDM03.03	Remedial actions to address risk management deviations	Risk impact communication	APO01.02 APO08.04 DSS04.02
			Risk-related root causes	DSS02.03 DSS03.01 DSS03.02 DSS03.03 DSS03.05 DSS04.02 MEA02.04 MEA04.04 MEA04.06

D. Component: People, Skills and Competencies		
Skill	**Related Guidance (Standards, Frameworks, Compliance Requirements)**	**Detailed Reference**
Business risk management	Skills Framework for the Information Age V6, 2015	BURM
Information assurance	Skills Framework for the Information Age V6, 2015	INAS
Risk management	e-Competence Framework (e-CF)—A common European Framework for ICT Professionals in all industry sectors—Part 1: Framework, 2016	E. Manage—E.3. Risk Management

E. Component: Principles, Policies and Procedures	
Relevant Policy	**Policy Description**
There are no small and medium enterprise-specific principles, policies and procedures for this objective.	

F. Component: Culture, Ethics and Behavior
Key Culture Elements
To support a transparent and participatory risk culture, senior management should set direction and demonstrate visible and genuine support for incorporation of risk practices throughout the enterprise. Management should encourage open communication and business ownership for I&T-related business risk. Desirable behaviors include aligning policies to the defined risk appetite, reporting risk trends to senior management and risk governing bodies, rewarding effective risk management, and proactively monitoring risk and progress on the risk action plan.

G. Component: Services, Infrastructure and Applications
• Crisis management services • Governance, risk and compliance (GRC) tools • Risk analysis tools • Risk intelligence services

Domain: Align, Plan and Organize Management Objective: APO13 — Managed Security	Focus Area: Small and Medium Enterprises
Description	
Define, operate and monitor an information security management system.	
Purpose	
Keep the impact and occurrence of information security incidents within the enterprise's risk appetite levels.	
Small and Medium Enterprise Focus Area Relevance	
A system for managing security and privacy can be integrated in the I&T management system, with special attention paid to possible security and privacy risk. The aim is to align information security with the overall enterprise approach and incorporate it in the information security management system (ISMS). Security and privacy risk can be managed as part of the I&T-related risk process. It is important to make sure that security and privacy are explicit in the I&T risk management approach.	

A. Component: Process		
Management Practice	**Small and Medium Enterprise-specific Metrics**	
APO13.01 Establish and maintain an information security management system (ISMS). Establish and maintain an information security management system (ISMS) that provides a standard, formal and continuous approach to information security management, enabling secure technology and business processes that are aligned with business requirements.	a. Percent of key security roles clearly defined	
Small and Medium Enterprise-specific Activities		**Capability Level**
1. Define the scope and boundaries of the ISMS in terms of the context and purpose of the organization, its location, assets and technology. Include details of, and justification for, any exclusions from the scope.		2
2. Define an ISMS in accordance with enterprise policy and aligned with the organization, its location, assets and technology.		
3. Align the ISMS with the overall enterprise approach to the management of security.		
4. Obtain management authorization to implement and operate or change the ISMS.		
5. Prepare and maintain a statement of applicability that describes the scope of the ISMS.		
6. Define and communicate information security management roles and responsibilities.		
7. Communicate the ISMS approach.		
Related Guidance (Standards, Frameworks, Compliance Requirements)	**Detailed Reference**	
HITRUST CSF version 9, September 2017	0.01 Information Security Management program	
ISO/IEC 20000-1:2011(E)	6.6 Information security management	
ITIL V3, 2011	Service Design, 4.7 Information Security Management	
National Institute of Standards and Technology Special Publication 800-37, Revision 2 (Draft), May 2018	3.3 Selection (Task 1); 3.4 Implementation (Task 1)	
National Institute of Standards and Technology Special Publication 800-53, Revision 5 (Draft), August 2017	3.17 Risk assessment (RA-2)	

A. Component: Process *(cont.)*		
Management Practice	**Small and Medium Enterprise-specific Metrics**	
APO13.02 Define and manage an information security and privacy risk treatment plan. Maintain an information security plan that describes how information security risk is to be managed and aligned with enterprise strategy and enterprise architecture. Ensure that recommendations for implementing security improvements are based on approved business cases, implemented as an integral part of services and solutions development, and operated as an integral part of business operation.	a. Percent of security and privacy solutions deviating from the plan	
Small and Medium Enterprise-specific Activities		**Capability Level**
1. Formulate and maintain an information security and privacy risk treatment plan aligned with strategic objectives and the privacy policy.		3
2. Develop proposals to implement the information security risk treatment plan, supported by suitable business cases, which include consideration of funding and allocation of roles and responsibilities.		
3. Implement information security training and awareness programs.		
4. Integrate the planning, design, implementation and monitoring of information security procedures and other controls capable of enabling prompt prevention, detection of security events and response to security and privacy incidents.		
5. Define how to measure the effectiveness of the selected management practices.		4
Related Guidance (Standards, Frameworks, Compliance Requirements)	**Detailed Reference**	
No related guidance for this management practice		
Management Practice	**Small and Medium Enterprise-specific Metrics**	
APO13.03 Monitor and review the information security management system (ISMS). Maintain and regularly communicate the need for, and benefits of, continuous improvement in information security. Collect and analyze data about the ISMS and improve its effectiveness. Correct nonconformities to prevent recurrence.	a. Percent of security- and privacy-related incidents caused by failure to adhere to the security plan b. Number of security- and privacy-related incidents c. Number of solutions developed and confirmed to align with the security plan	
Small and Medium Enterprise-specific Activities		**Capability Level**
1. Undertake regular reviews of the effectiveness of the ISMS, including ISMS policy and objectives and security practices. Take into account results of security audits, incidents, results from effectiveness measurements, and suggestions and feedback from all interested parties.		4
2. Conduct internal ISMS audits at planned intervals.		
3. Undertake a management review of the ISMS on a regular basis to ensure that the scope remains adequate and improvements in the ISMS process are identified.		
4. Record actions and events that could have an impact on the effectiveness or performance of the ISMS.		
5. Provide input to the maintenance of the security plans, taking into account the findings of monitoring and reviewing activities.		5
Related Guidance (Standards, Frameworks, Compliance Requirements)	**Detailed Reference**	
National Institute of Standards and Technology Special Publication 800-37, Revision 2 (Draft), May 2018	3.3 Selection (Task 3)	

B. Component: Organizational Structures						
Key Management Practice	Business Process Owners	Head of IT	Security Expert	IT Development Coordinator	IT Operations Coordinator	Privacy Officer
APO13.01 Establish and maintain an information security management system (ISMS).		R	A			
APO13.02 Define and manage an information security and privacy risk treatment plan.		R	A			R
APO13.03 Monitor and review the information security management system (ISMS).	R	R	A	R	R	R

C. Component: Information Flows and Items				
Management Practice	Small and Medium Enterprise-specific Inputs		Small and Medium Enterprise-specific Outputs	
	From	Description	Description	To
APO13.01 Establish and maintain an information security management system (ISMS).	Outside COBIT	Enterprise security approach	ISMS scope statement	DSS06.03
			ISMS policy	Internal
APO13.02 Define and manage an information security risk treatment plan.	APO02.04	Gaps and changes required to realize target capability	Information security risk treatment plan	All EDM All APO All BAI All DSS All MEA
	APO12.05	Project proposals for reducing risk	Information security business cases	APO05.02
APO13.03 Monitor and review the information security management system (ISMS).	DSS02.02	Classified and prioritized incidents and service requests	Recommendations for improving the information security management system (ISMS)	Internal
			ISMS audit reports	MEA02.01

D. Component: People, Skills and Competencies		
Skill	Related Guidance (Standards, Frameworks, Compliance Requirements)	Detailed Reference
Information security	Skills Framework for the Information Age V6, 2015	SCTY
Information security strategy development	e-Competence Framework (e-CF)—A common European Framework for ICT Professionals in all industry sectors - Part 1: Framework, 2016	D. Enable—D.1. Information Security Strategy Development

E. Component: Principles, Policies and Procedures	
Relevant Policy	Policy Description
Information security and privacy policy	Sets behavioral guidelines to protect corporate information, systems and infrastructure. Given that business requirements regarding security and storage are more dynamic than I&T risk management and privacy, their governance should be handled separately from that of I&T risk and privacy. For operational efficiency, synchronize information security policy with I&T risk and privacy policy.

F. Component: Culture, Ethics and Behavior
Key Culture Elements
Establish a culture of security and privacy awareness that encourages desirable behavior and implementation of security and privacy policies in daily practice. Provide sufficient security and privacy guidance, indicate security and privacy champions (including C-level executives, leaders in HR, and security and privacy professionals), and proactively support and communicate security and privacy programs, innovations and challenges.

G. Component: Services, Infrastructure and Applications
• Configuration management tools • Security and privacy awareness services • Third-party security assessment services

Domain: Align, Plan and Organize Management Objective: APO14 — Managed Data	Focus Area: Small and Medium Enterprises
Description	
Achieve and sustain effective management of the enterprise data assets across the data life cycle, from creation through delivery, maintenance and archiving.	
Purpose	
Ensure effective utilization of the critical data assets to achieve enterprise goals and objectives.	
Small and Medium Enterprise Focus Area Relevance	
Define a centrally managed data process for company data, including management of I&T-related data across the data life cycle, from creation through delivery, maintenance and archiving. This ensures effective utilization of the critical data assets to achieve enterprise goals and objectives.	

A. Component: Process		
Management Practice	**Small and Medium Enterprise-specific Metrics**	
APO14.01 Define and communicate the organization's data management strategy and roles and responsibilities. Define how to manage and improve the organization's data assets, in line with enterprise strategy and objectives. Communicate the data management strategy to all stakeholders. Assign roles and responsibilities to ensure that corporate data are managed as critical assets and the data management strategy is implemented and maintained in an effective and sustainable manner.	a. Number of roles and responsibilities identified to support management of data	
Small and Medium Enterprise-specific Activities		**Capability Level**
1. Specify roles and responsibilities to support the management of data for the enterprise.		2
2. Ensure that business and technology stakeholders collaboratively develop the organization's data management strategy, taking care that data management objectives, priorities and scope reflect enterprise objectives and are consistent with regulation.		3
3. Ensure that data management objectives, priorities and scope are approved by the executive committee.		
4. Communicate data management objectives, priorities and scope and adjust them as needed, based upon feedback.		
5. Research innovative business processes and emerging regulatory requirements to ensure that data management remains compatible with future business needs.		5
Related Guidance (Standards, Frameworks, Compliance Requirements)	**Detailed Reference**	
CMMI Data Management Maturity Model, 2014	Data Management Strategy - Data Management Strategy; Data Governance—Governance Management	
ITIL V3, 2011	Service Design, 5.2 Management of Data and Information	
The CIS Critical Security Controls for Effective Cyber Defense Version 6.1, August 2016	CSC 13: Data Protection	
Management Practice	**Small and Medium Enterprise-specific Metrics**	
APO14.02 Define and maintain a consistent business glossary. Create, approve, update and promote consistent business terms and definitions to foster shared data usage across the organization.	a. Level of acceptance of business glossary terms throughout the organization b. Number of synonyms for defined business glossary terminology	
Small and Medium Enterprise-specific Activities		**Capability Level**
1. Ensure that standard business terms are readily available and communicated to relevant stakeholders.		2
2. Ensure that each business term added to the business glossary has a unique name and unique definition.		
3. Use standard industry business terms and definitions, as appropriate, in the business glossary.		
4. Establish and document a process to define, manage, use and maintain the business glossary. For example, new initiatives should apply standard business terms as part of the data requirements definition process to ensure consistency of language.		
5. Ensure that the process for managing and maintaining the business glossary is followed. This will help achieve comparability of the content and facilitate data sharing across the organization.		3
Related Guidance (Standards, Frameworks, Compliance Requirements)	**Detailed Reference**	
CMMI Data Management Maturity Model, 2014	Data Governance - Business Glossary	
ISF, The Standard of Good Practice for Information Security 2016	IM1.1 Information Classification and Handling	

A. Component: Process *(cont.)*

Management Practice	Small and Medium Enterprise-specific Metrics
APO14.03 Establish the processes and infrastructure for metadata management. Establish the processes and infrastructure for specifying and extending metadata about the organization's data assets, fostering and supporting data sharing, ensuring compliant use of data, improving responsiveness to business changes and reducing data-related risk.	a. Number of identified inaccuracies in metadata b. Percent of metadata containing measures and metrics to evaluate accuracy and adoption

Small and Medium Enterprise-specific Activities	Capability Level
1. Establish and follow a metadata management process.	2
2. Ensure that metadata documentation captures data interdependencies.	
3. Establish and follow metadata categories, properties and standards.	
4. Validate metadata and any changes to metadata against the existing architecture.	3
5. Use measures and metrics to evaluate the accuracy and adoption of metadata.	4
6. Evaluate planned data changes for impact on the metadata repository. Continuously improve metadata capture, change and refinement processes.	5

Related Guidance (Standards, Frameworks, Compliance Requirements)	Detailed Reference
CMMI Data Management Maturity Model, 2014	Data Governance—Metadata Management
ISO/IEC 27002:2013/Cor.2:2015(E)	8.2 Information classification

Management Practice	Small and Medium Enterprise-specific Metrics
APO14.04 Define a data quality strategy. Define an integrated, organizationwide strategy to achieve and maintain the level of data quality (such as complexity, integrity, accuracy, completeness, validity, traceability and timeliness) required to support the business goals and objectives.	a. Number of data quality improvement efforts identified and recorded in a sequence plan b. Percent of stakeholders satisfied with the quality of data

Small and Medium Enterprise-specific Activities	Capability Level
1. Define a data quality strategy in collaboration with business and technology stakeholders. The strategy should facilitate moving from the current to the target state. It should also explicitly align with business objectives and the organization's data management strategy.	2
2. Ensure that data quality strategy is approved by executive management.	3
3. Ensure that the data quality strategy is followed across the organization and is accompanied by corresponding policies, processes and guidelines.	
4. Develop, monitor and maintain a sequence plan for data quality improvement efforts across the organization.	
5. To evaluate progress, monitor plans to meet the goals and objectives of the data quality strategy.	4
6. Systematically collect stakeholder reports of data quality issues. Include their expectations for improving data quality in the data quality strategy. Measure and monitor them.	5

Related Guidance (Standards, Frameworks, Compliance Requirements)	Detailed Reference
CMMI Cybermaturity Platform, 2018	DP.DR Safeguard Data at Rest; DP.DT Safeguard Data in Transit; DP.IP Integrity and Data Leak Prevention
CMMI Data Management Maturity Model, 2014	Data Quality - Data Quality Strategy

A. Component: Process *(cont.)*

Management Practice	Small and Medium Enterprise-specific Metrics
APO14.05 Establish data profiling methodologies, processes and tools. Implement standardized data profiling methodologies, processes, practices, tools and templates that can be applied across multiple data repositories and data stores.	a. Number of defined and implemented data templates, and their usage percentage b. Number of shared data sets with a defined data profile

Small and Medium Enterprise-specific Activities	Capability Level
1. Define and standardize data profiling methodologies, processes, practices, tools and results templates. Ensure that profiling processes are reusable and leveraged across multiple data stores and shared data repositories.	3
2. Identify core shared data sets that are regularly profiled and monitored.	
3. During a data profiling activity, compare actual issues to the statistically predicted issues based on historical profiling results.	4
4. Ensure that results are centrally stored, systematically monitored and analyzed with respect to statistics and metrics.	
5. Create real-time or near real-time automated profiling reports for all critical data feeds and repositories.	5

Related Guidance (Standards, Frameworks, Compliance Requirements)	Detailed Reference
CMMI Data Management Maturity Model, 2014	Data Quality—Data Profiling
National Institute of Standards and Technology Special Publication 800-53, Revision 5, August 2017	3.20 System and information integrity (SI-1)

Management Practice	Small and Medium Enterprise-specific Metrics
APO14.06 Ensure a data quality assessment approach. Provide a systematic approach to measure and evaluate data quality according to processes and techniques, and against data quality rules.	a. Number of identified issues in data quality assessment results b. Number of data quality assessment results that include recommendations for remediation

Small and Medium Enterprise-specific Activities	Capability Level
1. Periodically conduct data quality assessments, according to an approved frequency per the data quality assessment policy. Ensure that data governance determines the key set of attributes by subject area for data quality assessments.	4
2. Include recommendations for remediation, with supporting rationale, in data quality assessment results.	
3. Assess data quality, using established thresholds and targets for each selected quality dimension.	
4. Systematically generate data quality measurement reports, based on criticality of attributes and data volatility.	
5. Continuously review and improve data quality assessment and reporting processes.	5

Related Guidance (Standards, Frameworks, Compliance Requirements)	Detailed Reference
CMMI Data Management Maturity Model, 2014	Data Quality—Data Quality Assessment

Management Practice	Small and Medium Enterprise-specific Metrics
APO14.07 Define the data cleansing approach. Define the mechanisms, rules, processes, and methods to validate and correct data according to predefined business rules.	a. Percent of SLAs that include data quality criteria and hold data providers accountable for cleansed data

Small and Medium Enterprise-specific Activities	Capability Level
1. Establish and maintain a data cleansing policy.	2
2. Maintain data change history through cleansing activities.	3
3. Establish methods for correcting the data and define those methods within a plan. Methods may include multiple repository comparison, verification against a valid source, logic checks, referential integrity or range tolerance.	4
4. Include data quality criteria to hold data providers accountable for cleansed data in SLAs.	

Related Guidance (Standards, Frameworks, Compliance Requirements)	Detailed Reference
CMMI Data Management Maturity Model, 2014	Data Quality—Data Cleansing

A. Component: Process *(cont.)*		
Management Practice	**Small and Medium Enterprise-specific Metrics**	
APO14.08 Manage the life cycle of data assets. Ensure that the organization understands, maps, inventories and controls its data flows through business processes over the data life cycle, from creation or acquisition to retirement.	a. Number of shared data sets b. Time since last compliance check regarding mapping of business processes to data	
Small and Medium Enterprise-specific Activities		**Capability Level**
1. Map and align the requirements of data consumers and producers.		2
2. Define business process-to-data mappings. Maintain them and periodically review them for compliance.		3
3. Follow a defined process for collaborative agreements with respect to shared data and data usage within business processes.		
4. Implement data flows and full data-to-process life cycle maps for shared data for each major business process at the organizational level.		
5. Ensure that changes to shared data sets or target data sets for a specific business purpose are managed by data governance structures, with relevant stakeholder engagement.		
6. Use metrics to expand approved shared data reuse and eliminate process redundancy.		4
Related Guidance (Standards, Frameworks, Compliance Requirements)	**Detailed Reference**	
CMMI Data Management Maturity Model, 2014	Data Operations—Data Lifecycle Management	
Management Practice	**Small and Medium Enterprise-specific Metrics**	
APO14.09 Support data archiving and retention. Ensure that data maintenance satisfies organizational and regulatory requirements for availability of historical data. Ensure that legal and regulatory requirements for data archiving and retention are met.	a. Percent of unsuccessful attempts transferring data to archive	
Small and Medium Enterprise-specific Activities		**Capability Level**
1. Ensure that policies clearly define management of data history, including retention, destruction and audit trail requirements.		2
2. Ensure the existence of a defined method that guarantees accessibility to the historical data necessary to support business needs.		
3. Use policy and processes to control access, transmittal and modifications to historical and archived data.		
4. Ensure that the organization has a prescribed data warehouse repository that provides access to historical data for meeting analytics needs supporting business processes.		3
Related Guidance (Standards, Frameworks, Compliance Requirements)	**Detailed Reference**	
CMMI Data Management Maturity Model, 2014	Platform and Architecture—Historical Data, Retention and Archiving	
Management Practice	**Small and Medium Enterprise-specific Metrics**	
APO14.10 Manage data backup and restore arrangements. Manage availability of critical data to ensure operational continuity.	a. Percent of unsuccessful attempts backing up data b. Percent of successful attempts restoring backup data	
Small and Medium Enterprise-specific Activities		**Capability Level**
1. Define a schedule to ensure correct backup of all critical data, taking into account frequency, type of backup, security, privacy and other criteria.		2
2. Define requirements for on-site and off-site storage of backup data, taking into account volume, capacity and retention period, in alignment with the business requirements.		
3. Establish a testing schedule for backup data.		
4. Ensure that the data can be restored correctly without drastically impacting business.		
Related Guidance (Standards, Frameworks, Compliance Requirements)	**Detailed Reference**	
The CIS Critical Security Controls for Effective Cyber Defense Version 6.1, August 2016	CSC 10: Data Recovery Capability	

B. Component: Organizational Structures					
Key Management Practice	Head of IT	Security Expert	IT Development Coordinator	IT Operations Coordinator	Legal Department
APO14.01 Define and communicate the organization's data management strategy and roles and responsibilities.	A	R	R		
APO14.02 Define and maintain a consistent business glossary.	A	R	R		
APO14.03 Establish the processes and infrastructure for metadata management.	A	R	R	R	
APO14.04 Define a data quality strategy.	A	R	R		
APO14.05 Establish data profiling methodologies, processes and tools.	A	R	R		
APO14.06 Ensure a data quality assessment approach.	A	R	R		
APO14.07 Define the data cleansing approach.	A	R	R	R	
APO14.08 Manage the life cycle of data assets.	A	R	R		R
APO14.09 Support data archiving and retention.	A	R		R	R
APO14.10 Manage data backup and restore arrangements.	A	R	R		R

C. Component: Information Flows and Items				
Management Practice	Small and Medium Enterprise-specific Inputs		Small and Medium Enterprise-specific Outputs	
	From	Description	Description	To
APO14.01 Define and communicate the organization's data management strategy and roles and responsibilities.	APO01.07	Data classification guidelines	Data management strategy	APO03.02 APO14.10
	APO07.03	Skills and competencies matrix	Agreed roles and responsibilities for data management and data governance	Internal
	Outside COBIT	Enterprise strategy	Implementation plan for data management strategy	Internal
APO14.02 Define and maintain a consistent business glossary.	There are no small and medium enterprise-specific inputs for this practice.		Business glossary	APO14.03 BAI02.01
APO14.03 Establish the processes and infrastructure for metadata management.	APO03.02	Information architecture model	Metadata documentation	APO03.02
	APO14.02	Business glossary		
APO14.04 Define a data quality strategy.	APO01.07	Data security and control guidelines	Data quality strategy	APO14.05 APO14.06 APO14.07
	APO11.01	Quality management plans	Data quality improvement plan	Internal

C. Component: Information Flows and Items *(cont.)*				
Management Practice	Small and Medium Enterprise-specific Inputs		Small and Medium Enterprise-specific Outputs	
	From	Description	Description	To
APO14.05 Establish data profiling methodologies, processes and tools.	APO14.04	Data quality strategy	Data profiling methodologies, processes, practices, tools and results templates	Internal
APO14.06 Ensure a data quality assessment approach.	APO11.01	Quality management plans	Data quality assessment results	Internal
	APO14.04	Data quality strategy		
APO14.07 Define the data cleansing approach.	APO14.04	Data quality strategy	There are no small and medium enterprise-specific outputs for this practice.	
APO14.08 Manage the life cycle of data assets.	APO01.07	Data security and control guidelines	There are no small and medium enterprise-specific outputs for this practice.	
	DSS04.07	Backup data		
APO14.09 Support data archiving and retention.	DSS06.05	Retention requirements	Data archive	Internal
APO14.10 Manage data backup and restore arrangements.	APO01.07	Data security and control guidelines	Backup plan	DSS04.07
	APO14.01	Data management strategy	Backup test plan	DSS04.07

D. Component: People, Skills and Competencies		
Skill	**Related Guidance (Standards, Frameworks, Compliance Requirements)**	**Detailed Reference**
Data analysis	Skills Framework for the Information Age V6, 2015	DTAN
Data management	Skills Framework for the Information Age V6, 2015	DATM
Information assurance	Skills Framework for the Information Age V6, 2015	INAS
Information management	Skills Framework for the Information Age V6, 2015	IRMG

E. Component: Principles, Policies and Procedures	
Relevant Policy	**Policy Description**
There are no small and medium enterprise-specific principles, policies and procedures for this objective.	

F. Component: Culture, Ethics and Behavior
Key Culture Elements
Create a culture of shared responsibility for the organization's data assets. Acknowledge the potential value of data assets and ensure that roles and responsibilities are clear for governance and management of data assets.
Create awareness around data integrity, accuracy, completeness and protection to establish a culture of data quality. Relate data quality to the enterprise's core values. Continuously communicate the impact and risk of data loss. Ensure that employees understand the true cost of failing to implement a data quality culture.

G. Component: Services, Infrastructure and Applications

- Data modeling tools
- Data repositories

7.3 Build, Acquire and Implement (BAI)

01 Managed Programs

02 Managed Requirements Definition

03 Managed Solutions Identification and Build

04 Managed Availability and Capacity

05 Managed Organizational Change

06 Managed IT Changes

07 Managed IT Change Acceptance and Transitioning

08 Managed Knowledge

09 Managed Assets

10 Managed Configuration

11 Managed Projects

Page intentionally left blank

Domain: Build, Acquire and Implement Management Objective: BAI01 — Managed Programs	Focus Area: Small and Medium Enterprises
Description	
Manage all programs from the investment portfolio in alignment with enterprise strategy and in a coordinated way, based on a standard program management approach. Initiate, plan, control, and execute programs, and monitor expected value from the program.	
Purpose	
Realize desired business value and reduce the risk of unexpected delays, costs and value erosion. To do so, improve communications to and involvement of business and end users, ensure the value and quality of program deliverables and follow up of projects within the programs, and maximize program contribution to the investment portfolio.	
Small and Medium Enterprise Focus Area Relevance	
Small to medium enterprises may find this management objective less relevant than others in this guide if they have a limited number of IT staff and resources available and manage their investments on a project basis rather than on a program basis. These enterprises should consider implementing BAI11 *Managed Projects*. However, enterprises that are working with programs should find the guidance of this objective pertinent. Agile can be incorporated into program management practices in small to medium enterprises.	

A. Component: Process		
Management Practice	**Small and Medium Enterprise-specific Metrics**	
BAI01.01 Maintain a standard approach for program management. Maintain a standard approach for program management that enables governance and management review, decision-making and delivery-management activities. These activities should focus consistently on business value and goals (i.e., requirements, risk, costs, schedule and quality targets).	a. Percent of successful programs b. Percent of programs based on the defined standard approach	
Small and Medium Enterprise-specific Activities		**Capability Level**
1. Maintain and enforce a standard approach to program management, based on defined process and use of appropriate technology. Ensure that the approach covers the full life cycle and disciplines to be followed, including the management of scope, resources, risk, cost, quality, time, communication, stakeholder involvement, procurement, change control, integration and benefit realization.		2
2. Assign the responsibility for overall program or project management to one person who maintains the standard approach for program and project management across the organization. This person supports all programs and projects by creating and maintaining required project documentation templates, providing training and best practices for program/project managers, tracking metrics on the use of best practices for project management, etc. In some cases, the project management office (PMO) may also report program/project progress to senior management and/or stakeholders, help prioritize projects, and ensure all projects support the overall business objectives of the enterprise.		3
3. Evaluate lessons learned based on the use of the program management approach and update the approach accordingly.		4
Related Guidance (Standards, Frameworks, Compliance Requirements)	**Detailed Reference**	
No related guidance for this management practice		
Management Practice	**Small and Medium Enterprise-specific Metrics**	
BAI01.02 Initiate a program. Initiate a program to confirm expected benefits and obtain authorization to proceed. This includes agreeing on program sponsorship, confirming the program mandate through approval of the conceptual business case, appointing program board or committee members, producing the program brief, reviewing and updating the business case, developing a benefits realization plan, and obtaining approval from sponsors to proceed.	a. Percent of I&T initiatives/projects championed by business owners b. Percent of programs undertaken without approved business cases c. Percent of programs with stakeholders approving enterprise need, scope and planned outcome	

A. Component: Process *(cont.)*	
Small and Medium Enterprise-specific Activities	**Capability Level**
1. Agree on program sponsorship. Appoint a program board/committee with members who have strategic interest in the program, hold responsibility for investment decision making, will be significantly impacted by the program and will be required to enable delivery of the change.	2
2. Appoint a dedicated manager for the program, with the commensurate competencies and skills to manage the program effectively and efficiently.	
3. Develop a detailed business case for the program. Involve all key stakeholders in developing and documenting a complete understanding of the expected enterprise outcomes, how they will be measured, the full scope of initiatives required, the risk involved and the impact on all aspects of the enterprise. Identify and assess alternative courses of action to achieve the desired enterprise outcomes.	3
4. Develop a benefits realization plan that will be managed throughout the program to ensure that planned benefits always have owners and are achieved, sustained and optimized.	

Related Guidance (Standards, Frameworks, Compliance Requirements)	**Detailed Reference**
No related guidance for this management practice	

Management Practice	**Small and Medium Enterprise-specific Metrics**
BAI01.03 Manage stakeholder engagement. Manage stakeholder engagement to ensure an active exchange of accurate, consistent and timely information for all relevant stakeholders. This includes planning, identifying and engaging stakeholders and managing their expectations.	a. Percent of stakeholders effectively engaged

Small and Medium Enterprise-specific Activities	**Capability Level**
1. Identify, engage and manage stakeholders by establishing and maintaining appropriate levels of coordination, communication and liaison to ensure that they are involved in the program.	3
2. Analyze stakeholder interests and requirements.	
3. Follow a defined process for collaborative agreements with respect to shared data and data usage within business processes.	4

Related Guidance (Standards, Frameworks, Compliance Requirements)	**Detailed Reference**
PMBOK Guide Sixth Edition, 2017	Part 1: 10. Project communications management

Management Practice	**Small and Medium Enterprise-specific Metrics**
BAI01.04 Develop and maintain the program plan. Formulate a program to lay the initial groundwork. Position it for successful execution by formalizing the scope of the work and identifying deliverables that will satisfy goals and deliver value. Maintain and update the program plan and business case throughout the full economic life cycle of the program, ensuring alignment with strategic objectives and reflecting the current status and insights gained to date.	a. Percentage of program status reviews that do not meet value criteria b. Percent of active programs undertaken without valid and updated program value maps

Small and Medium Enterprise-specific Activities	**Capability Level**
1. Specify funding, cost, schedule and interdependencies of multiple program components.	2
2. Define and document the program plan covering all projects. Include what is needed to bring about changes to the enterprise; its purpose, mission, vision, values, culture, products and services; business processes; people skills and numbers; relationships with stakeholders, customers, suppliers and others; technology needs; and organizational restructuring required to achieve the program's expected enterprise outcomes.	3
3. Ensure that there is effective communication of program plans and progress reports among all projects and with the overall program. Ensure that any changes made to individual plans are reflected in the other enterprise program plans.	
4. Maintain the program plan to ensure that it is up to date and reflects alignment with current strategic objectives, actual progress and material changes to outcomes, benefits, costs and risk. Have the business drive the objectives and prioritize the work throughout to ensure that the program, as designed, will meet enterprise requirements. Review progress of individual projects and adjust the projects as necessary to meet scheduled milestones and releases.	
5. Throughout the program's economic life, update and maintain the business case and a benefits register to identify and define key benefits arising from undertaking the program.	
6. Prepare a program budget that reflects the full economic life cycle costs and the associated financial and nonfinancial benefits.	

Related Guidance (Standards, Frameworks, Compliance Requirements)	**Detailed Reference**
No related guidance for this management practice	

A. Component: Process *(cont.)*		
Management Practice	**Small and Medium Enterprise-specific Metrics**	
BAI01.05 Launch and execute the program. Launch and execute the program to acquire and direct the resources needed to accomplish the goals and benefits of the program as defined in the program plan. In accordance with stage-gate or release review criteria, prepare for stage-gate, iteration or release reviews to report progress and make the case for funding up to the following stage-gate or release review.	a. Percent of stakeholder sign-offs for stage-gate reviews of active programs b. Number of root cause analyses for deviations from the plan and necessary remedial actions addressed	
Small and Medium Enterprise-specific Activities		**Capability Level**
1. Plan, resource and commission the necessary projects required to achieve the program results, based on funding review and approvals at each stage-gate review.		3
2. Manage each program or project to ensure that decision-making and delivery activities focus on value by achieving business goals consistently, addressing risk and meeting stakeholder requirements.		
3. Establish agreed stages of the development process (development checkpoints). At the end of each stage, facilitate formal discussions of approved criteria with the stakeholders. After successful completion of functionality, performance and quality reviews, and before finalizing stage activities, obtain formal approval and sign-off from all stakeholders and the sponsor/business process owner.		
4. Undertake a benefits realization process throughout the program to ensure that planned benefits always have owners and are likely to be achieved, sustained and optimized. Monitor benefits delivery and report against performance targets at the stage-gate or iteration and release reviews. Perform root cause analysis for deviations from the plan and identify and address any necessary remedial actions.		4
5. Plan audits, quality reviews, phase/stage-gate reviews and reviews of realized benefits.		
Related Guidance (Standards, Frameworks, Compliance Requirements)	**Detailed Reference**	
No related guidance for this management practice		
Management Practice	**Small and Medium Enterprise-specific Metrics**	
BAI01.06 Monitor, control and report on the program outcomes. Monitor and control performance against plan throughout the full economic life cycle of the investment, covering solution delivery at the program level and value/outcome at the enterprise level. Report performance to the program steering committee and the sponsors.	a. Percent of expected program benefits achieved b. Percent of programs for which performance was monitored and timely remedial action taken when required	
Small and Medium Enterprise-specific Activities		**Capability Level**
1. Update operational I&T portfolios to reflect changes that result from the program in the relevant I&T service, asset or resource portfolios.		3
2. Monitor and control the performance of the overall program and the projects within the program, including contributions of the business and IT to the projects. Report in a timely, complete and accurate fashion. Reporting may include schedule, funding, functionality, user satisfaction, internal controls and acceptance of accountabilities.		4
3. Monitor and control IT services, assets and resources created or changed as a result of the program. Note implementation and in-service dates. Report to management on performance levels, sustained service delivery and contribution to value.		
4. Manage program performance against key criteria (e.g., scope, schedule, quality, benefits realization, costs, risk, velocity), identify deviations from the plan and take timely remedial action when required.		
5. Monitor individual project performance related to delivery of the expected capabilities, schedule, benefits realization, costs, risk or other metric. Identify potential impacts on program performance and take timely remedial action when required.		
6. Identify assurance tasks and practices required to support the accreditation of new or modified systems during program planning and include them in the integrated plans. Design the tasks to provide assurance that internal controls and security/privacy solutions meet the defined requirements.		
Related Guidance (Standards, Frameworks, Compliance Requirements)	**Detailed Reference**	
No related guidance for this management practice		

A. Component: Process *(cont.)*		
Management Practice	**Small and Medium Enterprise-specific Metrics**	
BAI01.07 Manage program quality. Prepare and execute a quality management plan, processes and practices that align with quality management standards. Describe the approach to program quality and implementation. The plan should be formally reviewed and agreed on by all parties concerned and incorporated into the integrated program plan.	a. Percent of program deliverables approved at each gate review	
Small and Medium Enterprise-specific Activities		**Capability Level**
1. To provide quality assurance for the program deliverables, identify ownership and responsibilities, quality review processes, success criteria and performance metrics.		3
2. Provide quality assurance for the program deliverables and identify ownership and responsibilities, quality review processes, success criteria, and performance metrics.		
3. Perform quality assurance and control activities in accordance with the quality management plan and QMS.		4
Related Guidance (Standards, Frameworks, Compliance Requirements)	**Detailed Reference**	
No related guidance for this management practice		
Management Practice	**Small and Medium Enterprise-specific Metrics**	
BAI01.08 Manage program risk. Eliminate or minimize specific risk associated with programs through a systematic process of planning, identifying, analyzing, responding to, monitoring and controlling the areas or events with the potential to cause unwanted change. Define and record any risk faced by program management.	a. Percent of programs without a proper risk assessment	
Small and Medium Enterprise-specific Activities		**Capability Level**
1. Ensure that the risk assessments include identifying, analyzing, responding to, mitigating, monitoring and controlling risk.		3
2. Assign to appropriately skilled personnel the responsibility for executing the risk management process within a program and ensuring that this is incorporated into the solution development practices. Consider allocating this role to an independent team or person, especially if an objective viewpoint is required or a program is considered critical.		
3. Perform the risk assessment of identifying and quantifying risk continuously throughout the program. Manage and communicate risk appropriately within the program governance structure.		
4. Identify owners for actions to avoid, accept or mitigate risk.		
Related Guidance (Standards, Frameworks, Compliance Requirements)	**Detailed Reference**	
No related guidance for this management practice		
Management Practice	**Small and Medium Enterprise-specific Metrics**	
BAI01.09 Close a program. Remove the program from the active investment portfolio when there is agreement that the desired value has been achieved or when it is clear it will not be achieved within the value criteria set for the program.	a. Percent of successfully closed programs that achieved desired value	
Small and Medium Enterprise-specific Activities		**Capability Level**
1. Bring the program to an orderly closure, including formal approval, disbanding of the program organization and supporting function, validation of deliverables, and communication of retirement.		3
2. Review and document lessons learned. Once the program is retired, remove it from the active investment portfolio. Move any resulting capabilities to an operational asset portfolio to ensure that value continues to be created and sustained.		4
3. Put accountability and processes in place to ensure that the enterprise continues to optimize value from the service, asset or resources. Additional investments may be required at some future time to ensure that this occurs.		5
Related Guidance (Standards, Frameworks, Compliance Requirements)	**Detailed Reference**	
National Institute of Standards and Technology Framework for Improving Critical Infrastructure Cybersecurity v1.1, April 2018	RS.IM Improvements	

B. Component: Organizational Structures

Key Management Practice	General Manager	Business Process Owners	Steering Committee (Projects)	Head of IT	IT Development Coordinator	IT Operations Coordinator
BAI01.01 Maintain a standard approach for program management.	A			R		
BAI01.02 Initiate a program.		R	A			
BAI01.03 Manage stakeholder engagement.		R	A			
BAI01.04 Develop and maintain the program plan.			A			
BAI01.05 Launch and execute the program.		R	A	R	R	R
BAI01.06 Monitor, control and report on the program outcomes.			A	R		
BAI01.07 Manage program quality.		R	A		R	
BAI01.08 Manage program risk.		R	A		R	
BAI01.09 Close a program.		R	A	R		

C. Component: Information Flows and Items

Management Practice	Small and Medium Enterprise-specific Inputs		Small and Medium Enterprise-specific Outputs	
	From	Description	Description	To
BAI01.01 Maintain a standard approach for program management.	AP003.04	• Implementation phase descriptions • Architecture governance requirements	Updated program management approaches	Internal
	AP005.04	Updated portfolios of programs, services and assets		
	AP010.04	Identified vendor delivery risk		
	EDM02.03	Requirements for stagegate reviews		
	EDM02.04	Actions to improve value delivery		

C. Component: Information Flows and Items *(cont.)*				
Management Practice	Small and Medium Enterprise-specific Inputs		Small and Medium Enterprise-specific Outputs	
	From	Description	Description	To
BAI01.02 Initiate a program.	APO03.04	• Resource requirements • Implementation phase descriptions	Program mandate and brief	APO05.02
	APO05.02	Program business case	Program concept business case	APO05.02
	APO07.03	Skills and competencies matrix	Program benefit realization plan	APO05.02 APO06.05
	BAI05.02	Common vision and goals		
BAI01.03 Manage stakeholder engagement.	There are no small and medium enterprise-specific inputs for this practice.		Results of stakeholder engagement effectiveness assessments	Internal
			Stakeholder engagement plan	Internal
BAI01.04 Develop and maintain the program plan.	APO05.02	Selected programs with ROI milestones	Program budget and benefits register	APO05.05 APO06.05
	APO07.03	Skills and competencies matrix	Resource requirements and roles	APO07.05 APO07.06
	APO07.05	Inventory of business and IT human resources	Program plan	Internal
	BAI05.02	Implementation team and roles		
	BAI05.03	Vision communication plan		
	BAI05.04	Identified quick wins		
	BAI07.03	Approved acceptance test plan		
	BAI07.05	Approved acceptance and release for production		
BAI01.05 Launch and execute the program.	BAI05.03	Vision communications	Results of program goal achievement monitoring	APO02.04
			Results of benefit realization monitoring	APO05.05 APO06.05
			Program audit plans	MEA04.02

C. Component: Information Flows and Items *(cont.)*				
Management Practice	Small and Medium Enterprise-specific Inputs		Small and Medium Enterprise-specific Outputs	
	From	Description	Description	To
BAI01.06 Monitor, control and report on the program outcomes.	APO05.01	Investment return expectations	Stage-gate review results	APO02.04 APO05.03 EDM02.02
	APO05.02	Business case assessments	Results of program performance reviews	MEA01.03
	APO05.03	Investment portfolio performance reports		
	APO05.05	• Benefit results and related communications • Corrective actions to improve benefit realization		
	APO07.05	• Resourcing shortfall analyses • Resource utilization records		
	BAI05.04	Communication of benefits		
	BAI06.03	Change request status reports		
	BAI07.05	Evaluation of acceptance results		
	EDM02.04	Feedback on portfolio and program performance		
BAI01.07 Manage program quality.	APO11.01	Quality management plans	Quality management plan	BAI02.04 BAI03.06 BAI07.01
	APO11.02	Customer requirements for quality management	Requirements for independent verification of deliverables	BAI07.03
BAI01.08 Manage program risk.	APO12.02	Risk analysis results	Program risk register	Internal
	BAI02.03	• Requirements risk register • Risk mitigation actions	Program risk assessment results	Internal
	Outside COBIT	Enterprise risk management (ERM) framework	Program risk management plan	Internal
BAI01.09 Close a program.	BAI07.08	• Post-implementation review report • Remedial action plan	Communication of program retirement and ongoing accountabilities	APO05.04 APO07.06

D. Component: People, Skills and Competencies		
Skill	**Related Guidance (Standards, Frameworks, Compliance Requirements)**	**Detailed Reference**
Benefits management	Skills Framework for the Information Age V6, 2015	BENM
Business plan development	e-Competence Framework (e-CF)—A common European Framework for ICT Professionals in all industry sectors—Part 1: Framework, 2016	A. Plan—A.3. Business Plan Development
Program management	Skills Framework for the Information Age V6, 2015	PGMG
Project and portfolio management	e-Competence Framework (e-CF)—A common European Framework for ICT Professionals in all industry sectors—Part 1: Framework, 2016	E. Manage—E.2. Project and Portfolio Management

E. Component: Principles, Policies and Procedures	
Relevant Policy	**Policy Description**
Program/project management policy	Guides management of risk related to programs and projects. Details management position and expectation regarding program and project management. Treats accountability, goals and objectives regarding performance, budget, risk analysis, reporting and mitigation of adverse events during program/project execution.

F. Component: Culture, Ethics and Behavior
Key Culture Elements
Ensure the organization understands and supports the value of enterprisewide program management. Establish an enterprisewide culture that supports consistent implementation of program management, taking into account organizational structure and business environment. Ensure the program office has a central view of all programs in the enterprise portfolio.

G. Component: Services, Infrastructure and Applications
Program management tool

Domain: Build, Acquire and Implement Management Objective: BAI02 — Managed Requirements Definition	Focus Area: Small and Medium Enterprises
Description	
Identify solutions and analyze requirements before acquisition or creation to ensure that they align with enterprise strategic requirements covering business processes, applications, information/data, infrastructure and services. Coordinate the review of feasible options with affected stakeholders, including relative costs and benefits, risk analysis, and approval of requirements and proposed solutions.	
Purpose	
Create optimal solutions that meet enterprise needs while minimizing risk.	
Small and Medium Enterprise Focus Area Relevance	
Requirements need to be formalized before selecting or building solutions in order to create solutions that meet enterprise needs. Agile can be incorporated into the requirements definition.	

A. Component: Process		
Management Practice	**Small and Medium Enterprise-specific Metrics**	
BAI02.01 Define and maintain business functional and technical requirements. Based on the business case, identify, prioritize, specify and agree on business information, functional, technical and control requirements covering the scope/understanding of all initiatives required to achieve the expected outcomes of the proposed I&T-enabled business solution.	a. Percent of projects where requirements are validated through approaches such as peer review, model validation or operational prototyping	
Small and Medium Enterprise-specific Activities		**Capability Level**
1. Express business requirements in terms of how the gap between current and desired business capabilities needs to be addressed and how the user (employee, client, etc.) will interact with and use the solution.		2
2. Specify and prioritize information, functional and technical requirements, based on the user experience design and confirmed stakeholder requirements.		
3. Include information control requirements in the business processes, automated processes and I&T environments to address information risk and to comply with laws, regulations and commercial contracts.		3
4. Confirm acceptance of key aspects of the requirements, including enterprise rules, user experience, information controls, business continuity, legal and regulatory compliance, auditability, ergonomics, operability and usability, safety, and supporting documentation.		
5. Validate all requirements through approaches such as peer review, model validation or operational prototyping.		4
Related Guidance (Standards, Frameworks, Compliance Requirements)	**Detailed Reference**	
ISF, The Standard of Good Practice for Information Security 2016	SD2.1 Specifications of Requirements	
ISO/IEC 27002:2013/Cor.2:2015(E)	14.1 Security requirements of information systems	
ITIL V3, 2011	Service Design, 5.1 Requirements engineering	
PMBOK Guide Sixth Edition, 2017	Part 1: 5. Project scope management	
Management Practice	**Small and Medium Enterprise-specific Metrics**	
BAI02.02 Perform a feasibility study and formulate alternative solutions. Perform a feasibility study of potential alternative solutions, assess their viability and select the preferred option. If appropriate, implement the selected option as a pilot to determine possible improvements.	a. Percent of requirements formally accepted for a go/no go decision	
Small and Medium Enterprise-specific Activities		**Capability Level**
1. Identify required actions for solution acquisition or development based on the enterprise architecture and take into account scope, time and/or budget limitations. Carefully consider whether to buy or build. Consider upgrading existing systems, doing nothing or applying manual solutions.		2
2. Review the alternative solutions with all stakeholders and select the most appropriate one based on feasibility criteria, including risk and cost.		
3. Translate the preferred course of action into a high-level acquisition/development plan identifying resources to be used and stages requiring a go/no-go decision.		3
4. Define and execute a feasibility study, pilot or basic working solution that clearly and concisely describes the alternative solutions and measures how these would satisfy the business and functional requirements. Include an evaluation of their technological and economic feasibility.		4
Related Guidance (Standards, Frameworks, Compliance Requirements)	**Detailed Reference**	
No related guidance for this management practice		

A. Component: Process *(cont.)*

Management Practice	Small and Medium Enterprise-specific Metrics
BAI02.03 Manage requirements risk. Identify, document, prioritize and mitigate functional, technical and information processing-related risk associated with the enterprise requirements, assumptions and proposed solution.	a. Percent of requirements risk not covered by an appropriate risk response

Small and Medium Enterprise-specific Activities	Capability Level
1. Identify quality, functional and technical requirements risk (e.g., due to lack of user involvement, unrealistic expectations, developers adding unnecessary functionality, unrealistic assumptions).	3
2. Determine appropriate risk response to requirements risk.	
3. Analyze the identified risk by estimating probability and impact on budget and schedule. Evaluate budgetary impact of appropriate risk response actions.	4

Related Guidance (Standards, Frameworks, Compliance Requirements)	Detailed Reference
No related guidance for this management practice	

Management Practice	Small and Medium Enterprise-specific Metrics
BAI02.04 Obtain approval of requirements and solutions. Coordinate feedback from affected stakeholders. At predetermined key stages, obtain approval and sign-off from the business sponsor or product owner regarding functional and technical requirements, feasibility studies, risk analyses and recommended solutions.	a. Percent of projects in which stakeholders approved the solution in relation to the business case

Small and Medium Enterprise-specific Activities	Capability Level
1. Ensure that the business sponsor or product owner makes the final choice of solution, acquisition approach and high-level design, based on the business case. Obtain necessary approvals from affected stakeholders (e.g., business process owner, IT lead).	3
2. Obtain quality reviews throughout and at the end of each key project stage, iteration or release to assess the results against the original acceptance criteria. Have business sponsors and other stakeholders sign off on each successful quality review.	4

Related Guidance (Standards, Frameworks, Compliance Requirements)	Detailed Reference
No related guidance for this management practice	

B. Component: Organizational Structures

Key Management Practice	Business Process Owners	Steering Committee (Projects)	Project Manager	Head of IT	IT Development Coordinator	IT Operations Coordinator	Privacy Officer
BAI02.01 Define and maintain business functional and technical requirements.	R	A	R		R		R
BAI02.02 Perform a feasibility study and formulate alternative solutions.	R	A	R		R		
BAI02.03 Manage requirements risk.	R	A	R	R	R	R	R
BAI02.04 Obtain approval of requirements and solutions.	R	A	R				R

C. Component: Information Flows and Items				
Management Practice	Small and Medium Enterprise-specific Inputs		Small and Medium Enterprise-specific Outputs	
	From	Description	Description	To
BAI02.01 Define and maintain business functional and technical requirements.	APO01.07	• Data classification guidelines • Data security and control guidelines • Data inventory	Requirements definition repository	BAI03.01 BAI03.02 BAI03.12 BAI04.01 BAI05.01
	APO03.01	Architecture principles and scope	Confirmed acceptance criteria from stakeholders	BAI03.01 BAI03.02 BAI03.12 BAI04.03 BAI05.01 BAI05.02
	APO03.02	Information architecture model	Record of requirement change requests	BAI03.09
	APO10.02	Vendor RFIs and RFPs		
	APO11.02	Acceptance criteria		
	APO14.02	Business glossary		
BAI02.02 Perform a feasibility study and formulate alternative solutions.	APO10.01	Vendor catalog	High-level acquisition/ development plan	APO10.02 BAI03.01
	APO10.02	• Vendor RFIs and RFPs • RFI and RFP evaluations • Decision results of vendor evaluations	Feasibility study report	BAI03.02 BAI03.03 BAI03.12
	APO11.02	Acceptance criteria		
BAI02.03 Manage requirements risk.	BAI02.01	Requirements definition repository	Requirements risk register	BAI03.02 BAI04.01 BAI05.01 BAI11.06
			Risk mitigation actions	BAI03.02 BAI05.01
BAI02.04 Obtain approval of requirements and solutions.	BAI11.05	Project quality management plan	Approved quality reviews	APO11.03
			Sponsor approvals of requirements and proposed solutions	BAI03.02 BAI03.03 BAI03.04

D. Component: People, Skills and Competencies		
Skill	Related Guidance (Standards, Frameworks, Compliance Requirements)	Detailed Reference
Application design	e-Competence Framework (e-CF)—A common European Framework for ICT Professionals in all industry sectors—Part 1: Framework, 2016	A. Plan—A.6. Application Design
Business analysis	Skills Framework for the Information Age V6, 2015	BUAN
Business process improvement	Skills Framework for the Information Age V6, 2015	BPRE
Needs identification	e-Competence Framework (e-CF)—A common European Framework for ICT Professionals in all industry sectors—Part 1: Framework, 2016	D. Enable—D.11. Needs Identification
Requirements definition and management	Skills Framework for the Information Age V6, 2015	REQM
User experience analysis	Skills Framework for the Information Age V6, 2015	UNAN

E. Component: Principles, Policies and Procedures	
Relevant Policy	**Policy Description**
Software development policy	Standardizes software development across the organization by listing all protocols and standards to be followed

F. Component: Culture, Ethics and Behavior
Key Culture Elements
Establish a culture that ensures consistent and robust processes for defining requirements. Ensure that the processes clearly align development requirements with enterprise strategic requirements.

G. Component: Services, Infrastructure and Applications
Requirements definition and documentation tools

Domain: Build, Acquire and Implement Management Objective: BAI03 – Managed Solutions Identification and Build	Focus Area: Small and Medium Enterprises
Description	
Establish and maintain identified products and services (technology, business processes and workflows) in line with enterprise requirements covering design, development, procurement/sourcing and partnering with vendors. Manage configuration, test preparation, testing, requirements management and maintenance of business processes, applications, information/data, infrastructure and services.	
Purpose	
Ensure agile and scalable delivery of digital products and services. Establish timely and cost-effective solutions (technology, business processes and workflows) capable of supporting enterprise strategic and operational objectives.	
Small and Medium Enterprise Focus Area Relevance	
Establish and maintain timely and cost-effective solutions for identified products and services (technology, business processes and workflows) covering design, development, procurement/sourcing and partnering with vendors to support enterprise strategic and operational objectives. Manage configuration, test preparation, testing, requirements management and maintenance of business processes, applications, information/data, infrastructure and services.	

A. Component: Process	
Management Practice	**Small and Medium Enterprise-specific Metrics**
BAI03.01 Design high-level solutions. Develop and document high-level designs for the solution in terms of technology, business processes and workflows. Use agreed and appropriate phased or rapid Agile development techniques. Ensure alignment with the I&T strategy and enterprise architecture. Reassess and update the designs when significant issues occur during detailed design or building phases, or as the solution evolves. Apply a user-centric approach; ensure that stakeholders actively participate in the design and approve each version.	a. Percent of stakeholder participation in the design and approval sign-off of each version

Small and Medium Enterprise-specific Activities	Capability Level
1. Establish a high-level design specification that translates the proposed solution into a high-level design for business processes, supporting services, workflows, applications, infrastructure, and information repositories capable of meeting business and enterprise architecture requirements.	2
2. Involve appropriately qualified and experienced user experience designers and IT specialists in the design process (internal or external resources) to make sure that the design provides a solution that optimally uses the proposed I&T capabilities to enhance the business process.	
3. Create a design authority at a level of detail that is appropriate for the solution and development method. Ensure that it is consistent with business, enterprise and I&T strategies; the enterprise architecture; the security plan; and applicable laws, regulations and contracts.	
4. After quality assurance approval, submit the final high-level design to the project stakeholders and the sponsor/business process owner for approval based on agreed-on criteria. This design will evolve throughout the project as understanding grows.	

Related Guidance (Standards, Frameworks, Compliance Requirements)	Detailed Reference
ISF, The Standard of Good Practice for Information Security 2016	SD2.2 System Design

Management Practice	Small and Medium Enterprise-specific Metrics
BAI03.02 Design detailed solution components. Develop, document and elaborate detailed designs progressively. Use agreed and appropriate phased or rapid Agile development techniques, addressing all components (business processes and related automated and manual controls, supporting I&T applications, infrastructure services and technology products, and partners/suppliers). Ensure that the detailed design includes internal and external service level agreements (SLAs) and operational level agreements (OLAs).	a. Percent of design review deficiencies b. Percent of in-process design changes

A. Component: Process *(cont.)*	
Small and Medium Enterprise-specific Activities	**Capability Level**
1. Progressively design business process activities and workflows that need to be performed in conjunction with the new application system to meet enterprise objectives, including the design of the manual control activities.	2
2. Design the application processing steps, including specification of transaction types and business processing rules, automated controls, data definitions/business objects, use cases, external interfaces, design constraints, and other requirements (e.g., licensing, legal, standards and internationalization/localization).	
3. Classify data inputs and outputs according to enterprise standards. Specify the source data collection design, documenting the data inputs (regardless of source) and validation for processing transactions as well as the methods for validation. Design the identified outputs, including data sources.	
4. Design system/solution interface, including any automated data exchange.	
5. Design data storage, location, retrieval and recoverability.	
6. Design appropriate redundancy, recovery and backup.	
7. Design the interface between the user and the system application so that it is easy to use and self-documenting.	3
8. Consider the impact of the solution's need for infrastructure performance, being sensitive to the number of computing assets, bandwidth intensity and time sensitivity of the information.	
9. Proactively evaluate for design weaknesses (e.g., inconsistencies, lack of clarity, potential flaws) throughout the life cycle, identifying improvements when required.	
10. Provide an ability to audit transactions and identify root causes of processing errors.	4

Related Guidance (Standards, Frameworks, Compliance Requirements)	Detailed Reference
ISF, The Standard of Good Practice for Information Security 2016	SD2.2 System Design

Management Practice	Small and Medium Enterprise-specific Metrics
BAI03.03 Develop solution components. Develop solution components progressively in a separate environment, in accordance with detailed designs following standards and requirements for development and documentation, quality assurance (QA), and approval. Ensure that all control requirements in the business processes, supporting I&T applications and infrastructure services, services and technology products, and partner/vendor services are addressed.	a. Percent of solution exceptions to design noted during stage reviews

Small and Medium Enterprise-specific Activities	Capability Level
1. Develop a detailed design for business processes, supporting services, applications, infrastructure and information repositories within a separate environment.	2
2. When third-party providers are involved with the solution development, ensure that maintenance, support, development standards and licensing are addressed and adhered to in contractual obligations.	
3. Track change requests and design, performance and quality reviews, ensuring active participation of all impacted stakeholders.	
4. Define and enforce basic documentation standards for all solution components and maintain version control over all developed components and associated documentation.	
5. Assess the impact of solution customization and configuration on the performance and efficiency of acquired solutions and on inter-operability with existing applications, operating systems and other infrastructure.	3
6. Adapt business processes as required to leverage the application capability.	
7. Ensure that responsibilities for using high security or restricted access infrastructure components are clearly defined and understood by those who develop and integrate infrastructure components. Monitor and evaluate their use.	4

Related Guidance (Standards, Frameworks, Compliance Requirements)	Detailed Reference
ISF, The Standard of Good Practice for Information Security 2016	SD1.2 System Development Environments
ISO/IEC 27002:2013/Cor.2:2015(E)	14.2 Security in development and support processes
ITIL V3, 2011	Service Strategy, 5.5 IT service strategy and application development
National Institute of Standards and Technology Special Publication 800-53, Revision 5 (Draft), August 2017	3.18 System and services acquisition (SA-3)

A. Component: Process ***(cont.)***

Management Practice	Small and Medium Enterprise-specific Metrics
BAI03.04 Procure solution components. Procure solution components, based on the acquisition plan, in accordance with requirements and detailed designs, architecture principles and standards, and the enterprise's overall procurement and contract procedures, QA requirements, and approval standards. Ensure that all legal and contractual requirements are identified and addressed by the vendor.	a. Percent of suppliers engaged in collaborative design

Small and Medium Enterprise-specific Activities	Capability Level
1. Create and maintain a practical approach and guidance for the acquisition of solution components, considering future flexibility for capacity additions, transition costs, risk and upgrades over the lifetime of the project.	3
2. Review and approve all acquisition proposals considering risk, costs, benefits and technical conformance with enterprise architecture standards.	
3. Assess and document the degree to which acquired solutions require adaptation of business process to leverage the benefits of the acquired solution. Do not inject technology if there is no clear idea about how to improve business processes.	
4. Use a standard selection process when acquiring IT products or services. Invite more than one vendor to bid. Obtain required approval at key decision points during the procurement process.	
5. Record receipt of all infrastructure and software acquisitions in an asset inventory.	4

Related Guidance (Standards, Frameworks, Compliance Requirements)	Detailed Reference
ISF, The Standard of Good Practice for Information Security 2016	SD2.3 Software Acquisition
National Institute of Standards and Technology Framework for Improving Critical Infrastructure Cybersecurity v1.1, April 2018	3.4 Buying Decisions
National Institute of Standards and Technology Special Publication 800-53, Revision 5 (Draft), August 2017	3.18 System and services acquisition (SA-4)

Management Practice	Small and Medium Enterprise-specific Metrics
BAI03.05 Build solutions. Install and configure solutions and integrate with business process activities. During configuration and integration of hardware and infrastructure software, implement control, security, privacy and auditability measures to protect resources and ensure availability and data integrity. Update the product or services catalogue to reflect the new solutions.	a. Gap between estimated and final development effort b. Percent of review defects

Small and Medium Enterprise-specific Activities	Capability Level
1. Integrate and configure business and IT solution components and information repositories in line with detailed specifications and quality requirements. Consider the role of users, business stakeholders and the process owner in the configuration of business processes.	2
2. Complete and update business process and operational manuals, where necessary, to account for any customization or special conditions unique to the implementation.	
3. Consider all relevant information control requirements in solution component integration and configuration, including implementation of business controls, where appropriate, into automated application controls such that processing is accurate, complete, timely, authorized and auditable.	3
4. Configure acquired application software to meet business processing requirements.	
5. Implement audit trails to ensure availability and integrity.	4
6. Consider when the effect of cumulative customizations and configurations (including minor changes that were not subjected to formal design specifications) require a high-level reassessment of the solution and associated functionality.	

Related Guidance (Standards, Frameworks, Compliance Requirements)	Detailed Reference
HITRUST CSF version 9, September 2017	10.05 Security in Development & Support Processes
ISF, The Standard of Good Practice for Information Security 2016	SD2.4 System Build

A. Component: Process *(cont.)*		
Management Practice	**Small and Medium Enterprise-specific Metrics**	
BAI03.06 Perform quality assurance (QA). Develop, resource and execute a QA plan aligned with the QMS to obtain the quality specified in the requirements definition and in the enterprise's quality policies and procedures.	a. Percent of reworked solution designs due to misalignment with requirements	
Small and Medium Enterprise-specific Activities		**Capability Level**
1. Define quality criteria for the solution, as well as how quality will be reviewed (based on solution requirements, enterprise policies, adherence to development methodologies, quality management procedures and acceptance criteria).		3
2. Employ code inspection, test-driven development practices, automated testing, continuous integration, walk-throughs and testing of applications as appropriate. Report on outcomes of the monitoring process and testing to the application software development team and IT management.		4
3. Monitor all quality exceptions and address all corrective actions. Maintain a record of all reviews, results, exceptions and corrections. Repeat quality reviews, where appropriate, based on the amount of rework and corrective action.		
Related Guidance (Standards, Frameworks, Compliance Requirements)	**Detailed Reference**	
ISF, The Standard of Good Practice for Information Security 2016	SD1.3 Quality Assurance	
Management Practice	**Small and Medium Enterprise-specific Metrics**	
BAI03.07 Prepare for solution testing. Establish a test plan and required environments to test the individual and integrated solution components. Include the business processes and supporting services, applications and infrastructure.	a. Percent of business users involved in creating test procedures	
Small and Medium Enterprise-specific Activities		**Capability Level**
1. Create a test environment that supports the full scope of the solution and reflects, as closely as possible, real-world conditions, including the business processes and procedures, range of users, transaction types, and deployment conditions.		2
2. Create test procedures that allow evaluation of the operation of the solution in real-world conditions. Ensure that the test procedures evaluate the adequacy of the solution and the controls and are approved by the sponsor/business process owner and project steering committee.		3
3. Document and save the test procedures and cases for future testing of the application.		4
Related Guidance (Standards, Frameworks, Compliance Requirements)	**Detailed Reference**	
CMMI Cybermaturity Platform, 2018	AD.DE Safeguard Development Environment	
National Institute of Standards and Technology Special Publication 800-53, Revision 5 (Draft), August 2017	3.10 Maintenance (MA-2, MA-3)	
Management Practice	**Small and Medium Enterprise-specific Metrics**	
BAI03.08 Execute solution testing. During development, execute testing continually (including control testing), in accordance with the defined test plan and development practices in the appropriate environment. Engage business process owners and end users in the test team. Identify, log and prioritize errors and issues identified during testing.	a. Number of errors found during testing b. Percent of tests to re-perform due to errors found c. Time and effort to perform tests, compared to total development time and effort	
Small and Medium Enterprise-specific Activities		**Capability Level**
1. Undertake testing of solutions and their components in accordance with the testing procedures. Include testers independent from the solution team, with representative business process owners and end users. Ensure that testing is conducted only within the development and test environments.		2
2. Use clearly defined test instructions, as defined in the test procedures, and consider the appropriate balance between automated scripted tests and interactive user testing.		
3. Identify, log and classify (e.g., minor, significant and mission-critical) errors during testing. Repeat tests until all significant errors have been resolved.		
4. Record testing outcomes and communicate results of testing to the sponsor/business process owner and project steering committee.		
5. Ensure that an audit trail of test results is maintained.		4

A. Component: Process *(cont.)*		
Related Guidance (Standards, Frameworks, Compliance Requirements)		
CMMI Cybermaturity Platform, 2018	AD.ST Secure Development Testing	
ISF, The Standard of Good Practice for Information Security 2016	SD2.5 System Testing; SD2.6 Security Testing	
National Institute of Standards and Technology Special Publication 800-53, Revision 5 (Draft), August 2017	3.18 System and services acquisition (SA-11)	
Management Practice	**Small and Medium Enterprise-specific Metrics**	
BAI03.09 Manage changes to requirements. Track the status of individual requirements (including all rejected requirements) throughout the project life cycle. Manage the approval of changes to requirements.	a. Number of tracked, approved changes that generate new errors b. Percentage of changes requested and made with respect to the initial requirements	
Small and Medium Enterprise-specific Activities		**Capability Level**
1. Assess the impact of all solution change requests on the solution development, the original business case and the budget, and categorize and prioritize them accordingly.		3
2. Track changes to requirements, enabling relevant stakeholders (sponsor/business process owners or project steering committee) to monitor, review and approve the changes.		
3. Ensure that the outcomes of the change process are fully understood and agreed on by the stakeholders.		
4. Apply change requests, maintaining the integrity of integration and configuration of solution components. Assess the impact of any major solution upgrade in terms of cost, benefits and risk involved.		
Related Guidance (Standards, Frameworks, Compliance Requirements)	**Detailed Reference**	
ISF, The Standard of Good Practice for Information Security 2016	SD2.9 Post-implementation Review	
Management Practice	**Small and Medium Enterprise-specific Metrics**	
BAI03.10 Maintain solutions. Develop and execute a plan for the maintenance of solution and infrastructure components. Include periodic reviews against business needs and operational requirements.	a. Percent of demands for maintenance that go unsatisfied	
Small and Medium Enterprise-specific Activities		**Capability Level**
1. Develop and execute a plan for the maintenance of solution components that includes periodic reviews against business needs and operational requirements such as patch management, upgrade strategies, risk, privacy, vulnerabilities assessment and security requirements.		2
2. Assess the significance of a proposed maintenance activity on current solution design, functionality and/or business processes. Consider risk, user impact and resource availability. Ensure that the business process owners understand the effect of designating changes as maintenance.		3
3. In the event of major changes to existing solutions that result in significant change in current designs and/or functionality and/or business processes, follow the development process used for new systems. For maintenance updates, use the change management process.		
4. Ensure that the pattern and volume of maintenance activities are analyzed periodically for abnormal trends indicating underlying quality or performance problems, cost/benefit of major upgrades, or major changes being qualified as maintenance.		4
Related Guidance (Standards, Frameworks, Compliance Requirements)	**Detailed Reference**	
ISO/IEC 27002:2013/Cor.2:2015(E)	14.3 Test data	
Management Practice	**Small and Medium Enterprise-specific Metrics**	
BAI03.11 Define IT products and services and maintain the service portfolio. Define and agree on new or changed IT products or services and service level options. Document new or changed product and service definitions and service level options to be updated in the products and services portfolio.	a. Percent of stakeholders signing off on new IT services b. Percent of new or changed service definitions and service level options documented in the services portfolio	

A. Component: Process *(cont.)*	
Small and Medium Enterprise-specific Activities	**Capability Level**
1. Propose definitions of the new or changed IT products and services to ensure that they are fit for purpose. Document the proposed definitions in the portfolio list of products and services.	3
2. Propose new or changed service level options (service times, user satisfaction, availability, performance, capacity, security, continuity, compliance and usability) to ensure that the IT products and services are fit for use. Document the proposed service options in the portfolio.	
Related Guidance (Standards, Frameworks, Compliance Requirements)	**Detailed Reference**
No related guidance for this management practice	
Management Practice	**Small and Medium Enterprise-specific Metrics**
BAI03.12 Design solutions based on the defined development methodology. Design, develop and implement solutions with the appropriate development methodology (i.e., waterfall, Agile or bimodal I&T), in accordance with the overall strategy and requirements.	a. Percent of solution development projects that apply selected development methodologies
Small and Medium Enterprise-specific Activities	**Capability Level**
1. Analyze and assess the impact of choosing a development methodology (i.e., waterfall, Agile, bimodal) on the available resources and architecture requirements.	3
2. Establish the appropriate development methodology and organizational approach that deliver the proposed solution efficiently and effectively and that are capable of meeting business, architecture and system requirements. Adapt processes to the chosen strategy, as appropriate.	
3. Establish the needed project teams as defined by the chosen development methodology and provide sufficient training.	
Related Guidance (Standards, Frameworks, Compliance Requirements)	**Detailed Reference**
ISF, The Standard of Good Practice for Information Security 2016	SD1.1 System Development Methodology

B. Component: Organizational Structures

Key Management Practice	Business Process Owners	Steering Committee (Projects)	Project Manager	Head of IT	IT Development Coordinator	IT Operations Coordinator	Privacy Officer
BAI03.01 Design high-level solutions.	R	A	R		R		
BAI03.02 Design detailed solution components.	R	A	R		R		
BAI03.03 Develop solution components.	R	A	R		R		
BAI03.04 Procure solution components.	R	A			R	R	
BAI03.05 Build solutions.	R	A	R		R		
BAI03.06 Perform quality assurance (QA).	R	A	R		R		
BAI03.07 Prepare for solution testing.	R	A			R	R	R
BAI03.08 Execute solution testing.	R	A			R	R	R
BAI03.09 Manage changes to requirements.	R	A	R		R		R
BAI03.10 Maintain solutions.	R		R	A	R		R
BAI03.11 Define IT products and services and maintain the service portfolio.				A			R
BAI03.12 Design solutions based on the defined development methodology.			R	A			

C. Component: Information Flows and Items				
Management Practice	Small and Medium Enterprise-specific Inputs		Small and Medium Enterprise-specific Outputs	
	From	Description	Description	To
BAI03.01 Design high-level solutions.	APO03.01	Architecture principles and scope	Approved high-level design specification	BAI04.03 BAI05.01
	APO04.03	Research analyses of innovation possibilities		
	APO04.04	Evaluations of innovation ideas		
	BAI02.01	• Requirements definition repository • Confirmed acceptance criteria from stakeholders		
	BAI02.02	High-level acquisition/ development plan		
BAI03.02 Design detailed solution components.	APO03.01	Architecture principles	Internal and external SLAs	BAI04.02
	APO03.02	• Baseline domain descriptions and architecture definition • Information architecture model	Approved detailed design specification	BAI04.03 BAI05.01
	APO04.06	Assessments of innovative approaches		
	BAI02.01	• Requirements definition repository • Confirmed acceptance criteria from stakeholders		
	BAI02.02	Feasibility study report		
	BAI02.03	• Requirements risk register • Risk mitigation actions		
	BAI02.04	Sponsor approvals of requirements and proposed solutions		
BAI03.03 Develop solution components.	BAI02.02	Feasibility study report	Documented solution components	BAI04.03 BAI05.05 BAI08.02 BAI08.03
	BAI02.04	Sponsor approvals of requirements and proposed solutions		

C. Component: Information Flows and Items *(cont.)*				
Management Practice	**Small and Medium Enterprise-specific Inputs**		**Small and Medium Enterprise-specific Outputs**	
	From	**Description**	**Description**	**To**
BAI03.04 Procure solution components.	BAI02.04	Sponsor approvals of requirements and proposed solutions	Approved acquisition approach	APO10.03
			Updates to asset inventory	BAI09.01
BAI03.05 Build solutions.	There are no small and medium enterprise-specific inputs for this practice.		Integrated and configured solution components	BAI06.01
BAI03.06 Perform quality assurance (QA).	BAI11.05	Project quality management plan	Quality review results, exceptions and corrections	APO11.04
			Quality assurance plan	APO11.04
BAI03.07 Prepare for solution testing.	There are no small and medium enterprise-specific inputs for this practice.		Test procedures	BAI07.03
BAI03.08 Execute solution testing.	There are no small and medium enterprise-specific inputs for this practice.		Test result logs	BAI07.03
BAI03.09 Manage changes to requirements.	APO04.05	Results and recommendations from proof-of-concept initiatives	Record of all approved and applied change requests	BAI06.03
	BAI02.01	Record of requirement change requests		
BAI03.10 Maintain solutions.	There are no small and medium enterprise-specific inputs for this practice.		Maintenance plan	APO08.05
			Updated solution components and related documentation	BAI05.05
BAI03.11 Define IT products and services and maintain the service portfolio.	APO02.04	Gaps and changes required to realize target capability	Updated service portfolio	APO05.04
	APO06.02	Budget allocations	Service definitions	EDM02.01 DSS01.03
	APO06.03	• I&T budget • Budget communications		
	APO08.05	Definition of potential improvement projects		
	BAI10.02	Configuration baseline		
	BAI10.03	Approved changes to baseline		

C. Component: Information Flows and Items *(cont.)*				
Management Practice	Small and Medium Enterprise-specific Inputs		Small and Medium Enterprise-specific Outputs	
	From	Description	Description	To
BAI03.12 Design solutions based on the defined development methodology.	APO07.03	Skills and competencies matrix	There are no small and medium enterprise-specific outputs for this practice.	
	BAI02.01	• Confirmed acceptance criteria from stakeholders • Requirements definition repository		
	BAI02.02	Feasibility study report		
	BAI10.02	Configuration baseline		

D. Component: People, Skills and Competencies		
Skill	Related Guidance (Standards, Frameworks, Compliance Requirements)	Detailed Reference
Application development	e-Competence Framework (e-CF)—A common European Framework for ICT Professionals in all industry sectors—Part 1: Framework, 2016	B. Build—B.1. Application Development
Business process testing	Skills Framework for the Information Age V6, 2015	BPTS
Component integration	e-Competence Framework (e-CF)—A common European Framework for ICT Professionals in all industry sectors—Part 1: Framework, 2016	B. Build—B.2. Component Integration
Database design	Skills Framework for the Information Age V6, 2015	DBDS
Documentation production	e-Competence Framework (e-CF)—A common European Framework for ICT Professionals in all industry sectors—Part 1: Framework, 2016	B. Build—B.5. Documentation Production
Hardware design	Skills Framework for the Information Age V6, 2015	HWDE
Porting/software configuration	Skills Framework for the Information Age V6, 2015	PORT
Programming/software development	Skills Framework for the Information Age V6, 2015	PROG
Release and deployment	Skills Framework for the Information Age V6, 2015	RELM
Solution architecture	Skills Framework for the Information Age V6, 2015	ARCH
Solution deployment	e-Competence Framework (e-CF)—A common European Framework for ICT Professionals in all industry sectors—Part 1: Framework, 2016	B. Build—B.4. Solution Deployment
Systems design	Skills Framework for the Information Age V6, 2015	DESN
Systems development management	Skills Framework for the Information Age V6, 2015	DLMG
Systems engineering	e-Competence Framework (e-CF)—A common European Framework for ICT Professionals in all industry sectors—Part 1: Framework, 2016	B. Build—B.6. Systems Engineering

D. Component: People, Skills and Competencies *(cont.)*		
Skill	**Related Guidance (Standards, Frameworks, Compliance Requirements)**	**Detailed Reference**
Systems installation/ decommissioning	Skills Framework for the Information Age V6, 2015	HSIN
Systems integration	Skills Framework for the Information Age V6, 2015	SINT
Testing	Skills Framework for the Information Age V6, 2015	TEST
Testing	e-Competence Framework (e-CF)—A common European Framework for ICT Professionals in all industry sectors—Part 1: Framework, 2016	B. Build—B.3. Testing
User experience design	Skills Framework for the Information Age V6, 2015	HCEV

E. Component: Principles, Policies and Procedures	
Relevant Policy	**Policy Description**
There are no small and medium enterprise-specific principles, policies and procedures for this objective.	

F. Component: Culture, Ethics and Behavior
Key Culture Elements
Establish an open, unbiased culture that fairly and objectively evaluates alternatives when investigating potential new solutions (including whether to build or buy).

G. Component: Services, Infrastructure and Applications
• Digital factory services, separating "fast IT" (the digital factory responsible for developing digital applications) from legacy core IT • Solution evaluation and selection services • Testing tools and services

Domain: Build, Acquire and Implement Management Objective: BAI04 — Managed Availability and Capacity	Focus Area: Small and Medium Enterprises
Description	
Balance current and future needs for availability, performance and capacity with cost-effective service provision. Include assessment of current capabilities, forecasting of future needs based on business requirements, analysis of business impacts, and assessment of risk to plan and implement actions to meet the identified requirements.	
Purpose	
Maintain service availability, efficient management of resources and optimization of system performance through prediction of future performance and capacity requirements.	
Small and Medium Enterprise Focus Area Relevance	
The description and purpose of this COBIT objective is fully applicable to SMEs. No SME-specific focus area relevance statement is required.	

A. Component: Process		
Management Practice	**Small and Medium Enterprise-specific Metrics**	
BAI04.01 Assess current availability, performance and capacity and create a baseline. Assess availability, performance and capacity of services and resources to ensure that cost-justifiable capacity and performance are available to support business needs and deliver against service level agreements (SLAs). Create availability, performance and capacity baselines for future comparison.	a. Percent of actual capacity usage b. Percent of actual availability levels c. Percent of actual performance levels	
Small and Medium Enterprise-specific Activities		**Capability Level**
1. Consider the following (current and forecasted) in the assessment of availability and capacity of services and resources: customer requirements, business priorities, business objectives, budget impact, resource utilization, IT capabilities and industry trends.		2
2. Identify and follow up on all incidents caused by inadequate performance or capacity.		3
3. Monitor actual performance and capacity usage against defined thresholds, supported where necessary with automated software.		4
4. Regularly evaluate the current levels of performance against SLAs.		
Related Guidance (Standards, Frameworks, Compliance Requirements)	**Detailed Reference**	
CMMI Cybermaturity Platform, 2018	DP.CP Capacity Planning	
ISF, The Standard of Good Practice for Information Security 2016	SY2.2 Performance and Capacity Management	
ISO/IEC 20000-1:2011(E)	6.5 Capacity management	
ITIL V3, 2011	Service Design, 4.4 Availability Management; 4.5 Capacity Management	
National Institute of Standards and Technology Special Publication 800-53, Revision 5 (Draft), August 2017	3.14 Planning (PL-10, PL-11)	
Management Practice	**Small and Medium Enterprise-specific Metrics**	
BAI04.02 Assess business impact. Identify important services to the enterprise. Map services and resources to business processes and identify business dependencies. Ensure that the impact of unavailable resources is fully agreed on and accepted by the customer. For vital business functions, ensure that availability requirements can be satisfied per service level agreement (SLA).	a. Percent of critical solutions and services assessed b. Percent of business process owners signing off on analysis results	

Build, Acquire and Implement

A. Component: Process *(cont.)*

Small and Medium Enterprise-specific Activities	Capability Level
1. Identify solutions or services that are critical in the availability and capacity management process.	2
2. Map the selected solutions or services to application(s) and infrastructure (IT and facility) on which they depend to enable a focus on critical resources for availability planning.	3
3. Create scenarios based on the collected data, describing future availability situations to illustrate a variety of potential capacity levels needed to achieve the availability performance objective.	4
4. Determine the impact of the scenarios on the business performance measures (e.g., revenue, profit, customer services) together with business process owners.	
5. Ensure that business process owners fully understand and agree to the results of this analysis. From the business owners, obtain a list of unacceptable risk scenarios that require a response to reduce risk to acceptable levels.	

Related Guidance (Standards, Frameworks, Compliance Requirements)	Detailed Reference
ISO/IEC 20000-1:2011(E)	6.3 Service continuity and availability management

Management Practice	Small and Medium Enterprise-specific Metrics
BAI04.03 Plan for new or changed service requirements. Plan and prioritize availability, performance and capacity implications of changing business needs and service requirements.	a. Percent of comparisons executed of actual demand on resources against forecasted supply and demand

Small and Medium Enterprise-specific Activities	Capability Level
1. Identify availability and capacity implications of changing business needs and improvement opportunities.	3
2. Perform comparisons of actual demand on resources against forecasted supply and demand to evaluate current forecasting techniques and make improvements where possible.	4
3. Prioritize needed improvements and create cost-justifiable availability and capacity plans.	5
4. Adjust the performance and capacity plans and SLAs based on realistic, new, proposed and/or projected business processes and supporting services, applications and infrastructure changes as well as reviews of actual performance and capacity usage, including workload levels.	

Related Guidance (Standards, Frameworks, Compliance Requirements)	Detailed Reference
ISO/IEC 20000-1:2011(E)	5. Design and transition of new changed services

Management Practice	Small and Medium Enterprise-specific Metrics
BAI04.04 Monitor and review availability and capacity. Monitor, measure, analyze, report and review availability, performance and capacity. Identify deviations from established baselines. Review trend analysis reports identifying any significant issues and variances. Initiate actions where necessary and ensure that all outstanding issues are addressed.	a. Number of events in which capacity has exceeded planned limits b. Percent of transaction peaks exceeding target performance

Small and Medium Enterprise-specific Activities	Capability Level
1. Monitor availability, performance and capacity workload on all information-related resources (people, applications, infrastructure).	3
2. Provide regular reporting of the results in an appropriate form for review by IT and business management and escalation to enterprise management when relevant.	4

Related Guidance (Standards, Frameworks, Compliance Requirements)	Detailed Reference
No related guidance for this management practice	

A. Component: Process *(cont.)*	
Management Practice	**Small and Medium Enterprise-specific Metrics**
BAI04.05 Investigate and address availability, performance and capacity issues. Address deviations by investigating and resolving identified availability, performance and capacity issues.	a. Percent of incidents caused by availability issues b. Percent of availability incidents solved by corrective actions

Small and Medium Enterprise-specific Activities	Capability Level
1. Obtain guidance from vendor product manuals to ensure an appropriate level of performance availability for peak processing and workloads.	3
2. Define an escalation procedure for swift resolution in case of emergency capacity and performance problems.	
3. Identify performance and capacity gaps based on monitoring current and forecasted performance.	4
4. Define corrective actions (e.g., shifting workload, prioritizing tasks or adding resources) when performance and capacity issues are identified.	5

Related Guidance (Standards, Frameworks, Compliance Requirements)	Detailed Reference
No related guidance for this management practice	

B. Component: Organizational Structures Key Management Practice	Executive Committee	Business Process Owners	Head of IT	IT Operations Coordinator
BAI04.01 Assess current availability, performance and capacity and create a baseline.		R	A	R
BAI04.02 Assess business impact.	A	R	R	R
BAI04.03 Plan for new or changed service requirements.		R	A	R
BAI04.04 Monitor and review availability and capacity.	A	R	R	R
BAI04.05 Investigate and address availability, performance and capacity issues.		R	A	R

C. Component: Information Flows and Items				
Management Practice	**Small and Medium Enterprise-specific Inputs**		**Small and Medium Enterprise-specific Outputs**	
	From	**Description**	**Description**	**To**
BAI04.01 Assess current availability, performance and capacity and create a baseline.	BAI02.01	Requirements definition repository	Evaluations against SLAs	APO09.05
	BAI02.03	Requirements risk register	Availability, performance and capacity baselines	Internal
BAI04.02 Assess business impact.	BAI03.02	Internal and external SLAs	Availability, performance and capacity business impact assessments	Internal
			Availability, performance and capacity scenarios	
BAI04.03 Plan for new or changed service requirements.	BAI02.01	Confirmed acceptance criteria from stakeholders	Performance and capacity plans	APO02.02
	BAI03.01	Approved high-level design specification	Prioritized improvements	APO02.02
	BAI03.02	Approved detailed design specification		
	BAI03.03	Documented solution components		

C. Component: Information Flows and Items *(cont.)*				
Management Practice	Small and Medium Enterprise-specific Inputs		Small and Medium Enterprise-specific Outputs	
	From	Description	Description	To
BAI04.04 Monitor and review availability and capacity.	There are no small and medium enterprise-specific inputs for this practice.		Availability, performance and capacity monitoring review reports	MEA01.03
BAI04.05 Investigate and address availability, performance and capacity issues.	There are no small and medium enterprise-specific inputs for this practice.		Corrective actions	APO02.02
			Emergency escalation procedure	DSS02.02
			Performance and capacity gaps	Internal

D. Component: People, Skills and Competencies		
Skill	Related Guidance (Standards, Frameworks, Compliance Requirements)	Detailed Reference
Availability management	Skills Framework for the Information Age V6, 2015	AVMT
Capacity management	Skills Framework for the Information Age V6, 2015	CPMG

E. Component: Principles, Policies and Procedures	
Relevant Policy	Policy Description
Availability management policy	Informs infrastructure planning in terms of availability, scalability, reliability and potential resilience. Includes guidelines to identify bandwidth, capacity and availability of services (prior to design and provisioning); establish SLAs; and implement continuous monitoring of circuits, traffic and response times.

F. Component: Culture, Ethics and Behavior
Key Culture Elements
For information-dependent enterprises, availability and capacity management are critical to successful operations. Establish a culture in which product and service availability and capacity are prioritized (in line with business requirements) and supported by processes and behaviors that not only identify required availability and capacity before design, but also consider them in provisioning. Consistently define SMART SLAs; continuously monitor circuits, traffic and response times. Perform regular testing of infrastructure for business continuity and disaster recovery.

G. Component: Services, Infrastructure and Applications
• Capacity planning tools • Provisioning services and tools • Service level monitoring tools

Domain: Build, Acquire and Implement Management Objective: BAI05 — Managed Organizational Change	Focus Area: Small and Medium Enterprises
Description	
Maximize the likelihood of successfully implementing sustainable enterprisewide organizational change quickly and with reduced risk. Cover the complete life cycle of the change and all affected stakeholders in the business and IT.	
Purpose	
Prepare and commit stakeholders for business change and reduce the risk of failure.	
Small and Medium Enterprise Focus Area Relevance	
Prepare the business for changes through implementation of new or planned change solutions. In general, the metrics defined for the practices can be used as attention points, but should not be included in key performance indicator (KPI) reporting because of their subjective character.	

A. Component: Process		
Management Practice	**Small and Medium Enterprise-specific Metrics**	
BAI05.01 Establish the desire to change. Understand the scope and impact of the desired change. Assess stakeholder readiness and willingness to change. Identify actions that will motivate stakeholder acceptance and participation to make the change work successfully.	a. Level of senior management involvement b. Level of stakeholder desire for the change	
Small and Medium Enterprise-specific Activities		**Capability Level**
1. Assess the scope and impact of the envisioned change, the various stakeholders who are affected, the nature of the impact on and involvement required from each stakeholder group, and the current readiness and ability to adopt the change.		2
2. Identify, leverage and communicate current pain points, negative events, risk, customer dissatisfaction and business problems, as well as initial benefits, future opportunities and rewards, and competitor advantages, as a foundation for establishing the desire to change.		
3. Issue key communications from the executive committee or CEO to demonstrate the commitment to the change.		
Related Guidance (Standards, Frameworks, Compliance Requirements)	**Detailed Reference**	
PROSCI® 3-Phase Change Management Process	Phase 1. Preparing for change—Define your change management strategy	
Management Practice	**Small and Medium Enterprise-specific Metrics**	
BAI05.02 Form an effective implementation team. Establish an effective implementation team by assembling appropriate members, creating trust, and establishing common goals and effectiveness measures.	a. Stakeholder satisfaction ratings of implementation team	
Small and Medium Enterprise-specific Activities		**Capability Level**
1. Identify and assemble an effective core implementation team. It should include appropriate members from business and IT who have the capacity to spend the required amount of time and can contribute knowledge and expertise, experience, credibility, and authority. Consider including external parties such as consultants to provide an independent view or to address skill gaps. Identify potential change agents within different parts of the enterprise with whom the core team can work to support the vision and cascade changes down.		3
2. Develop a common vision and goals that support enterprise objectives.		
Related Guidance (Standards, Frameworks, Compliance Requirements)	**Detailed Reference**	
PROSCI® 3-Phase Change Management Process	Phase 1. Preparing for change—Prepare your change management team	

A. Component: Process *(cont.)*

Management Practice	Small and Medium Enterprise-specific Metrics
BAI05.03 Communicate desired vision. Communicate the desired vision for the change in the language of those affected by it. The communication should be made by senior management and include the rationale for, and benefits of, the change; the impacts of not making the change; and the vision, the road map and the involvement required of the various stakeholders.	a. Number of questions pertaining to the change b. Stakeholder feedback on level of understanding of the change

Small and Medium Enterprise-specific Activities	Capability Level
1. Create a change story to explain why the change is needed, what happens if no action is taken, how the change affects different stakeholders, and how the teams can help.	2
2. Develop a vision communication plan to address the core audience groups, their behavioral profiles and information requirements, communication channels, and principles.	3
3. Deliver the communication at appropriate levels of the enterprise in accordance with the plan.	
4. Make all levels of leadership accountable for demonstrating the vision.	
5. Check understanding of the desired vision and respond to any issues highlighted by staff.	4

Related Guidance (Standards, Frameworks, Compliance Requirements)	Detailed Reference
No related guidance for this management practice	

Management Practice	Small and Medium Enterprise-specific Metrics
BAI05.04 Empower role players and identify short-term wins. Empower those with implementation roles by assigning accountability. Provide training and align organizational structures and HR processes. Identify and communicate short-term wins that are important from a change-enablement perspective.	a. Percent of quick wins identified and communicated

Small and Medium Enterprise-specific Activities	Capability Level
1. Identify, prioritize and deliver opportunities for quick wins. These could be related to current known areas of difficulty or external factors that need to be addressed urgently.	2
2. Leverage delivered quick wins by communicating the benefits to those impacted to show the vision is on track. Fine-tune the vision, keep leaders on board and build momentum.	
3. Identify and manage stakeholders who continue to resist needed change.	3

Related Guidance (Standards, Frameworks, Compliance Requirements)	Detailed Reference
No related guidance for this management practice	

Management Practice	Small and Medium Enterprise-specific Metrics
BAI05.05 Enable operation and use. Plan and implement all technical, operational and usage aspects so all those who are involved in the future state environment can exercise their responsibility.	a. Level of detail of operation and use plan

Small and Medium Enterprise-specific Activities	Capability Level
1. Develop a plan for operation and use of the change that communicates and builds on realized quick wins. Ensure that the plan covers a holistic view of the change and provides documentation (e.g., procedures), mentoring, training, coaching, knowledge transfer, enhanced immediate post-go-live support and ongoing support.	3
2. Implement the operation and use plan. Define and track success measures, including hard business measures and perception measures that indicate how people feel about a change, taking remedial action as necessary.	4

Related Guidance (Standards, Frameworks, Compliance Requirements)	Detailed Reference
PROSCI® 3-Phase Change Management Process	Phase 2. Managing change

A. Component: Process *(cont.)*		
Management Practice	**Small and Medium Enterprise-specific Metrics**	
BAI05.06 Embed new approaches. Embed new approaches by tracking implemented changes, assessing the effectiveness of the operation and use plan, and sustaining ongoing awareness through regular communication. Take corrective measures as appropriate (which may include enforcing compliance).	a. Level of user satisfaction with adoption of the change	
Small and Medium Enterprise-specific Activities		**Capability Level**
1. Make process owners accountable for normal day-to-day operations.		2
2. Celebrate successes and implement reward and recognition programs to reinforce the change.		3
3. Provide ongoing awareness through regular communication of the change and its adoption.		
4. Use performance measurement systems to identify root causes for low adoption and take corrective action.		4
Related Guidance (Standards, Frameworks, Compliance Requirements)	**Detailed Reference**	
PROSCI® 3-Phase Change Management Process	Phase 3. Reinforcing change	
Management Practice	**Small and Medium Enterprise-specific Metrics**	
BAI05.07 Sustain changes. Sustain changes through effective training of new staff, ongoing communication campaigns, continued commitment of top management, monitoring of adoption and sharing of lessons learned across the enterprise.	a. Percent of trainings and knowledge transfers performed on an ongoing basis	
Small and Medium Enterprise-specific Activities		**Capability Level**
1. Sustain and reinforce the change through regular communication demonstrating top management commitment.		2
2. Provide mentoring, training, coaching and knowledge transfer to new staff to sustain the change.		3
3. Perform periodic reviews of the operation and use of the change and identify improvements.		4
4. Capture lessons learned relating to implementation of the change and share knowledge across the enterprise.		5
Related Guidance (Standards, Frameworks, Compliance Requirements)	**Detailed Reference**	
PROSCI® 3-Phase Change Management Process	Phase 3. Reinforcing change	

B. Component: Organizational Structures

Key Management Practice	Executive Committee	General Manager	Operations Manager	Head Human Resources	Business Process Owners	Project Manager	Head of IT	IT Development Coordinator	IT Operations Coordinator
BAI05.01 Establish the desire to change.	R	A		R	R	R	R		
BAI05.02 Form an effective implementation team.					A	R	R	R	
BAI05.03 Communicate desired vision.					A	R	R		
BAI05.04 Empower role players and identify short-term wins.				R	A	R	R		
BAI05.05 Enable operation and use.			R		A		R	R	R
BAI05.06 Embed new approaches.			R		A		R	R	R
BAI05.07 Sustain changes.			R		A	R	R	R	R

C. Component: Information Flows and Items				
Management Practice	Small and Medium Enterprise-specific Inputs		Small and Medium Enterprise-specific Outputs	
BAI05.01 Establish the desire to change.	From	Description	Description	To
	APO11.02	Results of quality of service, including customer feedback	Communications from executive management committing to change	Internal
	BAI02.01	• Requirements definition repository • Confirmed acceptance criteria from stakeholders		
	BAI02.03	• Requirements risk register • Risk mitigation actions		
	BAI03.01	Approved high-level design specification		
	BAI03.02	Approved detailed design specification		
BAI05.02 Form an effective implementation team.	BAI02.01	Confirmed acceptance criteria from stakeholders	Implementation team and roles	BAI11.02
BAI05.03 Communicate desired vision.	There are no small and medium enterprise-specific inputs for this practice.		Vision communications	BAI01.05
BAI05.04 Empower role players and identify short-term wins.	Outside COBIT	Enterprise organizational structure	Communication of benefits	BAI01.06
BAI05.05 Enable operation and use.	BAI03.03	Documented solution components	Operation and use plan	APO08.04 BAI08.03 DSS01.01 DSS01.02 DSS06.02
	BAI03.10	Updated solution components and related documentation	Success measures and results	APO08.05 BAI07.07 BAI07.08 MEA01.03
BAI05.06 Embed new approaches.	There are no small and medium enterprise-specific inputs for this practice.		HR performance review results	APO07.04
			Awareness communications	Internal
BAI05.07 Sustain changes.	There are no small and medium enterprise-specific inputs for this practice.		Knowledge transfer plans	BAI08.02 BAI08.03

D. Component: People, Skills and Competencies		
Skill	Related Guidance (Standards, Frameworks, Compliance Requirements)	Detailed Reference
Business change management	e-Competence Framework (e-CF)—A common European Framework for ICT Professionals in all industry sectors—Part 1: Framework, 2016	E. Manage—E.7. Business Change Management
Change implementation planning and management	Skills Framework for the Information Age V6, 2015	CIPM
Organization design and implementation	Skills Framework for the Information Age V6, 2015	ORDI

E. Component: Principles, Policies and Procedures	
Relevant Policy	**Policy Description**
Organizational change management policy	Provides framework and outlines principles for managing organizational change. Reflects current legislation and provides good people-management practices; ensures consistent approach to managing change across the organization.

F. Component: Culture, Ethics and Behavior
Key Culture Elements
Realizing value from I&T-enabled investments requires more than delivering I&T solutions and services. It also requires changes to business processes, skills and competencies, culture and behavior, etc., all of which must be included in the business case for the investment. Leadership must create a culture of continuous change through flexibility, openness and confidence and establish appropriate change management support and communication.

G. Component: Services, Infrastructure and Applications
• Communication tools and channels • Surveying tools

Page intentionally left blank

Domain: Build, Acquire and Implement Management Objective: BAI06 — Managed IT Changes	Focus Area: Small and Medium Enterprises
Description	
Manage all changes in a controlled manner, including standard changes and emergency maintenance relating to business processes, applications and infrastructure. This includes change standards and procedures, impact assessment, prioritization and authorization, emergency changes, tracking, reporting, closure, and documentation.	
Purpose	
Enable fast and reliable delivery of change to the business. Mitigate the risk of negatively impacting the stability or integrity of the changed environment.	
Small and Medium Enterprise Focus Area Relevance	
The description and purpose of this COBIT objective is fully applicable to SMEs. No SME-specific focus area relevance statement is required.	

A. Component: Process	
Management Practice	**Small and Medium Enterprise-specific Metrics**
BAI06.01 Evaluate, prioritize and authorize change requests. Evaluate all requests for change to determine the impact on business processes and I&T services, and to assess whether change will adversely affect the operational environment and introduce unacceptable risk. Ensure that changes are logged, prioritized, categorized, assessed, authorized, planned and scheduled.	a. Percent of standard changes defined for each category b. Amount of rework caused by failed changes

Small and Medium Enterprise-specific Activities	Capability Level
1. Define a clear change management process to enable business and IT people to request changes to business process, infrastructure, systems or applications. Make sure that all such changes arise only through this process.	2
2. Identify standard changes by category (business process, infrastructure, operating systems, networks, all application systems, and if relevant, purchased/packaged application software).	
3. Prioritize all requested changes based on business and technical requirements; resources required; and legal, regulatory and contractual reasons for the requested change.	
4. Formally approve each change by business and IT stakeholders, as appropriate. Changes that are low-risk and relatively frequent should be pre-approved as standard changes.	
5. Plan and schedule all approved changes.	
6. Evaluate requests in a structured way. Include an impact analysis on business process, infrastructure, systems and applications, business continuity plans (BCPs), and service providers to ensure that all affected components have been identified. Assess the likelihood of adversely affecting the operational environment and the risk associated with implementing the change. Consider security, legal, contractual and compliance implications of the requested change. Consider also interdependencies among changes. Involve business in the assessment process, as appropriate.	3
7. Consider the impact of contracted services providers (e.g., of outsourced business processing, infrastructure, application development and shared services) on the change management process, including integration of the enterprise's organizational change management process with the change management processes of service providers and the impact on contractual terms and SLAs.	

Related Guidance (Standards, Frameworks, Compliance Requirements)	Detailed Reference
ISF, The Standard of Good Practice for Information Security 2016	SY2.4 Change Management
ISO/IEC 20000-1:2011(E)	9.2 Change management
ITIL V3, 2011	Service Transition, 4.2 Change Management
PMBOK Guide Sixth Edition, 2017	Part 1: 4.6 Perform Integrated Change Control

A. Component: Process *(cont.)*		
Management Practice	**Small and Medium Enterprise-specific Metrics**	
BAI06.02 Manage emergency changes. Carefully manage emergency changes to minimize further incidents. Ensure the emergency change is controlled and takes place securely. Verify that emergency changes are appropriately assessed and authorized after the change.	a. Percent of emergency changes not authorized after the incident b. Percent of total changes that are emergency fixes	
Small and Medium Enterprise-specific Activities		**Capability Level**
1. Define the conditions for launching an emergency change.		2
2. Integrate in the change management process the procedures for declaring, assessing and providing preliminary approval; for authorizing the emergency change; and for recording the emergency change.		
3. Verify that all emergency access arrangements for changes are appropriately authorized, documented and revoked after the change has been applied.		3
4. Monitor all emergency changes and conduct post-implementation reviews involving all concerned parties. The review should consider and initiate corrective actions based on root causes such as problems with business process, application system development and maintenance, development and test environments, documentation and manuals, and data integrity.		4
Related Guidance (Standards, Frameworks, Compliance Requirements)	**Detailed Reference**	
No related guidance for this management practice		
Management Practice	**Small and Medium Enterprise-specific Metrics**	
BAI06.03 Track and report change status. Maintain a tracking and reporting system to document rejected changes and communicate the status of approved, in-process and complete changes. Make certain that approved changes are implemented as planned.	a. Number and age of backlogged change requests	
Small and Medium Enterprise-specific Activities		**Capability Level**
1. Categorize change requests in the tracking process (e.g., rejected, approved but not yet initiated, approved and in process, and closed).		4
2. Monitor open changes to ensure that all approved changes are closed in a timely fashion, depending on priority.		
Related Guidance (Standards, Frameworks, Compliance Requirements)	**Detailed Reference**	
CMMI Cybermaturity Platform, 2018	IP.CC Apply Change Control	
Management Practice	**Small and Medium Enterprise-specific Metrics**	
BAI06.04 Close and document the changes. Whenever changes are implemented, update the solution, user documentation and procedures affected by the change.	a. Percent of errors found during the reviews of the related updates b. Percent of updates performed within a predefined time schedule	
Small and Medium Enterprise-specific Activities		**Capability Level**
1. Include changes into the documentation (e.g., business and IT operational procedures, configuration information, application documentation, help screens, and training materials).		2
2. Review modified documentation related to the change.		3
Related Guidance (Standards, Frameworks, Compliance Requirements)	**Detailed Reference**	
No related guidance for this management practice		

B. Component: Organizational Structures

Key Management Practice	Business Process Owners	Project Manager	Head of IT	Security Expert	IT Development Coordinator	IT Operations Coordinator	Privacy Officer
BAI06.01 Evaluate, prioritize and authorize change requests.	R		A	R	R	R	R
BAI06.02 Manage emergency changes.			A		R	R	R
BAI06.03 Track and report change status.	R	R	A		R	R	
BAI06.04 Close and document the changes.	R	R	A		R	R	

C. Component: Information Flows and Items

Management Practice	Small and Medium Enterprise-specific Inputs		Small and Medium Enterprise-specific Outputs	
	From	Description	Description	To
BAI06.01 Evaluate, prioritize and authorize change requests.	BAI03.05	Integrated and configured solution components	Change plan and schedule	BAI07.01
	DSS02.03	Approved service requests	Approved requests for change	BAI07.01
	DSS03.03	Proposed solutions to known errors	Impact assessments	Internal
	DSS03.05	Identified sustainable solutions		
	DSS04.08	Approved changes to the plans		
	DSS06.01	Root cause analyses and recommendations		
BAI06.02 Manage emergency changes.	There are no small and medium enterprise-specific inputs for this practice.		Post-implementation review of emergency changes	Internal
BAI06.03 Track and report change status.	BAI03.09	Record of all approved and applied change requests	Change request status reports	BAI10.03
BAI06.04 Close and document the changes.	There are no small and medium enterprise-specific inputs for this practice.		Change documentation	Internal

D. Component: People, Skills and Competencies

Skill	Related Guidance (Standards, Frameworks, Compliance Requirements)	Detailed Reference
Change management	Skills Framework for the Information Age V6, 2015	CHMG
Change support	e-Competence Framework (e-CF) - A common European Framework for ICT Professionals in all industry sectors - Part 1: Framework, 2016	C. Run - C.2. Change Support

E. Component: Principles, Policies and Procedures	
Relevant Policy	**Policy Description**
There are no small and medium enterprise-specific principles, policies and procedures for this objective.	

F. Component: Culture, Ethics and Behavior
Key Culture Elements
Leaders must create a culture of continuous improvement in IT solutions and services, recognizing that improvement requires them to understand the impact of technology change on the enterprise, its inherent risk and associated mitigation, and its cost. Leaders must balance the impact of change against its expected benefits and contribution to I&T strategy and enterprise objectives.

G. Component: Services, Infrastructure and Applications
• Configuration management tools • IT change management tools

Domain: Build, Acquire and Implement Management Objective: BAI07 — Managed IT Change Acceptance and Transitioning	Focus Area: Small and Medium Enterprises
Description	
Formally accept and make operational new solutions. Include implementation planning, system and data conversion, acceptance testing, communication, release preparation, promotion to production of new or changed business processes and I&T services, early production support, and a post-implementation review.	
Purpose	
Implement solutions safely and in line with the agreed expectations and outcomes.	
Small and Medium Enterprise Focus Area Relevance	
Adequate change acceptance and clear transition of responsibility post-development are crucial for successful change implementations. The implementation plan should minimally include a checklist of defined controls to be executed before implementing each change to ensure that the solutions are implemented safely and are in line with the agreed expectations and outcomes.	

A. Component: Process		
Management Practice	**Small and Medium Enterprise-specific Metrics**	
BAI07.01 Establish an implementation plan. Establish an implementation plan that covers system and data conversion, acceptance testing criteria, communication, training, release preparation, promotion to production, early production support, a fallback/back-up plan, and a post-implementation review. Obtain approval from relevant parties.	a. Number and percent of changes for which the checklist is completed b. Percent of components implemented as per plan	
Small and Medium Enterprise-specific Activities		**Capability Level**
1. Create a checklist that covers the sequence of implementation steps, resource requirements, interdependencies, criteria for management acceptance of the production implementation, installation verification requirements, transition activities for production support, and review of the need for updating business continuity plans.		2
2. Obtain commitment from external solution providers regarding their involvement in each step of the implementation.		
3. Identify and document the fallback and recovery processes.		
4. Confirm that the implementation steps are executed by technical and business stakeholders, as appropriate.		3
5. Formally review the technical and business risk associated with implementation and ensure that the key risk is considered and addressed in the planning process.		
Related Guidance (Standards, Frameworks, Compliance Requirements)	**Detailed Reference**	
ITIL V3, 2011	Service Transition, 4.1 Transition Planning and Support	

Build, Acquire and Implement

A. Component: Process *(cont.)*

Management Practice	Small and Medium Enterprise-specific Metrics
BAI07.02 Plan business process, system and data conversion. Prepare for business process, I&T service data and infrastructure migration as part of the enterprise's development methods. Include audit trails and a recovery plan should the migration fail.	a. Percent of successful conversions

Small and Medium Enterprise-specific Activities	Capability Level
1. Define a migration plan related to business processes, IT service data and infrastructure. In the development of the plan, consider, e.g., hardware, networks, operating systems, software, transaction data, master files, backups and archives, interfaces with other systems (both internal and external), possible compliance requirements, business procedures, and system documentation.	2
2. Consider all necessary adjustments to procedures, including revised roles and responsibilities and control procedures.	
3. Confirm that the data conversion plan does not require changes in data values unless absolutely necessary for business reasons. Document changes made to data values and obtain approval from the business process data owner.	
4. Plan retention of backup and archived data to conform to business needs and regulatory or compliance requirements.	
5. Rehearse and test the conversion before attempting a live conversion.	
6. Coordinate and verify the timing and completeness of the conversion cutover to guarantee a smooth, continuous transition with no loss of transaction data. Where necessary, in the absence of any other alternative, freeze live operations.	
7. Plan to back up all systems and data taken at the point prior to conversion. If possible, maintain audit trails to enable the conversion to be retraced and ensure that there is a recovery plan for rollback of migration and fallback to previous processing, should the migration fail.	
8. Incorporate in the data conversion plan methods for collecting, converting and verifying data to be converted, and identifying and resolving any errors found during conversion. Include comparing the original and converted data for completeness and integrity.	3
9. Consider the risk of conversion problems, business continuity planning, and fallback procedures in the business process, data and infrastructure migration plan where there are risk management, business needs or regulatory/compliance requirements.	

Related Guidance (Standards, Frameworks, Compliance Requirements)	Detailed Reference
ITIL V3, 2011	Service Transition, 4.1 Transition Planning and Support

Management Practice	Small and Medium Enterprise-specific Metrics
BAI07.03 Plan acceptance tests. Establish a test plan based on enterprisewide standards that define roles, responsibilities, and entry and exit criteria. Ensure that the plan is approved by relevant parties.	a. Number of documented test plans that include all testing phases and robust testing scenarios and are appropriate to the operational requirements and environment

A. Component: Process *(cont.)*	
Small and Medium Enterprise-specific Activities	**Capability Level**
1. Develop and document the test plan. Communicate and consult with appropriate business and IT stakeholders.	2
2. Ensure that the test plan reflects an assessment of risk from the project and that all functional and technical requirements are tested. Based on assessment of the risk of system failure and faults on implementation, ensure that the plan includes requirements for performance, stress, usability, pilot, security testing and privacy.	
3. Ensure that the test plan addresses the potential need for internal or external accreditation of outcomes of the test process (e.g., financial or regulatory requirements).	
4. Ensure that the test plan identifies necessary resources to execute testing and evaluate the results. Examples of resources include construction of test environments and use of staff time for the test group, including potential temporary replacement of test staff in the production or development environments. Ensure that stakeholders are consulted on the resource implications of the test plan.	
5. Confirm that the test plan considers test preparation (including site preparation), training requirements, installation or an update of a defined test environment, planning/performing/documenting/retaining test cases, error and problem handling, correction and escalation, and formal approval.	
6. Confirm that all test plans are approved by stakeholders, including business process owners and IT, as appropriate.	3
7. Ensure that the test plan establishes clear criteria for measuring the success of undertaking each testing phase. Consult the business and IT stakeholders in defining the success criteria. Determine that the plan establishes remediation procedures when the success criteria are not met. For example, in a case of significant failures in a testing phase, the plan should provide guidance on whether to proceed to the next phase, stop testing or postpone implementation.	

Related Guidance (Standards, Frameworks, Compliance Requirements)	Detailed Reference
No related guidance for this management practice	

Management Practice	Small and Medium Enterprise-specific Metrics
BAI07.04 Establish a test environment. Define and establish a secure test environment representative of the planned business process and IT operations environment in terms of performance, capacity, security, internal controls, operational practices, data quality, privacy requirements and workloads.	a. Percent of tests performed in a proper test environment

Small and Medium Enterprise-specific Activities	Capability Level
1. Create a database of test data that are representative of the production environment. Sanitize production environment data used in the test environment according to business needs and organizational standards. For example, consider whether compliance or regulatory requirements require that the data be anonymized or pseudonymized.	2
2. Protect sensitive test data and results against disclosure, including access, retention, storage and destruction.	3
3. Put in place a process to enable proper retention or disposal of test results, media and other associated documentation to enable adequate review and subsequent analysis or efficient retesting as required by the test plan. Take into account applicable regulatory or compliance requirements.	
4. Ensure that the test environment is representative of the future business and operational landscape, including business process procedures and roles, likely workload stress, operating systems, necessary application software, database management systems, and network and computing infrastructure found in the production environment.	
5. Ensure that the test environment is secure and incapable of interacting with production systems.	

Related Guidance (Standards, Frameworks, Compliance Requirements)	Detailed Reference
No related guidance for this management practice	

A. Component: Process *(cont.)*		
Management Practice	**Small and Medium Enterprise-specific Metrics**	
BAI07.05 Perform acceptance tests. Test changes independently, in accordance with the defined test plan, prior to migration to the live operational environment.	a. Percent of identified gaps between acceptance test results and the defined success criteria b. Percent of successful acceptance tests	
Small and Medium Enterprise-specific Activities		**Capability Level**
1. Review the log of errors found in the testing process by the development team, verifying that all errors have been remediated or formally accepted.		2
2. Ensure that testing of changes is undertaken in accordance with the testing plan. Ensure that the testing is designed and conducted by a test group independent from the development team. Consider the extent to which business process owners and end users are involved in the test group. Ensure that testing is conducted only within the test environment. Ensure that the tests and anticipated outcomes are in accordance with the defined success criteria set out in the testing plan. Consider using scripts to verify the extent to which the system meets security requirements.		3
3. Ensure that the independent test group assesses and approves each test script to confirm that it adequately addresses test success criteria set out in the test plan.		
4. Consider the appropriate balance between automated scripted tests and interactive user testing.		
5. Undertake tests of security in accordance with the test plan. Measure the extent of security weaknesses or loopholes. Consider the effect of security incidents since construction of the test plan. Consider the effect on access and boundary controls. Consider privacy.		
6. Undertake tests of system and application performance in accordance with the test plan. Consider a range of performance metrics (e.g., end-user response times and database management system update performance).		
7. When undertaking testing, ensure that the fallback and rollback elements of the test plan have been addressed.		
8. Identify, log and classify (e.g., minor, significant, mission-critical) errors during testing. Ensure that an audit trail of test results is available.		
9. Approve the acceptance with formal sign-off by the business process owners, third parties (as appropriate) and IT stakeholders prior to promotion.		
10. Communicate results of testing to stakeholders in accordance with the test plan to facilitate bug fixing and further quality enhancement.		
Related Guidance (Standards, Frameworks, Compliance Requirements)	**Detailed Reference**	
ITIL V3, 2011	Service Transition, 4.5 Service Validation and Testing	
Management Practice	**Small and Medium Enterprise-specific Metrics**	
BAI07.06 Promote to production and manage releases. Promote the accepted solution to the business and operations. Where appropriate, run the solution as a pilot implementation or in parallel with the old solution for a defined period and compare behavior and results. If significant problems occur, revert to the original environment based on the fallback/back-up plan. Manage releases of solution components.	a. Number and percent of releases not ready for release on schedule	
Small and Medium Enterprise-specific Activities		**Capability Level**
1. Prepare for transfer of business procedures and supporting services, applications and infrastructure from testing to the production environment in accordance with organizational change management policy.		2
2. Determine the extent of pilot implementation or parallel processing of the old and new systems in line with the implementation plan.		
3. Update relevant business process and system documentation, configuration information, and contingency plan documents as appropriate, before promotion to production.		
4. Ensure that all media libraries are updated promptly with the version of the solution component being transferred from testing to the production environment. Archive the existing version and its supporting documentation. Ensure that promotion to production of systems, application software and infrastructure is under configuration control.		
5. Where distribution of solution components is conducted electronically, control automated distribution to ensure that users are notified and that distribution is limited to authorized and correctly identified destinations. Ensure that the release process backup procedures include enabling review of the distribution of changes in the event of a malfunction or error.		
6. Where distribution takes physical form, keep a formal log of what items have been distributed, to whom, where they have been implemented, and when each has been updated.		
Related Guidance (Standards, Frameworks, Compliance Requirements)	**Detailed Reference**	
ISO/IEC 20000-1:2011(E)	9.3 Release and deployment management	
ITIL V3 2011	Service Transition, 4.4 Release and Deployment Management	

A. Component: Process *(cont.)*		
Management Practice	**Small and Medium Enterprise-specific Metrics**	
BAI07.07 Provide early production support. For an agreed period of time, provide early support to users and I&T operations to resolve issues and help stabilize the new solution.	a. Percent of additional staff resources provided for support	
Small and Medium Enterprise-specific Activities		**Capability Level**
1. Provide additional resources, as required, to end users and support personnel until the release has stabilized.		3
Related Guidance (Standards, Frameworks, Compliance Requirements)	**Detailed Reference**	
No related guidance for this management practice		
Management Practice	**Small and Medium Enterprise-specific Metrics**	
BAI07.08 Perform a post-implementation review. Conduct a post-implementation review to confirm outcome and results, identify lessons learned, and develop an action plan. Evaluate actual performance and outcomes of the new or changed service against expected performance and outcomes anticipated by the user or customer.	a. Number and percent of root cause analyses completed b. Percent of releases causing downtime	
Small and Medium Enterprise-specific Activities		**Capability Level**
1. Conduct post-implementation reviews to identify, assess and report on the extent to which enterprise requirements have been met; expected benefits have been realized; the system is considered usable; internal and external stakeholder expectations have been met; unexpected impacts on the enterprise have occurred; key risk has been mitigated; and the change management, installation and accreditation processes have been performed effectively and efficiently. Engage business process owners and third parties as appropriate.		3
2. Consult business process owners and IT technical management in the choice of metrics for measurement of success and achievement of requirements and benefits.		4
3. Agree on and implement an action plan to address issues identified in the post-implementation review. Engage business and IT stakeholders in the development of the action plan.		5
Related Guidance (Standards, Frameworks, Compliance Requirements)	**Detailed Reference**	
ITIL V3, 2011	Service Transition, 4.6 Change Evaluation	

B. Component: Organizational Structures					
Key Management Practice	Business Process Owners	Head of IT	IT Development Coordinator	IT Operations Coordinator	Privacy Officer
BAI07.01 Establish an implementation plan.	R	A	R		
BAI07.02 Plan business process, system and data conversion.	R	A	R		
BAI07.03 Plan acceptance tests.	R	A	R	R	R
BAI07.04 Establish a test environment.	R	A	R	R	
BAI07.05 Perform acceptance tests.	R	A	R	R	R
BAI07.06 Promote to production and manage releases.	R	A	R	R	
BAI07.07 Provide early production support.	R	A	R	R	
BAI07.08 Perform a post-implementation review.	R	A	R	R	

C. Component: Information Flows and Items				
Management Practice	Small and Medium Enterprise-specific Inputs		Small and Medium Enterprise-specific Outputs	
	From	Description	Description	To
BAI07.01 Establish an implementation plan.	BAI06.01	• Approved requests for change • Change plan and schedule	Completed implementation checklist	Internal
	BAI11.05	Project quality management plan		
BAI07.02 Plan business process, system and data conversion.	There are no small and medium enterprise-specific inputs for this practice.		Migration plan	DSS06.02
BAI07.03 Plan acceptance tests.	BAI03.07	Test plan	Approved acceptance test plan	BAI11.04
	BAI03.08	Test result logs		
	BAI11.05	Requirements for independent verification of project deliverables		

C. Component: Information Flows and Items *(cont.)*				
Management Practice	Small and Medium Enterprise-specific Inputs		Small and Medium Enterprise-specific Outputs	
	From	Description	Description	To
BAI07.04 Establish a test environment.	There are no small and medium enterprise-specific inputs for this practice.		Test data	Internal
			Operational test environment	Internal
BAI07.05 Perform acceptance tests.	There are no small and medium enterprise-specific inputs for this practice.		Test results log	Internal
BAI07.06 Promote to production and manage releases.	There are no small and medium enterprise-specific inputs for this practice.		Release plan	BAI10.01
			Release log	Internal
BAI07.07 Provide early production support.	APO11.02	Results of quality of service, including customer feedback	Supplemental support plan	APO08.04 APO08.05 DSS02.04
	BAI05.05	Success measures and results		
BAI07.08 Perform a post-implementation review.	APO11.03	• Results of quality monitoring • Root causes of quality delivery failures	Post-implementation review report	BAI11.09
	APO11.04	Results of quality reviews and audits		
	BAI05.05	Success measures and results		

D. Component: People, Skills and Competencies		
Skill	Related Guidance (Standards, Frameworks, Compliance Requirements)	Detailed Reference
Business process testing	Skills Framework for the Information Age V6, 2015	BPTS
Release and deployment	Skills Framework for the Information Age V6, 2015	RELM
Service acceptance	Skills Framework for the Information Age V6, 2015	SEAC
Testing	Skills Framework for the Information Age V6, 2015	TEST
User experience evaluation	Skills Framework for the Information Age V6, 2015	USEV

E. Component: Principles, Policies and Procedures	
Relevant Policy	Policy Description
There are no small and medium enterprise-specific principles, policies and procedures for this objective.	

F. Component: Culture, Ethics and Behavior
Key Culture Elements
Establish a culture that ensures timely communication of IT change requests to affected groups. Consult the affected groups regarding implementation and testing of changes.

G. Component: Services, Infrastructure and Applications
• IT change management tools • Release management tools • Testing tools and services

Page intentionally left blank

Domain: Build, Acquire and Implement Management Objective: BAI08 — Managed Knowledge	Focus Area: Small and Medium Enterprises
Description	
Maintain the availability of relevant, current, validated and reliable knowledge and management information to support all process activities and to facilitate decision making related to the governance and management of enterprise I&T. Plan for the identification, gathering, organizing, maintaining, use and retirement of knowledge.	
Purpose	
Provide the knowledge and information required to support all staff in the governance and management of enterprise I&T and allow for informed decision making.	
Small and Medium Enterprise Focus Area Relevance	
Coordinate knowledge and information sharing and management and maintain in a pragmatic way. Example metrics have been limited to avoid too formal processes related to this objective.	

A. Component: Process		
Management Practice	**Small and Medium Enterprise-specific Metrics**	
BAI08.01 Identify and classify sources of information for governance and management of I&T. Identify, validate and classify diverse sources of internal and external information required to enable governance and management of I&T, including strategy documents, incident reports and configuration information that progresses from development to operations before going live.	a. Number of validation remarks received, based on validation criteria	
Small and Medium Enterprise-specific Activities		**Capability Level**
1. Obtain knowledge requirements and sources of information from identified users.		2
2. Classify sources of information according to an agreed-on content classification scheme. Consider content types (procedures, processes, structures, concepts, policies, rules, facts, classifications), artifacts (documents, records, video, voice), and structured and unstructured information (experts, social media, email, voice mail, Rich Site Summary [RSS] feeds).		3
3. Collect and validate information based on information validation criteria (e.g., understandability, relevance, importance, integrity, accuracy, consistency, confidentiality, currency and reliability).		4
Related Guidance (Standards, Frameworks, Compliance Requirements)	**Detailed Reference**	
No related guidance for this management practice		
Management Practice	**Small and Medium Enterprise-specific Metrics**	
BAI08.02 Organize and contextualize information into knowledge Organize information based on classification criteria. Identify and create meaningful relationships among information elements and enable use of information. Identify owners, and leverage and implement enterprise-defined information levels of access to management information and knowledge resources.	a. Number of relationships identified between sources of information (tagging)	
Small and Medium Enterprise-specific Activities		**Capability Level**
1. Match sources of information, creating relationships between information sets (information tagging).		3
2. Create views to related data sets, considering stakeholder and organizational requirements.		
3. Publish and make knowledge accessible to relevant stakeholders based on roles and access mechanisms.		
Related Guidance (Standards, Frameworks, Compliance Requirements)	**Detailed Reference**	
COSO Enterprise Risk Management, June 2017	10. Information, Communication, and Reporting - Principle 18	

A. Component: Process *(cont.)*		
Management Practice	**Small and Medium Enterprise-specific Metrics**	
BAI08.03 Use and share knowledge. Propagate available knowledge resources to relevant stakeholders and communicate how these resources can be used to address different needs (e.g., problem solving, learning, strategic planning and decision making).	a. Number and percent of comments and feedback received on shared knowledge	
Small and Medium Enterprise-specific Activities		**Capability Level**
1. Create an environment, tools and artifacts that support the sharing and transfer of knowledge. Ensure appropriate access controls are in place, in line with defined knowledge classification.		2
2. Measure the use of knowledge tools and elements and evaluate the impact on operational processes.		4
3. Improve information and knowledge for operational processes that show knowledge gaps.		5
Related Guidance (Standards, Frameworks, Compliance Requirements)	**Detailed Reference**	
CMMI Cybermaturity Platform, 2018	PP.IS Apply Information Sharing; IR.ES Ensure Information Sharing	
ITIL V3, 2011	Service Transition, 4.7 Knowledge Management	
PMBOK Guide Sixth Edition, 2017	Part 1: 4.4 Manage project knowledge	
Management Practice	**Small and Medium Enterprise-specific Metrics**	
BAI08.04 Evaluate and update or retire information. Measure the use and evaluate the currency and relevance of information. Update information or retire obsolete information.	a. Frequency of update b. Level of satisfaction of knowledge by users	
Small and Medium Enterprise-specific Activities		**Capability Level**
1. Update outdated information that still has relevance and value to the organization. Identify related information that is no longer relevant to the enterprise's knowledge requirements and retire or archive according to agreed procedures.		4
Related Guidance (Standards, Frameworks, Compliance Requirements)	**Detailed Reference**	
No related guidance for this management practice		

B. Component: Organizational Structures

Key Management Practice	Operations Manager	Business Process Owners	Project Manager	Head of IT	IT Development Coordinator	IT Operations Coordinator	Privacy Officer	Legal Department	Compliance or Quality
BAI08.01 Identify and classify sources of information for governance and management of I&T.	R	R		A	R	R			
BAI08.02 Organize and contextualize information into knowledge.	R			A	R	R			
BAI08.03 Use and share knowledge.	R	R	R	A				R	
BAI08.04 Evaluate and update or retire information.	R	R	R	A	R	R	R		R

C. Component: Information Flows and Items				
Management Practice	Small and Medium Enterprise-specific Inputs		Small and Medium Enterprise-specific Outputs	
	From	Description	Description	To
BAI08.01 Identify and classify sources of information for governance and management of I&T.	Outside COBIT	Knowledge requirements and sources	Classification of information sources	Internal
BAI08.02 Organize and contextualize information into knowledge.	BAI03.03	Documented solution components	Published knowledge repositories	APO07.03
BAI08.03 Use and share knowledge.	BAI03.03	Documented solution components	Knowledge awareness and training schemes	APO07.03
	BAI05.05	Operation and use plan	Knowledge user database	Internal
BAI08.04 Evaluate and update or retire information.	There are no small and medium enterprise-specific inputs for this practice.		Rules for knowledge retirement	Internal

D. Component: People, Skills and Competencies		
Skill	Related Guidance (Standards, Frameworks, Compliance Requirements)	Detailed Reference
Information and knowledge management	e-Competence Framework (e-CF)—A common European Framework for ICT Professionals in all industry sectors—Part 1: Framework, 2016	D. Enable—D.10. Information and Knowledge Management

E. Component: Principles, Policies and Procedures	
Relevant Policy	Policy Description
There are no small and medium enterprise-specific principles, policies and procedures for this objective.	

F. Component: Culture, Ethics and Behavior
Key Culture Elements
Embed a knowledge-sharing culture in the enterprise. Proactively communicate the value of knowledge to encourage knowledge creation, use, reuse and sharing. Encourage the sharing and transfer of knowledge by identifying and leveraging motivational factors.

G. Component: Services, Infrastructure and Applications
• Collaboration platform • Knowledge repository

Page intentionally left blank

Domain: Build, Acquire and Implement Management Objective: BAI09 – Managed Assets	Focus Area: Small and Medium Enterprises
Description	
Manage I&T assets through their life cycle to make sure that their use delivers value at optimal cost, they remain operational (fit for purpose), and they are accounted for and physically protected. Ensure that those assets that are critical to support service capability are reliable and available. Manage software licenses to ensure that the optimal number are acquired, retained and deployed in relation to required business usage, and the software installed is in compliance with license agreements.	
Purpose	
Account for all I&T assets and optimize the value provided by their use.	
Small and Medium Enterprise Focus Area Relevance	
Manage I&T assets that have important economic or business value through their respective life cycles to make sure that their use delivers value at optimal cost, that they remain operational (fit for purpose), and that they are accounted for and physically protected. Ensure that assets which are critical to support service capability are reliable and available. Ensure that all I&T assets are accounted for and that the value provided is optimized by their effective and efficient use.	

A. Component: Process	
Management Practice	**Small and Medium Enterprise-specific Metrics**
BAI09.01 Identify and record current assets. Maintain an up-to-date, accurate record of all I&T assets that are required to deliver services and that are owned or controlled by the organization with an expectation of future benefit (including resources with economic value, such as hardware or software). Ensure alignment with configuration management and financial management.	a. Percent of assets that are fit for purpose b. Percent of assets accurately recorded in asset register c. Percent of current of assets in the inventory

Small and Medium Enterprise-specific Activities	Capability Level
1. Identify all owned assets in an asset register that records current status. Assets are reported on the balance sheet. They are bought or created to increase the value of the organization or benefit its operations (e.g., hardware, software).	2
2. Identify legal, regulatory or contractual requirements that need to be addressed when managing the asset.	
3. Periodically verify that the assets are still fit for purpose (i.e., in a useful condition).	
4. Ensure accounting for all assets.	3
5. Verify the existence of all owned assets by performing regular physical and logical inventory checks and reconciliation.	4

Related Guidance (Standards, Frameworks, Compliance Requirements)	Detailed Reference
CMMI Cybermaturity Platform, 2018	RI.AD Asset Discovery & Identification
ISF, The Standard of Good Practice for Information Security 2016	BA1.1 Business Application Register
ISO/IEC 27002:2013/Cor.2:2015(E)	8.1 Responsibility for assets
National Institute of Standards and Technology Special Publication 800-53, Revision 5 (Draft), August 2017	3.13 Physical and environmental protection (PE-9)
The CIS Critical Security Controls for Effective Cyber Defense Version 6.1, August 2016	CSC 1: Inventory of Authorized and Unauthorized Devices; CSC 2: Inventory of Authorized and Unauthorized Software

A. Component: Process *(cont.)*		
Management Practice	**Small and Medium Enterprise-specific Metrics**	
BAI09.02 Manage critical assets. Identify assets that are critical in providing service capability. Maximize their reliability and availability to support business needs.	a. Percent of critical assets b. Average downtime per critical asset	
Small and Medium Enterprise-specific Activities		**Capability Level**
1. Identify assets that are critical in providing service capability by referencing requirements in service definitions, SLAs and the configuration management system.		2
2. On a regular basis, consider the risk of failure or need for replacement of each critical asset.		
3. Communicate to affected customers and users the expected impact (e.g., performance restrictions) of maintenance activities.		
4. Incorporate planned downtime in an overall production schedule and schedule maintenance activities to minimize the adverse impact on business processes.		3
5. Schedule regular preventive maintenance, monitor performance, and, if required, provide alternative and/or additional assets to minimize the likelihood of failure.		
6. Establish the necessary maintenance agreements involving third-party access to organizational I&T facilities for on-site and off-site activities (e.g., outsourcing).		
7. Ensure that remote access services and user profiles (or other means used for maintenance or diagnosis) are active only when required.		
8. Monitor performance of critical assets by examining incident trends and, where necessary, take action to repair or replace.		
Related Guidance (Standards, Frameworks, Compliance Requirements)	**Detailed Reference**	
National Institute of Standards and Technology Framework for Improving Critical Infrastructure Cybersecurity v1.1, April 2018	ID.AM Asset Management	
National Institute of Standards and Technology Special Publication 800-53, Revision 5 (Draft), August 2017	3.13 Physical and environmental protection (PE-20)	
Management Practice	**Small and Medium Enterprise-specific Metrics**	
BAI09.03 Manage the asset life cycle. Manage assets from procurement to disposal. Ensure that assets are utilized as effectively and efficiently as possible and are accounted for and physically protected until appropriately retired.	a. Percent of unused assets disposed	
Small and Medium Enterprise-specific Activities		**Capability Level**
1. Procure all assets based on approved requests and in accordance with the enterprise procurement policy.		2
2. Source, receive, verify, test and record all assets in a controlled manner, including physical labelling, as required.		
3. Approve payments and complete the process with suppliers according to agreed-on contract conditions.		
4. Deploy assets following the standard implementation life cycle, including change management and acceptance testing.		3
5. Allocate assets to users, with acceptance of responsibilities and sign-off, as appropriate.		
6. Reallocate assets whenever needed, due to changes.		
7. Dispose of assets securely when they are no longer needed. For example, consider the permanent deletion of any data recorded on media devices. Also consider potential damage to the environment.		
Related Guidance (Standards, Frameworks, Compliance Requirements)	**Detailed Reference**	
CMMI Cybermaturity Platform, 2018	DP.ML Manage Asset Lifecycle	
ISF, The Standard of Good Practice for Information Security 2016	IM2.1 Document Management; PA1.1 Hardware Life Cycle Management	
ITIL V3, 2011	Service Transition, 4.3 Service Asset and Configuration Management	
National Institute of Standards and Technology Framework for Improving Critical Infrastructure Cybersecurity v1.1, April 2018	PR.MA Maintenance	

A. Component: Process *(cont.)*	
Management Practice	**Small and Medium Enterprise-specific Metrics**
BAI09.04 Optimize asset value. Regularly review the overall asset base to identify ways to optimize value in alignment with business needs.	a. Number of assets not utilized b. Number of assets replaced after review of cost and value

Small and Medium Enterprise-specific Activities	Capability Level
1. On a regular basis, review the overall asset base, considering whether it is aligned with business requirements.	3
2. Assess maintenance costs, consider reasonableness, and identify lower-cost options, including, where necessary, replacement with new alternatives.	4
3. Review warranties and consider value and replacement possibilities to determine lowest-cost options.	5
4. Use capacity and utilization statistics to identify underutilized or redundant assets that could be considered for disposal or replacement to lower costs.	

Related Guidance (Standards, Frameworks, Compliance Requirements)	Detailed Reference
No related guidance for this management practice	

Management Practice	Small and Medium Enterprise-specific Metrics
BAI09.05 Manage licenses. Manage software licenses to maintain the optimal number of licenses and support business requirements. Ensure that the number of licenses owned is sufficient to cover the installed software in use.	a. Percent of licenses still being paid for but not being used b. Percent of products and licenses that should be upgraded to achieve better value

Small and Medium Enterprise-specific Activities	Capability Level
1. Maintain a register of all purchased software licenses and associated license agreements.	2
2. On a regular basis, conduct an audit to identify all instances of installed licensed software.	3
3. Compare the number of installed software instances and the software actually used with the number of licenses owned, and reduce the number of licenses if possible.	4
4. On a regular basis, consider whether better value can be obtained by upgrading products and associated licenses.	5

Related Guidance (Standards, Frameworks, Compliance Requirements)	Detailed Reference
No related guidance for this management practice	

B. Component: Organizational Structures

Key Management Practice	Head of IT	Security Expert	IT Development Coordinator	IT Operations Coordinator	Privacy Officer	Compliance or Quality
BAI09.01 Identify and record current assets.	A			R		
BAI09.02 Manage critical assets.	A	R	R	R	R	R
BAI09.03 Manage the asset life cycle.	A			R		
BAI09.04 Optimize asset value.	A		R	R		
BAI09.05 Manage licenses.	A		R	R		

C. Component: Information Flows and Items				
Management Practice	Small and Medium Enterprise-specific Inputs		Small and Medium Enterprise-specific Outputs	
	From	Description	Description	To
BAI09.01 Identify and record current assets.	BAI03.04	Updates to asset inventory	Results of fit-for-purpose reviews	APO02.02
	BAI10.02	Configuration repository	Asset register	APO06.01 BAI10.03
			Results of physical inventory checks	BAI10.03 BAI10.04 DSS05.03
BAI09.02 Manage critical assets.	There are no small and medium enterprise-specific inputs for this practice.		Communications of planned maintenance downtime	APO08.04
			Maintenance agreements	Internal
BAI09.03 Manage the asset life cycle.	There are no small and medium enterprise-specific inputs for this practice.		Authorized asset retirements	BAI10.03
			Updated asset register	BAI10.03
			Approved asset procurement requests	Internal
BAI09.04 Optimize asset value.	There are no small and medium enterprise-specific inputs for this practice.		Opportunities to reduce asset costs or increase value	APO02.02
			Results of cost optimization reviews	APO02.02
BAI09.05 Manage licenses.	There are no small and medium enterprise-specific inputs for this practice.		Register of software licenses	BAI10.02
			Results of installed license audits	MEA03.03

D. Component: People, Skills and Competencies		
Skill	Related Guidance (Standards, Frameworks, Compliance Requirements)	Detailed Reference
Asset management	Skills Framework for the Information Age V6, 2015	ASMG
Systems installation/ decommissioning	Skills Framework for the Information Age V6, 2015	HSIN

E. Component: Principles, Policies and Procedures	
Relevant Policy	Policy Description
Asset management policy	Provides guidelines for asset life cycle management, asset protection measures, system classification and ownership, data ownership, and data classification

F. Component: Culture, Ethics and Behavior
Key Culture Elements
Establish a culture that identifies, assesses and reports the relative economic and strategic value of each asset to the enterprise in an open, consistent and transparent manner.

G. Component: Services, Infrastructure and Applications
Asset management tools

Domain: Build, Acquire and Implement Management Objective: BAI10 — Managed Configuration	Focus Area: Small and Medium Enterprises
Description	
Define and maintain descriptions and relationships among key resources and capabilities required to deliver I&T-enabled services. Include collecting configuration information, establishing baselines, verifying and auditing configuration information, and updating the configuration repository.	
Purpose	
Provide sufficient information about service assets to enable the service to be effectively managed. Assess the impact of changes and deal with service incidents.	
Small and Medium Enterprise Focus Area Relevance	
The description and purpose of this COBIT objective is fully applicable to SMEs. No SME-specific focus area relevance statement is required.	

A. Component: Process		
Management Practice	**Small and Medium Enterprise-specific Metrics**	
BAI10.01 Establish and maintain a configuration model. Establish and maintain a logical model of the services, assets, infrastructure and recording of configuration items (CIs), including the relationships among them. Include the CIs considered necessary to manage services effectively and to provide a single, reliable description of the assets in a service.	a. Percent of stakeholders validating the logical configuration model	
Small and Medium Enterprise-specific Activities		**Capability Level**
1. Define and agree on the scope and level of detail for configuration management (i.e., which services, assets and infrastructure configurable items to include) in line with the enterprise strategy, size, assets and activities.		3
2. Establish and maintain a logical model for configuration management, including information on CI types, CI attributes, relationship types, relationship attributes and status codes.		
Related Guidance (Standards, Frameworks, Compliance Requirements)	**Detailed Reference**	
CMMI Data Management Maturity Model, 2014	Supporting Processes - Configuration Management	
ISF, The Standard of Good Practice for Information Security 2016	SY1 System Configuration	
ISO/IEC 20000-1:2011(E)	9.1 Configuration management	
ITIL V3, 2011	Service Transition, 4.3 Service Asset and Configuration Management	
National Institute of Standards and Technology Special Publication 800-53, Revision 5 (Draft), August 2017	3.5 Configuration management (CM-6)	
Management Practice	**Small and Medium Enterprise-specific Metrics**	
BAI10.02 Establish and maintain a configuration repository and baseline. Establish and maintain a configuration management repository and create controlled configuration baselines.	a. Number of CIs listed in the repository	
Small and Medium Enterprise-specific Activities		**Capability Level**
1. Identify and classify CIs and populate the repository.		2
2. Create, review and formally agree on configuration baselines of a service, application or infrastructure.		3
Related Guidance (Standards, Frameworks, Compliance Requirements)	**Detailed Reference**	
CMMI Cybermaturity Platform, 2018	IP.CB Apply Configuration Baselines	
National Institute of Standards and Technology Special Publication 800-37, Revision 2 (Draft), May 2018	3.4 Implementation (Task 2)	
National Institute of Standards and Technology Special Publication 800-53, Revision 5 (Draft), August 2017	3.19 System and service acquisition (SA-10)	

A. Component: Process *(cont.)*		
Management Practice	**Small and Medium Enterprise-specific Metrics**	
BAI10.03 Maintain and control configuration items. Maintain an up-to-date repository of configuration items (CIs) by populating any configuration changes.	a. Frequency of changes/updates to the repository	
Small and Medium Enterprise-specific Activities		**Capability Level**
1. Regularly identify all changes to CIs.		2
2. Review proposed changes to CIs against the baseline to ensure completeness and accuracy.		3
3. Update configuration details for approved changes to CIs.		
Related Guidance (Standards, Frameworks, Compliance Requirements)	**Detailed Reference**	
National Institute of Standards and Technology Special Publication 800-53, Revision 5 (Draft), August 2017	3.5 Configuration management (CM-2)	
Management Practice	**Small and Medium Enterprise-specific Metrics**	
BAI10.04 Produce status and configuration reports. Define and produce configuration reports on status changes of configuration items.	a. Percent of accuracy of status changes of CIs against the baseline	
Small and Medium Enterprise-specific Activities		**Capability Level**
1. Identify reporting requirements from all stakeholders, including content, frequency and media.		3
2. Produce reports according to the identified requirements.		
Related Guidance (Standards, Frameworks, Compliance Requirements)	**Detailed Reference**	
National Institute of Standards and Technology Special Publication 800-53, Revision 5 (Draft), August 2017	3.5 Configuration management (CM-3)	
Management Practice	**Small and Medium Enterprise-specific Metrics**	
BAI10.05 Verify and review integrity of the configuration repository. Periodically review the configuration repository and verify completeness and correctness against the desired target.	a. Number of deviations between the configuration repository and live configuration b. Number of discrepancies relating to incomplete or missing configuration information	
Small and Medium Enterprise-specific Activities		**Capability Level**
1. Periodically verify live CIs against the configuration repository by comparing physical and logical configurations and using appropriate discovery tools, as required.		4
2. Report and review all deviations for approved corrections or action to remove any unauthorized assets.		
3. Periodically compare the degree of completeness and accuracy and take remedial action, as necessary, to improve the quality of the repository data.		5
Related Guidance (Standards, Frameworks, Compliance Requirements)	**Detailed Reference**	
National Institute of Standards and Technology Special Publication 800-53, Revision 5 (Draft), August 2017	3.5 Configuration management (CM-4)	

B. Component: Organizational Structures			
Key Management Practice	Head of IT	IT Development Coordinator	IT Operations Coordinator
BAI10.01 Establish and maintain a configuration model.	A		R
BAI10.02 Establish and maintain a configuration repository and baseline.	A	R	R
BAI10.03 Maintain and control configuration items.	A	R	R
BAI10.04 Produce status and configuration reports.	A		R
BAI10.05 Verify and review integrity of the configuration repository.	A	R	R

C. Component: Information Flows and Items				
Management Practice	Small and Medium Enterprise-specific Inputs		Small and Medium Enterprise-specific Outputs	
BAI10.01 Establish and maintain a configuration model.	**From**	**Description**	**Description**	**To**
	BAI07.06	Release plan	Logical configuration model	Internal
			Scope of configuration management model	Internal
BAI10.02 Establish and maintain a configuration repository and baseline.	BAI09.05	Register of software licenses	Configuration baseline	BAI03.11 BAI03.12
			Configuration repository	BAI09.01 DSS02.01
BAI10.03 Maintain and control configuration items.	BAI06.03	Change request status reports	Approved changes to baseline	BAI03.11
	BAI09.01	• Asset register • Results of physical inventory checks	Updated repository with CIs	Internal
	BAI09.03	• Updated asset register • Authorized asset retirements		
BAI10.04 Produce status and configuration reports.	BAI09.01	Results of physical inventory checks	Configuration status reports	DSS02.01
BAI10.05 Verify and review integrity of the configuration repository.	There are no small and medium enterprise-specific inputs for this practice.		Results of physical verification of CIs	Internal
			Results of repository completeness reviews	Internal

D. Component: People, Skills and Competencies		
Skill	**Related Guidance (Standards, Frameworks, Compliance Requirements)**	**Detailed Reference**
Configuration management	Skills Framework for the Information Age V6, 2015	CFMG

E. Component: Principles, Policies and Procedures	
Relevant Policy	**Policy Description**
There are no small and medium enterprise-specific principles, policies and procedures for this objective.	

F. Component: Culture, Ethics and Behavior
Key Culture Elements
Establish a culture that supports a structured approach to configuration management across departments in which users recognize the value of strict configuration management (e.g., avoiding version conflicts or duplicative effort) and apply the rules and procedures that were put in place.

G. Component: Services, Infrastructure and Applications
Configuration management tools and repositories

Domain: Build, Acquire and Implement Management objective: BAI11 — Managed Projects	Focus Area: Small and Medium Enterprises
Description	
Manage all projects that are initiated within the enterprise in alignment with enterprise strategy and in a coordinated way based on the standard project management approach. Initiate, plan, control and execute projects, and close with a post-implementation review.	
Purpose	
Realize defined project outcomes and reduce the risk of unexpected delays, costs and value erosion by improving communications to and involvement of business and end users. Ensure the value and quality of project deliverables and maximize their contribution to the defined programs and investment portfolio.	
Small and Medium Enterprise Focus Area Relevance	
The description and purpose of this COBIT objective is fully applicable to SMEs. No SME-specific focus area relevance statement is required.	

A. Component: Process		
Management Practice	**Small and Medium Enterprise-specific Metrics**	
BAI11.01 Maintain a standard approach for project management. Maintain a standard approach for project management that enables governance and management review, decision-making and delivery-management activities. These activities should focus consistently on business value and goals (i.e., requirements, risk, costs, schedule and quality targets).	a. Percent of successful projects based on the defined standard approach b. Time since last update of the project management approach, tools or templates	
Small and Medium Enterprise-specific Activities		**Capability Level**
1. Maintain and enforce a standard approach to project management aligned to the enterprise's specific environment. Ensure that the approach covers the management of scope, resources, risk, cost, quality and stakeholder involvement.		2
2. Provide appropriate project management training and consider certification for project managers.		3
3. Evaluate lessons learned on the use of the project management approach and update the good practices, tools and templates accordingly.		4
Related Guidance (Standards, Frameworks, Compliance Requirements)	**Detailed Reference**	
National Institute of Standards and Technology Special Publication 800-53, Revision 5 (Draft), August 2017	3.15 Program management (PM-2)	
Management Practice	**Small and Medium Enterprise-specific Metrics**	
BAI11.02 Start up and initiate a project. Define and document the nature and scope of the project to confirm and develop a common understanding of project scope among stakeholders. The definition should be formally approved by the project sponsors.	a. Percent of stakeholders approving project definition and scope statement	
Small and Medium Enterprise-specific Activities		**Capability Level**
1. To create a common understanding of project scope, provide stakeholders with a clear written statement defining the nature, scope and deliverables of every project.		2
2. Ensure that each project has a sponsor with sufficient authority to guarantee the correct execution of the project.		
3. Ensure that key stakeholders and sponsors agree on and accept the requirements for the project, including definition of project success (acceptance) criteria and KPIs.		
4. Appoint a dedicated manager for the project, with the required understanding of technology and business and the competencies and skills to manage the project effectively and efficiently.		
5. With the approval of stakeholders, maintain the project definition throughout the project, reflecting changing requirements.		
6. To track the execution of a project, put in place mechanisms such as regular reporting and stage-gate, release or phase reviews in a timely manner with appropriate approval.		
Related Guidance (Standards, Frameworks, Compliance Requirements)	**Detailed Reference**	
PMBOK Guide Sixth Edition, 2017	Part 1: 4.1 Develop project charter; Part 1: 6. Project schedule management	

A. Component: Process *(cont.)*

Management Practice	Small and Medium Enterprise-specific Metrics
BAI11.03 Manage stakeholder engagement. Manage stakeholder engagement to ensure an active exchange of accurate, consistent and timely information that reaches all relevant stakeholders. This includes planning, identifying and engaging stakeholders and managing their expectations.	a. Percent of stakeholders effectively engaged

Small and Medium Enterprise-specific Activities	Capability Level
1. Identify stakeholders and manage engagement by establishing and maintaining appropriate levels of coordination, communication and liaison to ensure that they are involved in the project.	3
2. Analyze stakeholder interests, requirements and engagement and take remedial actions as required.	4

Related Guidance (Standards, Frameworks, Compliance Requirements)	Detailed Reference
PMBOK Guide Sixth Edition, 2017	Part 1: 13. Project stakeholder management Part 1: 10. Project communications management

Management Practice	Small and Medium Enterprise-specific Metrics
BAI11.04 Develop and maintain the project plan. Establish and maintain a formal, approved, integrated project plan (covering business and IT resources) to guide project execution and control throughout the life of the project. The scope of projects should be clearly defined and tied to building or enhancing business capability.	a. Percent of milestones reached or tasks completed vs. the plan

Small and Medium Enterprise-specific Activities	Capability Level
1. Develop a project plan that provides information to enable management to control project progress progressively. Ensure that the plan includes details of project deliverables and acceptance criteria, required internal and external resources and responsibilities, clear work breakdown structures and work packages, estimates of resources required, milestones/release plan/phases, key dependencies, budget and costs, and identification of a critical path.	2
2. Maintain the project plan and any dependent plans (e.g., risk plan, quality plan) to ensure that they are up to date and reflect actual progress and approved material changes.	
3. Determine the activities, interdependencies, and collaboration and communication required within the project and among multiple projects that are linked.	
4. Ensure that each milestone is accompanied by a significant deliverable requiring review and sign-off.	
5. Establish a project baseline (e.g., cost, schedule, scope, quality) that is appropriately reviewed and approved.	

Related Guidance (Standards, Frameworks, Compliance Requirements)	Detailed Reference
PMBOK Guide Sixth Edition, 2017	Part 1: 4.2 Develop project management plan

Management Practice	Small and Medium Enterprise-specific Metrics
BAI11.05 Manage project quality. Prepare and execute a quality management plan, processes and practices that align with quality management standards. Describe the approach to project quality and implementation. The plan should be formally reviewed and agreed on by all parties concerned and incorporated into the integrated project plans.	a. Percent of quality reviews executed on the project

Small and Medium Enterprise-specific Activities	Capability Level
1. Organize quality assurance reviews of project deliverables. Identify ownership and responsibilities for quality review.	2
2. Identify assurance tasks and practices required to support the accreditation of new or modified systems during project planning and include them in the integrated plans.	3
3. Define any requirements for independent validation and verification of the quality of deliverables in the plan.	

Related Guidance (Standards, Frameworks, Compliance Requirements)	Detailed Reference
PMBOK Guide Sixth Edition, 2017	Part 1: 8. Project quality management

A. Component: Process *(cont.)*		
Management Practice	**Small and Medium Enterprise-specific Metrics**	
BAI11.06 Manage project risk. Eliminate or minimize specific risk associated with projects through a systematic process of planning, identifying, analyzing, responding to, monitoring and controlling the areas or events with potential to cause unwanted change. Define and record any risk faced by project management.	a. Percent of identified delays and issues b. Percent of projects with a documented risk register	
Small and Medium Enterprise-specific Activities		**Capability Level**
1. Assign to appropriately skilled personnel the responsibility for executing a project risk assessment within a project and ensuring that this is incorporated into the solution development practices. Consider allocating this role to an independent team, especially if an objective viewpoint is required or a project is considered critical.		2
2. Identify owners for actions to avoid, accept or mitigate risk.		
3. Reassess project risk periodically, including at initiation of each major project phase and as part of major change request assessments. Manage and communicate risk appropriately within the project governance structure.		3
4. Maintain and review a register of all potential project risk and a risk mitigation log of all project risk issues and resolution(s). Analyze the log periodically for trends and recurring problems to ensure that root causes are corrected.		
Related Guidance (Standards, Frameworks, Compliance Requirements)	**Detailed Reference**	
National Institute of Standards and Technology Special Publication 800-53, Revision 5 (Draft), August 2017	3.15 Program management (PM-4)	
PMBOK Guide Sixth Edition, 2017	Part 1: 11. Project risk management	
Management Practice	**Small and Medium Enterprise-specific Metrics**	
BAI11.07 Monitor and control projects. Measure project performance against key project performance criteria such as schedule, quality, cost and risk. Identify any deviations from expected targets. Assess the impact of deviations on the project and overall program and report results to key stakeholders.	a. Percent of deviations from plan addressed b. Frequency of project status reviews	
Small and Medium Enterprise-specific Activities		**Capability Level**
1. Establish and use a set of project criteria including, but not limited to, scope, expected outcome, schedule, quality, cost and level of risk.		2
2. Report to identified key stakeholders project progress, deviations from established key project criteria, and potential positive and negative effects on the project.		
3. Document and submit any necessary changes to the project's key stakeholders for their approval before adoption. Communicate revised criteria to project managers for use in future performance reports.		
4. Gain approval and sign-off from designated stakeholders on the deliverables produced in each iteration, release or project phase.		
5. Assess the project at agreed-on major stage-gates, releases or iterations and make formal go/no-go decisions based on predetermined critical success criteria.		3
6. Recommend and monitor remedial action, when required, in line with the project governance framework.		4
Related Guidance (Standards, Frameworks, Compliance Requirements)	**Detailed Reference**	
PMBOK Guide Sixth Edition, 2017	Part 1: 4.5 Monitor and control project work	

A. Component: Process *(cont.)*		
Management Practice	**Small and Medium Enterprise-specific Metrics**	
BAI11.08 Manage project resources and work packages. Manage project work packages by placing formal requirements on authorizing and accepting work packages and assigning and coordinating appropriate business and IT resources.	a. Number of resource issues (e.g., skills, capacity)	
Small and Medium Enterprise-specific Activities		**Capability Level**
1. Identify business and IT resource needs for the project and clearly map appropriate roles and responsibilities, with escalation and decision-making authorities agreed on and understood.		2
2. Identify required skills and time requirements for all individuals involved in the project phases in relation to defined roles. Staff the roles based on available skills information (e.g., IT skills matrix).		
3. Consider and clearly define the roles and responsibilities of other involved parties, including finance, legal, procurement, HR, internal audit and compliance.		
4. Clearly define and agree on the responsibility for procurement and management of third-party products and services and manage the relationships.		
5. Identify and authorize the execution of the work according to the project plan.		
6. Identify project plan gaps and provide feedback to the project manager to remediate.		3
Related Guidance (Standards, Frameworks, Compliance Requirements)	**Detailed Reference**	
PMBOK Guide Sixth Edition, 2017	Part 1: 4.3 Direct and manage project work	
Management Practice	**Small and Medium Enterprise-specific Metrics**	
BAI11.09 Close a project or iteration. At the end of each project, release or iteration, require the project stakeholders to ascertain whether the project, release or iteration delivered the required results in terms of capabilities and contributed as expected to program benefits. Identify and communicate any outstanding activities required to achieve planned results of the project and/or benefits of the program. Identify and document lessons learned for future projects, releases, iterations and programs.	a. Number of lessons learned documented at project closure review b. Level of stakeholder satisfaction expressed at project closure review c. Percent of outcomes with first-time acceptance	
Small and Medium Enterprise-specific Activities		**Capability Level**
1. Obtain stakeholder acceptance of project deliverables.		2
2. Define and apply key steps for project closure, including post-implementation reviews that assess whether a project attained desired results.		3
3. Identify, assign and track activities. Maintain relevant communications regarding completion of activities to ensure that the project delivers the required results and capabilities.		
4. Assign to appropriately skilled personnel the responsibility for executing a project risk assessment within a project and ensuring that this is incorporated into the solution development practices. Consider allocating this role to an independent team, especially if an objective viewpoint is required or a project is considered critical.		4
Related Guidance (Standards, Frameworks, Compliance Requirements)	**Detailed Reference**	
PMBOK Guide Sixth Edition, 2017	Part 1: 4.7 Close project or phase	

B. Component: Organizational Structures

Key Management Practice	General Manager	Business Process Owners	Steering Committee (Projects)	Project Manager	Head of IT	IT Development Coordinator
BAI11.01 Maintain a standard approach for project management.	A			R	R	
BAI11.02 Start up and initiate a project.		R	A	R		R
BAI11.03 Manage stakeholder engagement.			A	R	R	
BAI11.04 Develop and maintain the project plan.			A	R		
BAI11.05 Manage project quality.			A	R	R	
BAI11.06 Manage project risk.			A	R	R	
BAI11.07 Monitor and control projects.		R	A	R		R
BAI11.08 Manage project resources and work packages.		R	A	R		R
BAI11.09 Close a project or iteration.			A	R		

C. Component: Information Flows and Items

Management Practice	Small and Medium Enterprise-specific Inputs		Small and Medium Enterprise-specific Outputs	
	From	Description	Description	To
BAI11.01 Maintain a standard approach for project management.	APO03.04	Implementation phase descriptions	Updated project management approach	Internal
	APO10.04	Identified vendor delivery risk		
	EDM02.03	Requirements for stage-gate reviews		
	EDM02.04	Actions to improve value delivery		
BAI11.02 Start up and initiate a project.	There are no small and medium enterprise-specific inputs for this practice.		Project definition, including scope statement	Internal
BAI11.03 Manage stakeholder engagement.	There are no small and medium enterprise-specific inputs for this practice.		There are no small and medium enterprise-specific outputs for this practice.	
BAI11.04 Develop and maintain the project plan.	BAI07.03	Approved acceptance test plan	Reviewed and approved project plans	Internal

C. Component: Information Flows and Items *(cont.)*				
Management Practice	Small and Medium Enterprise-specific Inputs		Small and Medium Enterprise-specific Outputs	
BAI11.05 Manage project quality.	From	Description	Description	To
	APO11.01	Quality management plans	Project quality management plan	BAI02.04 BAI03.06 BAI07.01
	APO11.02	Customer requirements for quality management	Requirements for independent verification of project deliverables	BAI07.03
BAI11.06 Manage project risk.	APO12.02	Risk analysis results	Project risk register	Internal
	BAI02.03	• Requirements risk register • Risk mitigation actions		
BAI11.07 Monitor and control projects.	There are no small and medium enterprise-specific inputs for this practice.		Project progress reports	Internal
BAI11.08 Manage project resources and work packages.	There are no small and medium enterprise-specific inputs for this practice.		Project resource requirements	APO07.05 APO07.06
			Gaps in project planning	Internal
			Project roles and responsibilities	Internal
BAI11.09 Close a project or iteration.	BAI07.08	Post-implementation review report	Post-implementation review results	APO02.04
			Stakeholder project acceptance confirmations	Internal
			Project lessons learned	Internal

D. Component: People, Skills and Competencies		
Skill	Related Guidance (Standards, Frameworks, Compliance Requirements)	Detailed Reference
Portfolio, program and project support	Skills Framework for the Information Age V6, 2015	PROF
Project and portfolio management	e-Competence Framework (e-CF)—A common European Framework for ICT Professionals in all industry sectors—Part 1: Framework, 2016	E. Manage—E.2. Project and Portfolio Management
Project management	Skills Framework for the Information Age V6, 2015	PRMG

E. Component: Principles, Policies and Procedures	
Relevant Policy	Policy Description
Program/project management policy	Guides management of risk related to programs and projects. Details management position and expectation regarding program and project management. Treats accountability, goals and objectives regarding performance, budget, risk analysis, reporting and mitigation of adverse events during program/project execution.

F. Component: Culture, Ethics and Behavior
Key Culture Elements
Establish an enterprisewide project management culture that ensures consistent and optimal implementation of project management across the enterprise, taking into account organizational structure and business environment. Ensure that all initiatives are translated into projects (or changes, where minor in scope) and that no ad hoc actions occur outside the scope of project management.

G. Component: Services, Infrastructure and Applications
Project management tools

Page intentionally left blank

7.4 Deliver, Service and Support (DSS)

01 Managed Operations

02 Managed Service Requests and Incidents

03 Managed Problems

04 Managed Continuity

05 Managed Security Services

06 Managed Business Process Controls

Page intentionally left blank

Domain: Deliver, Service and Support Management Objective: DSS01 - Managed Operations	Focus Area: Small and Medium Enterprises
Description	
Coordinate and execute the activities and operational procedures required to deliver internal and outsourced I&T services. Include the execution of predefined standard operating procedures and the required monitoring activities.	
Purpose	
Deliver I&T operational product and service outcomes as planned.	
Small and Medium Enterprise Focus Area Relevance	
The level of detail and formality will depend on the criticality of the systems and the level of outsourcing of enterprise operating activities.	

A. Component: Process		
Management Practice	**Small and Medium Enterprise-specific Metrics**	
DSS01.01 Perform operational procedures. Maintain and perform operational procedures and operational tasks reliably and consistently.	a. Number of incidents caused by operational problems	
Small and Medium Enterprise-specific Activities		**Capability Level**
1. Develop and maintain operational procedures and related activities to support all delivered services.		2
2. Maintain a schedule of operational activities and perform the activities.		
3. Verify that all data expected for processing are received and processed completely, accurately and in a timely manner. Deliver output in accordance with enterprise requirements. Support restart and reprocessing needs. Ensure that users are receiving the right outputs in a secure and timely manner.		3
4. Manage the performance and throughput of the scheduled activities.		4
5. Monitor incidents and problems dealing with operational procedures and take appropriate action to improve reliability of operational tasks performed.		5
Related Guidance (Standards, Frameworks, Compliance Requirements)	**Detailed Reference**	
CMMI Cybermaturity Platform, 2018	TP.SE Safeguard Operational Environment	
HITRUST CSF version 9, September 2017	09.01 Document Operating Procedures	
ISO/IEC 27002:2013/Cor.2:2015(E)	12.1 Operational procedures and responsibilities	
ITIL V3, 2011	Service Operation, 4.1 Event Management	
National Institute of Standards and Technology Special Publication 800-53, Revision 5 (Draft), August 2017	3.13 Physical and environmental protection (PE-13, PE-14, PE-15)	
Management Practice	**Small and Medium Enterprise-specific Metrics**	
DSS01.02 Manage outsourced I&T services. Manage the operation of outsourced I&T services to maintain the protection of enterprise information and reliability of service delivery.	a. Percent of internal processes integrated with providers' processes	
Small and Medium Enterprise-specific Activities		**Capability Level**
1. Ensure that the enterprise's operational business and IT processing requirements—including security, privacy and priorities for service delivery—are adhered to in accordance with contracts and SLAs with third parties hosting or providing services.		3
2. Integrate critical internal IT management processes with those of outsourced service providers. Include, for example, performance and capacity planning, change management, configuration management, service request and incident management, problem management, security and privacy management, business continuity, and the monitoring of process performance and reporting.		
3. Plan for independent audit and assurance of the operational environments of outsourced providers to confirm that agreed-on requirements are being adequately addressed.		4
Related Guidance (Standards, Frameworks, Compliance Requirements)	**Detailed Reference**	
ISF, The Standard of Good Practice for Information Security 2016	SC1.2 Outsourcing	
ISO/IEC 20000-1:2011(E)	4.2 Governance of processes operated by other parties	

<table>
<tr><th colspan="3">A. Component: Process (cont.)</th></tr>
<tr><th>Management Practice</th><th colspan="2">Small and Medium Enterprise-specific Metrics</th></tr>
<tr><td>DSS01.03 Monitor I&T infrastructure.
Monitor the I&T infrastructure and related events. Store sufficient chronological information in operations logs to reconstruct and review time sequences of operations and other activities surrounding or supporting operations.</td><td colspan="2">a. Percent of critical operational event types covered by automatic detection systems
b. Percent of key infrastructure assets monitored</td></tr>
<tr><th colspan="2">Small and Medium Enterprise-specific Activities</th><th>Capability Level</th></tr>
<tr><td colspan="2">1. Log events, identifying the level of information to be recorded based on a consideration of risk and performance.</td><td>2</td></tr>
<tr><td colspan="2">2. Identify and maintain a list of infrastructure assets that need to be monitored based on service criticality and the relationship between configuration items and services that depend on them.</td><td rowspan="3">3</td></tr>
<tr><td colspan="2">3. Produce event logs and retain them for an appropriate period to assist in future investigations.</td></tr>
<tr><td colspan="2">4. Ensure that incident tickets are created in a timely manner when monitoring identified deviations from defined thresholds.</td></tr>
<tr><td colspan="2">5. Establish procedures for monitoring event logs and conduct regular reviews.</td><td>4</td></tr>
<tr><th>Related Guidance (Standards, Frameworks, Compliance Requirements)</th><th colspan="2">Detailed Reference</th></tr>
<tr><td>National Institute of Standards and Technology Special Publication 800-53, Revision 5 (Draft), August 2017</td><td colspan="2">3.10 Maintenance (MA-2, MA-3)</td></tr>
<tr><th>Management Practice</th><th colspan="2">Small and Medium Enterprise-specific Metrics</th></tr>
<tr><td>DSS01.04 Manage the environment.
Maintain measures for protection against environmental factors. Install specialized equipment and devices to monitor and control the environment.</td><td colspan="2">a. Percent of people trained to respond to environmental alarm procedures
b. Percentage of detection equipment monitored</td></tr>
<tr><th colspan="2">Small and Medium Enterprise-specific Activities</th><th>Capability Level</th></tr>
<tr><td colspan="2">1. Identify natural and man-made disasters that might occur in the area within which the IT facilities are located. Assess the potential effect on the IT facilities.</td><td rowspan="3">2</td></tr>
<tr><td colspan="2">2. Identify how I&T equipment, including mobile and off-site equipment, is protected against environmental threats.</td></tr>
<tr><td colspan="2">3. Keep the IT sites and server rooms clean and in a safe condition at all times (i.e., no mess, no paper or cardboard boxes, no filled dustbins, no flammable chemicals or materials).</td></tr>
<tr><td colspan="2">4. Situate and construct IT facilities to minimize and mitigate susceptibility to environmental threats (e.g., theft, air, fire, smoke, water, vibration, terror, vandalism, chemicals, explosives). Consider specific security zones and/or fireproof cells (e.g., locating production and development environments/servers away from each other).</td><td rowspan="2">3</td></tr>
<tr><td colspan="2">5. Compare measures and contingency plans against insurance policy requirements and report results. Address points of noncompliance in a timely manner.</td></tr>
<tr><td colspan="2">6. Regularly monitor and maintain devices that proactively detect environmental threats (e.g., fire, water, smoke, humidity).</td><td>4</td></tr>
<tr><th>Related Guidance (Standards, Frameworks, Compliance Requirements)</th><th colspan="2">Detailed Reference</th></tr>
<tr><td>National Institute of Standards and Technology Special Publication 800-37, Revision 2 (Draft), May 2018</td><td colspan="2">2.1 System and system elements; 3.2 Categorization (Task 5, 6)</td></tr>
</table>

A. Component: Process *(cont.)*		
Management Practice	**Small and Medium Enterprise-specific Metrics**	
DSS01.05 Manage facilities. Manage facilities, including power and communications equipment, in line with laws and regulations, technical and business requirements, vendor specifications, and health and safety guidelines.	a. Time since last test of the uninterruptible power supply's mechanisms b. Number of people trained on health and safety guidelines	
Small and Medium Enterprise-specific Activities		**Capability Level**
1. Examine the IT facilities' requirement for protection against power fluctuations and outages. Procure suitable uninterruptible supply equipment (e.g., batteries, generators) to support business continuity planning.		2
2. Regularly test the uninterruptible power supply's mechanisms and ensure that power can be switched to the supply without any significant effect on business operations.		
3. Ensure that the facilities housing the I&T systems have more than one source for dependent utilities (e.g., power, telecommunications, water, gas). Separate the physical entrance of each utility.		
4. Confirm that cabling external to the IT site is located underground or has suitable alternative protection. Determine that cabling within the IT site is contained within secured conduits and that wiring cabinet access is restricted to authorized personnel.		
5. Ensure that cabling and physical patching (data and phone) are structured and organized. Cabling and conduit structures should be documented (e.g., blueprint building plan and wiring diagrams).		
6. Educate personnel on a regular basis on health and safety laws, regulations, and relevant guidelines. Educate personnel on fire and rescue drills to ensure knowledge and actions taken in case of fire or similar incidents.		
7. Ensure that IT sites and equipment are maintained according to the supplier's recommended service intervals and specifications. Ensure that the maintenance is carried out only by authorized personnel.		3
8. Analyze the facilities housing's high-availability systems for redundancy and fail-over cabling requirements (external and internal).		
9. Ensure that IT sites and facilities are in ongoing compliance with relevant health and safety laws, regulations, guidelines, and vendor specifications.		
10. Record, monitor, manage and resolve facilities incidents in line with the I&T incident management process.		4
11. Analyze physical alterations to IT sites or premises to reassess the environmental risk (e.g., fire or water damage). Report results of this analysis to business continuity and facilities management.		
Related Guidance (Standards, Frameworks, Compliance Requirements)	**Detailed Reference**	
No related guidance for this management practice		

B. Component: Organizational Structures						
Key Management Practice	Chief Operating Officer	Chief Information Officer	Chief Technology Officer	Head IT Operations	Information Security Manager	Privacy Officer
DSS01.01 Perform operational procedures.	R	A	R	R		
DSS01.02 Manage outsourced I&T services.		A	R	R	R	R
DSS01.03 Monitor I&T infrastructure.		R	A	R	R	
DSS01.04 Manage the environment.		R	A	R	R	
DSS01.05 Manage facilities.		R	A	R	R	

C. Component: Information Flows and Items				
Management Practice	Small and Medium Enterprise-specific Inputs		Small and Medium Enterprise-specific Outputs	
DSS01.01 Perform operational procedures.	**From**	**Description**	**Description**	**To**
	BAI05.05	Operation and use plan	Backup log	Internal
			Operational schedule	Internal
DSS01.02 Manage outsourced I&T services.	APO09.03	• SLAs • OLAs	Independent assurance plans	MEA04.02
	BAI05.05	Operation and use plan		
DSS01.03 Monitor I&T infrastructure.	BAI03.11	Service definitions	Asset monitoring rules and event conditions	DSS02.01; DSS02.02
			Incident tickets	DSS02.02
			Event logs	Internal
DSS01.04 Manage the environment.	There are no small and medium enterprise-specific inputs for this practice.		Environmental policies	APO01.09
			Insurance policy reports	MEA03.03
DSS01.05 Manage facilities.	There are no small and medium enterprise-specific inputs for this practice.		Health and safety awareness	Internal
			Facilities assessment reports	MEA01.03

D. Component: People, Skills and Competencies		
Skill	**Related Guidance (Standards, Frameworks, Compliance Requirements)**	**Detailed Reference**
Database administration	Skills Framework for the Information Age V6, 2015	DBAD
Facilities management	Skills Framework for the Information Age V6, 2015	DCMA
IT infrastructure	Skills Framework for the Information Age V6, 2015	ITOP
Methods and tools	Skills Framework for the Information Age V6, 2015	METL
Service delivery	e-Competence Framework (e-CF)—A common European Framework for ICT Professionals in all industry sectors—Part 1: Framework, 2016	C. Run—C.3. Service Delivery
Storage management	Skills Framework for the Information Age V6, 2015	STMG

E. Component: Principles, Policies and Procedures	
Relevant Policy	**Policy Description**
Service management policy	Provides direction and guidance to ensure effective management and implementation of all I&T services to meet business and customer requirements, within a framework of performance measurement. Covers management of risk related to I&T services. (The ITIL V3 framework offers detailed guidance on service management and optimization of risk related to services.)

F. Component: Culture, Ethics and Behavior
Key Culture Elements
Create a culture of habitual excellence throughout the organization. Encourage employees to excel. Create an environment in which operational procedures deliver (more than) the necessary services while also allowing employees to question the status quo and try new ideas. Manage operational excellence through employee engagement and continuous improvement. Apply a customer-centric approach (for both internal and external customers).

G. Component: Services, Infrastructure and Applications
• Cloud hosting services • Infrastructure monitoring tools • Service level monitoring tools

Page intentionally left blank

Domain: Deliver, Service and Support Management Objective: DSS02 - Managed Service Requests and Incidents	Focus Area: Small and Medium Enterprises
Description	
Provide timely and effective response to user requests and resolution of all types of incidents. Restore normal service; record and fulfil user requests; and record, investigate, diagnose, escalate and resolve incidents.	
Purpose	
Achieve increased productivity and minimize disruptions through quick resolution of user queries and incidents. Assess the impact of changes and deal with service incidents. Resolve user requests and restore service in response to incidents.	
Small and Medium Enterprise Focus Area Relevance	
Ensure the impact on operations is reduced by actively managing incident responses. Incident response management should cover all corporate systems that are used in the enterprise's production environment, including IT assets. It also applies to all employees, assignees, interns and third parties who perform activities on the enterprise's premises.	

A. Component: Process		
Management Practice	**Small and Medium Enterprise-specific Metrics**	
DSS02.01 Define classification schemes for incidents and service requests. Define classification schemes and models for incidents and service requests.	a. Total number of service requests and incidents per priority level	
Small and Medium Enterprise-specific Activities		**Capability Level**
1. Define incident and service request classification and prioritization schemes and criteria for problem registration to ensure consistent approaches for handling, informing users and conducting trend analysis.		3
2. Define incident models for known errors to enable efficient and effective resolution.		
3. Define service request models according to service request type to enable self-help and efficient service for standard requests.		
4. Define incident escalation rules and procedures, especially for major incidents and security incidents.		
5. Define knowledge sources on incidents and requests and how to use them.		
Related Guidance (Standards, Frameworks, Compliance Requirements)	**Detailed Reference**	
CMMI Cybermaturity Platform, 2018	IA.IP Implement Incident Investigation Processes	
HITRUST CSF version 9, September 2017	11.01 Reporting Information Security Incidents and Weaknesses	
ISF, The Standard of Good Practice for Information Security 2016	TM2 Security Incident Management	
ISO/IEC 20000-1:2011(E)	8.1 Incident and service request management	
ISO/IEC 27002:2013/Cor.2:2015(E)	16. Information security incident management	
Management Practice	**Small and Medium Enterprise-specific Metrics**	
DSS02.02 Record, classify and prioritize requests and incidents. Identify, record and classify service requests and incidents and assign a priority according to business criticality and service agreements.	a. Frequency of evaluating the classification schema b. Number of service requests and incidents not categorized c. Percentage of service requirements and incidents with high priority	
Small and Medium Enterprise-specific Activities		**Capability Level**
1. Log all service requests and incidents, recording all relevant information, so that they can be handled effectively and a full historical record can be maintained.		2
2. Classify service requests and incidents by type and category to enable trend analysis.		
3. Prioritize service requests and incidents based on business impact and urgency.		
Related Guidance (Standards, Frameworks, Compliance Requirements)	**Detailed Reference**	
No related guidance for this management practice		

A. Component: Process *(cont.)*		
Management Practice	**Small and Medium Enterprise-specific Metrics**	
DSS02.03 Verify, approve and fulfill service requests. Select the appropriate request procedures and verify that the service requests fulfill defined request criteria. Obtain approval, if required, and fulfill the requests.	a. Mean elapsed time for handling each type of service request b. Percentage of service requests not fulfilled	
Small and Medium Enterprise-specific Activities		**Capability Level**
1. Verify justifications for service requests using, where possible, a predefined process flow and standard changes.		2
2. Obtain financial and functional approval or sign-off, if required, or use predefined approvals for agreed-on standard changes.		
3. Fulfill the requests by performing the selected request procedure, using, where possible, self-help automated menus and predefined request models for frequently requested items.		3
Related Guidance (Standards, Frameworks, Compliance Requirements)	**Detailed Reference**	
ITIL V3, 2011	Service Operation, 4.3 Request Fulfilment	
Management Practice	**Small and Medium Enterprise-specific Metrics**	
DSS02.04 Investigate, diagnose and allocate incidents. Identify and record incident symptoms, determine possible causes, and allocate for resolution.	a. Number of correctly determined symptom causes	
Small and Medium Enterprise-specific Activities		**Capability Level**
1. Identify and describe relevant symptoms to establish the most probable causes of the incidents. Reference available knowledge resources (including known errors and problems) to identify possible incident resolutions (temporary workarounds and/or permanent solutions).		2
2. Assign incidents to specialist functions if deeper expertise is needed, and engage the appropriate level of management, where and if needed.		
Related Guidance (Standards, Frameworks, Compliance Requirements)	**Detailed Reference**	
No related guidance for this management practice		
Management Practice	**Small and Medium Enterprise-specific Metrics**	
DSS02.05 Resolve and recover from incidents. Document, apply and test the identified solutions or workarounds. Perform recovery actions to restore the I&T-related service.	a. Percent of incidents resolved within agreed-on SLA b. Percent of stakeholder satisfaction with resolution and recovery from incident	
Small and Medium Enterprise-specific Activities		**Capability Level**
1. Select and apply the most appropriate incident resolutions (temporary workaround and/or permanent solution).		2
2. Record whether workarounds were used for incident resolution.		
3. Perform recovery actions, if required.		
4. Document incident resolution and assess if the resolution can be used as a future knowledge source.		3
Related Guidance (Standards, Frameworks, Compliance Requirements)	**Detailed Reference**	
ITIL V3, 2011	Service Operation, 4.2 Incident Management	
National Institute of Standards and Technology Framework for Improving Critical Infrastructure Cybersecurity v1.1, April 2018	RC.RP Recovery Planning	
National Institute of Standards and Technology Special Publication 800-53, Revision 5 (Draft), August 2017	3.9 Incident response (IR-4, IR-5, IR-6)	
The CIS Critical Security Controls for Effective Cyber Defense Version 6.1, August 2016	CSC 19: Incident Response and Management	

A. Component: Process *(cont.)*	
Management Practice	**Small and Medium Enterprise-specific Metrics**
DSS02.06 Close service requests and incidents. Verify satisfactory incident resolution and/or fulfilment of requests, and close.	a. Percent of user satisfaction with service request fulfilment b. Percent of incidents resolved within an agreed-on/acceptable period of time

Small and Medium Enterprise-specific Activities	Capability Level
1. Verify with the affected users that the service request has been fulfilled satisfactorily or the incident has been resolved satisfactorily and within an agreed-on/acceptable period of time.	2
2. Close service requests and incidents.	

Related Guidance (Standards, Frameworks, Compliance Requirements)	Detailed Reference
No related guidance for this management practice	

Management Practice	Small and Medium Enterprise-specific Metrics
DSS02.07 Track status and produce reports. Regularly track, analyze and report incidents and fulfilment of requests. Examine trends to provide information for continual improvement.	a. Number and percent of incidents causing disruption to business-critical processes

Small and Medium Enterprise-specific Activities	Capability Level
1. Monitor and track incident escalations and resolutions and request handling procedures to progress toward resolution or completion.	2
2. Agree with the business on incident reporting frequency requirements and medium.	3
3. Produce and distribute timely reports on resolution of incidents and fulfillment of service requests.	4
4. Analyze incidents and service requests by category and type to establish trends and identify patterns of recurring issues, SLA breaches or inefficiencies.	
5. Use information resulting from the analysis as input to continual improvement planning.	5

Related Guidance (Standards, Frameworks, Compliance Requirements)	Detailed Reference
CMMI Cybermaturity Platform, 2018	MI.IM Ensure Incident Mitigation; IR.IR Incident Reporting
National Institute of Standards and Technology Special Publication 800-53, Revision 5 (Draft), August 2017	3.9 Incident response (IR-7, IR-8)

B. Component: Organizational Structures

Key Management Practice	Business Process Owners	IT Development Coordinator	IT Operations Coordinator
DSS02.01 Define classification schemes for incidents and service requests.		R	A
DSS02.02 Record, classify and prioritize requests and incidents.			A
DSS02.03 Verify, approve and fulfill service requests.	R	R	A
DSS02.04 Investigate, diagnose and allocate incidents.	R		A
DSS02.05 Resolve and recover from incidents.		R	A
DSS02.06 Close service requests and incidents.			A
DSS02.07 Track status and produce reports.			A

C. Component: Information Flows and Items				
Management Practice	**Small and Medium Enterprise-specific Inputs**		**Small and Medium Enterprise-specific Outputs**	
	From	**Description**	**Description**	**To**
DSS02.01 Define classification schemes for incidents and service requests.	APO09.03	SLAs	Rules for incident escalation	Internal
	BAI10.02	Configuration repository	Incident and service request classification schemes and models	Internal
	BAI10.04	Configuration status reports		
DSS02.02 Record, classify and prioritize requests and incidents.	APO09.03	SLAs	Classified and prioritized incidents and service requests	APO08.03 APO09.04 APO13.03
	BAI04.05	Emergency escalation procedure	Incident and service request log	Internal MEA04.07
	DSS01.03	Incident tickets		
	DSS05.07	Security-related incident tickets		
DSS02.03 Verify, approve and fulfill service requests.	There are no small and medium enterprise-specific inputs for this practice.		Approved service requests	BAI06.01
			Fulfilled service requests	Internal
DSS02.04 Investigate, diagnose and allocate incidents.	BAI07.07	Supplemental support plan	Problem log	DSS03.01
			Incident symptoms	Internal
DSS02.05 Resolve and recover from incidents.	APO12.06	Risk-related incident response plans	Incident resolutions	DSS03.03 DSS03.04 DSS03.05 MEA04.07
	DSS03.03	Known error records		
	DSS03.04	Communication of knowledge learned		
DSS02.06 Close service requests and incidents.	There are no small and medium enterprise-specific inputs for this practice.		User confirmation of satisfactory fulfillment or resolution	APO08.03
			Closed service requests and incidents	APO08.03 APO09.04
DSS02.07 Track status and produce reports.	APO09.03	OLAs	Incident status and trends report	APO08.03 APO09.04 APO11.04 APO12.01 MEA01.03
			Request fulfillment status and trends report	APO08.03 APO09.04 APO11.04 MEA01.03

D. Component: People, Skills and Competencies		
Skill	**Related Guidance (Standards, Frameworks, Compliance Requirements)**	**Detailed Reference**
Application support	Skills Framework for the Information Age V6, 2015	ASUP
Customer service support	Skills Framework for the Information Age V6, 2015	CSMG
Incident management	Skills Framework for the Information Age V6, 2015	USUP
Network support	Skills Framework for the Information Age V6, 2015	NTAS
User support	e-Competence Framework (e-CF)—A common European Framework for ICT Professionals in all industry sectors—Part 1: Framework, 2016	C. Run—C.1. User Support

E. Component: Principles, Policies and Procedures	
Relevant Policy	**Policy Description**
Service request policy	States rationale and provides guidance for a service request/incident, including how it should be documented

F. Component: Culture, Ethics and Behavior
Key Culture Elements
Enable employees to identify incidents on a correct and timely basis and implement appropriate escalation paths. Encourage prevention. Respond to and resolve incidents immediately. Avoid a hero culture.

G. Component: Services, Infrastructure and Applications
Incident tracking tools and system

Page intentionally left blank

Domain: Deliver, Service and Support Management Objective: DSS03 - Managed Problems	Focus Area: Small and Medium Enterprises
Description	
Identify and classify problems and their root causes. Provide timely resolution to prevent recurring incidents. Provide recommendations for improvements.	
Purpose	
Increase availability, improve service levels, reduce costs, improve customer convenience and satisfaction by reducing the number of operational problems, and identify root causes as part of problem resolution.	
Small and Medium Enterprise Focus Area Relevance	
Ensure that enterprise processes for incident response and service request fulfillment are functioning well before focusing on problem management. In addition, ensure the processes for problem identification and solving are in place before starting on proactive problem management.	

A. Component: Process		
Management Practice	**Small and Medium Enterprise-specific Metrics**	
DSS03.01 Identify and classify problems. Define and implement criteria and procedures to identify and report problems. Include problem classification, categorization and prioritization.	a. Percent of major incidents for which problems were logged	
Small and Medium Enterprise-specific Activities		**Capability Level**
1. Identify problems through the correlation of incident reports, error logs and other problem identification resources.		2
2. Define priority levels through consultation with the business to ensure that problem identification and root cause analysis are handled in a timely manner according to the agreed-on SLAs. Base priority levels on business impact and urgency.		
3. Report the status of identified problems to the service desk so customers and IT management can be kept informed.		
4. Maintain a single problem management catalog to register and report problems identified and to establish audit trails of the problem management processes, including the status of each problem (i.e., open, reopen, in progress or closed).		3
Related Guidance (Standards, Frameworks, Compliance Requirements)	**Detailed Reference**	
ISO/IEC 20000-1:2011(E)	8.2 Problem management	
Management Practice	**Small and Medium Enterprise-specific Metrics**	
DSS03.02 Investigate and diagnose problems. Investigate and diagnose problems using relevant subject matter experts to assess and analyze root causes.	a. Number of identified problems classified as known errors b. Percent of problems investigated and diagnosed	
Small and Medium Enterprise-specific Activities		**Capability Level**
1. Identify problems that may be known errors by comparing incident data with the database of known and suspected errors (e.g., those communicated by external vendors) and classify appropriate problems as known errors.		3
2. Associate the affected configuration items to the established/known error.		
3. Communicate progress in resolving problems and monitor the impact of problems not solved.		
Related Guidance (Standards, Frameworks, Compliance Requirements)	**Detailed Reference**	
No related guidance for this management practice		
Management Practice	**Small and Medium Enterprise-specific Metrics**	
DSS03.03 Raise known errors. As soon as root causes of problems are identified, create known-error records, document appropriate workarounds and identify potential solutions.	a. Number of problems for which a satisfactory resolution that addressed root causes was found b. Percent of problems not resolved by problem owners	
Small and Medium Enterprise-specific Activities		**Capability Level**
1. As soon as the root causes of problems are identified, create known-error records and develop a suitable workaround.		2
2. Identify, evaluate, prioritize and process solutions to known errors based on a cost-benefit business case, business impact and urgency.		3
Related Guidance (Standards, Frameworks, Compliance Requirements)	**Detailed Reference**	
No related guidance for this management practice		

A. Component: Process *(cont.)*		
Management Practice	**Small and Medium Enterprise-specific Metrics**	
DSS03.04 Resolve and close problems. Identify and initiate sustainable solutions addressing the root cause. Raise change requests via the established change management process, if required, to resolve errors. Ensure that the personnel affected are aware of the actions taken and the plans developed to prevent future incidents from occurring.	a. Decrease in number of recurring incidents caused by unresolved problems b. Percent of workarounds defined for open problems	
Small and Medium Enterprise-specific Activities		**Capability Level**
1. Close problem records either after confirmation of successful elimination of the known error or after agreement with the business on how to alternatively handle the problem.		2
2. Inform the service desk of any ramifications of problem closure—for example, the schedule for fixing known errors and possible workarounds—and emphasize the fact that the problem will remain until the change is implemented. Outline the consequences of the approach taken. Keep affected users and customers informed as appropriate.		3
3. Review and confirm the success of resolutions of major problems.		4
4. Make sure the knowledge learned from the review is shared with the business process owner and other relevant stakeholders.		5
Related Guidance (Standards, Frameworks, Compliance Requirements)	**Detailed Reference**	
No related guidance for this management practice		
Management Practice	**Small and Medium Enterprise-specific Metrics**	
DSS03.05 Perform proactive problem management. Collect and analyze operational data (especially incident and change records) to identify emerging trends that may indicate problems. Log problem records to enable assessment.	a. Percent of problems logged as part of the proactive problem management activity	
Small and Medium Enterprise-specific Activities		**Capability Level**
1. Capture problem information related to I&T changes and incidents.		3
2. Ensure that process owners and IT management meet regularly to discuss known problems and future planned changes.		
3. Identify and initiate sustainable solutions (permanent fixes) addressing the root cause and raise change requests via the established change management processes.		
4. To enable the enterprise to monitor the total costs of problems, capture change efforts resulting from problem management process activities (e.g., fixes to problems and known errors) and report on them.		4
5. Monitor the problem resolution against business requirements and SLAs. Ensure the proper escalation of problems—for example, escalating to the IT management level according to agreed-on criteria, contacting external vendors or referring issues to the executive committee to increase the priority of an urgent request for change (RFC) to implement a temporary workaround.		
6. To optimize the use of resources and reduce workarounds, track problem trends.		5
Related Guidance (Standards, Frameworks, Compliance Requirements)	**Detailed Reference**	
CMMI Cybermaturity Platform, 2018	MI.IC Ensure Incident Containment	
ITIL V3, 2011	Service Operation, 4.4 Problem Management	

B. Component: Organizational Structures				
Key Management Practice	Executive Committee	Head of IT	IT Development Coordinator	IT Operations Coordinator
DSS03.01 Identify and classify problems.		A	R	R
DSS03.02 Investigate and diagnose problems.		A		R
DSS03.03 Raise known errors.		A		R
DSS03.04 Resolve and close problems.		A		R
DSS03.05 Perform proactive problem management.	R	A		R

C. Component: Information Flows and Items				
Management Practice	Small and Medium Enterprise-specific Inputs		Small and Medium Enterprise-specific Outputs	
	From	Description	Description	To
DSS03.01 Identify and classify problems.	APO12.06	Risk-related root causes	Problem classification scheme	DSS02.01
	DSS02.04	Problem log	Problem status reports	DSS02.07
			Problem register	Internal
DSS03.02 Investigate and diagnose problems.	APO12.06	Risk-related root causes	Problem resolution reports	DSS02.07
			Root causes of problems	Internal DSS03.05
DSS03.03 Raise known errors.	APO12.06	Risk-related root causes	Proposed solutions to known errors	BAI06.01
	DSS02.05	Incident resolutions	Known error records	DSS02.05
DSS03.04 Resolve and close problems.	DSS02.05	Incident resolutions	Communication of knowledge learned	APO08.04 DSS02.05
			Closed problem records	DSS02.06
DSS03.05 Perform proactive problem management.	APO12.06	Risk-related root causes	Identified sustainable solutions	BAI06.01
	DSS02.05	Incident resolutions	Problem resolution monitoring reports	DSS02.07 MEA04.07

D. Component: People, Skills and Competencies		
Skill	**Related Guidance (Standards, Frameworks, Compliance Requirements)**	**Detailed Reference**
Application support	Skills Framework for the Information Age V6, 2015	ASUP
Network support	Skills Framework for the Information Age V6, 2015	NTAS
Problem management	e-Competence Framework (e-CF)—A common European Framework for ICT Professionals in all industry sectors—Part 1: Framework, 2016	C. Run—C.4. Problem Management
Problem management	Skills Framework for the Information Age V6, 2015	PBMG

E. Component: Principles, Policies and Procedures	
Relevant Policy	**Policy Description**
There are no small and medium enterprise-specific principles, policies and procedures for this objective.	

F. Component: Culture, Ethics and Behavior
Key Culture Elements
Support a culture of proactive problem management (detection, action and prevention) with clearly defined roles and responsibilities. Ensure a transparent and open environment for reporting problems by providing independent reporting mechanisms and/or rewarding people who bring problems forward.

G. Component: Services, Infrastructure and Applications
Problem tracking/resolution system

Domain: Deliver, Service and Support Management Objective: DSS04 - Managed Continuity	Focus Area: Small and Medium Enterprises
Description	
Establish and maintain a plan to enable the business and IT organizations to respond to incidents and quickly adapt to disruptions. This will enable continued operations of critical business processes and required I&T services and maintain availability of resources, assets and information at a level acceptable to the enterprise.	
Purpose	
Adapt rapidly, continue business operations and maintain availability of resources and information at a level acceptable to the enterprise in the event of a significant disruption (e.g., threats, opportunities, demands).	
Small and Medium Enterprise Focus Area Relevance	
The description and purpose of this COBIT objective is fully applicable to SMEs. No SME-specific focus area relevance statement is required.	

A. Component: Process		
Management Practice	**Small and Medium Enterprise-specific Metrics**	
DSS04.01 Define the business continuity policy, objectives and scope. Define business continuity policy and scope, aligned with enterprise and stakeholder objectives, to improve business resilience.	a. Number of business processes included in business continuity scope b. Number of I&T services included in business continuity scope	
Small and Medium Enterprise-specific Activities		**Capability Level**
1. Identify internal and outsourced business processes and service activities that are critical to the enterprise operations or necessary to meet legal and/or contractual obligations.		2
2. Define and document the agreed-on minimum policy objectives and scope for business resilience.		
Related Guidance (Standards, Frameworks, Compliance Requirements)	**Detailed Reference**	
HITRUST CSF version 9, September 2017	12.01 Information Security Aspects of Business Continuity Management	
ISF, The Standard of Good Practice for Information Security 2016	BC1.1 Business Continuity Strategy; BC1.2 Business Continuity Programme	
ISO/IEC 27002:2013/Cor.2:2015(E)	17. Information security aspects of business continuity management	
National Institute of Standards and Technology Special Publication 800-53, Revision 5 (Draft), August 2017	3.6 Contingency planning (CP-1)	
Management Practice	**Small and Medium Enterprise-specific Metrics**	
DSS04.02 Maintain business resilience. Evaluate business resilience options and choose a cost-effective and viable strategy that will ensure enterprise continuity, disaster recovery and incident response in the face of a disaster or other major incident or disruption.	a. Total maximum downtime in occurrence of major incident or disruption per business process	
Small and Medium Enterprise-specific Activities		**Capability Level**
1. Identify potential scenarios likely to give rise to events that could cause significant disruptive incidents.		2
2. Conduct a business impact analysis to evaluate the impact over time of a disruption to critical business functions.		
3. Establish the minimum time required to recover a business process and supporting I&T based on an acceptable length of business interruption and maximum tolerable outage.		
4. Determine the conditions and owners of key decisions that will cause the continuity plans to be invoked.		
5. Assess the likelihood of threats that could cause loss of business continuity and identify measures that will reduce the likelihood and impact through improved prevention and increased resilience.		3
6. Identify resource requirements and costs for each strategic technical option and make strategic recommendations.		
7. Obtain executive business approval for selected strategic options.		4
Related Guidance (Standards, Frameworks, Compliance Requirements)	**Detailed Reference**	
ISF, The Standard of Good Practice for Information Security 2016	BC1.3 Resilient Technical Environments	
ITIL V3, 2011	Service Design, 4.6 IT Continuity Management	
National Institute of Standards and Technology Special Publication 800-53, Revision 5 (Draft), August 2017	3.6 Contingency planning (CP-2)	

A. Component: Process *(cont.)*		
Management Practice	**Small and Medium Enterprise-specific Metrics**	
DSS04.03 Develop and implement a business continuity response. Develop a business continuity plan (BCP) and disaster recovery plan (DRP) based on the strategy. Document all procedures necessary for the enterprise to continue critical activities in the event of an incident.	a. Number of critical business systems not covered by the plan	
Small and Medium Enterprise-specific Activities		**Capability Level**
1. Define the incident response actions and communications (internal, such as to employees, and external, such as to suppliers and customers) to be taken in the event of disruption. Define related roles and responsibilities, including accountability for policy and implementation.		2
2. Ensure that key suppliers and outsource partners have effective continuity plans in place. Obtain audited evidence as required.		
3. Define the conditions and recovery procedures that would enable resumption of business processing, including updating and reconciliation of information databases to preserve information integrity.		
4. Develop and maintain operational BCPs and DRPs detailing procedures to be followed to enable continued operation of critical business processes and/or arrangements for temporary processing, including links to plans of outsourced service providers.		
5. Define and document the resources required to support the continuity and recovery procedures, considering people, facilities and IT infrastructure.		
6. Define and document the information backup requirements required to support the plans, including plans and paper documents as well as data files, and consider the need for security and off-site storage.		
7. Distribute the plans and supporting documentation securely to appropriately authorized interested parties and make sure they are accessible under all disaster scenarios.		3
Related Guidance (Standards, Frameworks, Compliance Requirements)	**Detailed Reference**	
ISF, The Standard of Good Practice for Information Security 2016	BC1.4 Crisis Management; BC2.1 Business Continuity Planning	
National Institute of Standards and Technology Special Publication 800-53, Revision 5 (Draft), August 2017	3.6 Contingency planning (CP-6, CP-9, CP-10)	
Management Practice	**Small and Medium Enterprise-specific Metrics**	
DSS04.04 Exercise, test and review the business continuity plan (BCP) and disaster response plan (DRP). Test continuity on a regular basis to exercise plans against predetermined outcomes, uphold business resilience and allow innovative solutions to be developed.	a. Frequency of tests b. Number of exercises and tests that have achieved recovery objectives	
Small and Medium Enterprise-specific Activities		**Capability Level**
1. Define objectives for exercising and testing the BCP and DRP to verify completeness in addressing business risk.		2
2. Define and agree on stakeholder exercises that are realistic and validate continuity procedures. Include roles and responsibilities and data retention arrangements that result in minimum disruption to business processes.		
3. Schedule exercises and test activities as defined in the continuity plans.		3
4. Conduct a post-exercise debriefing and analysis to consider the achievement.		4
5. Develop recommendations for improving the current continuity plans based on the results of the review.		5
Related Guidance (Standards, Frameworks, Compliance Requirements)	**Detailed Reference**	
CMMI Cybermaturity Platform, 2018	PP.RS Develop and Maintain Response Plans; PP.RP Develop and Maintain Recovery Plans	
ISF, The Standard of Good Practice for Information Security 2016	BC2.3 Business Continuity Testing	
The CIS Critical Security Controls for Effective Cyber Defense Version 6.1, August 2016	CSC 20: Penetration Tests and Red Team Exercises	

A. Component: Process *(cont.)*	
Management Practice	**Small and Medium Enterprise-specific Metrics**
DSS04.05 Review, maintain and improve the continuity plans. Conduct a management review of the continuity capability at regular intervals to ensure its continued suitability, adequacy and effectiveness. Manage changes to the plans in accordance with the change control process to ensure that continuity plans are kept up to date and continually reflect actual business requirements.	a. Frequency of updating the continuity plans and executing the business impact assessments (BIAs)

Small and Medium Enterprise-specific Activities	Capability Level
1. Review the continuity plans and capability on a regular basis against any assumptions made and current business operational and strategic objectives.	3
2. Review the continuity plans on a regular basis to consider the impact of new or major changes to the enterprise organization, business processes, outsourcing arrangements, technologies, infrastructure, operating systems and application systems.	
3. Consider whether a revised BIA may be required, depending on the nature of the change.	
4. Recommend and communicate changes in policy, plans, procedures, infrastructure, and roles and responsibilities for management approval and processing via the IT change management process.	4

Related Guidance (Standards, Frameworks, Compliance Requirements)	Detailed Reference
No related guidance for this management practice	

Management Practice	Small and Medium Enterprise-specific Metrics
DSS04.06 Conduct continuity plan training. Provide all concerned internal and external parties with regular training sessions regarding procedures and their roles and responsibilities in case of disruption.	a. Percent of internal and external stakeholders that have received training

Small and Medium Enterprise-specific Activities	Capability Level
1. Roll out BCP and DRP awareness and training.	2
2. Develop competencies based on practical training including participation in exercises and tests.	3
3. Monitor skills and competencies based on the exercise and test results.	4

Related Guidance (Standards, Frameworks, Compliance Requirements)	Detailed Reference
National Institute of Standards and Technology Special Publication 800-53, Revision 5 (Draft), August 2017	3.6 Contingency planning (CP-4)

Management Practice	Small and Medium Enterprise-specific Metrics
DSS04.07 Manage backup arrangements. Maintain availability of business-critical information.	a. Percent of backup media transferred and stored securely b. Percent of successful and timely restorations from backup or alternate media copies c. Frequency with which archived data are tested for validity

Small and Medium Enterprise-specific Activities	Capability Level
1. Back up systems, applications, data and documentation according to a defined schedule, considering frequency (monthly, weekly, daily, etc.), mode of backup (e.g., disk mirroring for real-time backups vs. DVD-ROM for long-term retention), type of backup (e.g., full vs. incremental), type of media, use of automated online backups, data types (e.g., voice, optical), creation of logs, critical end-user computing data (e.g., spreadsheets), physical and logical location of data sources, security and access rights, privacy, and encryption.	2
2. Define requirements for on-site and off-site storage of backup data that meet the business requirements. Consider the accessibility required to back up data.	
3. Periodically test and refresh archived and backup data.	3
4. Ensure that systems, applications, data and documentation maintained or processed by third parties are adequately backed up or otherwise secured. Consider requiring return of backups from third parties. Consider escrow or deposit arrangements.	

A. Component: Process *(cont.)*	
Related Guidance (Standards, Frameworks, Compliance Requirements)	**Detailed Reference**
CMMI Cybermaturity Platform, 2018	IP.BP Apply Backup Processes
HITRUST CSF version 9, September 2017	09.05 Information Back-Up
ISF, The Standard of Good Practice for Information Security 2016	SY2.3 Backup
ISO/IEC 27002:2013/Cor.2:2015(E)	12.3 Backup
National Institute of Standards and Technology Special Publication 800-53, Revision 5 (Draft), August 2017	3.6 Contingency planning (CP-3)
The CIS Critical Security Controls for Effective Cyber Defense Version 6.1, August 2016	CSC 10: Data Recovery Capability
Management Practice	**Small and Medium Enterprise-specific Metrics**
DSS04.08 Conduct post-resumption review. Assess the adequacy of the business continuity plan (BCP) and disaster response plan (DRP) following successful resumption of business processes and services after a disruption.	a. Percentage of successful resumptions of business processes and services after an interruption

Small and Medium Enterprise-specific Activities	Capability Level
1. Assess adherence to the documented BCP and DRP.	4
2. Determine the effectiveness of the plans.	
3. Identify weaknesses or omissions in the plans and capabilities and make recommendations for improvement. Obtain management approval for any changes to the plans	5

Related Guidance (Standards, Frameworks, Compliance Requirements)	Detailed Reference
No related guidance for this management practice	

B. Component: Organizational Structures

Key Management Practice	Executive Committee	General Manager	Operations Manager	Business Process Owners	Head of IT	Security Expert	IT Development Coordinator	IT Operations Coordinator
DSS04.01 Define the business continuity policy, objectives and scope.	R		A	R	R	R		R
DSS04.02 Maintain business resilience.	R		A	R	R			R
DSS04.03 Develop and implement a business continuity response.		A	R	R	R			R
DSS04.04 Exercise, test and review the business continuity plan (BCP) and disaster response plan (DRP).		A	R	R	R			R
DSS04.05 Review, maintain and improve the continuity plans.			A	R	R	R		R
DSS04.06 Conduct continuity plan training.			A	R	R		R	R
DSS04.07 Manage backup arrangements.			A					R
DSS04.08 Conduct post-resumption review.			A	R	R	R		R

C. Component: Information Flows and Items				
Management Practice	Small and Medium Enterprise-specific Inputs		Small and Medium Enterprise-specific Outputs	
	From	Description	Description	To
DSS04.01 Define the business continuity policy, objectives and scope.	APO09.03	SLAs	Criticality of current continuity capabilities and gaps	Internal
DSS04.02 Maintain business resilience.	APO12.06	• Risk impact communication • Risk-related root causes	Approved strategic options	APO02.05
			BIAs	APO12.02
			Continuity requirements	Internal
DSS04.03 Develop and implement a business continuity response.	APO09.03	OLAs	BCP	Internal
DSS04.04 Exercise, test and review the business continuity plan (BCP) and disaster response plan (DRP).	There are no small and medium enterprise-specific inputs for this practice.		Test exercises	Internal
			Test results and recommendations	Internal
DSS04.05 Review, maintain and improve the continuity plans.	There are no small and medium enterprise-specific inputs for this practice.		Recommended changes to plans	Internal
DSS04.06 Conduct continuity plan training.	HR	List of personnel requiring training	Monitoring results of skills and competencies	APO07.03
			Training requirements	APO07.03
DSS04.07 Manage backup arrangements.	APO14.10	• Backup plan • Backup test plan	Test results of backup data	Internal
			Backup data	Internal APO14.08
DSS04.08 Conduct post-resumption review.	There are no small and medium enterprise-specific inputs for this practice.		Approved changes to the plans	BAI06.01
			Post-resumption review report	Internal

D. Component: People, Skills and Competencies		
Skill	Related Guidance (Standards, Frameworks, Compliance Requirements)	Detailed Reference
Continuity management	Skills Framework for the Information Age V6, 2015	COPL

E. Component: Principles, Policies and Procedures	
Relevant Policy	Policy Description
Business continuity policy	Outlines management's commitment to the BIA, business contingency plan (including trusted recovery), recovery requirements for critical systems, defined thresholds and triggers for contingencies, escalation plan, data recovery plan, training, and testing.

F. Component: Culture, Ethics and Behavior
Key Culture Elements
Embed the need for business resilience in the enterprise culture. Regularly and frequently update employees about core values, desired behaviors and strategic objectives to maintain the enterprise's composure and image in every situation. Regularly test business continuity procedures and disaster recovery.

G. Component: Services, Infrastructure and Applications
• External hosting services • Incident monitoring tools • Remote storage facility services

Domain: Deliver, Service and Support Management Objective: DSS05 - Managed Security Services	Focus Area: Small and Medium Enterprises
Description	
Protect enterprise information to maintain the level of information security risk acceptable to the enterprise in accordance with the security policy. Establish and maintain information security roles and access privileges. Perform security monitoring.	
Purpose	
Minimize the business impact of operational information security vulnerabilities and incidents.	
Small and Medium Enterprise Focus Area Relevance	
Establish the security guidelines and policies and define the required outcome for outside service providers. The practices and related activities can provide input to the contracts executed with the service provider(s).	

A. Component: Process	
Management Practice	**Small and Medium Enterprise-specific Metrics**
DSS05.01 Protect against malicious software. Implement and maintain preventive, detective and corrective measures (especially up-to-date security patches and virus control) across the enterprise to protect information systems and technology from malicious software (e.g., ransomware, malware, viruses, worms, spyware, spam).	a. Number of successful malware attacks b. Percent of employees failing tests on malicious attacks (e.g., test phishing mail)

Small and Medium Enterprise-specific Activities	Capability Level
1. Install and activate malicious software protection tools on all processing facilities, with malicious software definition files that are updated as required (automatically or semi-automatically).	2
2. Filter incoming traffic, such as email and downloads, to protect against unsolicited information (e.g., spyware, phishing emails).	
3. Communicate malicious software awareness and enforce prevention procedures and responsibilities. Conduct periodic training about malware in email and Internet usage. Train users to not open but report suspicious emails and to not install shared or unapproved software.	3
4. Distribute all protection software centrally (version and patch-level) using centralized configuration and IT change management.	
5. Regularly review and evaluate information on new potential threats (e.g., reviewing vendors' products and services security advisories).	4

Related Guidance (Standards, Frameworks, Compliance Requirements)	Detailed Reference
CMMI Cybermaturity Platform, 2018	DP.DC Detect Malicious Code; RI.VT Vulnerability and Threat Identification
HITRUST CSF version 9, September 2017	09.04 Protection Against Malicious & Mobile Code
SF, The Standard of Good Practice for Information Security 2016	TS1 Security Solutions
SO/IEC 27002:2013/Cor.2:2015(E)	12.2 Protection against malware
The CIS Critical Security Controls for Effective Cyber Defense Version 6.1, August 2016	CSC 4: Continuous Vulnerability Assessment and Remediation; CSC 8: Malware Defenses

A. Component: Process *(cont.)*	
Management Practice	**Small and Medium Enterprise-specific Metrics**
DSS05.02 Manage network and connectivity security. Use security measures and related management procedures to protect information over all methods of connectivity.	a. Percent of firewall breaches against number of firewall rules applied b. Number of vulnerabilities discovered

Small and Medium Enterprise-specific Activities	Capability Level
1. Allow only authorized devices to have access to corporate information and the enterprise network. Configure these devices to force password entry.	2
2. Implement network filtering mechanisms, such as firewalls and intrusion detection software, with appropriate policies to control inbound and outbound traffic.	
3. Apply approved security protocols to network connectivity.	
4. Configure network equipment in a secure manner.	
5. Establish trusted mechanisms to support the secure transmission and receipt of information.	3
6. Carry out periodic testing of system security to determine adequacy of system protection.	4

Related Guidance (Standards, Frameworks, Compliance Requirements)	Detailed Reference
CMMI Cybermaturity Platform, 2018	AC.MI Manage Network Integrity & Segregation; CM.MN Monitor Networks; AC.CP Manage Communication Protections
HITRUST CSF version 9, September 2017	01.04 Network Access Control
ISF, The Standard of Good Practice for Information Security 2016	PA2.3 Mobile Device Connectivity; NC1.1 Network Device Configuration
ISO/IEC 27002:2013/Cor.2:2015(E)	13.1 Network security management
National Institute of Standards and Technology Special Publication 800-53, Revision 5 (Draft), August 2017	3.20 System and information integrity (SI-8)
The CIS Critical Security Controls for Effective Cyber Defense Version 6.1, August 2016	CSC 9: Limitation and Control of Network Ports, Protocols, and Services; CSC 11: Secure Configurations for Network Devices such as Firewalls, Routers, and Switches

Management Practice	Small and Medium Enterprise-specific Metrics
DSS05.03 Manage endpoint security. Ensure that endpoints (e.g., laptop, desktop, server, and other mobile and network devices or software) are secured at a level that is equal to or greater than the defined security requirements for the information processed, stored or transmitted.	a. Number of incidents involving endpoint devices b. Number of unauthorized devices detected on the network or in the end-user environment c. Percent of individuals receiving security awareness training

Small and Medium Enterprise-specific Activities	Capability Level
1. Configure operating systems in a secure manner.	2
2. Implement device lockdown mechanisms.	
3. Manage remote access and control (e.g., mobile devices, teleworking).	
4. Manage network configuration in a secure manner.	
5. Implement network traffic filtering on endpoint devices.	
6. Provide physical protection of endpoint devices.	
7. Dispose of endpoint devices securely.	
8. Manage malicious access through email and web browsers by blocking certain websites, deactivating click-through on links for smartphone, etc.	
9. Encrypt information in storage according to its classification.	3

A. Component: Process *(cont.)*	
Related Guidance (Standards, Frameworks, Compliance Requirements)	**Detailed Reference**
CMMI Cybermaturity Platform, 2018	IP.MM Apply Mobile Device Management; TP.MP Apply Media Protection; DP.DP Detect Mobile Code and Browser Protection
ISF, The Standard of Good Practice for Information Security 2016	PM1.3 Remote Working; PA2.1 Mobile Device Configuration; PA2.4 Employee-owned Devices; PA2.5 Portable Storage Devices; NC1.6 Remote Maintenance
National Institute of Standards and Technology Special Publication 800-53, Revision 5 (Draft), August 2017	3.4 Assessment, authorization and monitoring (CA-8, CA-9); 3.19 System and communications protection (SC-10)
The CIS Critical Security Controls for Effective Cyber Defense Version 6.1, August 2016	CSC 3: Secure Configurations for Hardware and Software on Mobile Devices, Laptops, Workstations, and Servers; CSC 7: Email and Web Browser Protections

Management Practice	Small and Medium Enterprise-specific Metrics
DSS05.04 Manage user identity and logical access. Ensure that all users have information access rights in accordance with business requirements. Coordinate with business units that manage their own access rights within business processes.	a. Number of accounts vs. number of authorized users/staff b. Number of incidents relating to unauthorized access to information

Small and Medium Enterprise-specific Activities	Capability Level
1. Maintain user access rights in accordance with business function, process requirements and privacy policies. Align the management of identities and access rights to the defined roles and responsibilities, based on least-privilege, need-to-have and need-to-know principles.	2
2. Keep track of all changes to access rights (creation, modifications and deletions).	3
3. Segregate, reduce to the minimum number necessary, and actively manage privileged user accounts. Ensure supervision on all activity that is recorded on these accounts.	
4. Maintain an audit trail of access to information classified as highly sensitive.	4
5. Perform regular management review of all accounts and related privileges.	

Related Guidance (Standards, Frameworks, Compliance Requirements)	Detailed Reference
HITRUST CSF version 9, September 2017	10.03 Cryptographic Controls
ISF, The Standard of Good Practice for Information Security 2016	PM1.1 Employment Life Cycle; SA1 Access Management
ISO/IEC 27002:2013/Cor.2:2015(E)	7.3 Termination and change of employment; 9. Access control
ITIL V3, 2011	Service Operation, 4.5 Access Management
National Institute of Standards and Technology Special Publication 800-53, Revision 5 (Draft), August 2017	3.1 Access control (AC-11, AC-12); 3.11 Media protection (MP-2, MP-4, MP-7); 3.13 Physical and environmental protection (PE-2, PE-3, PE-6)
The CIS Critical Security Controls for Effective Cyber Defense Version 6.1, August 2016	CSC 1: Inventory of Authorized and Unauthorized Devices; CSC 2: Inventory of Authorized and Unauthorized Software; CSC 5: Controlled Use of Administrative Privileges; CSC 16: Account Monitoring and Control

A. Component: Process *(cont.)*		
Management Practice	**Small and Medium Enterprise-specific Metrics**	
DSS05.05 Manage physical access to I&T assets. Define and implement procedures (including emergency procedures) to grant, limit and revoke access to premises, buildings and areas, according to business need. Access to premises, buildings and areas should be justified, authorized, logged and monitored. This requirement applies to all persons entering the premises, including staff, temporary staff, clients, vendors, visitors or any other third party.	a. Number of physical security-related incidents b. Frequency of training on physical security	
Small and Medium Enterprise-specific Activities		**Capability Level**
1. Define and monitor all entry points to IT sites. Register all visitors, including contractors and vendors, to the site.		2
2. Instruct all personnel to display visible identification at all times. Prevent the issuance of identity cards or badges without proper authorization.		
3. Require visitors to be escorted at all times while on-site. If an unaccompanied, unfamiliar individual who is not wearing staff identification is identified, alert security personnel.		
4. Restrict access to sensitive IT infrastructure by establishing perimeter restrictions, such as fences, walls, and security devices on interior and exterior doors.		
5. Manage requests for access to the computing facilities. Ensure that access requests are completed and authorized by management, and that request records are retained.		3
6. Conduct regular physical security awareness training.		
Related Guidance (Standards, Frameworks, Compliance Requirements)	**Detailed Reference**	
CMMI Cybermaturity Platform, 2018	AC.MA Manage Access; ID.DI Determine Impacts	
HITRUST CSF version 9, September 2017	01.01 Business Requirement for Access Control; 01.02 Authorized Access to Information Systems; 02.0 Human Resources Security	
ISF, The Standard of Good Practice for Information Security 2016	NC1.2 Physical Network Management	
ISO/IEC 27002:2013/Cor.2:2015(E)	11. Physical and environmental security	
Management Practice	**Small and Medium Enterprise-specific Metrics**	
DSS05.06 Manage sensitive documents and output devices. Establish appropriate physical safeguards, accounting practices and inventory management regarding sensitive I&T assets, such as special forms, negotiable instruments, special-purpose printers or security tokens.	a. Number of stolen or lost output devices	
Small and Medium Enterprise-specific Activities		**Capability Level**
1. Establish an inventory of sensitive documents and output devices and conduct regular reconciliations.		2
2. Establish appropriate physical safeguards over special forms and sensitive devices.		
3. Assign access privileges to sensitive documents and output devices based on the least-privilege principle, balancing risk and business requirements.		3
4. Destroy sensitive information and protect output devices (e.g., degaussing of electronic media, physical destruction of memory devices, making shredders or locked paper baskets available to destroy special forms and other confidential papers).		
5. Establish procedures to govern the receipt, use, removal and disposal of special forms and output devices into, within and out of the enterprise.		
6. Put cryptographic controls in place to ensure the protection of sensitive information (confidentiality, authenticity, integrity, etc.).		

A. Component: Process *(cont.)*	
Related Guidance (Standards, Frameworks, Compliance Requirements)	**Detailed Reference**
CMMI Cybermaturity Platform, 2018	CM.Ph Monitor Physical
HITRUST CSF version 9, September 2017	01.06 Application & Information Access Control; 01.07 Mobile Computing & Teleworking; 08.0 Physical & Environmental Security; 10.03 Cryptographic Controls; 10.04 Security of System Files
ISF, The Standard of Good Practice for Information Security 2016	IR2.3 Business Impact Assessment - Confidentiality Requirements; IR2.4 Business Impact Assessment - Integrity Requirements; IR2.5 Business Impact Assessment - Availability Requirements; IM2.2 Sensitive Physical Information; PA2.2 Enterprise Mobility Management
ISO/IEC 27002:2013/Cor.2:2015(E)	10. Cryptography
National Institute of Standards and Technology Special Publication 800-53, Revision 5 (Draft), August 2017	3.1 Access control (AC-2, AC-3, AC-4, AC-5, AC-6, AC-13, AC-24); 3.7 Identification and authentication (IA-2, IA-10, IA-11)
The CIS Critical Security Controls for Effective Cyber Defense Version 6.1, August 2016	CSC 15: Wireless Access Control
Management Practice	**Small and Medium Enterprise-specific Metrics**
DSS05.07 Manage vulnerabilities and monitor the infrastructure for security-related events. Using a portfolio of tools and technologies (e.g., intrusion detection tools), manage vulnerabilities and monitor the infrastructure for unauthorized access. Ensure that security tools, technologies and detection are integrated with general event monitoring and incident management.	a. Percent of periodic tests of environmental security devices b. Percent of security incident tickets created in a timely manner when monitoring identifies potential security incidents

Small and Medium Enterprise-specific Activities	Capability Level
1. Continually use a set of supported technologies, services and assets (e.g., vulnerability scanners, fuzzers and sniffers, protocol analyzers) to identify information security vulnerabilities and gaps that could lead to compliance issues.	2
2. Define and communicate the nature and characteristics of potential security-related incidents so they can be easily recognized and their impacts understood.	
3. Ensure that security and privacy-related incident tickets are created in a timely manner when monitoring identifies potential incidents.	
4. Log security-related events, identifying the level of information to be recorded based on a consideration of risk. Retain them for an appropriate period to assist in future investigations.	3

Related Guidance (Standards, Frameworks, Compliance Requirements)	Detailed Reference
ISF, The Standard of Good Practice for Information Security 2016	IR2.6 Threat Profiling
National Institute of Standards and Technology Special Publication 800-53, Revision 5 (Draft), August 2017	3.7 Identification and authentication (IA-3); 3.11 Media protection (MP-1); 3.13 Physical and environmental protection (PE-5); 3.19 System and communications protection (SC-15)
The CIS Critical Security Controls for Effective Cyber Defense Version 6.1, August 2016	Maintenance, Monitoring, and Analysis of Audit Logs

B. Component: Organizational Structures							
Key Management Practice	Head Human Resources	Business Process Owners	Head of IT	Security Expert	IT Development Coordinator	IT Operations Coordinator	Privacy Officer
DSS05.01 Protect against malicious software.		R	A	R	R	R	
DSS05.02 Manage network and connectivity security.			A	R	R	R	
DSS05.03 Manage endpoint security.			A	R	R	R	
DSS05.04 Manage user identity and logical access.	R	R	A	R		R	R
DSS05.05 Manage physical access to I&T assets.			A	R		R	R
DSS05.06 Manage sensitive documents and output devices.	R		A	R		R	R
DSS05.07 Manage vulnerabilities and monitor the infrastructure for security-related events.			A	R		R	R

C. Component: Information Flows and Items				
Management Practice	Small and Medium Enterprise-specific Inputs		Small and Medium Enterprise-specific Outputs	
DSS05.01 Protect against malicious software.	From	Description	Description	To
	There are no small and medium enterprise-specific inputs for this practice.		Measures taken to protect for potential threats	APO12.02 APO12.03
DSS05.02 Manage network and connectivity security.	APO01.07	Data classification guidelines	Implemented network filtering mechanisms	Internal
DSS05.03 Manage endpoint security.	APO03.02	Information architecture model	Security guidelines for endpoint devices	Internal
	BAI09.01	Results of physical inventory checks		
	DSS06.06	Reports of violations		
DSS05.04 Manage user identity and logical access.	APO03.02	Information architecture model	Results of reviews of user accounts and privileges	Internal
			Approved user access rights	Internal

C. Component: Information Flows and Items *(cont.)*				
Management Practice	Small and Medium Enterprise-specific Inputs		Small and Medium Enterprise-specific Outputs	
DSS05.05 Manage physical access to I&T assets.	From	Description	Description	To
	There are no small and medium enterprise-specific inputs for this practice.		Access logs	DSS06.03 MEA04.07
			Approved access requests	Internal
DSS05.06 Manage sensitive documents and output devices.	APO03.02	Information architecture model	Access privileges	Internal
			Inventory of sensitive documents and devices	Internal
DSS05.07 Manage vulnerabilities and monitor the infrastructure for security-related events.	There are no small and medium enterprise-specific inputs for this practice.		Security incident tickets	DSS02.02
			Security event logs	Internal

D. Component: People, Skills and Competencies		
Skill	**Related Guidance (Standards, Frameworks, Compliance Requirements)**	**Detailed Reference**
Information security	Skills Framework for the Information Age V6, 2015	SCTY
Information security management	e-Competence Framework (e-CF)—A common European Framework for ICT Professionals in all industry sectors—Part 1: Framework, 2016	E. Manage— E.8. Information Security Management
Penetration testing	Skills Framework for the Information Age V6, 2015	PENT
Security administration	Skills Framework for the Information Age V6, 2015	SCAD

E. Component: Principles, Policies and Procedures	
Relevant Policy	**Policy Description**
Information security policy	Sets guidelines to protect corporate information and associated systems and infrastructure

F. Component: Culture, Ethics and Behavior
Key Culture Elements
Create a culture of awareness regarding users and their responsibilities for maintaining security and privacy practices.

G. Component: Services, Infrastructure and Applications

- Directory services
- Email filtering systems
- Identity and access management system
- Security awareness services
- Security information and event management (SIEM) tools
- Security operations center (SOC) services
- Third-party security assessment services
- URL filtering systems

Page intentionally left blank

Domain: Deliver, Service and Support Management Objective: DSS06 - Managed Business Process Controls	Focus Area: Small and Medium Enterprises
Description	
Define and maintain appropriate business process controls to ensure that information related to and processed by in-house or outsourced business processes satisfies all relevant information control requirements. Identify the relevant information control requirements. Manage and operate adequate input, throughput and output controls (application controls) to ensure that information and information processing satisfy these requirements.	
Purpose	
Maintain information integrity and the security of information assets handled within business processes in the enterprise or its outsourced operation.	
Small and Medium Enterprise Focus Area Relevance	
Ensure that required business controls are identified and that decisions to automate or manually execute controls are documented in operational procedures. Ensure that responsibility for executing controls is defined and that traceability for correcting errors and exceptions at the source is established. Use a pragmatic approach, such as version control for documents and data records and logging of transactions.	

A. Component: Process		
Management Practice	**Small and Medium Enterprise-specific Metrics**	
DSS06.01 Align control activities embedded in business processes with enterprise objectives. Continually assess and monitor the execution of business process activities and related controls (based on enterprise risk), to ensure that processing controls align with business needs.	a. Percent of completed inventory of critical processes and key controls	
Small and Medium Enterprise-specific Activities		**Capability Level**
1. Identify and document the necessary control activities for key business processes to satisfy control requirements for strategic, operational, reporting and compliance objectives.		2
2. Prioritize control activities based on the inherent risk to the business and identify key controls.		
3. Ensure ownership of key control activities.		
4. Implement automated controls.		3
5. Continually monitor control activities on an end-to-end basis to identify opportunities for improvement.		4
6. Continually improve the design and operation of business process controls.		5
Related Guidance (Standards, Frameworks, Compliance Requirements)	**Detailed Reference**	
National Institute of Standards and Technology Special Publication 800-37, Revision 2 (Draft), May 2018	3.1 Preparation (Task 10, 11)	
The CIS Critical Security Controls for Effective Cyber Defense Version 6.1, August 2016	CSC 14: Controlled Access Based on the Need to Know	
Management Practice	**Small and Medium Enterprise-specific Metrics**	
DSS06.02 Control the processing of information. Operate the execution of the business process activities and related controls, based on enterprise risk. Ensure that information processing is valid, complete, accurate, timely and secure (i.e., reflects legitimate and authorized business use).	a. Number of incidents and audit report findings indicating failure of key controls b. Percent of coverage of key controls within test plans	
Small and Medium Enterprise-specific Activities		**Capability Level**
1. Take necessary actions to implement the business controls into the business activities.		2
2. Ensure adequate segregation of duties regarding the execution and approval of transactions.		
3. Maintain the integrity and validity of data throughout the processing cycle. Ensure that detection of erroneous transactions does not disrupt processing of valid transactions.		3
4. Handle output in an authorized manner, deliver it to the appropriate recipient and protect the information during transmission. Verify the accuracy and completeness of the output.		
5. Maintain the integrity of data during unexpected interruptions in business processing and confirm data integrity after processing failures.		

A. Component: Process *(cont.)*	
Related Guidance (Standards, Frameworks, Compliance Requirements)	**Detailed Reference**
HITRUST CSF version 9, September 2017	13.01 Openness and Transparency; 13.02 Individual Choice and Participation
ISF, The Standard of Good Practice for Information Security 2016	BA1.4 Information Validation
Management Practice	**Small and Medium Enterprise-specific Metrics**
DSS06.03 Manage roles, responsibilities, access privileges and levels of authority. Manage business roles, responsibilities, levels of authority and segregation of duties needed to support the business process objectives. Authorize access to all information assets related to business information processes, including those under the custody of the business, IT and third parties. This ensures that the business knows where the data are and who is handling data on its behalf.	a. Number of incidents and audit findings due to violations related to access or separation of duties b. Percent of business process roles with assigned access rights and levels of authority

Small and Medium Enterprise-specific Activities	Capability Level
1. Allocate roles and responsibilities based on approved job descriptions and business process activities.	2
2. Allocate to the defined job roles appropriate levels of authority for approval of transactions, transaction limits and any other business rules.	
3. Allocate roles for sensitive activities and ensure that there is a clear segregation of duties.	
4. Allocate access rights and privileges based on the minimum that is required to perform job activities, based on pre-defined job roles. Remove or revise access rights immediately if the job role changes or a staff member leaves the business process area.	3
5. Provide awareness and training regarding roles and responsibilities on a regular basis, so that everyone understands his or her responsibilities; the importance of controls; and the security, integrity, confidentiality and privacy of enterprise information in all its forms.	
6. Ensure administrative privileges are sufficiently and effectively secured, tracked and controlled to prevent misuse.	
7. Periodically review access control definitions, logs and exception reports to ensure that all access privileges are valid and aligned with current staff members and their allocated roles.	4

Related Guidance (Standards, Frameworks, Compliance Requirements)	Detailed Reference
HITRUST CSF version 9, September 2017	13.04 Collection, Use and Disclosure
ISO/IEC 27002:2013/Cor.2:2015(E)	7. Human resource security
The CIS Critical Security Controls for Effective Cyber Defense Version 6.1, August 2016	CSC 5: Controlled Use of Administrative Privileges
Management Practice	**Small and Medium Enterprise-specific Metrics**
DSS06.04 Manage errors and exceptions. Manage business process exceptions and errors and facilitate remediation, executing defined corrective actions and escalating as necessary. This treatment of exceptions and errors provides assurance of the accuracy and integrity of the business information process.	a. Frequency of processing inefficiencies due to incomplete data entry b. Numbers of data processing errors that were efficiently remediated

Small and Medium Enterprise-specific Activities	Capability Level
1. Review errors, exceptions and deviations.	2
2. Follow up, correct, approve and resubmit source documents and transactions.	
3. Maintain evidence of remedial actions.	
4. Define and maintain procedures to assign ownership for errors and exceptions, correct errors, override errors and handle out-of-balance conditions.	3
5. Report relevant business information process errors in a timely manner to perform root cause and trending analysis.	4

Related Guidance (Standards, Frameworks, Compliance Requirements)	Detailed Reference
No related guidance for this management practice	

A. Component: Process *(cont.)*		
Management Practice	**Small and Medium Enterprise-specific Metrics**	
DSS06.05 Ensure traceability and accountability for information events. Ensure that business information can be traced to an originating business event and associated with accountable parties. This discoverability provides assurance that business information is reliable and has been processed in accordance with defined objectives.	a. Number of incidents for which transaction history cannot be recovered b. Percent of completeness of traceable transaction log	
Small and Medium Enterprise-specific Activities		**Capability Level**
1. Define how traceability of information can be guaranteed by logging transactions, keeping versions of changes, etc.		2
2. Capture source information, supporting evidence and the record of transactions.		
3. Define retention requirements to meet operational, financial reporting and compliance needs. Ensure that the retention requirements are based on business requirements.		3
4. Dispose of source information, supporting evidence and the record of transactions in accordance with the retention policy.		
Related Guidance (Standards, Frameworks, Compliance Requirements)	**Detailed Reference**	
No related guidance for this management practice		
Management Practice	**Small and Medium Enterprise-specific Metrics**	
DSS06.06 Secure information assets. Secure information assets accessible by the business through approved methods, including information in electronic form (e.g., portable media devices, user applications and storage devices, or other methods that create new assets in any form), information in physical form (e.g., source documents or output reports) and information during transit. This benefits the business by providing end-to-end safeguarding of information.	a. Number of cases in which sensitive transaction data were delivered to the wrong recipient b. Frequency of compromised integrity of critical data	
Small and Medium Enterprise-specific Activities		**Capability Level**
1. Restrict use, distribution and physical access of information according to its classification.		2
2. Provide acceptable use awareness and training.		
3. Apply data classification and acceptable use and security policies and procedures to protect information assets under the control of the business.		3
4. Identify and implement processes, tools and techniques to reasonably verify compliance.		
5. Report to business and other stakeholders on violations and deviations.		4
Related Guidance (Standards, Frameworks, Compliance Requirements)	**Detailed Reference**	
CMMI Cybermaturity Platform, 2018	AC.MP Manage Access Permissions	
The CIS Critical Security Controls for Effective Cyber Defense Version 6.1, August 2016	CSC 18: Application Software Security	

B. Component: Organizational Structures										
Key Management Practice	Executive Committee	General Manager	Head Human Resources	Business Process Owners	Head of IT	Security Expert	IT Development Coordinator	IT Operations Coordinator	Privacy Officer	Legal Department
DSS06.01 Align control activities embedded in business processes with enterprise objectives.	R	A		R	R					
DSS06.02 Control the processing of information.				R	A	R				R
DSS06.03 Manage roles, responsibilities, access privileges and levels of authority.			A	R	R	R	R	R	R	
DSS06.04 Manage errors and exceptions.		A		R	R	R				
DSS06.05 Ensure traceability and accountability for information events.				R	A	R	R	R		
DSS06.06 Secure information assets.				R	A	R		R	R	

C. Component: Information Flows and Items				
Management Practice	Small and Medium Enterprise-specific Inputs		Small and Medium Enterprise-specific Outputs	
	From	Description	Description	To
DSS06.01 Align control activities embedded in business processes with enterprise objectives.	APO01.07	Data classification guidelines	List of required controls on business processes	
DSS06.02 Control the processing of information.	BAI05.05	Operation and use plan	Processing control reports	Internal
	BAI07.02	Migration plan		
DSS06.03 Manage roles, responsibilities, access privileges and levels of authority.	APO11.01	QMS roles, responsibilities and decision rights	Allocated levels of authority	APO01.05
	APO13.01	ISMS scope statement	Allocated roles and responsibilities	APO01.05
	DSS05.05	Access logs	Allocated access rights	APO07.04
DSS06.04 Manage errors and exceptions.	There are no small and medium enterprise-specific inputs for this practice.		Error reports and root cause analysis	Internal
			Evidence of error correction and remediation	MEA02.04
DSS06.05 Ensure traceability and accountability for information events.	There are no small and medium enterprise-specific inputs for this practice.		Record of transactions	Internal
			Retention requirements	Internal APO14.09
DSS06.06 Secure information assets.	There are no small and medium enterprise-specific inputs for this practice.		Reports of violations	DSS05.03

D. Component: People, Skills and Competencies		
Skill	**Related Guidance (Standards, Frameworks, Compliance Requirements)**	**Detailed Reference**
Information security	Skills Framework for the Information Age V6, 2015	SCTY
Security administration	Skills Framework for the Information Age V6, 2015	SCAD

E. Component: Principles, Policies and Procedures	
Relevant Policy	**Policy Description**
There are no small and medium enterprise-specific principles, policies and procedures for this objective.	

F. Component: Culture, Ethics and Behavior
Key Culture Elements
Create a culture that embraces the need for sound controls in business processes, building them into applications in development or requiring them in applications bought or accessed as a service. Encourage all employees to have a controls consciousness to protect all assets of the organization (e.g., paper records and facilities).

G. Component: Services, Infrastructure and Applications
• Automated application controls • Event log auditing tools

Page intentionally left blank

7.5 Monitor, Evaluate and Assess (MEA)

01 Managed Performance and Conformance Monitoring

02 Managed System of Internal Control

03 Managed Compliance With External Requirements

04 Managed Assurance

Page intentionally left blank

Domain: Monitor, Evaluate and Assess Management Objective: MEA01 — Managed Performance and Conformance Monitoring	Focus Area: Small and Medium Enterprises
Description	
Collect, validate and evaluate enterprise and alignment goals and metrics. Monitor that processes and practices are performing against agreed performance and conformance goals and metrics. Provide reporting that is systematic and timely.	
Purpose	
Provide transparency of performance and conformance and drive achievement of goals.	
Small and Medium Enterprise Focus Area Relevance	
Provide consistent and systematic reporting from all operational management objectives on their performance and conformance as defined in each objective. This is essential for providing transparency on achievements of the objectives.	

A. Component: Process	
Management Practice	**Small and Medium Enterprise-specific Metrics**
MEA01.01 Establish a monitoring approach. Engage with stakeholders to establish and maintain a monitoring approach to define the objectives, scope and method for measuring business solution and service delivery and contribution to enterprise objectives. Integrate this approach with the corporate performance management system.	a. Percent of processes with defined goals and metrics b. Percent of processes under monitoring and with established metrics

Small and Medium Enterprise-specific Activities	Capability Level
1. Identify stakeholders (e.g., management, process owners and users).	2
2. Agree with stakeholders on requirements for monitoring management objectives.	
3. Align the approach for IT with the enterprise approach and the tools to be used for data gathering and reporting (if applicable, e.g., business intelligence applications).	
4. Agree on types of goals and metrics (e.g., conformance, performance, value, risk), taxonomy (classification and relationships between goals and metrics), and data (evidence) retention.	
5. Periodically validate the approach used and identify new or changed stakeholders, requirements and resources.	3

Related Guidance (Standards, Frameworks, Compliance Requirements)	Detailed Reference
CMMI Data Management Maturity Model, 2014	Supporting Processes - Measurement and Analysis
SF, The Standard of Good Practice for Information Security 2016	SI2 Security Performance
ISO/IEC 27001:2013/Cor.2:2015(E)	9.1 Monitoring, measurement, analysis and evaluation
ISO/IEC 27004:2016(E)	6. Characteristics; 7. Types of measures; 8. Processes
ISO/IEC 38500:2015(E)	5.5 Principle 4: Performance; 5.6 Principle 5: Conformance
National Institute of Standards and Technology Special Publication 800-37, Revision 2 (Draft), May 2018	3.1 Preparation (Task 13); 3.3 Selection (Task 2); 3.7 Monitoring (Task 1)
National Institute of Standards and Technology Special Publication 800-53, Revision 5 (Draft), August 2017	3.4 Assessment, authorization and monitoring (CA-2, CA-7); 3.20 System and information integrity (SI-4)

A. Component: Process *(cont.)*		
Management Practice	**Small and Medium Enterprise-specific Metrics**	
MEA01.02 Set performance and conformance targets. Work with stakeholders to define, periodically review, update and approve performance and conformance targets within the performance measurement system.	a. Percent of processes monitoring their goals and metrics	
Small and Medium Enterprise-specific Activities		**Capability Level**
1. Define and periodically review with each process owner a limited number of goals and metrics to measure performance and conformance of their processes.		2
2. Evaluate whether the goals and metrics are adequate, i.e., specific, measurable, achievable, relevant and time-bound (SMART).		
3. Communicate proposed changes to performance and conformance targets and tolerances (relating to metrics) with key due diligence stakeholders (e.g., legal, audit, HR, ethics, compliance, finance).		3
Related Guidance (Standards, Frameworks, Compliance Requirements)	**Detailed Reference**	
CMMI Data Management Maturity Model, 2014	Supporting Processes - Process Management	
National Institute of Standards and Technology Special Publication 800-53, Revisionv5 (Draft), August 2017	3.4 Assessment, authorization and monitoring (CA-5)	
Management Practice	**Small and Medium Enterprise-specific Metrics**	
MEA01.03 Collect and process performance and conformance data. Collect and process timely and accurate data aligned with enterprise approaches.	a. Percent of critical processes monitored	
Small and Medium Enterprise-specific Activities		**Capability Level**
1. Collect data from defined processes—automated, where possible.		2
2. Assess efficiency (effort in relation to insight provided) and appropriateness (usefulness and meaning) and validate integrity (accuracy and completeness) of collected data.		
3. Aggregate data to support measurement of agreed-on metrics.		
4. Use suitable tools and systems for the processing and analysis of data.		3
Related Guidance (Standards, Frameworks, Compliance Requirements)	**Detailed Reference**	
National Institute of Standards and Technology Special Publication 800-53, Revision 5 (Draft), August 2017	3.20 System and information integrity (SI-2)	
Management Practice	**Small and Medium Enterprise-specific Metrics**	
MEA01.04 Analyze and report performance. Periodically review and report performance against targets. Use a method that provides a succinct all-around view of I&T performance and fits within the enterprise monitoring system.	a. Percent of performance reports delivered as scheduled b. Percent of processes with assured output meeting targets within tolerances	
Small and Medium Enterprise-specific Activities		**Capability Level**
1. Design process performance reports that are concise, easy to understand and tailored to management needs. Facilitate effective, timely decision making (e.g., scorecards, traffic light reports) and ensure that the cause-and-effect relationships between goals and metrics are communicated in an understandable manner.		3
2. Distribute reports to the relevant stakeholders.		
3. Analyze the cause of deviations against targets, initiate remedial actions, assign responsibilities for remediation, and follow up.		4
4. At appropriate times, review all deviations and search for root causes, where necessary. Document the issues for further guidance if the problem recurs. Document results.		
5. Where feasible, integrate performance and compliance into individual staff members' performance objectives and link achievement of performance targets to the organizational reward compensation system.		
6. Analyze trends in performance and compliance and take appropriate action.		
7. Recommend changes to the goals and metrics, where appropriate.		5
Related Guidance (Standards, Frameworks, Compliance Requirements)	**Detailed Reference**	
CMMI Data Management Maturity Model, 2014	Supporting Processes - Measurement and Analysis	
National Institute of Standards and Technology Special Publication 800-53, Revision 5 (Draft), August 2017	3.3 Audit and accountability (AU-6)	

A. Component: Process *(cont.)*		
Management Practice	**Small and Medium Enterprise-specific Metrics**	
MEA01.05 Ensure the implementation of corrective actions. Assist stakeholders in identifying, initiating and tracking corrective actions to address anomalies.	a. Number of recurring anomalies b. Number of corrective actions implemented	
Small and Medium Enterprise-specific Activities		**Capability Level**
1. Review management responses, options and recommendations to address issues and major deviations.		4
2. Ensure that the assignment of responsibility for corrective action is maintained.		
3. Track the results of actions committed.		5
4. Report the results to the stakeholders.		
Related Guidance (Standards, Frameworks, Compliance Requirements)	**Detailed Reference**	
ITIL V3, 2011	Continual Service Improvement, 4.1 The 7-Step Improvement Process	
National Institute of Standards and Technology Special Publication 800-37, Revision 2 (Draft), May 2018	3.7 Monitoring (Task 3)	
National Institute of Standards and Technology Special Publication 800-53, Revision 5 (Draft), August 2017	3.3 Audit and accountability (AU-5)	

B. Component: Organizational Structures									
Key Management Practice	**Executive Committee**	**General Manager**	**Financial Manager**	**Operations Manager**	**Business Process Owners**	**Head of IT**	**IT Development Coordinator**	**IT Operations Coordinator**	**Compliance or Quality**
MEA01.01 Establish a monitoring approach.	R	A	R	R		R			R
MEA01.02 Set performance and conformance targets.	A				R	R	R	R	R
MEA01.03 Collect and process performance and conformance data.					R	R	R	R	A
MEA01.04 Analyze and report performance.					R	R	R	R	A
MEA01.05 Ensure the implementation of corrective actions.					R	R	R	R	A

C. Component: Information Flows and Items				
Management Practice	**Small and Medium Enterprise-specific Inputs**		**Small and Medium Enterprise-specific Outputs**	
	From	**Description**	**Description**	**To**
MEA01.01 Establish a monitoring approach.	EDM05.01	• Evaluation of enterprise reporting requirements • Reporting and communications principles	Approved monitoring goals and metrics	Internal
			Monitoring requirements	Internal
	EDM05.02	Rules for validating and approving mandatory reports		
	EDM05.03	Assessment of reporting effectiveness		

C. Component: Information Flows and Items *(cont.)*				
Management Practice	Small and Medium Enterprise-specific Inputs		Small and Medium Enterprise-specific Outputs	
MEA01.02 Set performance and conformance targets.	**From**	**Description**	**Description**	**To**
	APO01.11	Performance goals and metrics for process improvement tracking	Monitoring targets	All APO All BAI All DSS All MEA
MEA01.03 Collect and process performance and conformance data.	APO01.11	Process capability assessments	Processed monitoring data	Internal
	APO05.03	Investment portfolio performance reports		
	APO09.04	Service level performance reports		
	APO10.05	Results of vendor compliance monitoring review		
	BAI01.06	Results of program performance reviews		
	BAI04.04	Availability, performance and capacity monitoring review reports		
	BAI05.05	Success measures and results		
	DSS01.05	Facilities assessment reports		
	DSS02.07	• Incident status and trends report • Request fulfillment status and trends report		
MEA01.04 Analyze and report performance.	There are no small and medium enterprise-specific inputs for this practice.		Performance reports	All APO All BAI All DSS All MEA EDM01.03
MEA01.05 Ensure the implementation of corrective actions.	MEA01.04	Performance reports	Remedial actions and assignments	All APO All BAI All DSS All MEA
			Status and results of actions	EDM01.03

D. Component: People, Skills and Competencies		
Skill	**Related Guidance (Standards, Frameworks, Compliance Requirements)**	**Detailed Reference**
Conformance review	Skills Framework for the Information Age V6, 2015	CORE
ICT quality management	e-Competence Framework (e-CF)—A common European Framework for ICT Professionals in all industry sectors—Part 1: Framework, 2016	E. Manage—E.6. ICT Quality Management
Quality assurance	Skills Framework for the Information Age V6, 2015	QUAS

E. Component: Principles, Policies and Procedures	
Relevant Policy	**Policy Description**
Self-assessment policy	Provides guidance for management in assessing operations as part of the continuous improvement program. Often used to report internally to executives or board on current capabilities, progress and improvement, based on business requirements. Assessments may be used during or after a process improvement program (i.e., to assess progress after completing an improvement).

F. Component: Culture, Ethics and Behavior
Key Culture Elements
To achieve the organization's goals and optimize performance, promote a culture of continuous improvement of business and I&T processes.

G. Component: Services, Infrastructure and Applications
• Performance measurement system (e.g., balanced scorecard, skills management tools) • Self-assessment tools

Page intentionally left blank

Domain: Monitor, Evaluate and Assess Management Objective: MEA02 — Managed System of Internal Control	Focus Area: Small and Medium Enterprises
Description	
Continuously monitor and evaluate the control environment, including self-assessments and self-awareness. Enable management to identify control deficiencies and inefficiencies and to initiate improvement actions. Plan, organize and maintain standards for internal control assessment and process control effectiveness.	
Purpose	
Obtain transparency for key stakeholders on the adequacy of the system of internal controls and thus provide trust in operations, confidence in the achievement of enterprise objectives and an adequate understanding of residual risk.	
Small and Medium Enterprise Focus Area Relevance	
Perform self-assessments that include appropriate substantiation of effective internal controls in preparation for internal and external audits.	

A. Component: Process	
Management Practice	**Small and Medium Enterprise-specific Metrics**
MEA02.01 Monitor internal controls. Continuously monitor, benchmark and improve the I&T control environment and control framework to meet organizational objectives.	a. Percent of controls environment and framework being monitored and improved to meet organizational objectives

Small and Medium Enterprise-specific Activities	Capability Level
1. Identify the boundaries of the internal control system (e.g., consider how organizational internal controls take into account outsourced and/or offshore development or production activities).	3
2. Assess the status of internal controls by external service providers and confirm that service providers comply with legal and regulatory requirements and contractual obligations.	
3. Perform internal control monitoring and evaluation activities for I&T in line with enterprise internal control activities.	
4. Ensure that control exceptions are promptly reported, followed up and analyzed, and appropriate corrective actions are prioritized and implemented according to the risk management profile (e.g., classify certain exceptions as a key risk and others as a non-key risk).	4
5. Consider independent evaluations of the internal control system (e.g., by internal audit or peers).	
6. Regularly evaluate the performance of the control framework, benchmarking against industry accepted standards and good practices.	5

Related Guidance (Standards, Frameworks, Compliance Requirements)	Detailed Reference
HITRUST CSF version 9, September 2017	09.10 Monitoring
ISO/IEC 38502:2017(E)	5.5 Governance and internal control
National Institute of Standards and Technology Special Publication 800-53, Revision 5 (Draft), August 2017	3.3 Audit and accountability (AU-2)

A. Component: Process *(cont.)*

Management Practice	Small and Medium Enterprise-specific Metrics
MEA02.02 Review effectiveness of business process controls. Review the operation of controls, including monitoring and test evidence, to ensure that controls within business processes operate effectively. Include activities to maintain evidence of the effective operation of controls through mechanisms such as periodic testing, continuous monitoring, independent assessments, command and control centers, and network operation centers. This evidence assures the enterprise that controls meet requirements related to business, regulatory and social responsibilities.	a. Percent of controls being monitored and tested to ensure that controls within business processes operate effectively

Small and Medium Enterprise-specific Activities	Capability Level
1. Understand and prioritize risk to organizational objectives.	3
2. Identify key controls and develop a strategy suitable for validating controls.	
3. Identify information that will indicate whether the internal control environment is operating effectively.	
4. Maintain evidence of control effectiveness.	4
5. Develop and implement cost-effective procedures to obtain this information in line with applicable information quality criteria.	

Related Guidance (Standards, Frameworks, Compliance Requirements)	Detailed Reference
No related guidance for this management practice	

Management Practice	Small and Medium Enterprise-specific Metrics
MEA02.03 Perform control self-assessments. Encourage management and process owners to improve controls proactively through a continuing program of self-assessment that evaluates the completeness and effectiveness of management's control over processes, policies and contracts.	a. Number of self-assessments performed b. Percent of identified gaps in self-assessments vs. industry standards or good practices

Small and Medium Enterprise-specific Activities	Capability Level
1. Define an agreed-on, consistent approach for performing control self-assessments.	3
2. Plan the communication of results of the self-assessment process to business, IT and general management and the board. Consider internal audit standards in the design of self-assessments.	
3. Determine the frequency of periodic self-assessments, considering the overall effectiveness and efficiency of ongoing monitoring.	
4. Assign responsibility for self-assessment to appropriate individuals to ensure objectivity and competence.	
5. Compare the results of the self-assessments against industry standards and good practices.	4
6. Summarize and report outcomes of self-assessments and benchmarking for remedial actions.	5

Related Guidance (Standards, Frameworks, Compliance Requirements)	Detailed Reference
ISO/IEC 27001:2013/Cor.2:2015(E)	9.3 Management review
National Institute of Standards and Technology Special Publication 800-37, Revision 2 (Draft), May 2018	3.7 Monitoring (Task 2)

Management Practice	Small and Medium Enterprise-specific Metrics
MEA02.04 Identify and report control deficiencies. Identify control deficiencies and analyze and identify their underlying root causes. Escalate control deficiencies and report to stakeholders.	a. Time between internal control deficiency occurrence and reporting b. Time between exception identification and agreed-on actions addressed

Small and Medium Enterprise-specific Activities	Capability Level
1. Define procedures for escalation of control exceptions, root cause analysis, and reporting to process owners and I&T stakeholders.	3
2. Consider related enterprise risk to establish thresholds for escalation of control exceptions and breakdowns.	
3. Identify, report and log control exceptions, and assign responsibility for resolving them and reporting on the status.	
4. Follow up on all exceptions to ensure that agreed-on actions have been addressed.	4
5. Identify, initiate, track and implement remedial actions arising from control assessments and reporting.	5

Related Guidance (Standards, Frameworks, Compliance Requirements)	Detailed Reference
No related guidance for this management practice	

B. Component: Organizational Structures

Key Management Practice	Financial Manager	Business Process Owners	Head of IT	IT Development Coordinator	IT Operations Coordinator	Privacy Officer	Compliance or Quality
MEA02.01 Monitor internal controls.		R	R	R	R	R	A
MEA02.02 Review effectiveness of business process controls.	R	R	R				A
MEA02.03 Perform control self-assessments.		R	R	R	R	R	A
MEA02.04 Identify and report control deficiencies.		R	R	R	R	R	A

C. Component: Information Flows and Items

Management Practice	Small and Medium Enterprise-specific Inputs		Small and Medium Enterprise-specific Outputs	
	From	Description	Description	To
MEA02.01 Monitor internal controls.	APO12.04	Results of third-party risk assessments	Results of internal control monitoring and reviews	EDM01.03 All AP All BAI All DS All MEA
	APO13.03	Information security management system (ISMS) audit reports		
	Outside COBIT	Industry standards and good practices		
	APO11.04	Results of quality reviews and audits		
MEA02.02 Review effectiveness of business process controls.	BAI05.06	Compliance audit results	Evidence of control effectiveness	Internal
	BAI05.07	Reviews of operational use		
MEA02.03 Perform control self-assessments.	There are no small and medium enterprise-specific inputs for this practice.		Self-assessment plans and criteria	All APO All BAI All DSS All MEA
			Results of self-assessments	Internal
MEA02.04 Identify and report control deficiencies.	APO11.03	Root causes of failure to deliver quality	Remedial actions	All APO All BAI All DSS All MEA
	APO12.06	Risk-related root causes	Control deficiencies	All APO All BAI All DSS All MEA
	DSS06.04	Evidence of error correction and remediation		

D. Component: People, Skills and Competencies		
Skill	**Related Guidance (Standards, Frameworks, Compliance Requirements)**	**Detailed Reference**
Risk management	e-Competence Framework (e-CF)—A common European Framework for ICT Professionals in all industry sectors—Part 1: Framework, 2016	E. Manage—E.3. Risk Management

E. Component: Principles, Policies and Procedures	
Relevant Policy	**Policy Description**
Internal control self-assessment guidance	Provides guidance on continuous monitoring of internal controls to identify deficiencies and gaps in effectiveness, determine their root causes, initiate plans of action, and set corrective milestones for reporting to stakeholders

F. Component: Culture, Ethics and Behavior
Key Culture Elements
Promote awareness of the importance of an effective control environment. Encourage a proactive risk- and self-aware culture, including commitment to self-assessment and independent assurance reviews.

G. Component: Services, Infrastructure and Applications
• COBIT and related products/tools • Third-party internal control assessment services

Domain: Monitor, Evaluate and Assess Management Objective: MEA03 — Managed Compliance With External Requirements	Focus Area: Small and Medium Enterprises
Description	
Evaluate that I&T processes and I&T-supported business processes are compliant with laws, regulations and contractual requirements. Obtain assurance that the requirements have been identified and complied with; integrate IT compliance with overall enterprise compliance.	
Purpose	
Ensure that the enterprise is compliant with all applicable external requirements.	
Small and Medium Enterprise Focus Area Relevance	
Identify external compliance requirements specific to the enterprise. Provide all required reporting, both on compliance and corrective actions to obtain external assurance. Obtain independent confirmation of compliance with each required objective.	

A. Component: Process		
Management Practice	**Small and Medium Enterprise-specific Metrics**	
MEA03.01 Identify external compliance requirements. On a continuous basis, monitor changes in local and international laws, regulations and other external requirements and identify mandates for compliance from an I&T perspective.	a. Frequency of compliance requirements reviews b. Percentage of new compliance requirements identified	
Small and Medium Enterprise-specific Activities		**Capability Level**
1. Assign responsibility for identifying and monitoring any changes of legal, regulatory and other external contractual requirements relevant to the use of IT resources and the processing of information.		2
2. Identify all potential compliance requirements and assess the impact on I&T activities in areas such as data flow, privacy, internal controls, financial reporting, industry-specific regulations, intellectual property, health and safety.		
3. Assess the impact of I&T-related legal and regulatory requirements on third-party contracts related to IT operations, service providers and business trading partners.		
4. Obtain independent counsel, where appropriate, on changes to applicable laws, regulations and standards.		3
5. Maintain an up-to-date list of all relevant legal, regulatory and contractual requirements, their impact and required actions.		
Related Guidance (Standards, Frameworks, Compliance Requirements)	**Detailed Reference**	
CMMI Cybermaturity Platform, 2018	BC.RR Determine Legal / Regulatory Requirements	
HITRUST CSF version 9, September 2017	06.01 Compliance with Legal Requirements	
ISF, The Standard of Good Practice for Information Security 2016	SM2.3 Legal and Regulatory Compliance	
Management Practice	**Small and Medium Enterprise-specific Metrics**	
MEA03.02 Optimize response to external requirements. Review and adjust policies, principles, standards, procedures and methodologies to ensure that legal, regulatory and contractual requirements are addressed and communicated. Consider adopting and adapting industry standards, codes of good practice, and good practice guidance.	a. Average time between identification of external compliance issues and resolution	
Small and Medium Enterprise-specific Activities		**Capability Level**
1. Regularly review and adjust policies, procedures and methodologies to ensure necessary compliance and address enterprise risk using external experts, as required.		3
2. Communicate new and changed requirements to all relevant personnel.		
Related Guidance (Standards, Frameworks, Compliance Requirements)	**Detailed Reference**	
King IV Report on Corporate Governance for South Africa, 2016	Part 5.4: Governance functional areas - Principle 13	

A. Component: Process *(cont.)*		
Management Practice	**Small and Medium Enterprise-specific Metrics**	
MEA03.03 Confirm external compliance. Confirm compliance of policies, principles, standards, procedures and methodologies with legal, regulatory and contractual requirements.	a. Number of critical noncompliance issues identified per year b. Percent of process owners signing off, confirming compliance	
Small and Medium Enterprise-specific Activities		**Capability Level**
1. Address compliance gaps on a timely basis.		3
2. Periodically evaluate business and IT processes and activities to ensure adherence to applicable legal, regulatory and contractual requirements.		
3. Regularly review for recurring patterns of compliance failures and assess lessons learned.		4
4. Based on review and lessons learned, improve policies, procedures, methodologies, and associated processes and activities.		5
Related Guidance (Standards, Frameworks, Compliance Requirements)	**Detailed Reference**	
No related guidance for this management practice		
Management Practice	**Small and Medium Enterprise-specific Metrics**	
MEA03.04 Obtain assurance of external compliance. Obtain and report assurance of compliance and adherence with policies, principles, standards, procedures and methodologies. Confirm that corrective actions to address compliance gaps are closed in a timely manner.	a. Number of compliance reports obtained b. Percent of service provider compliance as indicated by independent reviews c. Time between identifying corrective action and addressing compliance gap	
Small and Medium Enterprise-specific Activities		**Capability Level**
1. Obtain regular confirmation of business and IT process owners' compliance with internal policies.		3
2. If required, obtain assertions from third-party I&T service providers on levels of their compliance with applicable laws and regulations.		
3. If required, obtain assertions from business partners on levels of their compliance with applicable laws and regulations as they relate to intercompany electronic transactions.		
4. Monitor and report on noncompliance issues and, where necessary, investigate the root cause.		4
Related Guidance (Standards, Frameworks, Compliance Requirements)	**Detailed Reference**	
CMMI Data Management Maturity Model, 2014	Supporting Processes - Process Quality Assurance	
ISO/IEC 27002:2013/Cor.2:2015(E)	18. Compliance	

B. Component: Organizational Structures											
Key Management Practice	**General Manager**	**Financial Manager**	**Operations Manager**	**Business Process Owners**	**Head of IT**	**IT Development Coordinator**	**IT Operations Coordinator**	**Privacy Officer**	**Legal Department**	**Compliance or Quality**	**Audit**
MEA03.01 Identify external compliance requirements.				R	R			R	R	A	R
MEA03.02 Optimize response to external requirements.	R	R	R	R	R	R	R	R	R	R	A
MEA03.03 Confirm external compliance.	R	R	R	R	R			R	R	A	
MEA03.04 Obtain assurance of external compliance.					R				R	A	

C. Component: Information Flows and Items				
Management Practice	Small and Medium Enterprise-specific Inputs		Small and Medium Enterprise-specific Outputs	
MEA03.01 Identify external compliance requirements.	**From**	**Description**	**Description**	**To**
	Outside COBIT	Potential legal and regulatory requirements	Log of required compliance actions	Internal
			Compliance requirements register	Internal
MEA03.02 Optimize response to external requirements.	There are no small and medium enterprise-specific inputs for this practice.		Communications of changed compliance requirements	EDM01.01 All APO All BAI All DSS All MEA
			Updated I&T policies and procedures	APO01.09 APO01.11
MEA03.03 Confirm external compliance.	BAI09.05	Results of installed license audits	Compliance confirmations	EDM01.03
	DSS01.04	Insurance policy reports	Identified compliance gaps	MEA04.08
MEA03.04 Obtain assurance of external compliance.	EDM05.02	Rules for validating and approving mandatory reports	There are no small and medium enterprise-specific outputs for this practice.	

D. Component: People, Skills and Competencies		
Skill	**Related Guidance (Standards, Frameworks, Compliance Requirements)**	**Detailed Reference**
Information security	Skills Framework for the Information Age V6, 2015	SCTY

E. Component: Principles, Policies and Procedures	
Relevant Policy	**Policy Description**
Compliance policy	Identifies regulatory, contractual and internal compliance requirements. Explains the process to assess compliance with regulatory, contractual and internal requirements. Lists roles and responsibilities for different activities in the process and provides guidance on metrics to measure compliance. Obtains compliance reports and confirms compliance or corrective actions to address remediation of compliance gaps in a timely manner.

F. Component: Culture, Ethics and Behavior
Key Culture Elements
Promote a compliance-aware culture, including zero tolerance of noncompliance with legal and regulatory requirements.

G. Component: Services, Infrastructure and Applications
• Regulatory Watch services • Third-party compliance assessment services

Page intentionally left blank

Domain: Monitor, Evaluate and Assess Management Objective: MEA04 — Managed Assurance	Focus Area: Small and Medium Enterprises
Description	
Plan, scope and execute assurance initiatives to comply with internal requirements, laws, regulations and strategic objectives. Enable management to deliver adequate and sustainable assurance in the enterprise by performing independent assurance reviews and activities.	
Purpose	
Enable the organization to design and develop efficient and effective assurance initiatives, providing guidance on planning, scoping, executing and following up on assurance reviews, using a road map based on well-accepted assurance approaches.	
Small and Medium Enterprise Focus Area Relevance	
The description and purpose of this COBIT objective is fully applicable to SMEs. No SME-specific focus area relevance statement is required.	

A. Component: Process		
Management Practice	**Small and Medium Enterprise-specific Metrics**	
MEA04.01 Ensure that assurance providers are independent and qualified. Ensure that the entities performing assurance are independent from the function, groups or organizations in scope. The entities performing assurance should demonstrate an appropriate attitude and appearance, competence in the skills and knowledge necessary to perform assurance, and adherence to codes of ethics and professional standards.	a. Percent of processes receiving independent review b. Number of certifications and years of proven experience of assurance providers	
Small and Medium Enterprise-specific Activities		**Capability Level**
1. Establish competency and qualification of assurance providers.		2
2. Establish adherence to applicable codes of ethics and standards (e.g., Code of Professional Ethics of ISACA) and industry- and geography-specific assurance standards, such as the IT audit and assurance standards of ISACA and the International Auditing and Assurance Standards Board's (IAASB's) International Framework for Assurance Engagements (IAASB Assurance Framework).		
Related Guidance (Standards, Frameworks, Compliance Requirements)	**Detailed Reference**	
HITRUST CSF version 9, September 2017	06.03 Information System Audit Considerations	
Management Practice	**Small and Medium Enterprise-specific Metrics**	
MEA04.02 Develop risk-based planning of assurance initiatives. Determine assurance objectives based on assessments of the internal and external environment and context, the risk of not achieving enterprise goals, and the opportunities associated achievement of the same goals.	a. Percent of assurance initiatives following approved assurance program and plan standards b. Percent of assurance plan initiatives based on risk	
Small and Medium Enterprise-specific Activities		**Capability Level**
1. Understand the enterprise strategy and priorities.		2
2. Document the internal and external context of the enterprise. Understanding the internal context will help the assurance professional to better assess the enterprise goals and the relative importance of enterprise and alignment goals, as well as the most important threats to these goals. In turn, this will assist in defining a better and more relevant scope for the assurance engagement.		
3. Develop an overall yearly plan for assurance initiatives containing the consolidated assurance objectives.		3
Related Guidance (Standards, Frameworks, Compliance Requirements)	**Detailed Reference**	
King IV Report on Corporate Governance for South Africa, 2016	Part 5.4: Governance functional areas—Principle 15	

A. Component: Process *(cont.)*		
Management Practice	**Small and Medium Enterprise-specific Metrics**	
MEA04.03 Determine the objectives of the assurance initiative. Define and agree with all stakeholders on the objectives of the assurance initiative.	a. Percent of objectives achieved through the assurance initiative	
Small and Medium Enterprise-specific Activities		**Capability Level**
1. Define the assurance objective of the assurance initiative by identifying the stakeholders of the assurance initiative and their interests.		2
2. Agree on the high-level objectives and the organizational boundaries of the assurance engagement.		
3. Consider using the COBIT goals cascade and its different levels to express the assurance objective.		3
4. Ensure that the assurance engagement addresses all three value objective components: delivering benefits that support strategic objectives, minimizing the risk that strategic objectives are not achieved and optimizing resource levels required to achieve the strategic objectives.		
Related Guidance (Standards, Frameworks, Compliance Requirements)	**Detailed Reference**	
CMMI Data Management Maturity Model, 2014	Supporting Processes - Process Quality Assurance	
Management Practice	**Small and Medium Enterprise-specific Metrics**	
MEA04.04 Define the scope of the assurance initiative. Define and agree with all stakeholders on the scope of the assurance initiative, based on the assurance objectives.	a. Number of engagement plans that clearly indicate the information to be collected and stakeholders to be interviewed	
Small and Medium Enterprise-specific Activities		**Capability Level**
1. Define all governance components in scope of the review (principles, policies and procedures; processes; organizational structures; culture, ethics and behavior; information; and services, infrastructure and applications).		2
2. Based on the scope definition, define an engagement plan, considering information to be collected and stakeholders to be interviewed.		3
3. Confirm and refine the scope based on an understanding of the enterprise architecture.		
4. Refine the scope of the assurance engagement based on available resources.		
Related Guidance (Standards, Frameworks, Compliance Requirements)	**Detailed Reference**	
CMMI Cybermaturity Platform, 2018	TP.LA Apply Logging and Audit Processes	
Management Practice	**Small and Medium Enterprise-specific Metrics**	
MEA04.05 Define the work program for the assurance initiative. Define a detailed work program for the assurance initiative, structured according to the management objectives and governance components in scope.	a. Number of controls reviewed vs. total existing controls	
Small and Medium Enterprise-specific Activities		**Capability Level**
1. Define detailed steps for collecting and evaluating information from management controls within scope.		2
2. Ensure that the detailed steps include an assessment of the definition and application of good practices, relate to control design, achieve control objectives, and address control effectiveness.		
3. Understand the context of the management objectives and the supporting management controls that are put in place. Understand how these management controls contribute to the achievement of the alignment goals and enterprise goals.		
4. Understand all stakeholders and their interests.		
5. Agree on the expected good practices for the management controls.		3
6. Should a management control be weak, define possibilities to identify residual risk (in preparation for reporting).		
7. Understand the life cycle stage of the management controls and agree on expected values.		
Related Guidance (Standards, Frameworks, Compliance Requirements)	**Detailed Reference**	
No related guidance for this management practice		

A. Component: Process *(cont.)*		
Management Practice	**Small and Medium Enterprise-specific Metrics**	
MEA04.06 Execute the assurance initiative, focusing on design effectiveness. Execute the planned assurance initiative. Validate and confirm the design of the internal controls in place. Additionally, and specifically in internal audit assignments, consider the cost-effectiveness of the governance component design.	a. Percent of assurance initiatives that consider cost effectiveness of design b. Percentage of assurance initiatives completed on time	
Small and Medium Enterprise-specific Activities		**Capability Level**
1. Refine the understanding of the IT assurance subject.		2
2. Refine the scope of the IT assurance subject.		
3. Observe/inspect and review the management control approach. Validate the design with the control owner, considering completeness, relevancy, timeliness and measurability.		3
4. Confirm with the control owner that responsibilities for the governance component and overall accountability have been assigned. Test whether accountability and responsibilities are understood and accepted. Verify that the right skills and the necessary resources are available.		
5. Reconsider the balance of prevention vs. detection and correction types of management control activities.		
6. Consider the effort spent in maintaining the management controls vs. their cost/effectiveness.		
Related Guidance (Standards, Frameworks, Compliance Requirements)	**Detailed Reference**	
ISF, The Standard of Good Practice for Information Security 2016	SI1 Security Audit	
ISO/IEC 27001:2013/Cor.2:2015(E)	9.2 Internal audit	
Management Practice	**Small and Medium Enterprise-specific Metrics**	
MEA04.07 Execute the assurance initiative, focusing on operating effectiveness. Execute the planned assurance initiative. Test whether the internal controls in place are appropriate and sufficient. Test the outcome of the key management objectives in scope of the assurance initiative.	a. Percent of assurance initiatives that test whether the internal controls in place are appropriate and sufficient, and test the outcome of the key management objectives in scope b. Percent of stakeholder satisfaction with the execution of the assurance initiative	
Small and Medium Enterprise-specific Activities		**Capability Level**
1. Assess whether the expected outcomes of in-scope management controls are achieved (i.e., assess the effectiveness of each management control).		3
2. Ensure that the assurance professional tests the outcome or effectiveness of the management control by looking for direct and indirect evidence of the impact on the management control goals. This implies the direct and indirect substantiation of measurable contribution of management to the alignment goals, thereby recording direct and indirect evidence of achieving the expected outcomes.		
3. Ensure that the assurance professional obtains direct or indirect evidence for selected items/periods by applying a selection of testing techniques to assess whether the management control under review is working effectively. Ensure that the assurance professional also performs a limited review of the adequacy of the management control results and determines the level of substantive testing and additional work needed to provide assurance that the management control's performance is adequate.		
4. Investigate whether a management control can be made more efficient and its design can be made more effective by optimizing steps or looking for synergies with other management controls.		
Related Guidance (Standards, Frameworks, Compliance Requirements)	**Detailed Reference**	
ISF, The Standard of Good Practice for Information Security 2016	SI1 Security Audit	
SO/IEC 27001:2013/Cor.2:2015(E)	9.2 Internal audit	

A. Component: Process *(cont.)*	
Management Practice	**Small and Medium Enterprise-specific Metrics**
MEA04.08 Report and follow up on the assurance initiative. Provide positive assurance opinions, where appropriate, and recommendations for improvement relating to identified operational performance, external compliance and internal control weaknesses.	a. Percent of stakeholder acceptance of the assurance report b. Percent of stakeholder acceptance of recommendations for improvement relating to identified operational performance, external compliance and internal control weaknesses

Small and Medium Enterprise-specific Activities	Capability Level
1. Document the impact of control weaknesses.	2
2. Communicate with management during execution of the initiative so there is a clear understanding of the work performed and to ensure agreement with and acceptance of the preliminary findings and recommendations.	
3. Provide management with a report (aligned with the terms of reference, scope and agreed reporting standards) that supports the results of the initiative and enables a clear focus on key issues and important actions.	3
4. Supervise the assurance activities and make sure the work done is complete, meets objectives and is of acceptable quality. Revise the approach or detailed steps if quality gaps occur.	4

Related Guidance (Standards, Frameworks, Compliance Requirements)	Detailed Reference
No related guidance for this management practice	

Management Practice	Small and Medium Enterprise-specific Metrics
MEA04.09 Follow up on recommendations and actions. Agree on, follow up and implement the identified recommendations for improvement.	a. Number of recurring weaknesses b. Percent of identified weaknesses resolved as planned

Small and Medium Enterprise-specific Activities	Capability Level
1. Agree on and implement within the organization the actions that need to be taken to resolve identified weaknesses and gaps.	2
2. Follow up within the organization to assess whether corrective actions were taken and internal control weaknesses were resolved.	

Related Guidance (Standards, Frameworks, Compliance Requirements)	Detailed Reference
No related guidance for this management practice	

B. Component: Organizational Structures

Key Management Practice	General Manager	Operations Manager	Business Process Owners	Head of IT	IT Operations Coordinator	Legal	Audit
MEA04.01 Ensure that assurance providers are independent and qualified.			R	R		R	A
MEA04.02 Develop risk-based planning of assurance initiatives.		R	R	R		R	A
MEA04.03 Determine the objectives of the assurance initiative.		R	R	R		R	A
MEA04.04 Define the scope of the assurance initiative.		R	R	R		R	A
MEA04.05 Define the work program for the assurance initiative.		R	R	R		R	A
MEA04.06 Execute the assurance initiative, focusing on design effectiveness.		R	R	R	R	R	A
MEA04.07 Execute the assurance initiative, focusing on operating effectiveness.		R	R	R	R	R	A
MEA04.08 Report and follow up on the assurance initiative.		R	R	R		R	A
MEA04.09 Follow up on recommendations and actions.	A	R	R	R	R	R	R

C. Component: Information Flows and Items				
Management Practice	Small and Medium Enterprise-specific Inputs		Small and Medium Enterprise-specific Outputs	
	From	Description	Description	To
MEA04.01 Ensure that assurance providers are independent and qualified.	Outside COBIT	Assurance provider qualifications	Results of assurance provider evaluations	Internal
MEA04.02 Develop risk-based planning of assurance initiatives.	DSS01.02	Independent assurance plans	Assurance plans	EDM01.03 All APO All BAI All DSS All MEA
			Assessment criteria	Internal
MEA04.03 Determine the objectives of the assurance initiative.	MEA04.02	Assurance plans	Assurance objectives and expected benefits	Internal
MEA04.04 Define the scope of the assurance initiative.	APO11.03	Root causes of failure to deliver quality	Assurance review scope	Internal
	APO12.06	Risk-related root causes	Engagement plan	Internal
	MEA03.04	Reports of noncompliance issues and root causes		
MEA04.05 Define the work program for the assurance initiative.	APO12.04	Risk analysis and risk profile reports for stakeholders	Refined scope	Internal
			Detailed assurance work program	MEA04.06
MEA04.06 Execute the assurance initiative, focusing on design effectiveness.	APO12.06	Risk-related root causes	Documented design of internal controls	MEA04.07
	MEA04.05	Detailed assurance work program		
MEA04.07 Execute the assurance initiative, focusing on operating effectiveness.	DSS02.02	Incident and service request log	Control effectiveness testing	MEA04.08 MEA04.09
	DSS02.05	Incident resolutions		
	DSS03.05	Problem resolution monitoring reports		
	DSS05.05	Access logs		
	MEA04.06	Documented design of internal controls		
MEA04.08 Report and follow up on the assurance initiative.	MEA03.03	Identified compliance gaps	Assurance review report	EDM05.03 All APO All BAI All DSS All MEA
	MEA04.07	Control effectiveness testing	Assurance review results	EDM05.03 All APO All BAI All DSS All MEA MEA04.09
MEA04.09 Follow up on recommendations and actions.	MEA04.07	Control effectiveness testing	Remedial actions	All APO All BAI All DSS All MEA
	MEA04.08	Assurance review results		

D. Component: People, Skills and Competencies		
Skill	**Related Guidance (Standards, Frameworks, Compliance Requirements)**	**Detailed Reference**
A number of core principles, described by the Institute of Internal Auditors®, support the effectiveness and efficiency of the (internal) audit function. These principles include, among others, the importance of independence, effective communication skills, proactiveness, etc.	Core Principles for the Professional Practice of Internal Auditing, The Institute of Internal Auditors	IIA website—Standards & Guidance - Core Principles
Risk management	e-Competence Framework (e-CF)—A common European Framework for ICT Professionals in all industry sectors—Part 1: Framework, 2016	E. Manage—E.3. Risk Management

E. Component: Principles, Policies and Procedures	
Relevant Policy	**Policy Description**
Internal audit charter	Provides independence to undertake audit reviews and report findings and recommendations directly to top management. The internal audit function should be a separate entity reporting either to the chief executive officer or chief operating officer. With respect to I&T, the charter should stipulate that the function is responsible for reviewing both general and application controls to determine whether the controls have been designed in accordance with management direction, established standards and procedures, and known legal requirements, and whether the controls are operating effectively to provide reliability and security over the data being processed (i.e., confidentiality, integrity and availability). The charter should stipulate that the internal audit function is responsible for reviewing the design, development and implementation of new systems or major modifications of existing systems.

F. Component: Culture, Ethics and Behavior
Key Culture Elements
Create a culture that embraces internal audit and assurance findings and recommendations, based on root cause analysis. Leaders must ensure that internal audit and assurance are involved in strategic initiatives and recognize the need for (and value of) audit and assurance reports.

G. Component: Services, Infrastructure and Applications
• Assurance engagement tools • Event log auditing tools • Third-party assurance provisioning services

APPENDIX A
Suitability Test

One way to determine whether this guide is applicable to the target enterprise is to execute a suitability test, which consists of two tests designed to assess an enterprise's suitability for implementing control over I&T based on this SME guidance:

- The first test is about "staying in the blue zone," which means the enterprise is considered an SME.
  - This test helps the enterprise determine whether this book's SME guidance for governance and management of I&T is appropriate for its needs or if it should instead consider the full COBIT guidance.
  - If the results from the assessment are mainly contained in the blue zone, the enterprise is most likely suited to use this SME guidance. If the results are not primarily in the blue zone, it nevertheless remains management's decision whether to use this guide's approach anyway. However, management should remain conscious of the control assumptions described previously, as certain content that appears in the full COBIT publications (metrics, activities, inputs/outputs) is not retained in this SME guidance.
- The second test of the suitability tool is about "watching the heat."
  - This test can help assess the exception situations referred to in the first test.
  - The more the enterprise is in the red zone, the more it needs to consider going beyond this SME guidance and instead using *COBIT® 2019 Framework: Governance and Management Objectives*.

Staying in the Blue Zone

This test focuses on the organizational structure of an enterprise and the importance and criticality of I&T. It evaluates the following conditions:

- A simple command structure
- Short communications path
- Limited span of control
- I&T sophistication
  - I&T's strategic importance
  - I&T expenditures
  - Limited segregation of responsibilities

This SME guidance is most suitable for organizations in which:

- The I&T environment is not particularly complex.
- The I&T expenditure is not very significant.
- I&T is not strategically important.
- The use of I&T is not leading-edge.

The dimensions of this suitability test are as follows:

- **Simple command structure**—This dimension measures the degree to which authority, rules and control are institutionalized in the enterprise. This command structure varies from very informal and verbal to strictly formal and documented. Long-term/short-term orientation and the strategic/tactical direction imposed by the command structure are evaluated. The presence of more formal and documented structures and longer-term strategic views suggests that higher levels of control are needed.

- **Short communication path**—The communication path component indicates how many layers are situated between the head of the entity (HOE) and the (IT) staff. This illustrates how directly, quickly and efficiently the HOE can communicate with the (IT) staff and is measured by determining how well the HOE knows the staff's IT-related responsibilities. This assumes that the more direct the communication path, the better the IT-related responsibilities are known. The enterprise may need to look for control requirements beyond the COBIT SME guidance if the HOE does not know most people's IT responsibilities.
- **Span of control**—While the previous step assessed the degree to which the HOE knows everyone's IT-related responsibilities, this dimension measures the influence the HOE has on those responsibilities. This influence is rated by indicating which IT-related responsibilities the HOE effectively directs and monitors—from not directing and monitoring IT-related responsibilities to directing and monitoring every IT-related responsibility. Not knowing IT responsibilities of key personnel is an indicator that a larger control framework is required.
- **I&T sophistication**—The I&T sophistication component refers to the profile of the enterprise regarding the adoption of new technologies and the complexity of the I&T environment relative to its industry and peers. This profile ranges from being a pioneer that adopts new technologies well before the industry in a complex I&T environment, to being a laggard that adopts new technologies well behind industry peers while keeping the infrastructure simple. Taking a technology leadership position and working in a complex I&T environment evoke the possibility of greater risk and wider control requirements.
- **I&T strategic importance**—This dimension evaluates how dependent the enterprise is on I&T to operate and function and to achieve competitive advantages and success. This dimension is the equivalent of the traditional McFarlan quadrant 1, which positions enterprises based on current and future dependency on I&T. From the moment I&T is critical to support current operations, additional controls may be needed to manage that criticality.
- **I&T expenditure**—The I&T expenditure component is closely linked to the I&T sophistication and I&T strategic importance dimensions and ranks the enterprise based on its I&T expenditure relative to profit and compared to peers. Furthermore, the increasing trend of the total I&T expenditure is considered. If I&T expenditure increases yearly, surpasses profits or differs significantly from industry peers, it is prudent to consider stronger controls. Not-for-profit enterprises usually can avoid referring to profits and instead judge I&T expenditures based on peer expenditures and their own expenditure trends.
- **Segregation**—The segregation dimension checks whether the responsibilities not only for building, operating and influencing I&T solutions, but also for monitoring them, are overly concentrated in one person or instead are distributed properly to more people. There is insufficient segregation when a single person executes too many of these functions. The fact that management has implemented a certain degree of segregation indicates a level of concern and risk that is more consistent with a larger control framework.

Figure A.1 lists the questions to pose for the first part of the test and an example outcome.

Figure A.1—COBIT SME Suitability Test: Assessment 1

Suitability Assessment (1)

<<Stay in the Blue Zone>>

Simple command structure (SCS)

1. CS is informal and verbal, only short term and tactical.

2. CS is primarily informal and verbal, somewhat short-term, but largely medium-term oriented, and still primarily tactical.

3. CS is primarily formal and documented, begins looking at the long term, but is more medium-term oriented, somewhat tactical, with strategic views emerging.

4. CS is strictly formal and documented, covers short, medium and long term, and is strategy oriented.

Short communications path (SCP)

1. HOE (head of the entity) knows everyone's IT-related responsibilities.

2. HOE knows most people's IT-related responsibilities.

3. HOE only knows IT-related responsibilities for key personnel.

4. HOE does not know all IT-related responsibilities of key personnel.

Segregation (SEG)

1. Those who monitor have at least two other functions (build, operate or influence).

2. Those who monitor have at most building or operating as other functions. Those who influence can also have building and operating functions.

3. Monitoring is totally segregated, but building and operating can be executed by the same person. Those who influence have at most operating or building as other functions.

4. At most, influencing and monitoring are executed by one person.

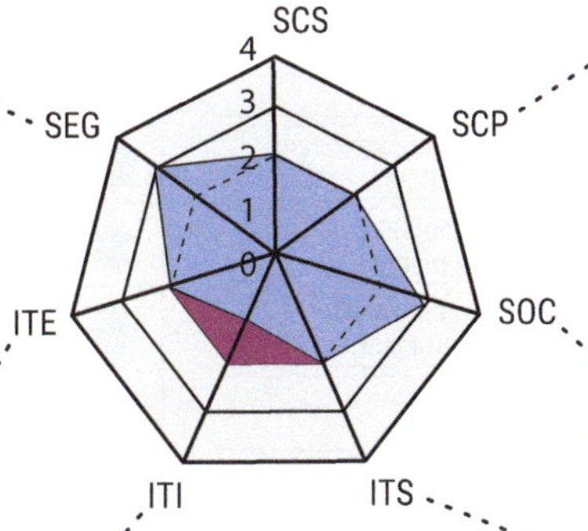

Span of control (SOC)

1. HOE directs and monitor everyone's IT-related responsibilities.

2. HOE directs and monitors most people's IT-related responsibilities.

3. HOE directs and monitors only key personnel's IT-related responsibilities.

4. HOE does not direct and monitor all IT-related responsibilities of key personnel.

IT Expenditure (ITE)

1. I&T expenditure is not more than profits and not much different from peers.

2. I&T expenditure is different from peers and only marginally increasing every year.

3. I&T expenditure is more than profits or significantly different from peers, and shows an annual increasing trend.

4. I&T expenditure is significantly more than the entity's profits.

IT Strategic Importance (ITI)

1. Reliable I&T are not critical to the functioning of the enterprise and are not likely to become strategically important.

2. Reliable I&T support is critical to the enterprise's current operation, but the application development portfolio is not fundamental to the enterprise's ability to compete.

3. Uninterrupted functioning of I&T is not absolutely critical to achieving current objectives, but applications and technology under development will be critical to future competitive success.

4. Reliable I&T support is critical to the enterprise's current operation, and applications and technology under development are critical to future competitive success.

I&T Leadership (ITS)

1. Laggard, well behind in technology adoption, with a simple I&T infrastructure.

2. Follower, adopting technology after peers, using more but still standard components.

3. Leader, adopting technology before peers, customizing and integrating solutions.

4. Pioneer, early adopter of new, emerging technology, well ahead of the industry, highly complex I&T environment.

Source: Adapted from ISACA, *COBIT® Quickstart, 2nd Edition*, USA, 2007

Watch the Heat

Answers to questions in the second test will help determine if this SME guide is suitable for the enterprise. The evaluation is predicated on the schema in **figure A.2**. Answers will generate appropriate advice, as follows:

- If the majority of answers coincide with red circles, the user should implement *COBIT® 2019 Framework: Governance and Management Objectives*.
- If the majority of answers coincide with green circles, the user should implement this SME guide.
- If answers coincide with a mix of red, yellow and green circles, the user can still apply this SME guide, but might also refer to *COBIT® 2019 Framework: Governance and Management Objectives* for some objectives.

Figure A.2—COBIT SME Suitability Test: Assessment 2

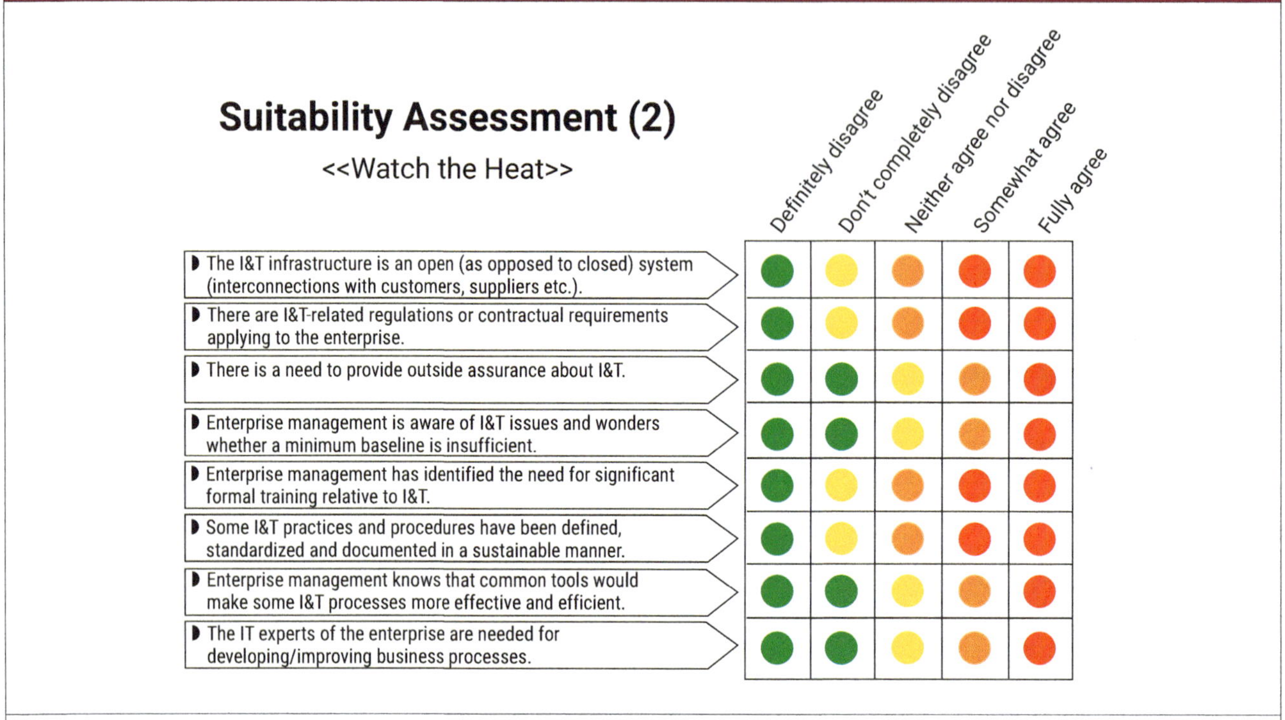

Source: Adapted from ISACA, *COBIT® Quickstart, 2nd Edition*, USA, 2007

Example outcomes of the second test are shown in **figures A.3** and **A.4**.

Outcome advice [example 1]: *COBIT SME guidance may be useful for controlling the I&T environment, but conditions exist that need to be monitored. If they deteriorate, fuller application of COBIT may be required.*

Figure A.3—COBIT SME Suitability Test: Assessment 2, Example 1

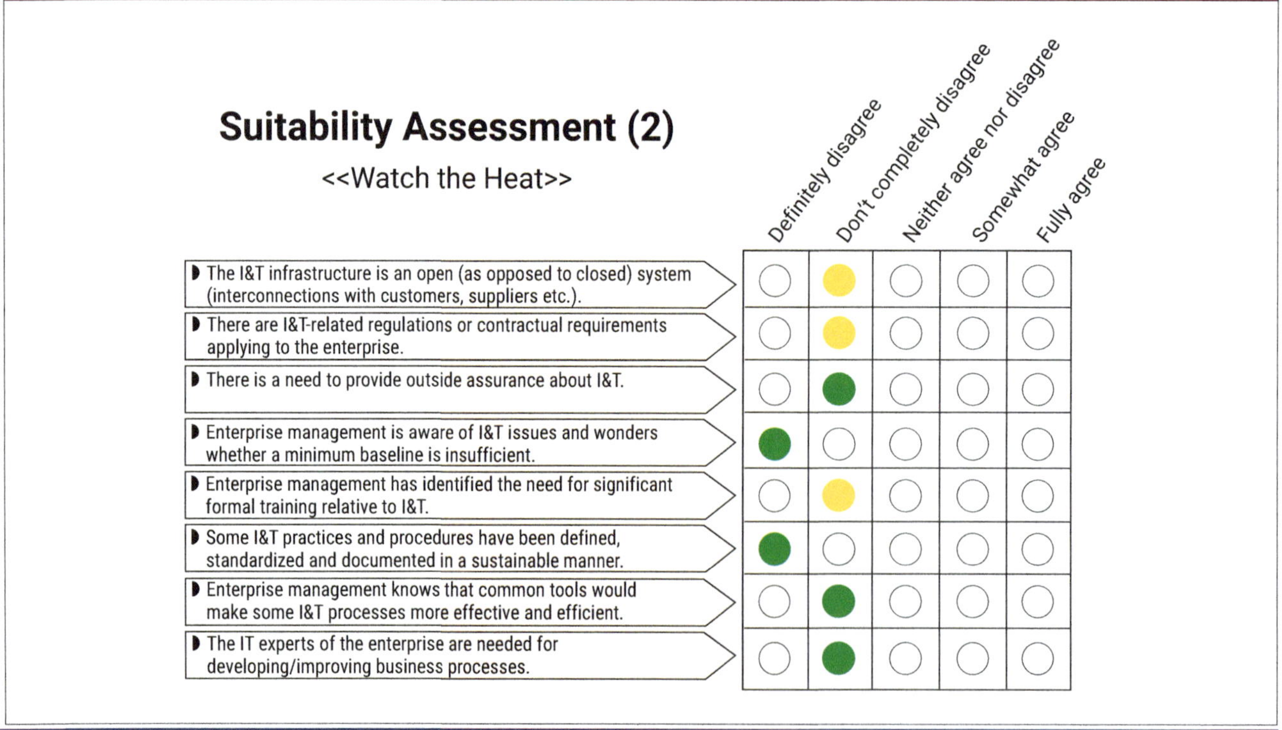

Outcome advice [example 2]: *Conditions exist that require a thorough review of full COBIT for application to the I&T environment of the enterprise.*

Figure A.4—COBIT SME Suitability Test: Assessment 2, Example 2

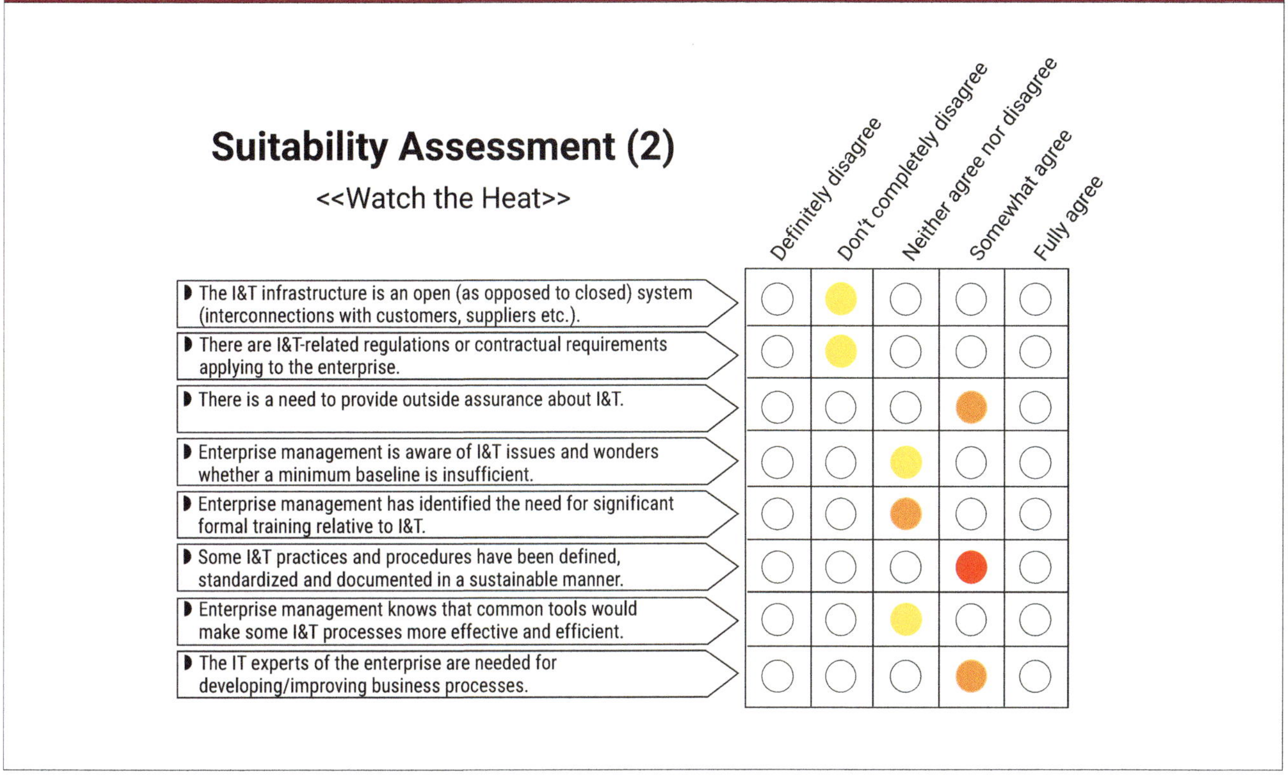

Page intentionally left blank

APPENDIX B
Design Factors

Design factors include any combination of the following (**figure B.1**).

Figure B.1—COBIT Design Factors

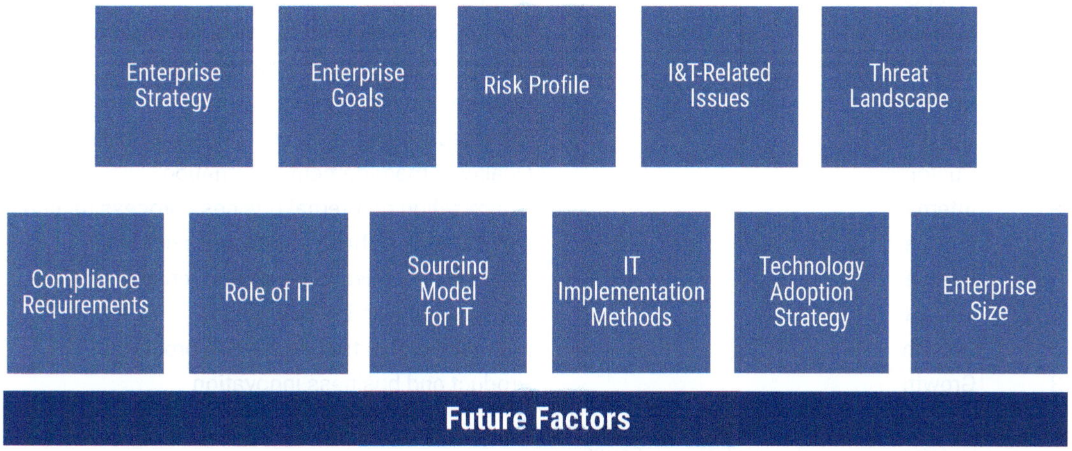

Source: ISACA, *COBIT® 2019 Framework: Introduction and Methodology*, USA, 2018, *https://store.isaca.org/s/store#/store/browse/detail/a2S4w000004Ko5dEAC*

Explanation of Design Factors

1. **Enterprise strategy**—Enterprises can have different strategies, which can be expressed as one or more of the archetypes shown in **figure B.2**. Organizations typically have a primary strategy and, at most, one secondary strategy.

Figure B.2—Enterprise Strategy Design Factor

Strategy Archetype	Explanation
Growth/Acquisition	The enterprise has a focus on growing (revenues).[12]
Innovation/Differentiation	The enterprise has a focus on offering different and/or innovative products and services to their clients.[13]
Cost Leadership	The enterprise has a focus on short-term cost minimization.[14]
Client Service/Stability	The enterprise has a focus on providing stable and client-oriented service.[15]

Source: ISACA, *COBIT® 2019 Framework: Introduction and Methodology*, USA, 2018, *https://store.isaca.org/s/store#/store/browse/detail/a2S4w000004Ko5dEAC*

[12] Corresponds with prospector in the Miles-Snow typology. See "Miles and Snow's Typology of Defender, Prospector, Analyzer, and Reactor," Elibrary, *https://ebrary.net/3737/management/miles_snows_typology_defender_prospector_analyzer_reactor*. See also Miles, R.; C. Snow; A. Meyer; H. Coleman; "Organizational Strategy, Structure, and Process," *The Academy of Management Review*, Vol. 3, No. 3, July 1978, *www.jstor.org/stable/257544?seq=8#metadata_info_tab_contents*.

[13] See Reeves, M.; C. Love; P. Tillmanns; "Your Strategy Needs a Strategy," *Harvard Business Review*, September 2012, *https://hbr.org/2012/09/your-strategy-needs-a-strategy*, specifically regarding visionary and shaping.

[14] Corresponds to cost leadership; see University of Cambridge, "Porter's Generic Competitive Strategies (ways of competing)," Institute for Manufacturing (IfM) Management Technology Policy, *https://www.ifm.eng.cam.ac.uk/research/dstools/porters-generic-competitive-strategies/*. Also corresponds to operational excellence; see Treacy, M.; F. Wiersema, "Customer Intimacy and Other Value Disciplines," *Harvard Business Review*, January/February 1993, *https://hbr.org/1993/01/customer-intimacy-and-other-value-disciplines*.

[15] Corresponds with defenders in the Miles-Snow typology. See *op cit* Miles, R.; C. Snow; A. Meyer; H. Coleman; "Organizational Strategy, Structure, and Process."

2. **Enterprise goals** supporting the enterprise strategy—Enterprise strategy is realized by the achievement of (a set of) enterprise goals. These goals are defined in the COBIT framework, structured along the balanced scorecard (BSC) dimensions and include the elements shown in **figure B.3**.

Figure B.3—Enterprise Goals Design Factor

Reference	Balanced Scorecard (BSC) Dimension	Enterprise Goal
EG01	Financial	Portfolio of competitive products and services
EG02	Financial	Managed business risk
EG03	Financial	Compliance with external laws and regulations
EG04	Financial	Quality of financial information
EG05	Customer	Customer-oriented service culture
EG06	Customer	Business-service continuity and availability
EG07	Customer	Quality of management information
EG08	Internal	Optimization of internal business process functionality
EG09	Internal	Optimization of business process costs
EG10	Internal	Staff skills, motivation and productivity
EG11	Internal	Compliance with internal policies
EG12	Growth	Managed digital transformation programs
EG13	Growth	Product and business innovation

Source: ISACA, *COBIT® 2019 Framework: Introduction and Methodology*, USA, 2018, *https://store.isaca.org/s/store#/store/browse/detail/a2S4w000004Ko5dEAC*

Section 4.6 contains more information on the COBIT goals cascade, which is the detailed elaboration of this design factor.

3. **Risk profile** of the enterprise and current issues in relation to I&T—The risk profile identifies the sort of I&T-related risk to which the enterprise is currently exposed and indicates which areas of risk are exceeding the risk appetite. The risk categories[16] listed in **figure B.4** merit consideration.

Figure B.4—Risk Profile Design Factor (IT Risk Categories)

Reference	Risk Category	Example Risk Scenarios
1	IT investment decision making, portfolio definition and maintenance	A. Programs selected for implementation misaligned with corporate strategy and priorities B. Failure of IT-related Investments to support digital strategy of the enterprise C. Selection of wrong software (in terms of cost, performance, features, compatibility, redundancy, etc.) for acquisition and implementation D. Selection of wrong infrastructure (in terms of cost, performance, features, compatibility, etc.) for implementation E. Duplication or important overlaps between different investment initiatives F. Long-term incompatibility between new investment programs and enterprise architecture G. Misallocation, inefficient management and/or competition for resources without alignment to business priorities
2	Program and projects lifecycle management	A. Failure of senior management to terminate failing projects (due to cost explosion, excessive delays, scope creep, changed business priorities) B. Budget overruns for I&T projects C. Lack of quality of I&T projects D. Late delivery of I&T projects E. Failure of third-party outsourcers to deliver projects as per contractual agreements (any combination of exceeded budgets, quality problems, missing functionality, late delivery)
3	IT cost and oversight	A. Extensive dependency on, and use of, user-created, user-defined, user-maintained applications and ad hoc solutions B. Excess cost and/or ineffectiveness of I&T-related purchases outside of the I&T procurement process C. Inadequate requirements leading to ineffective Service Level Agreements (SLAs) D. Lack of funds for I&T related investments

[16] Modified from ISACA, *Risk IT Practitioner Guide, 2nd Edition*, Chapter 5, USA, 2020, *https://store.isaca.org/s/store#/store/browse/detail/a2S4w000004Ko9XEAS.* See also ISACA, *COBIT® 2019 Design Guide: Designing an Information and Technology Governance Solution*, USA, 2018, *https://store.isaca.org/s/store#/store/browse/detail/a2S4w000004Ko9bEAC.*

Figure B.4—Risk Profile Design Factor (IT Risk Categories) *(cont.)*		
Reference	**Risk Category**	Example Risk Scenarios
4	IT expertise, skills and behavior	A. Lack or mismatch of IT-related skills within IT (e.g., due to new technologies or working methods) B. Lack of business understanding by IT staff that affects service delivery/project quality C. Inability to recruit and retain IT staff D. Recruitment of unsuitable profiles because of lack of due diligence in the recruitment process E. Lack of I&T training F. Overreliance for I&T services on key staff
5	Enterprise/IT architecture	A. Complex, inflexible enterprise architecture (EA), obstructing further evolution and expansion, and leading to missed business opportunities B. Failure to timely adopt and exploit new infrastructure or abandon obsolete infrastructure C. Failure to timely adopt and exploit new software (functionality, optimization, etc.) or to abandon obsolete applications D. Undocumented EA leading to inefficiencies and duplications E. Excessive number of exceptions on enterprise architecture standards
6	IT operational infrastructure incidents	A. Accidental damaging of IT equipment B. Errors by IT staff (during backup, during upgrades of systems, during maintenance of systems, etc.) C. Incorrect information input by IT staff or system users D. Destruction of data center (sabotage, etc.) by staff E. Theft of device with sensitive data F. Theft of a key infrastructure component G. Erroneous configuration of hardware components H. Intentional tampering with hardware (security devices, etc.) I. Abuse of access rights from prior roles to access IT infrastructure J. Loss of backup media or backups not checked for effectiveness K. Loss of data by cloud provider L. Operational-service interruption by cloud providers

Figure B.4—Risk Profile Design Factor (IT Risk Categories) *(cont.)*

Reference	Risk Category	Example Risk Scenarios
7	Unauthorized actions	A. Tampering with software B. Intentional modification or manipulation of software leading to incorrect data C. Intentional modification or manipulation of software leading to fraudulent actions D. Unintentional modification of software leading to inaccurate results E. Unintentional configuration and change-management errors
8	Software adoption/usage problems	A. Nonadoption of new application software by users B. Inefficient use of new software by users
9	Hardware incidents	A. System instability in wake of installing new infrastructure, leading to operational incidents (e.g., BYOD program) B. Inability of systems to handle transaction volumes when user volumes increase C. Inability of systems to handle load when new applications or initiatives are deployed D. Utilities failure (telecom, electricity) E. Hardware failure due to overheating and/or other environmental conditions like humidity F. Damaging of hardware components leading to destruction of data by internal staff G. Loss/disclosure of portable media containing sensitive data (CD, USB-drives, portable disks, etc.) H. Extended resolution time or support delays in case of hardware incidents
10	Software failures	A. Inability to use the software to realize desired outcomes (e.g., failure to make required business model or organizational changes) B. Implementation of immature software (early adopters, bugs, etc.) C. Operational glitches when new software is made operational D. Regular software malfunctioning of critical application software E. Obsolete application software (outdated, poorly documented, expensive to maintain, difficult to extend, not integrated in current architecture, etc.) F. Inability to revert back to former versions in case of operational issues with a new version G. Software-induced corrupted data(base) leading to inaccessible data

Figure B.4—Risk Profile Design Factor (IT Risk Categories) *(cont.)*		
Reference	**Risk Category**	Example Risk Scenarios
11	Logical attacks (hacking, malware, etc.)	A. Unauthorized (internal) users trying to break into systems B. Service interruption due to denial-of-service (DoS) attack C. Website defacement D. Malware attack E. Industrial espionage F. Hacktivism G. Disgruntled employee implements a time bomb which leads to data loss H. Company data stolen through unauthorized access gained by a phishing attack I. Foreign government attacks on critical systems
12	Third-party/supplier incidents	A. Inadequate performance of outsourcer in large-scale, long-term outsourcing arrangement (e.g., through lack of supplier due diligence regarding financial viability, delivery capability and sustainability of supplier's service) B. Accepting unreasonable terms of business from IT suppliers C. Inadequate support and services delivered by vendors, not in line with SLA D. Noncompliance with software license agreements (use and/or distribution of unlicensed software) E. Inability to transfer to alternative suppliers due to overreliance or overdependence on current supplier F. Purchase of IT services (especially cloud services) by the business without consultation /involvement of IT, resulting in inability to integrate the service with inhouse services. G. Inadequate or unenforced SLA to obtain agreed services and penalties in case of noncompliance
13	Noncompliance	A. Noncompliance with national or international regulations (e.g., privacy, accounting, manufacturing, environmental, etc.) B. Lack of awareness of potential regulatory changes that may have a business impact C. Operational obstacles caused by regulations D. Failure to comply with internal procedures
14	Geopolitical issues	A. Lack of access due to disruptive incident in other premises B. Government interference and national policies impacting the business C. Targeted action from government-sponsored groups or agencies

Figure B.4—Risk Profile Design Factor (IT Risk Categories) *(cont.)*		
Reference	**Risk Category**	Example Risk Scenarios
15	Industrial action	A. Lack of access due to disruptive incident in other premises B. Government interference and national policies impacting the business C. Targeted action from government-sponsored groups or agencies
16	Acts of nature	A. Earthquake destroying or damaging important IT infrastructure B. Tsunami destroying critical premises C. Major storms and tropical cyclone or tornado damaging critical infrastructure D. Major wildfire E. Flooding F. Rising water table leaving critical location unusable G. Rising temperature rendering critical locations uneconomical to operate
17	Technology-based innovation	A. Failure to identify new and important technology trends B. Failure to appreciate the value and potential of new technologies C. Failure to adopt and exploit new technologies in a timely manner (functionality, process optimization, etc.) D. Failure to provide technology support new business models
18	Environmental	A. Environmentally unfriendly equipment (e.g., power consumption, packaging)
19	Data and information management	A. Discovery of sensitive information by unauthorized persons due to inefficient retaining/archiving/disposing of information B. Intentional illicit or malicious modification of data C. Unauthorized disclosure of sensitive information through email or social media D. Loss of IP and/or leakage of competitive information
Source: ISACA, *COBIT® 2019 Framework: Introduction and Methodology*, USA, 2018, *https://store.isaca.org/s/store#/store/browse/detail/a2S4w000004Ko5dEAC*		

4. **I&T-related issues**—A related method for an I&T risk assessment for the enterprise is to consider which I&T-related issues it currently faces which I&T-related risk has materialized. The most common of such issues[17] includes those in **figure B.5**.

[17] *Op cit* ISACA, *COBIT® 2019 Implementation Guide: Implementing and Optimizing an Information and Technology Governance Solution*, Section 3.3.1 Typical Pain Points

Figure B.5—I&T-Related Issues Design Factor	
Reference	**Description**
A	Frustration between different IT entities across the organization because of a perception of low contribution to business value
B	Frustration between business departments (i.e., the IT customer) and the IT department because of failed initiatives or a perception of low contribution to business value
C	Significant IT-related incidents, such as data loss, security breaches, project failure and application errors, linked to IT
D	Service delivery problems by the IT outsourcer(s)
E	Failures to meet IT-related regulatory or contractual requirements
F	Regular audit findings or other assessment reports about poor IT performance or reported IT quality or service problems
G	Substantial hidden and rogue IT spending, that is, IT spending by user departments outside the control of the normal IT investment decision mechanisms and approved budgets
H	Duplication or overlaps between various initiatives, or other forms of wasted resources
I	Insufficient IT resources, staff with inadequate skills or staff burnout/dissatisfaction
J	IT-enabled changes or projects frequently failing to meet business needs and delivered late or over budget
K	Reluctance by board members, executives or senior management to engage with IT, or a lack of committed business sponsorship for IT
L	Complex IT operating model and/or unclear decision mechanisms for IT-related decisions
M	Excessively high cost of IT
N	Obstructed or failed implementation of new initiatives or innovations caused by the current IT architecture and systems
O	Gap between business and technical knowledge, which leads to business users and information and/or technology specialists speaking different languages
P	Regular issues with data quality and integration of data across various sources
Q	High level of end-user computing, creating (among other problems) a lack of oversight and quality control over the applications that are being developed and put in operation
R	Business departments implementing their own information solutions with little or no involvement of the enterprise IT department[18]
S	Ignorance of and/or noncompliance with privacy regulations
T	Inability to exploit new technologies or innovate using I&T
Source: ISACA, *COBIT® 2019 Framework: Introduction and Methodology*, USA, 2018, *https://store.isaca.org/s/store#/store/browse/detail/a2S4w000004Ko5dEAC*	

5. **Threat landscape**—The threat landscape under which the enterprise operates can be classified as shown in **figure B.6.**

Figure B.6—Threat Landscape Design Factor	
Threat Landscape	**Explanation**
Normal	The enterprise is operating under what are considered normal threat levels.
High	Due to its geopolitical situation, industry sector or particular profile, the enterprise is operating in a high-threat environment.
Source: ISACA, *COBIT® 2019 Framework: Introduction and Methodology*, USA, 2018, *https://store.isaca.org/s/store#/store/browse/detail/a2S4w000004Ko5dEAC*	

[18] This issue is related to end-user computing, which often stems from dissatisfaction with IT solutions and services.

6. **Compliance requirements**—The compliance requirements to which the enterprise is subject can be classified according to the figures listed in **figure B.7**.

Figure B.7—Compliance Requirements Design Factor

Regulatory Environment	Explanation
Low compliance requirements	The enterprise is subject to a minimal set of regular compliance requirements that are lower than average.
Normal compliance requirements	The enterprise is subject to a set of regular compliance requirements that are common across different industries.
High compliance requirements	The enterprise is subject to higher-than-average compliance requirements, most often related to industry sector or geopolitical conditions.

Source: ISACA, *COBIT® 2019 Framework: Introduction and Methodology*, USA, 2018, *https://store.isaca.org/s/store#/store/browse/detail/a2S4w000004Ko5dEAC*

7. **Role of IT**—The role of IT for the enterprise can be classified as indicated in **figure B.8**.

Figure B.8—Role of IT Design Factor

Role of IT	Explanation
Support	IT is not crucial for the running and continuity of the business processes and services, nor for their innovation.
Factory	When IT fails, there is an immediate impact on the running and continuity of the business processes and services. However, IT is not seen as a driver for innovating business processes and services.
Turnaround	IT is seen as a driver for innovating business processes and services. At this moment, however, there is not a critical dependency on IT for the current running and continuity of the business processes and services.
Strategic	IT is critical for both running and innovating the organization's business processes and services.

Source: ISACA, *COBIT® 2019 Framework: Introduction and Methodology*, USA, 2018, *https://store.isaca.org/s/store#/store/browse/detail/a2S4w000004Ko5dEAC*

8. **Sourcing model for IT**—The sourcing model the enterprise adopts can be classified as shown in figure **B.9**.

Figure B.9—Sourcing Model for IT Design Factor

Sourcing Model	Explanation
Outsourcing	The enterprise calls upon the services of a third party to provide IT services.
Cloud	The enterprise maximizes the use of the cloud for providing IT services to its users.
Insourced	The enterprise provides for its own IT staff and services.
Hybrid	A mixed model is applied, combining the other three models in varying degrees.

Source: ISACA, *COBIT® 2019 Framework: Introduction and Methodology*, USA, 2018, *https://store.isaca.org/s/store#/store/browse/detail/a2S4w000004Ko5dEAC*

9. **IT implementation methods**—The methods the enterprise adopts can be classified as noted in **figure B.10**.

Figure B.10—IT Implementation Methods Design Factor

IT Implementation Method	Explanation
Agile	The enterprise uses Agile development working methods for its software development.
DevOps	The enterprise uses DevOps working methods for software building, deployment and operations.
Traditional	The enterprise uses a more classic approach to software development (waterfall) and separates software development from operations.
Hybrid	The enterprise uses a mix of traditional and modern IT implementation, often referred to as "bimodal IT."

Source: ISACA, *COBIT® 2019 Framework: Introduction and Methodology*, USA, 2018, *https://store.isaca.org/s/store#/store/browse/detail/a2S4w000004Ko5dEAC*

10. **Technology adoption strategy**—The technology adoption strategy can be classified as listed in **figure B.11**.

Figure B.11—Technology Adoption Strategy Design Factor

Technology Adoption Strategy	Explanation
First mover	The enterprise generally adopts new technologies as early as possible and tries to gain first-mover advantage.
Follower	The enterprise typically waits for new technologies to become mainstream and proven before adopting them.
Slow adopter	The enterprise is very late with adoption of new technologies.

Source: ISACA, *COBIT® 2019 Framework: Introduction and Methodology*, USA, 2018, *https://store.isaca.org/s/store#/store/browse/detail/a2S4w000004Ko5dEAC*

11. **Enterprise size**—Two categories, as shown in **figure B.12**, are identified for the design of an enterprise's governance system.

Figure B.12—Enterprise Size Design Factor

Enterprise Size	Explanation
Large enterprise (default)	Enterprise with more than 250 full-time employees (FTEs)
Small and medium enterprise	Enterprise with 50 to 250 FTEs

Source: ISACA, *COBIT® 2019 Framework: Introduction and Methodology*, USA, 2018, *https://store.isaca.org/s/store#/store/browse/detail/a2S4w000004Ko5dEAC*

APPENDIX C
Applying Design Factors

Example: Medium-Sized Innovative Company

This case study posits a hypothetical medium-sized innovative company responsible for developing appliances for the automotive sector. It is intended to help practitioners use the COBIT® 2019 companion governance system design tool kit.[19]

The enterprise is relatively small, with only 150 employees, and its claim to fame is its fast innovation. It is critically dependent on IT for product development and manufacturing of appliances. The enterprise is both a user and a developer of software. It is very eager to benefit from every newly available technology. It has made a strategic choice to outsource all infrastructure-related IT services and migrate to the cloud.

Step 1: Understanding the Enterprise Context and Strategy

The first step of the governance design workflow is to summarize the external and internal context of the enterprise.

Step 1.1: Understanding Enterprise Strategy

A primary focus on innovation and differentiation and a secondary focus on growth/acquisition are depicted in **figure C.1.**

Figure C.1—Design Factor 1 *Enterprise Strategy*

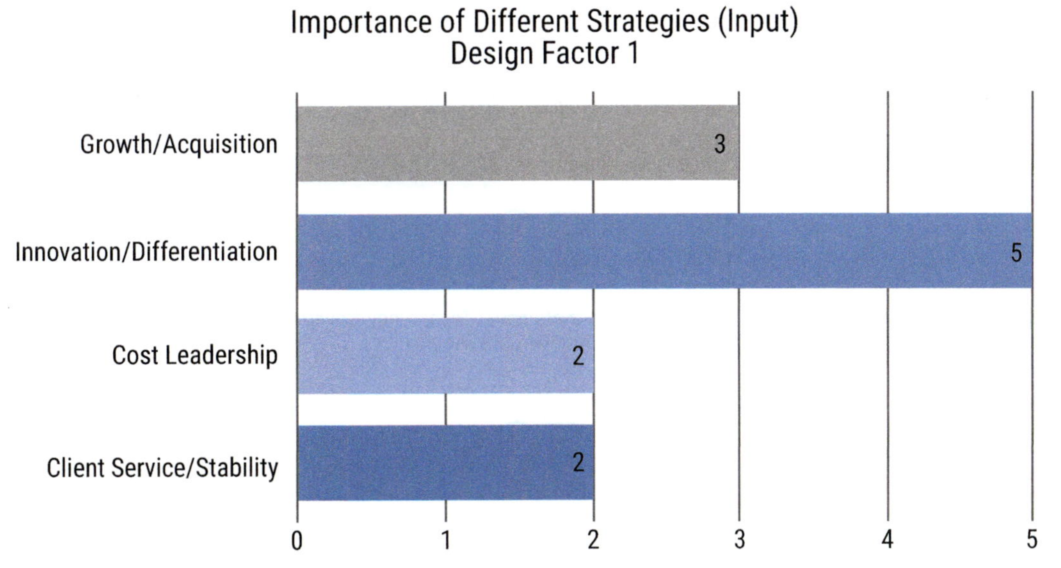

Source: ISACA, *COBIT® 2019 Design Guide: Designing an Information and Technology Governance Solution*, USA, 2018, *https://store.isaca.org/s/store#/store/browse/detail/a2S4w000004Kq7AEAS*

[19] The COBIT® 2019 governance system design tool kit may be downloaded at *https://www.isaca.org/-/media/files/isacadp/project/isaca/knowledge-and-insights/zips/cobit-2019-design-toolkit_tkt_eng_1218.zip?la=en&hash=0E8BC92071EF5FDF474A979F75A0F78CBC775E54.*

Step 1.2: Understanding Enterprise Goals

The enterprise has ranked the 13 generic EGs on a scale from 1 to 5, as depicted in **figure C.2**, which shows that EG01 *Portfolio of competitive products and services* and EG13 *Product and business innovation* are the highest-ranked enterprise goals.

Figure C.2—Design Factor 2 *Enterprise Goals*

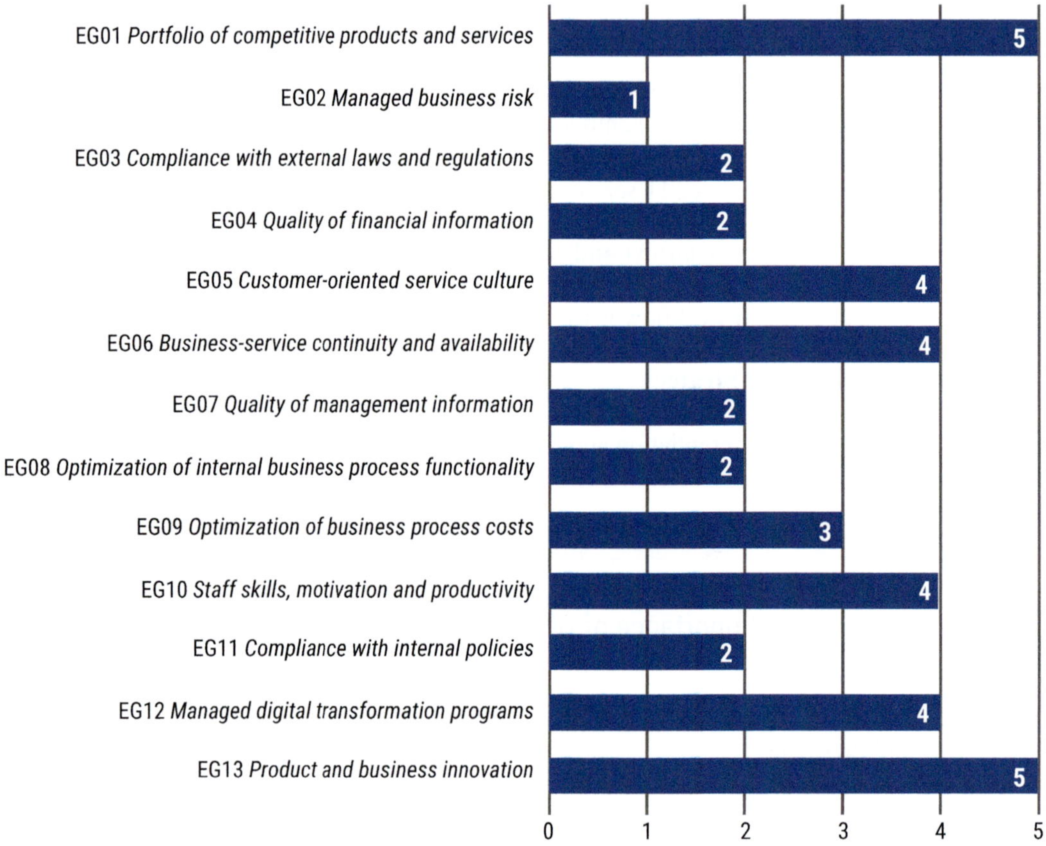

Source: ISACA, *COBIT® 2019 Design Guide: Designing an Information and Technology Governance Solution*, USA, 2018, *https://store.isaca.org/s/store#/store/browse/detail/a2S4w000004Kq7AEAS*

Step 1.3: Understanding the Risk Profile

A high-level risk analysis resulted in a risk profile that identifies the highest-risk categories (shown with red dots in the risk-rating column in **figure C.3**). They are:

- IT investment decision making, portfolio definition and maintenance
- Technology-based innovation

Figure C.3—Design Factor 3 *Risk Profile*

Design Factor 3 *Risk Profile*

Risk Scenario Category	Impact (1-5)	Likelihood (1-5)	Risk Rating
IT investment decision making, portfolio definition and maintenance	5	3	🔴
Program and projects lifecycle management	4	2	🟢
IT cost and oversight	5	1	🟢
IT expertise, skills and behavior	4	2	🟢
Enterprise/IT architecture	2	2	🟢
IT operational infrastructure incidents	3	3	🟡
Unauthorized actions	2	2	🟢
Software adoption/usage problems	2	1	⚫
Hardware incidents	4	2	🟢
Software failures	4	2	🟢
Logical attacks (hacking, malware, etc.)	3	4	🟡
Third-party/supplier incidents	5	2	🟡
Noncompliance	1	1	⚫
Geopolitical issues	1	1	⚫
Industrial action	2	1	⚫
Acts of nature	2	1	⚫
Technology-based innovation	5	3	🔴
Environmental	3	1	⚫
Data and information management	3	3	🟡

🔴	Very High Risk
🟡	High Risk
🟢	Normal Risk
⚫	Low Risk

Source: ISACA, *COBIT® 2019 Design Guide: Designing an Information and Technology Governance Solution*, USA, 2018, *https://store.isaca.org/s/store#/store/browse/detail/a2S4w000004Kq7AEAS*

Step 1.4: Understanding Current I&T-Related Issues

An analysis of the current situation (on a scale of importance from 1 to 3) resulted in an assessment of current I&T-related issues, as depicted in **figure C.4**. The following are perceived to be important issues to the enterprise:

- Service delivery problems with I&T outsourcers
- Insufficient I&T resources
- Obstructed or failed implementations
- Data quality issues

Figure C.4—Step 1.4: I&T-Related Issues

Value	Importance (1-3)
Frustration between different IT entities across the organization because of a perception of low contribution to business value	✔
Frustration between business departments (i.e., the IT customer) and the IT department because of failed initiatives or a perception of low contribution to business value	✔
Significant IT-related incidents, such as data loss, security breaches, project failure and application errors, linked to IT	!
Service delivery problems by the IT outsourcer(s)	X
Failures to meet IT-related regulatory or contractual requirements	✔
Regular audit findings or other assessment reports about poor IT performance or reported IT quality or service problems	✔
Substantial hidden and rogue IT spending, that is, IT spending by user departments outside the control of the normal IT investment decision mechanisms and approved budgets	✔
Duplications or overlaps between various initiatives, or other forms of wasted resources	✔
Insufficient IT resources, staff with inadequate skills or staff burnout/dissatisfaction	X
IT-enabled changes or projects frequently failing to meet business needs and delivered late or over budget	!
Reluctance by board members, executives or senior management to engage with IT, or a lack of committed business sponsorship for IT	✔
Complex IT operating model and/or unclear decision mechanisms for IT-related decisions	✔
Excessively high cost of IT	!
Obstructed or failed implementation of new initiatives or innovations caused by the current IT architecture and systems	X
Gap between business and technical knowledge, which leads to business users and information and/or technology specialists speaking different languages	!
Regular issues with data quality and integration of data across various sources	X
High level of end-user computing, creating (among other problems) a lack of oversight and quality control over the applications that are being developed and put in operation	✔
Business departments implementing their own information solutions with little or no involvement of the enterprise IT department	✔
Ignorance of and/or noncompliance with privacy regulations	✔
Inability to exploit new technologies or innovate using I&T	!

✔	No Issue
!	Issue
X	Serious Issue

Source: ISACA, *COBIT® 2019 Design Guide: Designing an Information and Technology Governance Solution*, USA, 2018, *https://store.isaca.org/s/store#/store/browse/detail/a2S4w000004Kq7AEAS*

Step 2: Determining the Initial Scope of the Governance System

At this point, it is possible to combine the resulting governance and management priorities from the previous steps to produce initial priorities for governance and management objectives in the governance system. The summary overview, presented in **figure C.5**, contains the calculated relative importance to the example enterprise of each of the 40 COBIT® 2019 governance and management objectives.

Figure C.5—Importance of the COBIT Objectives to the Example Enterprise

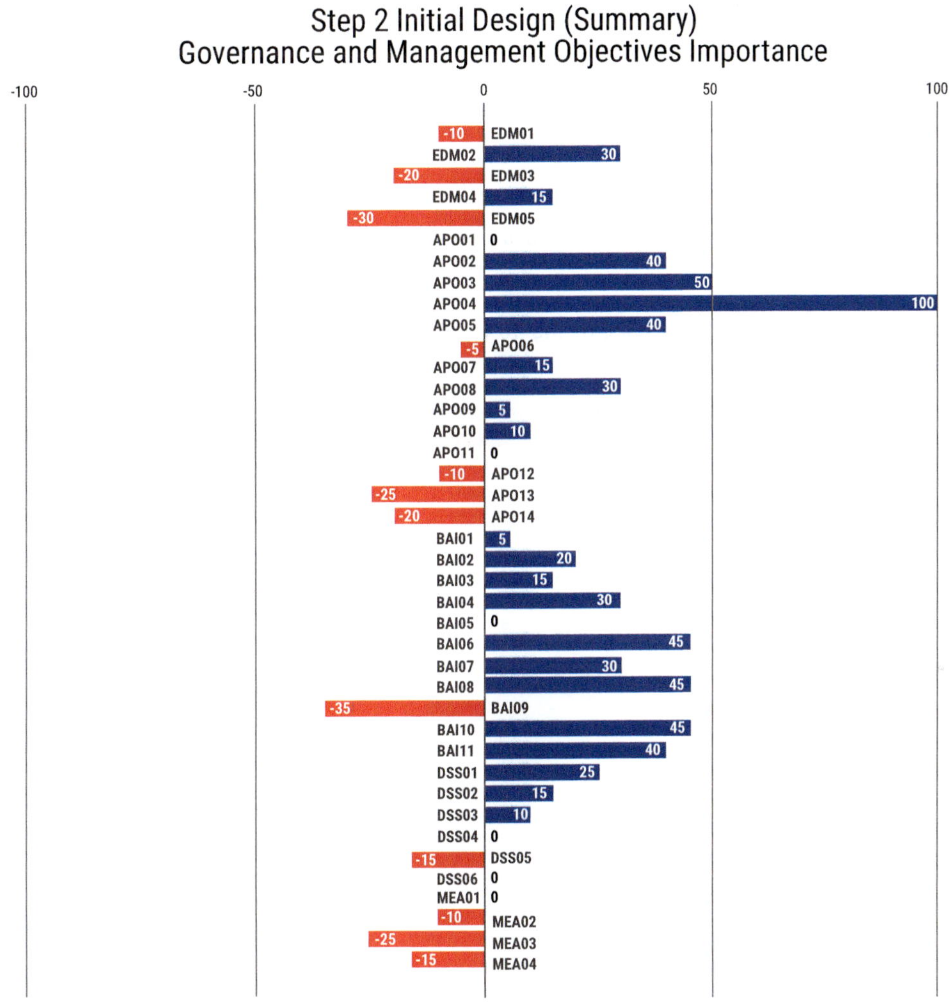

Source: ISACA, *COBIT® 2019 Design Guide: Designing an Information and Technology Governance Solution*, USA, 2018, *https://store.isaca.org/s/store#/store/browse/detail/a2S4w000004Kq7AEAS*

The next step will determine which refinements are required to this initial scope of the governance system.

Step 3: Refining the Scope of the Governance System

In step 3, refinements to the initial scope are identified based on the remaining set of design factors to be analyzed. (Not all design factors are necessarily applicable to each enterprise, so some may be ignored.)

Step 3.1: Threat Landscape

The percentage (**figure C.6**) indicates which portion of enterprise operations is subject to a high threat landscape.

Figure C.6—Importance of the Threat Landscape

Value	Importance (100%)
High	20
Normal	80

Source: ISACA, *COBIT® 2019 Design Guide: Designing an Information and Technology Governance Solution*, USA, 2018, *https://store.isaca.org/s/store#/store/browse/detail/a2S4w000004Kq7AEAS*

Figure C.7 summarizes the relative importance of the 40 COBIT objectives to the example enterprise. As noted in the figure, the variances are quite small.

Figure C.7—Impact of the Threat Landscape on COBIT Objectives for the Example Enterprise

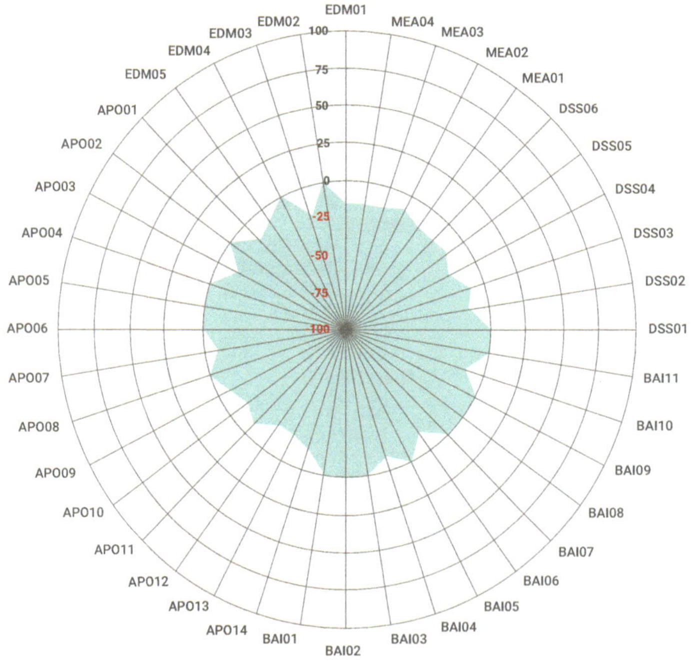

Source: ISACA, *COBIT® 2019 Design Guide: Designing an Information and Technology Governance Solution*, USA, 2018, *https://store.isaca.org/s/store#/store/browse/detail/a2S4w000004Kq7AEAS*

Step 3.2: Compliance Requirements

Since this is a small enterprise, only one percentage is indicated: 100 percent for normal compliance (**figure C.8**).

Figure C.8—Importance of Compliance Requirements

Value	Importance (100%)
High	0%
Normal	100%
Low	0%

Source: ISACA, *COBIT® 2019 Design Guide: Designing an Information and Technology Governance Solution*, USA, 2018, *https://store.isaca.org/s/store#/store/browse/detail/a2S4w000004Kq7AEAS*

Again, the impact on the objectives can be ignored, as they are all at the same level (**figure C.9**).

Figure C.9—Impact of Compliance Requirements on COBIT Objectives for the Example Enterprise

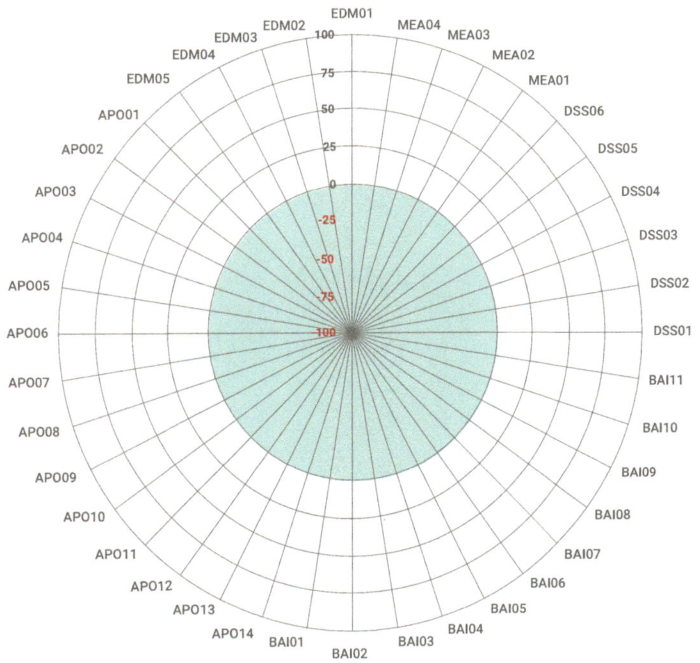

Source: ISACA, *COBIT® 2019 Design Guide: Designing an Information and Technology Governance Solution*, USA, 2018, *https://store.isaca.org/s/store#/store/browse/detail/a2S4w000004Kq7AEAS*

Step 3.3: Role of IT

Since the enterprise develops its own software, the strategic value and factory activities related to IT are very important (**figure C.10**).

Figure C.10—Importance of the Role of IT

Value	Importance (1–5)
Support	2
Factory	5
Turnaround	3
Strategic	5

Source: ISACA, *COBIT® 2019 Design Guide: Designing an Information and Technology Governance Solution*, USA, 2018, *https://store.isaca.org/s/store#/store/browse/detail/a2S4w000004Kq7AEAS*

The impact on the objectives is a little more nuanced than in the two previous figures, but it is still not very important (**figure C.11**). Importance level 5 would be the highest level of importance for each value in this figure.

Figure C.11—Impact of the Role of IT on COBIT Objectives for the Example Enterprise

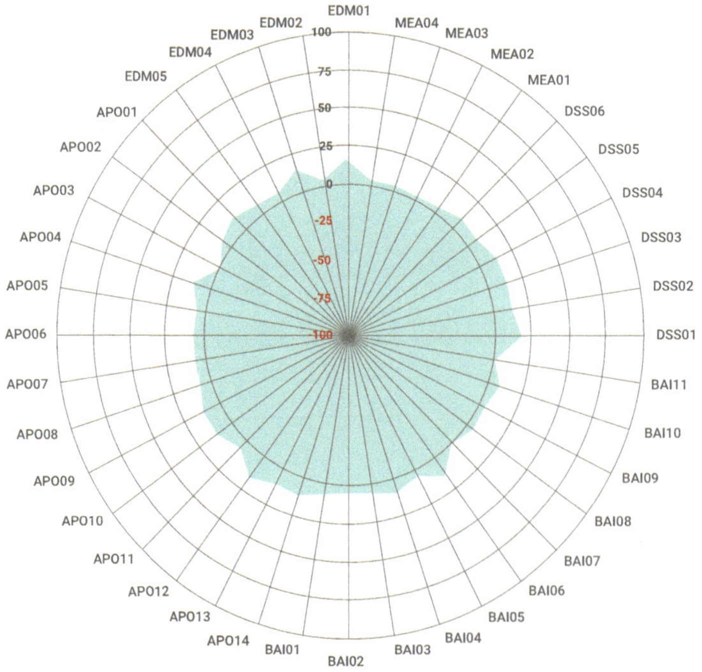

Source: ISACA, *COBIT® 2019 Design Guide: Designing an Information and Technology Governance Solution*, USA, 2018, *https://store.isaca.org/s/store#/store/browse/detail/a2S4w000004Kq7AEAS*

Step 3.4: Sourcing Model for IT

As the enterprise outsources IT and moves to the cloud, the percentages in **figure C.12** were used to evaluate its sourcing model for IT.

Figure C.12—Importance of Sourcing Models for IT

Value	Importance (100%)
Outsourcing	50%
Cloud	40%
Insourcing	10%

Source: ISACA, *COBIT® 2019 Design Guide: Designing an Information and Technology Governance Solution*, USA, 2018, *https://store.isaca.org/s/store#/store/browse/detail/a2S4w000004Kq7AEAS*

This results in more distinctions among impacts on the objectives. APO09 *Managed Service Agreements*, APO10 *Managed Vendors*, APO12 *Managed Risk* and MEA01 *Managed Performance and Conformance Monitoring* become more important (**figure C.13**).

Figure C.13—Impact of Sourcing Models for IT on COBIT Objectives for the Example Enterprise

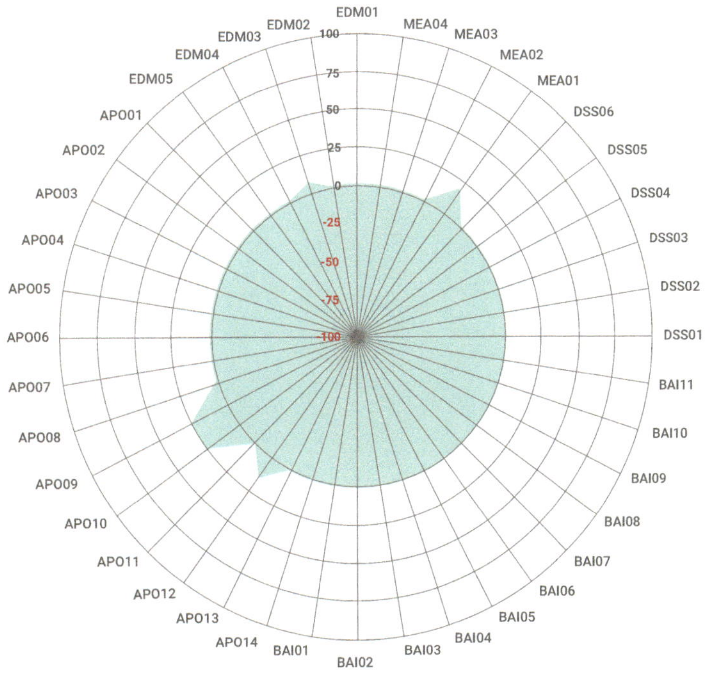

Source: ISACA, *COBIT® 2019 Design Guide: Designing an Information and Technology Governance Solution*, USA, 2018, *https://store.isaca.org/s/store#/store/browse/detail/a2S4w000004Kq7AEAS*

Step 3.5: IT Implementation Methods

Since the example enterprise is evolving toward DevOps, 100 percent importance was assigned to this option (**figure C.14**).

Figure C.14—Importance of IT Implementation Methods

Value	Importance (100%)
Agile	0%
DevOps	100%
Traditional	0%

Source: ISACA, *COBIT® 2019 Design Guide: Designing an Information and Technology Governance Solution*, USA, 2018, *https://store.isaca.org/s/store#/store/browse/detail/a2S4w000004Kq7AEAS*

This importance of some objectives is very clear now and spread over all domains, except for EDM (**figure C.15**).

Figure C.15—Impact of IT Implementation Methods on COBIT Objectives for the Example Enterprise

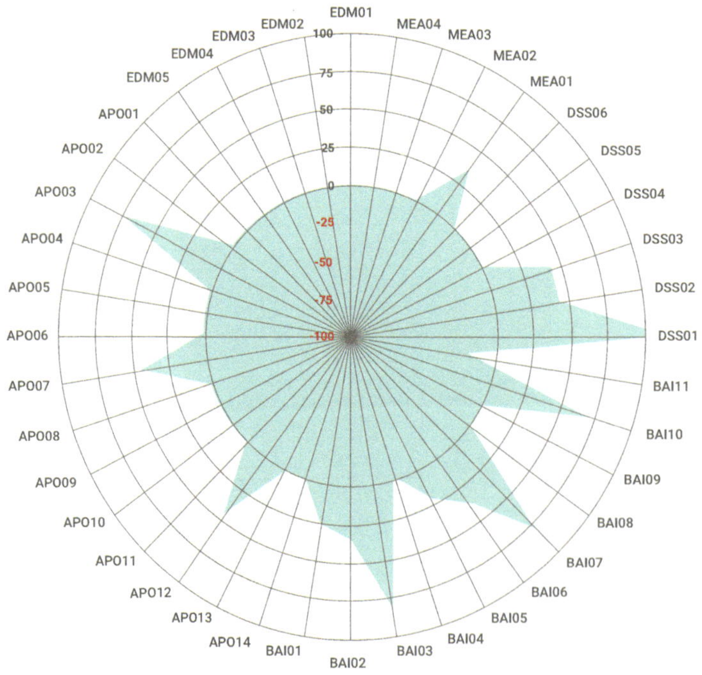

Source: ISACA, *COBIT® 2019 Design Guide: Designing an Information and Technology Governance Solution*, USA, 2018, *https://store.isaca.org/s/store#/store/browse/detail/a2S4w000004Kq7AEAS*

Step 3.6: Technology Adoption Strategy

For this innovative company, 100 percent is assigned to the first mover option (**figure C.16**).

Figure C.16—Importance of Technology Adoption Strategy

Value	Importance (100%)
First mover	100%
Follower	0%
Slow adopter	0%

Source: ISACA, *COBIT® 2019 Design Guide: Designing an Information and Technology Governance Solution*, USA, 2018, *https://store.isaca.org/s/store#/store/browse/detail/a2S4w000004Kq7AEAS*

The outcome is now even more dispersed, with a lot of importance for human resources (APO07) and budget and cost (APO08). Other APO objectives reflect a degree of importance as well (**figure C.17**).

Figure C.17—Impact of Technology Adoption Strategy on COBIT Objectives for the Example Enterprise

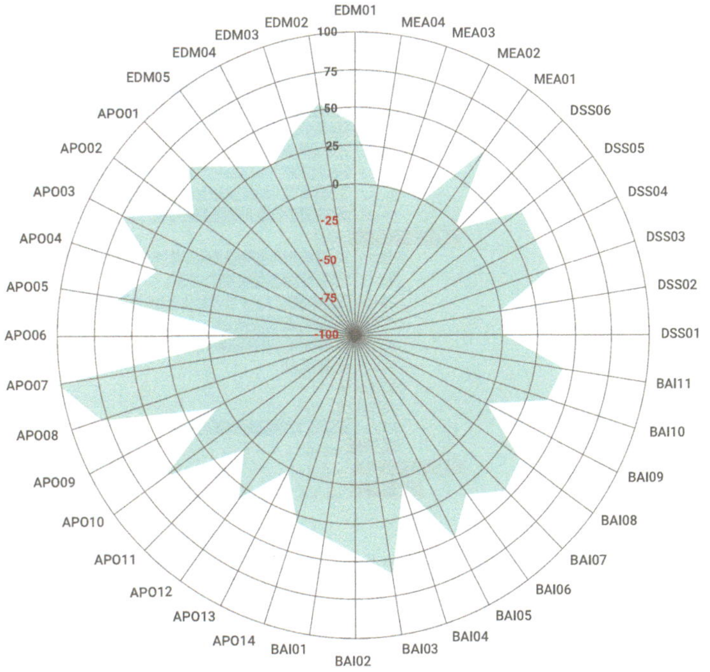

Source: ISACA, *COBIT® 2019 Design Guide: Designing an Information and Technology Governance Solution*, USA, 2018, *https://store.isaca.org/s/store#/store/browse/detail/a2S4w000004Kq7AEAS*

Step 4: Concluding the Governance Solution Design

The last step in the design process requires discussion of all inputs from previous steps to resolve conflicts and reach a conclusion. The resulting governance system reflects careful consideration of all inputs, taking into account that these inputs sometimes conflict, and choices had to be made.

Governance and Management Objectives

At this point, it is possible to add the governance and management priorities resulting from steps 3.1 through 3.7 to the results obtained from the initial governance system design in steps 2.1 through 2.4. This synthesis results in the adjusted priorities for governance and management objectives in the governance system shown in **figure C.18**.

Figure C.18—Overall Result From All Design Factors

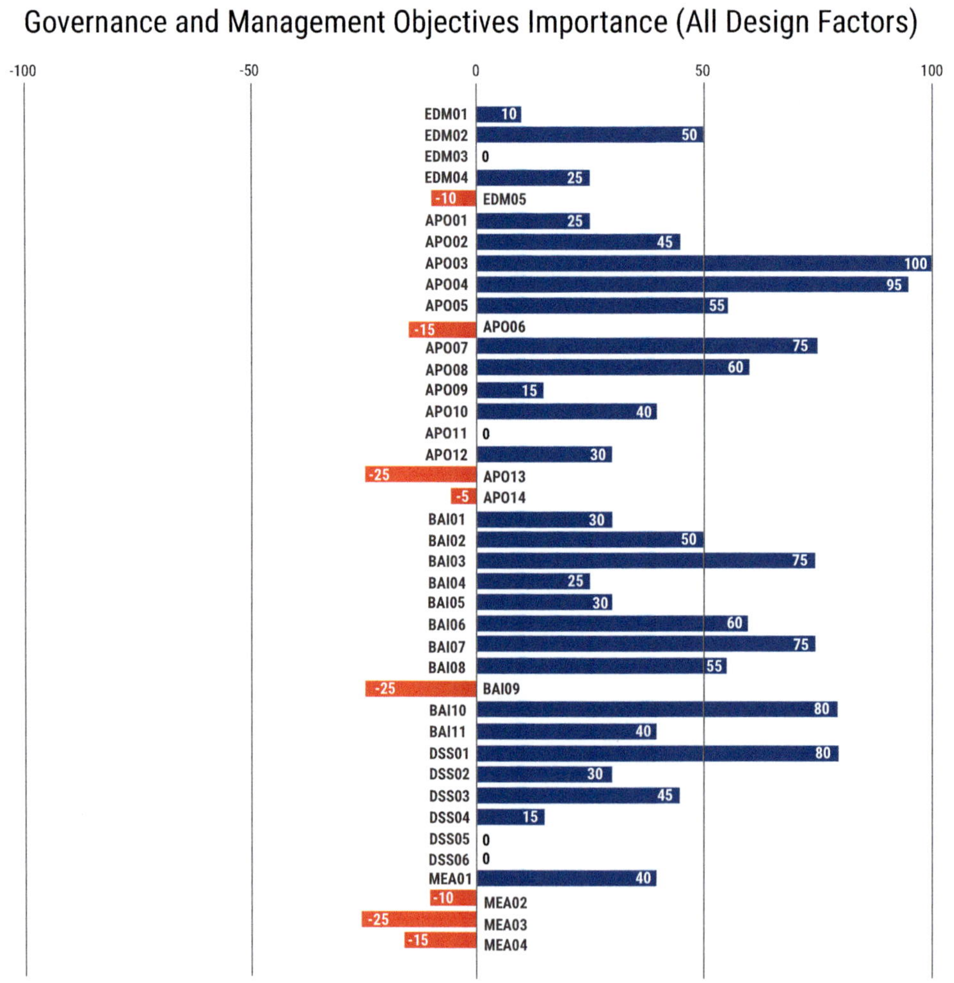

Source: ISACA, *COBIT® 2019 Design Guide: Designing an Information and Technology Governance Solution*, USA, 2018, *https://store.isaca.org/s/store#/store/browse/detail/a2S4w000004Kq7AEAS*

A comparison of this result to the initial scope supports the following observations:

- Overall, most governance/management objectives have gained significant importance after taking into account the additional design factors. This can be explained by the innovative character and strategic role of I&T.
- APO03 *Managed Enterprise Architecture* (100) and APO04 *Managed Innovation* (95) are still the most important objectives, although the enterprise architecture has gained a lot of importance compared to the first result.
- The DSS objectives have gained a lot of importance, as has MEA01 *Managed Performance and Conformance Monitoring.*
- The increased importance of BAI objectives is related to the strategic importance of IT and the creative role the enterprise wants to have in its development processes.

To confirm this rating, the outcome needs to be discussed with the management team, with the goal of obtaining agreement or changing the relative importance and deciding on the priority for the 40 COBIT objectives.

Page intentionally left blank

APPENDIX D

Goals Cascade—Overview

Introduction

Enterprises exist to create value for their stakeholders. Enterprises have many stakeholders, and creating value means different—and sometimes conflicting—things to each of them. Governance is about negotiating and deciding among different stakeholders' value interests. Thus, the governance system should consider all stakeholders when making benefit, risk and resource assessment decisions.

In the goals cascade, stakeholder needs cascade to enterprise goals (EGs). EGs then cascade to alignment goals (AGs). Each governance or management objective (see Chapter 5) supports the achievement of a set of AGs related to EGs.

Concept of the Goals Cascade

Stakeholder needs must be transformed into an enterprise's actionable strategy. The goals cascade (**figure D.1**) supports prioritization of governance and management objectives based on prioritization of EGs.

Figure D.1—COBIT Goals Cascade

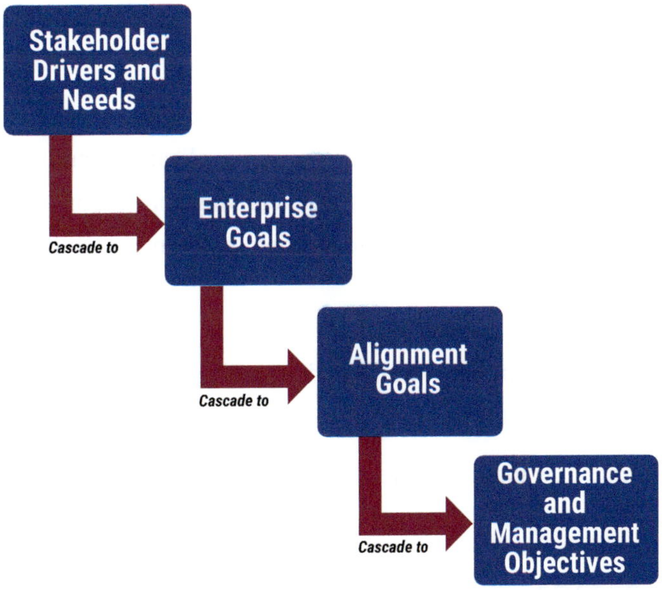

Source: ISACA, *COBIT® 2019 Framework: Introduction and Methodology*, USA, 2018, *https://store.isaca.org/s/store#/store/browse/detail/a2S4w000004Ko5dEAC*

The first step in the goals cascade is to identify the most relevant EGs (see the following list).

These EGs are related to AGs. After doing the mapping exercise (see section 4.1.2 in this chapter), the enterprise will have a list of AGs linked to the objectives. This cascading mechanism will enable the enterprise to identify its highest priority objectives and its highest priority I&T-related processes.

Enterprise goals include:

- **EG01**—Portfolio of competitive products and services
- **EG02**—Managed business risk
- **EG03**—Compliance with external laws and regulations
- **EG04**—Quality of financial information
- **EG05**—Customer-oriented service culture
- **EG06**—Business service continuity and availability
- **EG07**—Quality of management information
- **EG08**—Optimization of internal business process functionality
- **EG09**—Optimization of business process costs
- **EG10**—Staff skills, motivation and productivity
- **EG11**—Compliance with internal policies
- **EG12**—Managed digital transformation programs
- **EG13**—Product and business innovation

Alignment goals include:

- **AG01**—I&T compliance and support for business compliance with external laws and regulations
- **AG02**—Managed I&T-related risk
- **AG03**—Realized benefits from I&T-enabled investments and services portfolio
- **AG04**—Quality of technology-related financial information
- **AG05**—Delivery of I&T services in line with business requirements
- **AG06**—Agility to turn business requirements into operational solutions
- **AG07**—Security of information, processing infrastructure and applications, and privacy
- **AG08**—Enabling and supporting business processes by integrating applications and technology
- **AG09**—Delivering programs on time, on budget and meeting requirements and quality standards
- **AG10**—Quality of I&T management information
- **AG11**—I&T compliance with internal policies
- **AG12**—Competent and motivated staff with mutual understanding of technology and business
- **AG13**—Knowledge, expertise and initiatives for business innovation

The tables of Appendix E illustrate how these EGs are linked to the AGs, and how the AGs relate to governance and management objectives.

Executing the Goals Cascade

The method for executing the goals cascade comprises the following steps:

- Indicate the most important EGs shown in Appendix E, **figure E.1**.
  - Limit the number of EGs to three or four—no more than five.
- Based on this selection, find the most important AGs by traversing the rows in Appendix E, **figure E.1** and indicating all AGs with a P (primary, important) or S (secondary, less important) relationship.

Example Metrics

Example metrics for all EGs and AGs are defined in Appendix F.

Applying the mapping tables in reverse (objectives → AGs → EGs) will produce a list of example metrics that can guide the enterprise in the definition of tailored metrics for each objective.

Page intentionally left blank

APPENDIX E

Goals Cascade—Mapping Tables

Mapping Table: Enterprise Goals–Alignment Goals

Figure E.1—Mapping Table: Enterprise Goals–Alignment Goals

		EG01 Portfolio of competitive products and services	EG02 Managed business risk	EG03 Compliance with external laws and regulations	EG04 Quality of financial information	EG05 Customer-oriented service culture	EG06 Business service continuity and availability	EG07 Quality of management information	EG08 Optimization of internal business process functionality	EG09 Optimization of business process costs	EG10 Staff skills, motivation and productivity	EG11 Compliance with internal policies	EG12 Managed digital transformation programs	EG13 Product and business innovation
AG01	I&T compliance and support for business compliance with external laws and regulations		S	P								S		
AG02	Managed I&T-related risk		P				S							
AG03	Realized benefits from I&T-enabled investments and services portfolio	S				S			S	S			P	
AG04	Quality of technology-related financial information				P			P		P				
AG05	Delivery of I&T services in line with business requirements	P				S	S		S				S	
AG06	Agility to turn business requirements into operational solutions	P				S			S				S	S
AG07	Security of information, processing infrastructure and applications, and privacy		P				P							
AG08	Enabling and supporting business processes by integrating applications and technology	P				P			S		S		P	S
AG09	Delivering programs on time, on budget and meeting requirements and quality standards	P				S			S	S			P	S
AG10	Quality of I&T management information				P			P		S				
AG11	I&T compliance with internal policies		S	P								P		
AG12	Competent and motivated staff with mutual understanding of technology and business					S					P			
AG13	Knowledge, expertise and initiatives for business innovation	P		S									S	P

Source: ISACA, *COBIT® 2019 Framework: Governance and Management Objectives*, USA, 2018, *https://store.isaca.org/s/store#/store/browse/detail/a2S4w000004Ko5aEAC*

Mapping Table: Alignment Goals–Governance and Management Objectives

Figure E.2—Mapping Table: Alignment Goals–Governance and Management Objectives

		AG01	AG02	AG03	AG04	AG05	AG06	AG07	AG08	AG09	AG10	AG11	AG12	AG13
		I&T compliance and support for business compliance with external laws and regulations	Managed I&T-related risk	Realized benefits from I&T-enabled investments and services portfolio	Quality of technology-related financial information	Delivery of I&T services in line with business requirements	Agility to turn business requirements into operational solutions	Security of information, processing infrastructure and applications, and privacy	Enabling and supporting business processes by integrating applications and technology	Delivering programs on time, on budget and meeting requirements and quality standards	Quality of I&T management information	I&T compliance with internal policies	Competent and motivated staff with mutual understanding of technology and business	Knowledge, expertise and initiatives for business innovation
EDM01	Ensured governance framework setting and maintenance	P	S	P					S			S		
EDM02	Ensured benefits delivery			P		S	S		S					S
EDM03	Ensured risk optimization	S	P					P				S		
EDM04	Ensured resource optimization			S		S	S		S	P			S	
EDM05	Ensured stakeholder engagement				S						P	S		
APO01	Managed I&T management framework	S	S	P		S		S	S	S	S	P		
APO02	Managed strategy			S		S	S		P				S	S
APO03	Managed enterprise architecture			S		S	P	S	P					
APO04	Managed innovation			S			P		S				S	P
APO05	Managed portfolio			P		P	S		S	S				
APO06	Managed budget and costs			S	P					P	S			
APO07	Managed human resources			S		S				S			P	P
APO08	Managed relationships			S		P	P		S	S			P	P
APO09	Managed service agreements					P			S					
APO10	Managed vendors					P	S			S				
APO11	Managed quality			S	S	S				P	P			
APO12	Managed risk		P					P						
APO13	Managed security	S	S					P						
APO14	Managed data	S	S		S			S			P			
BAI01	Managed programs			P			S		S	P				
BAI02	Managed requirements definition			S		P	P		S	P			S	
BAI03	Managed solutions identification and build			S		P	P		S	P				
BAI04	Managed availability and capacity					P		S		S				
BAI05	Managed organizational changes			P		S	S		P	P			S	
BAI06	Managed IT changes		S			S	P		S					
BAI07	Managed IT change acceptance and transitioning		S				P			S				
BAI08	Managed knowledge			S			S		S	S			P	P
BAI09	Managed assets				P						S			
BAI10	Managed configuration					S		P						
BAI11	Managed projects			P		S	P			P				
DSS01	Managed operations					P			S					
DSS02	Managed service requests and incidents		S			P		S						
DSS03	Managed problems		S			P		S						
DSS04	Managed continuity		S			P		P						
DSS05	Managed security services	S	P			S		P				S		
DSS06	Managed business process controls		S			S		S	P			S		
MEA01	Managed performance and conformance monitoring	S		S		P				S	P	S		
MEA02	Managed system of internal control	S	S		S	S		S		S	S	P		
MEA03	Managed compliance with external requirements	P										S		
MEA04	Managed assurance	S	S		S	S		S			S	P		

Source: ISACA, *COBIT® 2019 Framework: Governance and Management Objectives*, USA, 2018, *https://store.isaca.org/s/store#/store/browse/detail/a2S4w000004Ko5aEAC*

APPENDIX F
Example Metrics

Example Metrics for Enterprise Goals

Figure F.1—Example Metrics for Enterprise Goals

Reference	BSC Dimension	Enterprise Goal	Example Metrics
EG01	Financial	Portfolio of competitive products and services	• Percent of products and services that meet or exceed targets in revenues and/or market share • Percent of products and services that meet or exceed customer satisfaction targets • Percent of products and services that provide competitive advantage • Time-to-market for new products and services
EG02	Financial	Managed business risk	• Percent of critical business objectives and services covered by risk assessment • Ratio of significant incidents that were not identified in risk assessment vs. total incidents • Appropriate frequency of update of risk profile
EG03	Financial	Compliance with external laws and regulations	• Cost of regulatory noncompliance, including settlements and fines • Number of regulatory noncompliance issues causing public comment or negative publicity • Number of noncompliance matters noted by regulators or supervisory authorities • Number of regulatory noncompliance issues related to contractual agreements with business partners
EG04	Financial	Quality of financial information	• Satisfaction survey of key stakeholders regarding the transparency, clarity and accuracy of enterprise financial information • Cost of regulatory noncompliance with finance-related regulations
EG05	Customer	Customer-oriented service culture	• Number of customer service disruptions • Percent of business stakeholders satisfied that customer service delivery meets agreed levels • Number of customer complaints • Trend of customer satisfaction survey results
EG06	Customer	Business service continuity and availability	• Number of customer service or business process interruptions causing significant incidents • Business cost of incidents • Number of business processing hours lost due to unplanned service interruptions • Percent of complaints as a function of committed service-availability targets

Figure F.1—Example Metrics for Enterprise Goals *(cont.)*			
Reference	**BSC Dimension**	**Enterprise Goal**	**Example Metrics**
EG07	Customer	Quality of management information	• Degree of board and executive management satisfaction with decision-making information • Number of incidents caused by incorrect business decisions based on inaccurate information • Time to provide supporting information to enable effective business decisions • Timeliness of management information
EG08	Internal	Optimization of internal business process functionality	• Satisfaction levels of board and executive management with business process capabilities • Satisfaction levels of customers with service delivery capabilities • Satisfaction levels of suppliers with supply chain capabilities
EG09	Internal	Optimization of business process costs	• Ratio of cost vs. achieved service levels • Satisfaction levels of board and executive management with business processing costs
EG10	Internal	Staff skills, motivation and productivity	• Staff productivity compared to benchmarks • Level of stakeholder satisfaction with staff expertise and skills • Percent of staff whose skills are insufficient relative to competencies required for their roles • Percent of satisfied staff
EG11	Internal	Compliance with internal policies	• Number of incidents related to noncompliance with policy • Percent of stakeholders who understand policies • Percent of policies supported by effective standards and working practices
EG12	Growth	Managed digital transformation programs	• Number of programs on time and within budget • Percent of stakeholders satisfied with program delivery • Percent of business transformation programs stopped • Percent of business transformation programs with regular reported status updates
EG13	Growth	Product and business innovation	• Level of awareness and understanding of business innovation opportunities • Stakeholder satisfaction with levels of product and innovation expertise and ideas • Number of approved product and service initiatives resulting from innovative ideas

Source: ISACA, *COBIT® 2019 Framework: Introduction and Methodology*, USA, 2018, *https://store.isaca.org/s/store#/store/browse/detail/a2S4w000004Ko5dEAC*

Example Metrics for Alignment Goals

Figure F.2—Example Metrics for Alignment Goals			
Reference	**I&T BSC Dimension**	**Alignment Goal**	**Metrics**
AG01	Financial	I&T compliance and support for business compliance with external laws and regulations	• Cost of I&T noncompliance, including settlements and fines, and the impact of reputational loss • Number of I&T-related noncompliance issues reported to the board or causing public comment or embarrassment • Number of noncompliance issues relating to contractual agreements with I&T service providers
AG02	Financial	Managed I&T-related risk	• Appropriate frequency of update of risk profile • Percent of enterprise risk assessments including I&T-related risk • Number of significant I&T-related incidents that were not identified in a risk assessment
AG03	Financial	Realized benefits from I&T-enabled investments and services portfolio	• Percent of I&T-enabled investments for which claimed benefits in the business case are met or exceeded • Percent of I&T services for which expected benefits (as stated in the service level agreements) are realized
AG04	Financial	Quality of technology-related financial information	• Satisfaction of key stakeholders regarding the level of transparency, understanding and accuracy of I&T financial information • Percent of I&T services with defined and approved operational costs and expected benefits
AG05	Customer	Delivery of I&T services in line with business requirements	• Percent of business stakeholders satisfied that I&T service delivery meets agreed service levels • Number of business disruptions due to I&T service incidents • Percent of users satisfied with the quality of I&T service delivery
AG06	Customer	Agility to turn business requirements into operational solutions	• Level of satisfaction of business executives with I&T's responsiveness to new requirements • Average time-to-market for new I&T-related services and applications • Average time to turn strategic I&T objectives into an agreed and approved initiative • Number of critical business processes supported by up-to-date infrastructure and applications
AG07	Internal	Security of information processing, infrastructure and applications, and privacy	• Number of confidentiality incidents causing financial loss, business disruption or public embarrassment • Number of availability incidents causing financial loss, business disruption or public embarrassment • Number of integrity incidents causing financial loss, business disruption or public embarrassment

Figure F.2—Example Metrics for Alignment Goals *(cont.)*

Reference	I&T BSC Dimension	Alignment Goal	Metrics
AG08	Internal	Enabling and supporting business processes by integrating applications and technology	• Time to execute business services or processes • Number of I&T-enabled business programs delayed or incurring additional cost due to technology integration issues • Number of business process changes that need to be delayed or reworked because of technology integration issues • Number of applications or critical infrastructures operating in silos and not integrated
AG09	Internal	Delivery of programs on time, on budget and meeting requirements and quality standards	• Number of programs/projects on time and within budget • Number of programs needing significant rework due to quality defects • Percent of stakeholders satisfied with program/project quality
AG10	Internal	Quality of I&T management information	• Level of user satisfaction with quality and timeliness and availability of I&T-related management information, taking into account available resources • Ratio and extent of erroneous business decisions in which erroneous or unavailable I&T-related information was a key factor • Percentage of information meeting quality criteria
AG11	Internal	I&T compliance with internal policies	• Number of incidents related to noncompliance with I&T-related policies • Number of exceptions to internal policies • Frequency of policy review and update
AG12	Learning and Growth	Competent and motivated staff with mutual understanding of technology and business	• Percent of I&T-savvy business people (i.e., those having the required knowledge and understanding of I&T to guide, direct, innovate and see opportunities of I&T for their domain of expertise) • Percent of business-savvy I&T people (i.e., those having the required knowledge and understanding of relevant business domains to guide, direct, innovate and see opportunities of I&T for the business domain) • Number or percentage of business people with technology management experience
AG13	Learning and Growth	Knowledge, expertise and initiatives for business innovation	• Level of business executive awareness and understanding of I&T innovation possibilities • Number of approved initiatives resulting from innovative I&T ideas • Number of innovation champions recognized/awarded

Source: ISACA, *COBIT® 2019 Framework: Introduction and Methodology*, USA, 2018, *https://store.isaca.org/s/store#/store/browse/detail/a2S4w000004Ko5dEAC*

APPENDIX G
Organizational Structures

Overview and Descriptions

The roles and organizational structures shown in **figure G.1** are included in the organizational structures component for the attribution of process accountabilities and responsibilities. The name and level of involvement that is applied to each role or structure can differ across enterprises. It is key for each enterprise to identify the appropriate mapping to its own context and structures based on the descriptions and attribution of involvement.

Figure G.1—SME Organizational Structures Roles and Descriptions

Role/Structure	Description
Board	The group of the most senior executives and/or non-executive directors of the enterprise who are accountable for the governance of the enterprise and have overall control of its resources
Executive Committee	A group of senior executives appointed by the board to ensure that the board is involved in, and kept informed of, major decisions. The committee is accountable for managing the portfolios of I&T-enabled investments, I&T services and I&T assets, ensuring that value is delivered and risk is managed. The committee is normally chaired by a board member.
General Manager	Typically, the highest-function ranking manager who is in charge of the total management of the enterprise
Financial Manager	The most senior manager of the enterprise who is accountable for all aspects of financial management, including financial risk and controls and reliable and accurate accounts
Operations Manager	The most senior manager of the enterprise who is accountable for operation of the enterprise
Security Manager	The most senior manager responsible for all aspects of security management across the enterprise
Security Expert	An individual responsible for aspects of security management in the enterprise
Business Process Owner	An individual accountable for the performance of a process in realizing its objectives, driving process improvement and approving process changes
Steering Committee	A group of stakeholders and experts who are accountable for guidance of projects, including management and monitoring of plans, allocation of resources, delivery of benefits and value, and management of project risk
Project Manager	The manager responsible for the guidance of a specific project, coordinating and delegating time, budget, resources and tasks across the project team
Head Human Resources	The most senior manager of an enterprise who is accountable for planning and policies with respect to all human resources in that enterprise
Head of IT	The most senior manager of the enterprise who is responsible for aligning I&T and business strategies and accountable for planning, resourcing and managing the delivery of I&T services and solutions to support enterprise objectives
IT Development Coordinator	A senior individual accountable for I&T-related solution development processes
IT Operations Coordinator	A senior individual accountable for the I&T operational environments and infrastructure
Privacy Officer	Individual responsible for monitoring risk and business impact of privacy laws and for guiding and coordinating the implementation of policies and activities that ensure compliance with privacy directives (In some enterprises, the position may be referenced as the data protection officer.)
Legal Department	The function in the enterprise responsible for guidance on legal and regulatory matters
Compliance or Quality	The function in the enterprise responsible for all guidance on external compliance
Audit	The function in the enterprise responsible for provision of internal audits

Page intentionally left blank

APPENDIX H
References to Other Standards

Detailed List of References

The following standards and guidance contribute to the detailed references to the 40 core COBIT® 2019 governance and management objectives.

- CIS® Center for Internet Security®, *The CIS Critical Security Controls for Effective Cyber Defense*, Version 6.1, August 2016
- CMMI® Cybermaturity Platform, 2018
- CMMI® Data Management Maturity (DMM)℠ model, 2014
- Committee of Sponsoring Organizations (COSO) Enterprise Risk Management (ERM) Framework, June 2017
- European Committee for Standardization (CEN), *e-Competence Framework (e-CF) – A common European Framework for ICT Professionals in all industry sectors – Part 1: Framework*, EN 16234-1:2016
- HITRUST® Common Security Framework, version 9, September 2017
- Information Security Forum (ISF), *The Standard of Good Practice for Information Security 2016*
- International Organization for Standardization / International Electrotechnical Commission (ISO/IEC) standards
  - ISO/IEC 20000-1:2011(E)
  - ISO/IEC 27001:2013/Cor.2:2015(E)
  - ISO/IEC 27002:2013/Cor.2:2015(E)
  - ISO/IEC 27004:2016(E)
  - ISO/IEC 27005:2011(E)
  - ISO/IEC 38500:2015(E)
  - ISO/IEC 38502:2017(E)
- Information Technology Infrastructure Library (ITIL®) v3, 2011
- Institute of Internal Auditors® (IIA®), "Core Principles for the Professional Practice of Internal Auditing"
- *King IV Report on Corporate Governance*™, 2016
- US National Institute of Standards and Technology (NIST) standards
  - *Framework for Improving Critical Infrastructure Cybersecurity* V1.1, April 2018
  - Special Publication 800-37, Revision 2 (Draft), May 2018
  - Special Publication 800-53, Revision 5 (Draft), August 2017
- *A Guide to the Project Management Body of Knowledge: PMBOK® Guide Sixth Edition*, 2017
- PROSCI® 3-Phase Change Management Process
- Scaled Agile Framework for Lean Enterprises (SAFe®)
- Skills Framework for the Information Age (SFIA®) V6, 2015
- The Open Group IT4IT® Reference Architecture, version 2.0
- The Open Group Standard TOGAF® version 9.2, 2018

Page intentionally left blank

9781604209006